Pierre Choderlos de Laclos

Pierre Choderlos de Laclos was born in Amiens, France, on October 19, 1741. He embarked on a military career, serving as an officer at Grenoble from 1769 to 1775, where he observed the dissolution of the local nobility. Laclos wrote, "after having written some poetry and studied a profession which would not lead me to any great advancement, I resolved to write a work that would cause a great commotion and go on reverberating in the world after I was gone." So in 1782 he wrote his most important work of fiction, the celebrated *Les Liaisons Dangereuses*. The novel so scandalized the French aristocracy that, while read avidly by all, it was often disguised as a missal. André Gide, a great admirer of the book, wrote, "there is no doubt that Laclos was hand in hand with Satan." Fifty editions of the book were published during Laclos's lifetime.

In 1784 Laclos married Solange Marie Duperré, the sister of an admiral. Secretly an influential member of the Jacobin Club, Laclos remained in the army all his life. He worked as the secretary of commands for the Duc d'Orléans. Later the treason of one of his superiors, Dumouriez, made Laclos suspect and he was arrested. Only the fall of Robespierre and the end of the Reign of Terror saved him from the guillotine.

Appointed a brigadier general under Napoleon, he commanded the artillery of the Army of the Rhine, then that of the Army of Italy. In 1803 he was transferred to Murat's corps in Naples and placed in charge of the defense of Taranto, where he died of dysentery in 1803.

Bantam Classics
Ask your bookseller for classics by these international writers:

Anton Chekhov
Dante
Fyodor Dostoevsky
Alexandre Dumas
Gustave Flaubert
Johann Wolfgang von Goethe
Victor Hugo
Henrik Ibsen
Franz Kafka
Pierre Choderlos de Laclos
Gaston Leroux
Niccolo Machiavelli
Thomas Mann
Edmond Rostand
Marie-Henri Beyle de Stendhal
Leo Tolstoy
Ivan Turgenev
Jules Verne
Voltaire

Les Liaisons Dangereuses by Pierre Choderlos de Laclos

Translated by
Lowell Bair

With an Introduction by
André Maurois

This translation was originally
published as
Dangerous Liaisons

BANTAM BOOKS
NEW YORK · TORONTO · LONDON · SYDNEY · AUCKLAND

LES LIAISONS DANGEREUSES
A Bantam Book

PRINTING HISTORY
Les Liaisons Dangereuses *was first published in 1782.*
A Bantam Classic / January 1962

New Classic edition / March 1989

This translation was originally published as
Dangerous Liaisons.

Cover painting ''Love Letters'' by
Jean Honoré Fragonard. Courtesy of
The Frick Collection, New York.

ISBN 0-553-21372-5

Published simultaneously in the United States and Canada

Bantam Books are published by Bantam Books, a division of Bantam
Doubleday Dell Publishing Group, Inc. Its trademark, consisting of the
words ''Bantam Books'' and the portrayal of a rooster, is Registered in
U.S. Patent and Trademark Office and in other countries. Marca
Registrada. Bantam Books, 666 Fifth Avenue, New York, New York 10103.

PRINTED IN THE UNITED STATES OF AMERICA

O 0 9 8 7 6 5 4 3 2

INTRODUCTION
By André Maurois
Of the French Academy

Here is a book which has had a strange destiny. It is famous, and considered to be one of the finest French novels. And yet for a long time the place granted to its author in histories of literature was small, sometimes nonexistent. Saint-Beuve, who speaks of the most unknown writers, devotes only a few words to him; Faguet, in studying the authors of the eighteenth century, neglects him. Others acknowledge *Les Liaisons Dangereuses*, but as an accursed book which smells of brimstone. Gide boasted of liking it, but in the same way that he boasted of being a friend of the devil.

Is it, then, such a scandalous work? It is written in a pure, abstract language which recalls that of Racine, of La Rochefoucauld, and sometimes even (I could cite examples), that of Bossuet. It does not contain one obscene word, and when it describes daring situations or scenes, it does so with a discretion which surprises our contempories. In comparison with any page by Hemingway, Caldwell or Françoise Sagan, Laclos appears to be an author for the pure in heart. Then why has he caused such fear and indignation while at the same time arousing the admiration of the literate public? That is what we shall try to explain.

I
THE AUTHOR

Laclos, or rather Choderlos de Laclos, is one of those writers who owe their glory to a single book. If it had not been for *Les Liaisons Dangereuses*, he would have been completely forgotten. He had a soul à la Stendhal, ready for any audacious action, but he went through life masked and difficult to seize. It is known that he was cold, witty without being gracious, "a tall, thin, sallow-faced gentleman, always wearing a black coat." Stendhal himself, who met him toward the end of his life, recalled an old artillery general at army headquarters in Milan, "to whom I paid court," he said, "because of *Les Liaisons Dangereuses*."

Nothing seemed to prepare young Lieutenant Laclos to create a French Lovelace. From 1769 to 1775 he was an officer at Grenoble, one of the best garrisons in France for those who sought amusement. There he observed the local nobility, whose morals were extremely lax. "The young men received money from their rich mistresses, and with that money they dressed themselves magnificently and supported their poor mistresses." But Laclos himself did not have the reputation of behaving in this manner. One of his biographers states that, just as Stendhal made war in the Quartermaster Corps, Laclos made love in the Intelligence Service. He liked to talk with ladies and have them confide in him. Ladies are more willing to confide in these noncombatant observers than in great conquerors, and are quite skillful at relating their love affairs. Henry James and Marcel Proust, and even Tolstoy, made great use of feminine chatter. Great novels are sometimes made from little bits of gossip.

Laclos was an admirer of Richardson and Rousseau. He had read and reread *Clarissa* and *La Nouvelle Héloïse*. This gave him a novelistic technique. Grenoble gave him characters and anecdotes. It is believed that a certain Marquise de la Tour du Pin-Montauban was the original of the Marquise de Merteuil. If we must accept *Les Liaisons Dangereuses* as an accurate picture of the nobility of Grenoble in the eighteenth century, that nobility was terribly depraved. But novelists often present as the mores of their time "what is actually nothing but the story of a score of fops and harlots." The rest of the city led normal family lives, but led them discreetly, while a handful of cynics and libertines filled conversations and newspapers with the scandal of their adventures.

It must be added that Laclos, who had been ennobled by a fluke, and only recently, did not like "high society" and took pleasure in denouncing its horrors. In 1782, the Revolution was already brewing in many minds. A poor officer like Laclos resented those great noblemen whose military careers had been so unjustly easy. He had not even been allowed to go to America with Rochambeau to seek glory. That was reserved for the great families: Ségur, Lauzun, Nouailles. *Les Liaisons Dangereuses* is, as a novel, something like what *The Marriage of Figaro* was as a drama: a pamphlet against an immoral, powerful and envied class. Laclos refrains from talking politics, but the reader is made to despise—and to draw certain conclusions.

The book made a great stir. Fifty editions of it were published during Laclos' lifetime. Efforts were made to identify the characters. At a time when the nobility was as revolutionary as the bourgeoisie, this bombshell was a source of pleasant excitement. It is interesting to note that a social class, whether it be the nobility or the bourgeoisie, gives better treatment to those who decry it than to those who praise it. Everyone, at Versailles as well as in Paris, wanted to know the author. His colonel became worried. An officer who was a novelist and a cynic. . . . It did not seem proper. But Laclos was an excellent artilleryman, and the cannon obtained indulgence for the novel. Some of his readers regretted that he had painted such a black picture, but he was praised for his knowledge of the passions, his gift for plot, his skill in creating unforgettable characters, and the naturalness of his style.

The surprising part of it is that this gifted author stopped writing after one triumph. He had been an amateur of genius; he became a provincial officer again. Still more surprising, that roué, that Machiavelli of sentiment, married and became a faithful, loving, tender-hearted husband. At the age of forty-three he singled out a young lady from La Rochelle, Mademoiselle Solange Marie Duperré, sister of the admiral. She had read *Les Liaisons Dangereuses* and said, "Monsieur de Laclos will never set foot in our drawing room." This statement was reported to Laclos. "Within six months," he said, "I will marry Mademoiselle Duperré."

This, at least, was like Valmont, the hero of *Les Liaisons Dangereuses*. He seduced Solange Duperré and got her pregnant. But he "made amends" by marrying her—not at all in Valmont's style—and he was the most sentimental of husbands. "For nearly twenty years now," he later wrote to his wife, "I have owed my happiness to you. The past is the guarantee of the future." "I see with pleasure that you at last feel loved, but allow me to tell you that you should have been sure of it for the past twelve years." He praised her for being "an adorable mistress, an excellent wife and a tender mother." When she began to put on weight: "The more there is of you, the better."

A thoroughly conjugal Lovelace! He even planned to write a second novel in which he would prove that there was no happiness outside of the family. The difficulty of arousing interest without romantic vicissitudes led him to give up this plan. He was no doubt right to do so. Good marriages make bad novels. André Gide was glad that Laclos had abandoned a plan so contrary to his genius, and did not believe that that prodigious creator of diabolical characters could have sincerely loved virtue. "There is no doubt," wrote Gide, "that Laclos was hand in hand with Satan." I am not so sure. More simply, Laclos had realized that Satan would help him to find readers. As he himself said, "after having written some poetry and studied a profession which would not lead me to any great advancement, I resolved to write a work that would be off the beaten path, a work that would cause a great commotion and go on reverberating in the world after I was gone." If this was his goal, he achieved it.

The Vicomte de Noailles, an admirer of Laclos, had introduced him to the Duc d'Orléans, who made him the secretary of his commands. At the time of the Revolution, in the house of this prince whom he dominated (insofar as one can dominate such a changeable mind), Laclos carried out rather "Satanic" intrigues against the king and queen. The duke hoped to overthrow the sovereigns by means of riots, and obtain the regency of the kingdom. Laclos egged him on and tried to help him.

His secret passions were more violent. He entered the Jacobin Club and became an influential member. In 1792, Danton sent him to the army as a member of old Marshal Lückner's staff, in order to forestall that foreign soldier's defection. Laclos, an excellent officer, reorganized the army and paved the way for the victory at Valmy. But the treason of his leader, Dumouriez, made Laclos suspect and he was arrested. The fall of Robespierre and the end of the Reign of Terror saved him from the guillotine. Having been appointed a brigadier general in the time of Bonaparte, he commanded the artillery of the Army of the Rhine, then that of the Army of Italy. In 1803 he was transferred to Murat's corps in Naples and placed in charge of the defense of Taranto. He died there of dysentery. Thus ended the strange career of a talented officer who made his name illustrious by writing a novelistic masterpiece.

II
THE NOVEL AND ITS CHARACTERS

It was natural that a reader of *Clarissa* should have thought of writing a novel in the form of letters. It is a somewhat artificial form. The essentials of life take place in conversations and actions, but letters can relate and describe them. They allow the author to show his subtlety. In a letter, there is both what it says and what it hides. It betrays and reveals. Laclos was very proud of the variety of styles he gave to his characters. It is not so striking as he thought. They all express themselves in the wonderful style of the French eighteenth century, that period when a young girl fresh out of a convent school wrote in a way that shames the writers of our own day.

Two groups of characters confront each other in this book: the monsters and the victims. The monsters are the Marquise de Merteuil, a dissolute, cynical and treacherous great lady who, when she has reasons for avenging herself, does not hesitate to break all the rules which constitute morality for others; and the Vicomte de Valmont, a professional Don Juan, an expert in feminine conquests, often radio-controlled by Madame de Merteuil, sometimes in rebellion against her. The victims are Madame de Tourvel, a beautiful, devout and prudish middle-class wife who would like to love her husband in peace; Cécile Volanges, an ignorant young girl, sensual without realizing it, whose mother wants her to marry the "old" Comte de Gercourt (he is thirty-six), but who loves the young Chevalier Danceny; and finally this Danceny, who loves Cécile, but whom Madame de Merteuil, without loving him, has taken as her lover.

The liaisons are therefore multiple and entangled. Gercourt, who is to marry young Cécile, has been Madame de Merteuil's lover and has betrayed her. She wants to take vengeance on him, and for this purpose she intends to make use of Valmont, who was also once her lover, but has remained her friend. Between Valmont and Madame de Merteuil there is no hypocrisy. They have taken pleasure together, they will perhaps do so again, and it has been and will be without any passion. They get along with each other in carrying out certain operations, as gangsters might do: without mutual confidence, but with professional esteem.

What does Madame de Merteuil ask of Valmont? That he seduce Cécile Volanges and make her his mistress before her marriage to Gercourt. The latter will thus play a ludicrous part. Moreover, there is nothing unpleasant about the service Valmont is being asked to perform, quite the contrary. Cécile is fifteen and very pretty—why not pluck the rosebud? Valmont is not enthusiastic at first. Seducing a naïve girl who knows nothing is a project unworthy of his talents. He has embarked on an undertaking that will bring him more glory and pleasure: the conquest of the inaccessible, saintly and austere Madame de Tourvel. The surrender of that pious woman is the goal to which he aspires. His strategy will be to speak to her not of love, but of religion.

In the hope of converting him, she will consent to receive him. The devil makes himself a hermit to make himself a lover.

Soon the three intrigues become intertwined. Young Danceny, driven away by Cécile's mother, asks Valmont to deliver letters to his beloved. The betrayal of a friend adds a certain spice to the seduction of an innocent girl. Valmont begins to desire Cécile. On the pretext of delivering Danceny's letters to her, he goes into her bedroom at night, steals a kiss, then much more, and so becomes the lover of a charming girl who is bewildered by what is happening to her, for her body has acquired a taste for Valmont while her heart still belongs to Danceny.

This success does not prevent Valmont from pursuing his conquest of Madame de Tourvel. He finally reaches the point of speaking to her of love. She tries to flee; her resistance exacerbates Valmont's desire. He has every reason to think he will triumph, for the poor woman has fallen madly in love with him. How will he obtain the final victory? The oldest tricks are the best. He pretends to be in despair. He says he is going to withdraw to a monastery. "I shall either possess you or die," he says, and when she continues to elude him he murmurs in a sinister tone, "So be it, then: death!" She falls unconscious into his arms. He has won.

The victims' misfortunes have been consummated. It is now time for the punishment of the guilty. In yielding to Valmont, Madame de Tourvel had thought she was assuring his salvation. He seemed to be sincerely in love with her. But how could the Marquise de Merteuil tolerate the triumph of virtue—or of passion? She makes fun of Valmont and challenges him to break off with Madame de Tourvel. This challenge excites Valmont; he will abandon Madame de Tourvel and try to win back the marquise. Out of pure vanity, he breaks off with the admirable woman he has just conquered, sending her an outrageously brutal letter dictated by the marquise. Disillusioned and reduced to despair, Madame de Tourvel "sinks into self-disgust" and soon dies of remorse.

But Madame de Merteuil quarrels with Valmont and reveals the truth about Cécile Volanges to Danceny. Danceny challenges Valmont to a duel and kills him. Cécile, dishonored, enters a convent. There still remains Madame de Merteuil. She is also terribly punished. She has been engaged in a lawsuit that will decide her entire fortune; she loses it and finds herself ruined. She catches smallpox; she survives, but is disfigured, loses one eye and is truly hideous. "O great Nemesis!" as Lord Byron would have said. "Who could fail to shudder in thinking of the misfortunes that can be caused by a single dangerous association?" Thus ends this extremely immoral morality play. The stage is strewn with corpses. One is reminded of the dénouement of *Hamlet*.

III
LOVE IS WAR

Are these dark adventures plausible? It is certain that the mores of the time were quite free. In high society, a husband and wife seldom saw each other. They lived in the same house, that was all. Deep feeling was rare; it was considered ridiculous. Two lovers who loved each other too much spread "constraint and boredom" around them. They refused to play the game. In this extreme license, morality lost but society gained. "The coquettishness of the men and the women," says Besenval, "maintained their vivacity and provided stimulating adventures every day." There was little jealousy: "A man and a woman attract each other, come together, part, come together again."

All these revels were kept rather secret, however. In public, everything—demeanor, gestures, vocabulary—remained respectable. Their freedom of action was never reflected in speech. "Even at their keenest moments, Laclos's characters speak the language of Marivaux." Appearances remained irreproachable. A husband who caught his wife in the act said gently, "Such imprudence, Madame! If it were anyone but me. . . ." In those days, the English nobility was no more prudish than the French nobility. In some respects, Valmont is Byron, who, moreover, had read Laclos and did his best to imitate his hero.

Reread the correspondence between Byron and Lady Melbourne. You will see that they speak of the games of love in the same tone as Valmont and Madame de Merteuil. They have the same impudent, detached attitude toward their victims. Their problems are not sentimental, but technical. What must one say and do to make a woman surrender? It is a question of tactics, not of love. There is one difference: Byron was less hardened than Valmont. He sometimes spared, out of pity, a willing woman to whom he was attracted, such as Lady Frances Webster. Sometimes, also, he threw his heart into the game. He seduced his half-sister Augusta, but he loved her.

Madame de Merteuil, however, is as ignorant of pity as of

love. Valmont himself ruins the innocent Cécile's life without remorse. Is it natural, is it possible that a human being should be so malicious? And above all, is it conceivable that he should be so cruel in love when, in most people, this sentiment engenders tenderness and attachment to the partner? Here lies the whole drama of Don Juan, a personage who has inspired an enormous literature and to whom women have always been strongly drawn.

How is a Don Juan formed? Why is Valmont so cruel? The case of Byron helps us a little to understand. Byron was a sentimentalist until he was betrayed by the woman who was his first love. He spent his whole life taking vengeance on all women for this betrayal. In his conquests, vanity and the spirit of revenge played a much greater part than desire. Valmont is like those dictators who attack innocent countries to show that they have a good army. His vocabulary is that of the warrior, sometimes that of the geometer, never that of the lover.

"So far, my fair friend, I believe you will find that I acted with a purity of method which will please you, and you will see that I in no way departed from the true principles of that kind of warfare which we have often observed to be so similar to the other kind. Judge me, then, as you would judge Turenne or Frederick. I forced the enemy to fight when she wanted to avoid action; by skillful maneuvers I gave myself the choice of terrain and disposition; I inspired her with confidence, so that I could overtake her more easily in her retreat; I made confidence give way to terror before joining battle; I left nothing to chance, except for consideration of a great advantage in case of victory, and the certainty of resources in case of defeat; finally, I did not join battle until I had an assured retreat by which I could cover and hold everything I had previously conquered."

A lover like Valmont is a strategist; he has also been compared to a matador. A woman's fall and his possession of her are equivalent to the kill. In the case of women who, like Cécile and Madame de Tourvel, are not willing, it is made possible only by skillful maneuvers. It is a whole "dramatic game." Just as the matador does not like to fight a sluggish bull, the Valmont type of Don Juan needs spirited resistance and tears for his pleasure. Or, borrowing an image from another sport: "Let the obscure poacher kill the deer he has ambushed: the real hunter must bring it to bay . . ." "It is not enough for me to possess her, it is my will that she shall give herself to me."

"It is my will." For this is definitely an exercise of will. Reread carefully Letter 81, in which Madame de Merteuil tells

Valmont the story of her life. No life was ever more rigorously planned. Her slightest gestures, the expressions of her face, her voice—everything is under control. She procures pledges of security against her lovers: she always has some means of ruining them. "When I have foreseen breaking off . . . I have been able to smother in advance, beneath ridicule or calumny, any credence those dangerous men might have obtained." In reading this famous and terrible letter, one thinks of the ferocious diplomats of the Renaissance, and also of Stendhal's heroes. But the men and women of the Renaissance sharpened their will for the conquest of power. Madame de Merteuil, Valmont and those like them have only one goal: sex—or sexual vengeance.

It may seem excessive to place such great means in action for such an end. All that strategy and calculation to win such a frivolous prize! "That a woman capable of that kind of energy," writes Malraux, "a woman to whom Stendhal would have given great designs, should concern herself so long with making sure that a lover who has left her will be cuckolded in advance—this would be a singular story if the book were only the application of a will to sexual ends. But it is something quite different: an erotization of the will. Will and sexuality are mingled, multiply each other. . . ." Since in Laclos pleasure is bound up with the ideas of war, hunting and constraint, it is not separate from the will. It is the same in Stendhal. Julien Sorel (in *The Red and the Black*) forces himself, despite the danger, to take Madame de Rênal's hand and to climb up to Mathilde's bedroom, and his pleasure comes much more from these victories over himself than from the contact of that flesh. But, unlike Laclos, Stendhal is not censured by moralists; he respects religion and passion.

It must also be said that in Stendhal's time the Revolution and the Empire supplied the will with other objects that were worthier of it. In the society of the eighteenth century, and particularly in provincial garrisons, energetic people had almost no other outlet for their energy than amorous conquest. At Versailles, power was obtained by means that were internal to the court; most men had no opportunity for political activity. Officers did little fighting, and only for a few months a year. Love became the great activity and, if one may say so, the great sport. At La Rochelle, Laclos himself truly hunted down Solange Duperré. The Revolution finally gave him a chance to devote his will and intelligence to more important objects. Then he changed. When Baudelaire took notes on *Les Liaisons Dangereuses* he wrote, "The Revolution was made by voluptuous men. Licentious books therefore comment on and explain the Revolution.''

While they were still part of a vain and idle society, the same people who later, when they were caught up in a great drama, made it a point of honor to die bravely (and that frivolous French nobility faced the scaffold with admirable courage) placed their ''glory'' in the conquests of love, and even, like Madame de Merteuil, in the triumphs of malice. She seeks domination and vengeance much more than pleasure. In her childhood she must have had some feelings of inferiority which she can now soothe only by the cruelest revenges. Ruining men and women, placing them in tragic or ridiculous situations: such is her happiness.

She enjoys it all the more because, by her efforts as a ''female Tartuffe,'' she has succeeded in presenting herself to the world as a virtuous woman. She carries hypocrisy to the point of genius and for that reason considers herself superior to Valmont. ''What have you done,'' she writes to him, ''that I have not surpassed a thousand times?'' We are reminded of Corneille:

> Et qu'a fait après tout ce grand nombre d'années
> Que ne puisse égaler une de mes journées?*

It was indeed the same ''point of honor'' which, in the days of the Cid, led noble lords to run their swords through one another and which, in Laclos's time, summoned the two sexes to oppose each other in combats without mercy.

Let us turn to the victims. Cécile is perhaps Laclos's master-piece. Nothing is more difficult for a novelist to depict than an adolescent girl. As soon as Cécile leaves her convent school, she is taken in hand by Madame de Merteuil, who understands her ''education.'' ''She is really delightful! She has neither character nor principles . . . I do not think she will ever be noted for her sentiments, but everything about her indicates the keenest sensa-tions. Although she is neither quick-witted nor cunning, she has a certain natural duplicity, if one may so describe it, which sometimes surprises even me, and which will be all the more successful since her face is the image of candor and ingenuous-ness. . . . You may take my word for it: no one was ever more susceptible to a surprise attack on the senses.''

And Valmont, after his easy victory: ''I did not go back to my

---

*''And what, after all, has that great number of years done that one of my days cannot equal?''

room until dawn. I was in great need of rest and sleep, but I sacrificed them both to my desire to be present at breakfast this morning. I am passionately fond of watching reactions and expressions the next morning. You cannot imagine what they were like this time. There was such embarrassment in her demeanor! She had such difficulty in walking! She kept her eyes lowered, and they were so big, with such dark rings around them! That round face had grown so much longer! Nothing could have been more amusing.'' Hangmen are often voluptuous.

There remains Madame de Tourvel, who refuses to fight. Tender, sincere and faithful, she can only die of love and disgust. But she is a middle-class woman while Madame de Merteuil is a great lady, and this, as we have already indicated, is one of the keys to the book, which denounces the depravity of high society. The Revolution was carried out against political abuses, but also against corrupt morals. Puritanism has its faults; it darkens life; but it gives singular strength to the ruling class. The libertinism of rulers engenders envy, anger, contempt and finally revolt on the part of those who are ruled.

IV
Moral or Immoral?

Is *Les Liaisons Dangereuses* an immoral book? We have seen that many critics have seemed to think so, and have relegated this incontestable masterpiece to the category of licentious books. In his preface, Laclos defends himself against such judgments. "It appears to me at least," he says, "that it is a service to morality to expose the means used by those who have bad morals to corrupt those whose morals are good." He flatters himself with having demonstrated two important truths: "The first is that any woman who consents to receive an immoral man into her society will eventually become his victim; the second is that a mother is imprudent, at the very least, if she allows anyone other than herself to have her daughter's confidence." He adds that a good mother, and an intelligent woman, said to him after having read the manuscript, "I think I would be doing my daughter a real service if I gave her this book on her wedding day," and that if all mothers thought this way he would always be glad he had published it.

This manner of presenting things would be a little naïve if Laclos really believed in it. It is true that the wicked are punished at the end of his work: they lose a lawsuit, catch smallpox or die in a duel. This, no doubt, proves that crime does not pay. But virtue is treated no better, and the saintly Madame de Tourvel ends as badly as Madame de Merteuil. And above all it is not certain that the reader will be turned away from bad morals by those who here exemplify them. It may be that he will envy the violence of their pleasures more than he will fear the rigors of their punishments. The vigor of those wills, the infallibility of those calculations and the penetrating intelligence of those roués may arouse more admiration than repulsion in some people. Despite St. Helena, reading a life of Napoleon has never disgusted a young man ambitious for power.

Giraudoux has clearly seen that "the beauty, the subject and the scandal of the book" is the Valmont-Merteuil couple, a kind of marriage of Evil which unites the two most seductive libertines in literature, the handsomest and most adroit man, the most charming and subtle woman. "It is the spectacle of this superb combination unleashed in the hunt for pleasure that is new, the equality of man and woman in the exercise of their passions. They are endowed with all the qualities required of the perfect couple: absolute confidence, secrecy with regard to the rest of mankind. . . . Nothing is more moving in stories of animals than the hunting pair, whether they be foxes or lions. And nothing is more satisfying for the spirit of Evil than the sight of the beautiful Merteuil and the handsome Valmont beating up game for each other, because for both of them victory has less value than confidence, and when each of them has felled his prey it is largely for the other that he takes his pleasure."

Baudelaire absolves Laclos for a subtler reason. He denies that Laclos is more immoral than the authors of our time; he is only franker. "Has morality become loftier in the nineteenth century?" Baudelaire asks himself, and he answers, "No, it is only that the energy of evil has declined, and silliness has taken the place of wit." Baudelaire thinks that it was no more blamable to go to so much trouble for what one admitted to be a trifle than to mingle sex with the language of worship. He judges Laclos to be healthier and more sincere than George Sand or Musset. "People did not damn themselves any more than they do today, but they damned themselves less foolishly. . . . In reality, Satanism has won. Satan has made himself ingenuous. Self-aware evil was less atrocious and closer to cure than self-ignorant evil."

It is true that a serious moralist always paints an immoral world because it is his role to put us on guard against the world as it is. If nature were moral, moralists would be useless. But nature is immoral, or amoral. Natural instincts push living beings to hunting, fighting and mating. It is societies that have imposed morals. When these morals are hypocritical, the courageous moralist becomes frightened, because he depicts the truth and the truth about man is frightening. However, when this moralist expresses himself, as he often does, in thoughts or maxims, without presenting any personages, his harshness appears less crudely. But imagine, as you read La Rochefoucauld, the novels that could be built on his maxims. You will find a hundred subjects as cruel as that of *Les Liaisons Dangereuses*.

Another and stronger reason has helped to back up the accusation of immorality. It is that Laclos dealt a very hard blow to the legend of feminine resistance. George Bernard Shaw later took up this idea that in love it is often the woman who is the hunter and the man who is the quarry. Madame de Merteuil guides Valmont, dictates his most important letters and makes fun of him if he in turn ventures to give her advice. "Here, as in life," says Baudelaire, "the palm for perversity goes to the woman." Valmont might have given way to tender feelings for Madame de Tourvel if Madame de Merteuil had not spurred him to overcome the obstacle. Now if women of the Merteuil type know they are superior to men, they do not like others to know it, except for a very intimate accomplice. Feeling much better protected by a mask of sentimentality, even of innocence, they have always condemned the novelists or playwrights who have unmasked them. Dumas *fils* discovered this at his expense.

Laclos was obdurate on this point all his life. When someone said to him, "You create monsters in order to combat them; women like Madame de Merteuil do not exist," he replied, "Then why all this commotion? When Don Quixote armed himself to go off to fight windmills, did anyone take it into his head to defend him? He was pitied; he was not accused. . . . If no woman has ever plunged into debauchery while pretending to devote herself to love; if no woman has ever facilitated and even instigated the seduction of her 'friend'; if no woman has ever set out to ruin a lover who has become unfaithful too soon—if none of those things has ever happened, then I was wrong to write. . . . But who would dare to deny the everyday truth?" A heretic and an apostate!

Once again, is this novel moral, as its author claimed it to be? I believe it teaches a morality, not by the torrent of catastrophes that befall the wicked at the end, but rather by the futility of their pleasures. These people are constructed by a merciless geometer; they act only by principles and reasoning. Applying logic to what ought to be dictated by intuition, feigning passions that are not felt, coldly studying the weaknesses of others in order to dominate them: such is the game played by Valmont and Madame de Merteuil.

Can it bring happiness? Laclos's novel clearly shows that it cannot. Not that pleasure does not contain a substantial and delightful reality. But Madame de Merteuil herself finally acknowledges that physical pleasures are monotonous if they are not animated by the strength of sentiments. "Have you not yet noticed," she writes, "that, while pleasure is indeed the sole motive for the union of the two sexes, it is not sufficient to form a bond between them, and that if it is preceded by desire, which attracts, it is none the less followed by disgust, which repels?"

The answer to these questions is that we must take advantage of the moment when desire embellishes everything to attach sentiments to this instinct, and also the social bond of marriage. The human race has had the wonderful intuition of constraining man to take a binding oath at a time when desire makes it more acceptable to him. Don Juan, or Valmont, says, "No chains for me; it is the constant renewal of desire and pleasures that gives life its value." *Les Liaisons Dangereuses* shows that this kind of life does not bring happiness, and also that it is not desire which makes Don Juans; it is imagination and pride.

It must be pointed out, to be complete, that the female readers of *Les Liaisons Dangereuses* had given at least an equal success to *La Nouvelle Héloïse*, in which the idea of virtue is always present. The cynicism of Laclos's heroes does not seem to have been shaken by Rousseau's noble declamations. One must pass through the Revolution and the Empire in order to understand how Laclos's harsh callousness and Rousseau's ardors, melted and combined by a newer genius, were later to produce *The Red and the Black* and *The Charterhouse of Parma*.

LES LIAISONS DANGEREUSES

or

Letters Collected from within a Social Group,
and Published for the Instruction of Others

by

Monsieur C . . . de L . . .

I have seen the morals of my time, and I have published these letters.

—Jean-Jacques Rousseau
     Preface to *La Nouvelle Héloïse*

⁓ Publisher's Foreword ⁓

We consider it our duty to notify the public that despite the title of this work and what the editor says about it in his preface, we do not guarantee the authenticity of the collection, and we even have good reason to believe that it is only a novel.

Moreover, it seems to us that although the author has sought plausibility, he has foolishly destroyed it himself by the period in which he has set the events he is now making public. Indeed, some of the characters he presents have such bad morals that it is impossible to suppose that they could have lived in our age—this age of philosophy in which, as everyone knows, enlightenment has spread on all sides, making all men so honorable and all women so modest and reserved.

It is therefore our opinion that if the events reported in this work have any basis of truth, they could have happened only in other places and at other times; and we strongly condemn the author, who, apparently seduced by the hope of arousing greater interest by setting his work in his own time and country, has dared to depict, in our attire and with our customs, morals which are so foreign to us.

In order that we may at least do everything in our power to protect the overly credulous reader from being misled in this matter, we shall support our opinion with a line of reasoning which we present to him with confidence, for it seems to us victorious and unanswerable: it is that the same causes would certainly not fail to produce the same effects, and yet nowadays we never see a young lady with an income of sixty thousand francs who becomes a nun, or a magistrate's young and pretty wife who dies of sorrow.

∾ Editor's Preface ∾

Although the public may find this work, or rather this collection, too voluminous, it contains only a very small number of the letters composing the correspondence from which it is drawn. When I was requested to put this correspondence in order by those into whose hands it had fallen, and whose intention I knew was to publish it, I asked nothing in return for my efforts except permission to omit anything that seemed useless to me, and I have tried to retain only those letters which seemed necessary either for the understanding of the events or for the development of the characters. If to this slight task is added that of placing the letters I have retained in an order that is nearly always chronological, and if inserting a few short notes, most of which have no other object than to indicate the sources of quotations or to explain my reasons for some of the omissions I have taken the liberty of making, my whole share in this work will be known. My purpose went no further.*

I had proposed more extensive changes, nearly all relating to the purity of the diction or the style, which will be found quite faulty. I would also have liked to have permission to cut some of the letters that are too long, several of which deal separately, and almost without transition, with matters that are totally unrelated. This labor, which was not accepted, would no doubt have been insufficient to give merit to the work, but it would at least have removed some of its defects.

I was told that the intention was to publish the letters themselves, not merely a work based on them, and that it would be as contrary to plausibility as to truth that the nine or ten people who took part in the correspondence should all have written with equal purity. And when I replied that this was so far from being the case that there was not one of them who had not made serious mistakes which could not fail to be criticized, I was told

---

*I must also state that I have suppressed or changed the names of all the persons mentioned in these letters, and that if among the names I have substituted for them there are any that belong to someone, this is only an error on my part from which no inference should be drawn.

that any sensible reader would surely expect to find mistakes in a collection of letters by private individuals, since of all those published so far by various eminent authors, and even by certain Academicians, there was none that was not open to this reproach to some extent. These reasons did not convince me, and I considered them, as I still do, easier to give than to accept; but the decision was not mine to make, so I gave in. I merely reserved the right to protest and declare my disagreement, which I now do.

As for any merit this work may have, perhaps I ought not to express myself on the subject, since my opinion should not and cannot influence that of anyone else. However, those who like to have a good idea of what to expect when they begin a book may continue reading this preface; others will do better to go directly to the work itself: they already know enough about it.

What I first wish to say is that, while I was in favor of publishing these letters, as I have admitted, I am far from hoping that they will be successful. This sincerity on my part must not be mistaken for the affected modesty of an author, for I declare with the same frankness that I would not have concerned myself with this collection if it had not seemed to me worthy of being offered to the public. Let us try to resolve this apparent contradiction.

The merit of a work is composed of either its usefulness or its charm, or of both, if it has them; but its success, which is not always a proof of merit, often depends more on the choice of a subject than on its execution, more on the aggregate of objects presented than on the manner in which they are treated. Now since this collection contains, as the title indicates, the letters of an entire group of people, there is a diversity of interests which weakens the reader's own interest. Furthermore, since nearly all the sentiments here expressed are feigned or dissimulated, they can arouse only the interest of curiosity, which is always far below the interest of sentiment; the latter makes one less inclined to indulgence and more aware of faults to be found in details when these details are constantly opposed to the sole desire one wishes to satisfy.

These defects are perhaps compensated for by a quality which also arises from the nature of the work, namely, the variety of styles, a merit which an author achieves with difficulty, but which here occurs spontaneously, and at least saves the reader from the boredom of uniformity. Some readers may also attribute a certain importance to the rather large number of new or little-known observations that are scattered through the letters. This, I believe, is all that can be expected from them in the way of charm, even if they are judged with the greatest indulgence.

The usefulness of the work will perhaps be more contested, yet it seems to me easier to establish. It appears to me at least that it is a service to morality to expose the means used by those who have bad morals to corrupt those whose morals are good, and I believe these letters can effectively contribute to that end. They also provide a proof and an example of two important truths which are so neglected that one might think them to be unknown: the first is that any woman who consents to receive an immoral man into her society will eventually become his victim; the second is that a mother is imprudent, at the very least, if she allows anyone other than herself to have her daughter's confidence. And young people of both sexes may learn here that the friendship which seems to be granted to them so easily by those who have bad morals is never anything but a dangerous snare, and is as fatal to their happiness as to their virtue. But abuse, which is always so close to good, seems to me too greatly to be feared here, and far from recommending this book for young people, I consider it important that they should be kept away from it and all others like it. It seems to me that the time when it may cease to be dangerous and become useful was quite clearly understood, for her own sex, by a mother who is not only witty but sensible. "I think I would be doing my daughter a real service," she said to me after she had read the manuscript of this correspondence, "if I gave her this book on her wedding day." If all mothers think this way about it, I shall always be glad I have published it.

But even if this favorable supposition is accepted, it still seems to me that this collection will please only a few. Depraved men and women will find it to their interest to decry a work that may harm them; and since they are not lacking in adroitness, they may be clever enough to induce the most rigorous moralists, alarmed by the picture of immortality that I have not been afraid to present, to side with them.

The so-called freethinkers will take no interest in a pious woman, because her very piety will make them regard her as foolish, while the pious will be angered to see virtue succumb, and will complain that religion is shown with too little power.

On the other hand, readers of delicate taste will be disgusted by the faulty and oversimplified style of some of these letters, while most readers, misled by the idea that everything which appears in print is the fruit of careful effort, will think they see in other letters the labored manner of an author who shows himself behind the character through whose mouth he speaks.

Finally, it will perhaps be rather commonly said that each thing is of value only in its proper place, and that while the excessively polished style of authors usually deprives social letters of some of their charm, the negligences of such letters become real defects and make them unbearable when they are printed.

I frankly confess that all these objections may be well founded; I also think I could answer them, and without exceeding the length of a preface. But it must be realized that if it were necessary to answer everything, the book would have to be unable to answer anything, and that if I had judged this to be the case, I would have suppressed both the preface and the book.

≈ PART ONE ≈

≈ *From Cécile Volanges to Sophie Carnay at the Ursuline Convent of* ———

Paris, August 3, 17—

As you can see, my dear friend, I've kept my word, and hats and pompons don't take up all my time—there will always be some left over for you. Yet I've seen more finery only today than we saw in the whole four years we spent together, and I think the haughty Tanville* will be more upset by my first visit, when I intend to ask for her, than she used to think she upset us whenever she came to see us in her best clothes. Mama has asked my opinion about everything, and she treats me much less like a schoolgirl than she used to. I have my own maid. I have a bedroom and a study at my disposal, and I'm writing this to you on a very pretty writing desk. I've been given the key to it and I can lock up anything I like in it. Mama says I'll see her every day when she gets up, that I can wait till dinner time to arrange my hair, because we'll always be alone, and that she'll tell me every day when she wants me to meet her in the afternoon. The rest of the time is my own, and I have my harp, my drawing and my books, the same as in the convent, except that Mother Perpétue isn't here to scold me, and I can do nothing all day long if I want to. But since my Sophie isn't here to talk and laugh with me, I may as well keep myself busy.

It's not yet five o'clock and I'm not supposed to meet Mama till seven—plenty of time, if I had anything to tell you! But so

---

*A pupil in the same convent.

far no one has talked to me about anything, and if it weren't for the preparations I see being made, and all the seamstresses who come here for me, I'd think there were no plans at all for my marriage, and that it was only another of good old Joséphine's* silly stories. Yet Mama has told me so many times that a young lady must stay in convent until she's married, and now she's taken me out of it, so Joséphine must be right.

A carriage has just stopped in front of our door and Mama has sent word to me that she wants me to come to her immediately. Can it be *he*? I'm not dressed, my hands are trembling and my heart is pounding. I asked my maid if she knew who was with my mother. "Why, it's Monsieur C——," she said. And she laughed! Oh, I think it's *he*! I'll be sure to come back and tell you what has happened. At least I know his name now. I mustn't keep him waiting. Good-by for a little while.

How you're going to laugh at your poor Cécile! Oh, I was so ashamed! But you would have been taken in the same as I was. When I walked into Mama's room I saw a gentleman dressed in black standing beside her. I greeted him as well as I could and stood still, unable to move. You can imagine how closely I examined him! "Madame," he said to my mother as he bowed to me, "you have a charming daughter and I appreciate your kindness more than ever." When I heard this outspoken remark I began to tremble so much that I couldn't stand up. I found an armchair and sat down in it, blushing deeply and terribly disconcerted. No sooner had I sat down than he was at my knees. Your poor Cécile lost her head. As Mama herself said, I was frightened out of my wits. I leapt to my feet and screamed—the way I did on the day of the thunderstorm. Mama burst out laughing and said, "What's the matter with you? Sit down and let Monsieur measure your foot." Yes, my dear friend, the gentleman was a shoemaker. I can't tell you how ashamed I was. Fortunately no one else was there but Mama. When I'm married, I don't think I'll ever use that shoemaker again.

You must admit that we're very well informed! Good-by. It's nearly six o'clock and my maid has just told me that I must get dressed. Good-by, my dear Sophie; I love you as though I were still at the convent.

P.S.—I don't know by whom to send this letter, so I'll wait till Joséphine comes.

---

*The doorkeeper of the convent.

LETTER 2

~ *From the Marquise de Merteuil to the Vicomte de Valmont
at the Château de* ———

Paris, August, 4, 17—

Come back, my dear Vicomte, come back: what are you
doing, what *can* you be doing at the house of an old aunt whose
entire estate is entailed to you? Leave at once; I need you. A
wonderful idea has occurred to me and I am willing to let you
carry it out. These few words should be enough for you and,
only too honored by my choice, you should eagerly come to
receive my orders on your knees; but you abuse my kindness
even now that you are no longer making use of it, and in the
choice between everlasting hatred and excessive indulgence, it is
your good fortune that my kindness has prevailed. I shall therefore tell you my plans; but swear to me as a faithful knight that
you will not become involved in any other adventure until you
have brought this one to a close. It is worthy of a hero: you will
be serving both love and vengeance, and you will also have one
more *rouerie*** to put in your memoirs; yes, in your memoirs, for
I want them to be printed, and I shall undertake the task of writing
them. But let us leave this and return to the matter at hand.

Madame de Volanges is arranging a marriage for her daughter.
It is still a secret, but she told me about it yesterday. And whom
do you think she has chosen to be her son-in-law? The Comte de
Gercourt. Who would ever have thought that Gercourt would
some day be my cousin? I am furious. . . . Have you not
guessed why? Oh, how dense you are! Have you forgiven him
for that affair with the *Intendante*?** And have *I* not still more
reason to complain of him, monster that you are?*** But I am
becoming calmer, and the hope of vengeance soothes my soul.

---

*The words "*roué*" and "*rouerie*," which are fortunately falling into disuse in good
society, were employed quite frequently at the time when these letters were written.

**A title designating the wife of the Administrator of a province. (Translator's note.)

***To understand this passage, the readers must know that the Comte de Gercourt had
left the Marquise de Merteuil for the *Intendante* de———, who had given up the Vicomte
de Valmont for him, and that it was then that the Marquise and the Vicomte became
attached to each other. Since all this occurred much earlier than the events dealt with in
these letters, the entire correspondence relating to it has been omitted.

You and I have both been annoyed a hundred times by the importance that Gercourt attaches to his future wife, and by the foolish presumptuousness which makes him believe he will avoid the inevitable fate. You know his ridiculous prejudice in favor of a cloistered education, and his still more ridiculous preconception about the modesty of blonde women. I am willing to bet, in fact, that despite little Cécile Volanges' income of sixty thousand francs, he would never have agreed to marry her if she had been a brunette, or if she had not been educated in a convent. Let us prove to him that he is a fool. She will make a fool of him sooner or later, I have no doubt of that; but it would be amusing if it were to happen at the very beginning. How delightful it would be for us to hear boasting the next day, for he will boast, you may be sure of it! And then, if you have succeeded in training that little girl, the chances are excellent that Gercourt will become the talk of Paris, the same as anyone else.

Furthermore, the heroine of this new adventure is worthy of your best efforts: she is really pretty, and only fifteen; a rosebud, incredibly awkward and not at all affected, but you men are not afraid of that; and then she has a certain languid look which promises a great deal. If to all this you add the fact that I am commending her to you, your course will be clear: you will thank me and obey me.

You will receive this letter tomorrow morning. I demand that you come to see me at seven o'clock tomorrow evening. I shall receive no one until eight, not even the reigning Chevalier; his mind is inadequate for such an important matter. You can see that love has not blinded me. At eight o'clock I shall release you, and you will return to have supper with the fair young lady, for I have invited her and her mother to supper. Good-by; it is past noon: I shall soon cease to concern myself with you.

LETTER 3

~ *From Cécile Volanges to Sophie Carnay*

Paris, August 4, 17—

I still know nothing, my dear friend. Mama had many guests for supper last night. Although it was to my interest to examine them, especially the men, I was very bored. All of them, men and women alike, were constantly looking at me and whispering to each other. I could see they were talking about me and it made me blush, I couldn't help it. I wish I could have, because I've noticed that other women don't blush when people look at them; or perhaps the rouge they wear makes it impossible to see the redness of their cheeks when they become embarrassed, because it must be very hard not to blush when a man stares at you.

What upset me most was not knowing what they thought about me. I think I heard the word "pretty" several times, but I clearly heard the word "awkward," and it must be true, because the lady who said it is a relative and friend of my mother; she even seemed to have a sudden feeling of friendship for me. She was the only person who talked to me all evening. Tomorrow we're going to have supper at her house.

After supper I also heard one man say to another, and I'm sure he was talking about me, "We'll have to let her ripen, then this winter we'll see." Perhaps he's the man I'm going to marry; but if so, it won't happen till four months from now! I wish I knew.

Joséphine has just arrived and she says she's in a hurry, but I want to tell you about another "awkwardness" of mine. Oh, I think that lady is right!

After supper they all began to gamble. I sat down beside Mama. I don't know how it happened, but I fell asleep almost immediately. I was awakened by loud laughter. I don't know if they were laughing at me, but I think they were. Mama let me go up to my room, and I was glad—it was after eleven o'clock! Good-bye, my dear Sophie; always love your Cécile. I assure you the world is not so amusing as we used to imagine.

LETTER 4

〜 *From the Vicomte de Valmont to the Marquise de Merteuil in Paris*

Château de ———, August 5, 17—

Your orders are charming and your way of giving them is more charming still; you would make despotism attractive. As you know, this is not the first time I have been sorry that I am no longer your slave, and although you now call me a monster, I never recall without pleasure the days when you used to honor me with sweeter names. Often I wish to deserve them again, and to end by giving the world an example of constancy with you. But we are called to greater things; our destiny is to conquer, and we must follow it. Perhaps we shall met again at the end, for let me tell you without offending you, my fair Marquise, that you have been at least keeping pace with me; and since we have been each preaching the faith separately, after parting for the happiness of the world, it seems to me that in this mission of love you have made more converts than I. I know your zeal, your ardent fervor; and if that god judged us by our works, you would some day be the patron saint of a large city, while your friend would at most be a village saint. This language surprises you, does it not? But for the past week, I have neither heard nor spoken any other, and it is in order to make myself more fluent in it that I find myself forced to disobey you.

Do not be angry; and listen to me. You already share all the secrets of my heart, and I am now going to confide to you the greatest project I have ever conceived. What are you proposing to me? To seduce a young girl who has seen nothing and knows nothing, who would be delivered to me defenseless, so to speak, who will not fail to be carried away by the first homage that is paid to her, and who will perhaps be led more swiftly by curiosity than by love. There are dozens of other men who could succeed with her as well as I. That is not the case with the enterprise in which I am now engaged: its success promises me as much glory as pleasure. Even the god of love who is preparing my crown hesitates between myrtle and laurel, or rather he will unite them both to honor my triumph. You yourself, my fair friend, will be overcome with reverent respect, and you will say enthusiastically, "There's a man after my own heart!"

You know Madame de Tourvel, her piety, her conjugal love and her stern principles. That is what I am attacking, that is the foe worthy of me, that is the goal I intend to achieve,

> *And if I do not carry off the prize of conquering her,*
> *I shall still have the honor of having dared to try.*

One may quote bad poetry when it is by a great poet.*

---

*La Fontaine.

I must also tell you that her husband, the magistrate, is in Burgundy because of an important lawsuit (I hope to make him lose a still more important case). His inconsolable wife is to remain here for the entire period of her painful temporary widowhood. A Mass every day, a few visits to the poor of the district, prayers morning and evening, solitary walks, pious conversations with my old aunt, and sometimes a dreary game of whist: such were to be her only diversions; but I am preparing more efficacious ones for her. My guardian angel has let me come here for her happiness and my own. How insane I was! I regretted the twenty-four hours I was sacrificing to a conventional visit. What a terrible punishment it would be if I were forced to return to Paris! Fortunately it takes four to play whist, and since there is no one here but the local priest, my eternal aunt urged me to sacrifice a few days to her. You may be sure I consented. You cannot imagine how she has been flattering me since then, and especially how edified she has been to see me regularly at prayer and at Mass with her. She does not suspect which divinity I am worshiping.

And so for the past four days I have been in the grip of a powerful passion. You know how keenly I desire and devour obstacles; but what you do not know is how much solitude adds to the ardor of desire. I now have only one idea; I think about it during the day and dream about it at night. I must have this woman, to save myself from the ridiculousness of being in love with her, for how far may one not be led by thwarted desire? O exquisite possession, I beg you to hasten for my happiness, and still more for my peace of mind! How fortunate we are that women defend themselves so badly! Otherwise we would be only their timid slaves. I now have a feeling of gratitude to women of easy virtue which naturally brings me to your feet. I prostrate myself before you to obtain forgiveness, and I now end this long letter. Good-by, my lovely friend—without rancor.

LETTER 5

～ *From the Marquise de Merteuil to the Vicomte de Valmont*

Paris, August 7, 17—

Are you aware, Vicomte, that your letter is singularly insolent, and that I have every right to be angry with you? But it clearly proves to me that you have lost your head, and that alone saves you from my indignation. As a generous and sympathetic friend, I shall forget my outrage and concern myself only with your danger; and, however boring it may be to reason, I shall yield to the need you now have of it.

You hope to possess Madame de Tourvel? What a ridiculous whim! I see in it the stubbornness that makes you desire only what you think you cannot get. What kind of a woman is she? Regular features, if you like, but no expression; a fairly good figure, but without grace; always laughably dressed, with bundles of shawls over her chest and a bodice that comes up to her chin! Let me tell you as a friend that it would not take two women like her to make you lose all the respect in which you are held. Remember the day when she took up the collection in Saint-Roche and you thanked me so much for having taken you here to see the spectacle. I can still see her, giving her hand to that tall bean pole with long hair, ready to fall at every step, holding the ten-foot handle of her basket, constantly bumping someone's head with it, and blushing with each bow. Who would have thought then that you would some day desire that woman? Come, Vicomte, you yourself should blush! Come to your senses! I promise you secrecy.

Besides, think of the annoyances that are awaiting you! Who is the rival you must combat? A husband! Do you not feel humiliated by the very word? What a disgrace if you fail! And how little glory if you succeed! I shall go further: you can expect no pleasure. Can there be any with prudes? I am speaking of those who are sincere: they are reserved even in the midst of pleasure, and they offer you only a half-enjoyment. That complete abandonment of oneself, that delirium of sensuality in which pleasure is purified by its excess, those treasures of love are unknown to them. Assuming the best, I predict that your Madame de Tourvel will think she has done everything for you when she has treated you like her husband, and even in the most tender conjugal relations the two parties always remain separate. Here it is still worse: your prude is pious, and with that simple-minded piety which condemns a woman to eternal childhood. Perhaps you will surmount that obstacle, but do not flatter yourself that you will destroy it: you may vanquish the love of God, but not the fear of the devil; and when you hold your mistress in your arms and feel her heart palpitating, it will be from fright, not from love. If you had known her sooner, you might have been able to make something of her; but she is now twenty-two, and has been married for almost two years. Believe me, Vicomte, when a woman has become "fossilized" to that extent, she must be abandoned to her fate; she will never be anything but mediocre.

And yet it is for the sake of this fine creature that you refuse to obey me, that you are burying yourself in your aunt's tomb, and that you are giving up a delightful adventure which would do you great honor! By what fate does it happen that Gercourt must always have some advantage over you? I am now talking to you good-naturedly, but at this moment I am tempted to believe that you do not deserve your reputation; and above all I am tempted to withdraw my confidence from you. I could never become accustomed to telling my secrets to Madame de Tourvel's lover.

However, I will tell you that little Cécile Volanges has already turned one head. Young Danceny is madly in love with her. He has sung with her; and I must admit that she sings better than any schoolgirl from a convent should. They are to practice many duets, and I think she would gladly be in unison with him; but Danceny is only a child who will waste his time in making love and will never complete anything. The girl is also quite shy, and in any case it will be much less amusing than you could have made it, so I am in a bad temper and I shall surely quarrel with the Chevalier when he arrives. I advise him to be gentle, because at this moment it would cause me no pain to break off with him. I am sure that if I had the good sense to leave him now, he would be in despair; and nothing amuses me so much as amorous despair. He would call me treacherous, and the word "treacherous" has always given me pleasure: after "cruel," it is the word that is sweetest to a woman's ears, and it is less painful to deserve. Seriously, I am going to prepare to break off with him. And you are the cause of it! I place it on your conscience. Good-by. Ask your Madame de Tourvel to pray for me.

LETTER 6

~ *From the Vicomte de Valmont to the Marquise de Merteuil in Paris*

Château de ———, August 9, 17—

So there is no woman in the world who does not abuse the power she has been able to acquire! Even you, whom I have so often called my indulgent friend, have finally ceased to be so: you do not hesitate to attack me through the object of my affections! With what strokes you have dared to paint Madame de Tourvel! . . . Any man would have paid for that insolent audacity with his life, and it would have given rise to at least some kind of vengeance against any woman but you. I beg you never again to subject me to such a rigorous test; I cannot guarantee that I would endure it. In the name of friendship, wait until I have had that woman if you want to disparage her. Do you not know that only sensual pleasure has the right to remove the blindfold from the eyes of love?

But what am I saying? Does Madame de Tourvel need any illusions? No, she needs only to be herself in order to be adorable. You reproach her with dressing badly and you are quite right: all clothing is detrimental to her, anything that hides her is unbecoming. It is in the unconstraint of casual attire that she is truly ravishing. Thanks to the oppressively hot weather we are having, a plain linen morning gown allows me to see her rounded, supple figure. Her breasts are covered only by a single piece of muslin, and my furtive but penetrating glances have already seized their enchanting shape. You say her face has no expression. But what should it express at times when nothing is speaking to her heart? No, unlike our coquettish women, she does not have that false gaze which sometimes seduces and always deceives us. She does not know how to cover the emptiness of a phrase with an affected smile, and even though she has the most beautiful teeth in the world, she laughs only at what amuses her. But you should see the image of open, spontaneous gaiety she presents in her playful moments, and the pure joy and compassionate kindness that shine from her eyes when she hastens to help the unfortunate! And above all you should see the touching embarrassment of unfeigned modesty that appears on her celestial face at the slightest word of praise or the mildest attempt to win her favor. She is reserved and pious, and from that you judge her to be cold and lifeless? I think otherwise. What an amazing sensibility she must have to be able to extend it even to her husband, and go on loving a man who is always absent! What stronger proof could you desire? And yet I have been able to obtain another.

I arranged a walk with her so that we came to a ditch that had to be crossed; and although she is very agile she is even more timid: as you can imagine, a prude is afraid to jump the ditch!* She had to accept my help. I held that modest woman in my arms. Our preparations and the crossing of my old aunt had made her burst into laughter, but as soon as I took hold of her, my adroit awkwardness made our arms intertwine. I pressed her chest to mine, and in that short moment I felt her heart beat faster. An attractive blush spread over her face and her modest embarrassment clearly showed me that *her heart was palpitating from love, not from fright*. However, my aunt was as mistaken as you: she said, "The child was afraid." But the "child's" charming candor would not permit her to lie, and she guilelessly replied, "Oh, no, but . . ." That was enough to enlighten me. From that moment my painful anxiety gave way to sweet hope. I shall have that woman; I shall take her away from the husband who profanes her; I shall even dare to ravish her from the God she adores. What an exquisite pleasure to be alternately an object and the conquerer of her remorse! Far be it from me to destroy the prejudices that assail her: they will add to my happiness and my glory! I hope that she will believe in virtue but sacrifice it to me, that her sins will horrify her without being able to restrain her, that she will be tormented by a thousand terrors and be able to forget and overcome them only in my arms. Then, I admit, if she says to me, "I adore you," she alone of all women will be worthy of speaking those words. I shall truly be the god she has preferred.

Let us be frank: in our cold and facile arrangements, what we call happiness is scarcely even a pleasure. Shall I confess it to you? I thought my heart had withered, and, finding that I had nothing left but my senses, I was complaining of premature old age. Madame de Tourvel has given me back the charming illusions of youth. With her I have no need of sensual pleasure in order to be happy. The only thing that alarms me is the time this adventure will take, for I am afraid to leave anything to chance. I recall my successful boldness in the past, but I cannot bring myself to use it now. If I am to be truly happy, she must give herself to me; and that is no small matter.

I am sure you would admire my prudence. I have not yet spoken the word "love," but we have already come to "confidence" and "interest." To deceive her as little as possible, and

---

*The reader will recognize here the bad taste for puns which was beginning to spread when these letters were written and has since made so much progress. [Translator's note: *"Sauter le fossé"* means literally "to jump the ditch," and figuratively "to take the plunge," or "to take a decisive step."]

especially to forestall any gossip that may reach her, I myself
have told her, as though accusing myself, some of my best
known exploits. You would laugh to see how candidly she
preaches to me. She says she wants to convert me. She still has
no idea of what it will cost her to attempt it. She is far from
thinking that in "pleading for the unfortunate women I have
ruined," to use her language, she is pleading her own cause in
advance. This idea came to me yesterday in the middle of one of
her sermons, and I could not resist the pleasure of interrupting
her to assure her that she was speaking like a prophet. Good-by,
my fair friend. You can see that I am not lost beyond recall.

P.S.—By the way, has the poor Chevalier killed himself in
despair? You are really a hundred times worse than I, and you
would humiliate me if I had any vanity.

LETTER 7

~· *From Cécile Volanges to Sophie Carnay**

August 7, 17—

If I haven't told you anyhthing about my marriage, it's because I don't know any more about it than I did the first day. I'm
getting used to not thinking about it, and I'm quite satisfied with
the way I'm living. I spend a great deal of time practicing my
singing and my harp. I seem to like them better now that I have
no teacher—or rather now that I have a better one. The Chevalier
Danceny, the gentleman I spoke to you about, and with whom I
sang in Madame de Merteuil's house, is kind enough to come
here every day and sing with me for hours on end. He's very
nice. He sings like an angel. He writes very pretty melodies and
also writes words for them. What a pity he's a Knight of Malta!
If he married, I think his wife would be very happy. . . . He has
a charming gentleness. He never seems to pay compliments, yet

---

*In order not to tax the reader's patience, many letters from this daily correspondence
have been omitted; the only ones that have been retained are those which seemed
necessary for a thorough understanding of the events that took place within this group of
people. For the same reason, all of Sophie Carnay's letters have been omitted, as well as
a number of those from the other actors in these adventures.

everything he says is flattering. He's always finding fault with me, in music as well as anything else, but his criticisms are mingled with so much gaiety and interest that it's impossible not to be grateful to him. When he only looks at you, he seems to be saying something pleasant. And in addition to all this, he's extremely gracious. Yesterday, for example, he was invited to an important concert but he preferred to stay at our house all evening. I was glad, because no one talks to me when he's not here, and I'm bored; but when he's here, we sing and talk together. He always has something to say to me. He and Madame de Merteuil are the only two people who seem pleasant to me. But good-by, my dear friend; I've promised to learn for today an arietta with a very difficult accompaniment and I don't want to break my word. I'm going to practice it till he comes.

LETTER 8

~ *From Madame de Tourvel to Madame de Volanges*

Château de ———, August 9, 17—

No one could be more grateful than I, Madame, for the confidence you have shown in me, or take a greater interest than I in the future of Mademoiselle de Volanges. It is with all my soul that I wish her the happiness of which I am sure she is worthy, and I rely on your prudence to obtain it for her. I do not know the Comte de Gercourt, but since he has been honored by your choice, I can only form a very high opinion of him. I shall limit myself, Madame, to wishing that this marriage will prove to be as happy as my own, which was also your work, and for which I am more grateful to you every day. May your daughter's happiness be your reward for the happiness you have procured for me, and may the best of friends be also the happiest of mothers!

I am truly sorry that I am unable to offer you the homage of these sincere wishes in person, and to make the acquaintance of Mademoiselle de Volanges as soon as I desire. Having experienced your truly maternal kindness, I have a right to expect from her the tender friendship of a sister. I beg you, Madame, to ask it of her on my behalf, until I am in a position to deserve it.

I plan to remain in the country during the entire period of

Monsieur de Tourvel's absence. I am taking this time to enjoy
and profit from the company of the worthy Madame de Rosemonde.
She is still charming: her great age has robbed her of nothing;
her memory is intact and she has retained all her gaiety. Only her
body is eighty-four; her mind is only twenty.

Our retirement is brightened by her nephew, the Vicomte de
Valmont, who has been kind enough to sacrifice a few days to
us. I had known him only by his reputation, and it had not made
me wish to know him in person, but it seems to me that he is
better than it. Here, where he is not spoiled by the whirl of
society, he talks sensibly with astonishing ease, and confesses
his faults with rare candor. He speaks to me with great confidence, and I preach to him with great severity. Knowing him as
you do, you will admit that his conversion would be a fine
achievement; but I am sure that, despite his promises, a week in
Paris will make him forget all my sermons. His stay here will at
least be that much time taken from his usual conduct; and in
view of the way he has lived, I think that the best thing he can
do is to do nothing at all. He knows I am writing to you and has
asked me to give you his respectful regards. Accept mine also,
and never doubt the sincere feelings with which I have the honor
of being, etc.

LETTER 9

～ *From Madame de Volanges to Madame de Tourvel*

August 11, 17—

I have never doubted, my fair young friend, either your friendship for me or your sincere interest in everything that concerns
me. It is not in order to clear up this point, which I hope is
settled forever between us, that I am replying to your reply, but I
consider it my inescapable duty to speak to you about the
Vicomte de Valmont.

I must confess that I never expected to find his name in one of
your letters. What can you and he have in common? You do not
know that man—where could you have acquired any idea of
what a libertine's soul is like? You speak of his ''rare candor'';
yes, Valmont's candor must indeed be very rare! He is even more
false and dangerous than he is charming and seductive. Since his

earliest youth, he has never taken a step or said a word without a plan in mind, and he has never had a plan that was not dishonorable or criminal. My friend, you know me; you know that among the virtues I have tried to acquire, forbearance is the one I cherish most. And so, if Valmont were carried away by fiery passions, or if, like countless others, he had been led astray by the errors of his age, I would pity the man himself while condemning his conduct, and I would wait in silence for the time when a fortunate change would bring him the esteem of decent people. But Valmont is not like that: his conduct is the result of his principles. He knows how to calculate all the atrocities that a man can allow himself to commit without compromising himself; and in order to be cruel and malicious without danger, he has chosen women as his victims. I shall not stop to count those he has seduced; but how many has he not ruined? In the quiet, retiring life you lead, these scandalous stories do not reach you. I could tell you some that would make you shudder, but your gaze, as pure as your soul, would be sullied by such pictures; certain that Valmont will never be dangerous to you, you have no need of such weapons with which to defend yourself. The only thing I have to tell you is that of all the women to whom he has devoted his efforts, whether successfully or not, there is not one who has not had reason to complain of him. The Marquise de Merteuil is the only exception to this general rule: she alone was able to resist him and hold his wickedness in check. I confess that this episode in her life is the one which does her the greatest honor in my eyes, and it has been sufficient to exonerate her fully in the eyes of everyone for certain indiscretions with which she was reproached at the beginning of her widowhood.*

Be all that as it may, my dear friend, my age, my experience and above all my friendship authorize me to point out to you that people in society are beginning to notice Valmont's absence, and that if it is known that he has spent some time alone with you and his aunt, your reputation will be in his hands, which is the greatest misfortune that can befall a woman. I therefore advise you to urge his aunt not to retain him any longer; and if he insists on staying, I think you should not hesitate to leave. But why should he stay? What is he doing there in the country? If you had his movements watched, I am sure you would discover that he has simply taken a more convenient

---

*Madame de Volanges's error shows us that, like other scoundrels, Valmont did not reveal his accomplices.

refuge for some evil act he is planning in that vicinity. But since it is impossible to remedy the evil, let us be satisfied with preserving ourselves from it.

Good-by, my dear friend. My daughter's marriage has been delayed a little. The Comte de Gercourt, whom we had been expecting to arrive any day, has written to me that his regiment is being sent to Corsica, and since there are still operations of war, it will be impossible for him to return before winter. It distresses me, but it also gives me the hope that we shall have the pleasure of seeing you at the wedding; I was sorry that it was going to take place without you. Good-by; I am, without compliment and without reserve, entirely yours.

P.S.—Give my best regards to Madame de Rosemonde, whom I still love as much as she deserves.

LETTER 10

~ *From the Marquise de Merteuil to the Vicomte de Valmont*

August 12, 17—

Are you being sulky with me, Vicomte? Or are you dead? Or, which would be almost the same thing, are you living only for your Madame de Tourvel? That woman, who has "given you back the illusions of youth," will soon give you back its ridiculous prejudices as well. You are already timid and slavish; you might as well be in love. You have given up your "successful boldness." You are therefore acting without principles and leaving everything to chance, or rather to caprice. Have you forgotten that love, like medicine, is only the art of aiding nature? As you can see, I am beating you with your own weapons; but I take no pride in it, because it is beating a fallen man. You tell me that "she must give herself to you." Well, no doubt she must, and so she will give herself to you like the others, with the difference that she will do so with bad grace. But to make sure that she will end by giving herself, the best means is to begin by taking her. That ridiculous distinction is a raving of love! I say "love" because you are in love. To speak to you otherwise would be to deceive you; it would be hiding your illness from you. Tell me, languishing lover, do you think you raped those other women you have had? However much a woman wants to give herself, however eager she may be, she still needs a pretext, and is there any more convenient pretext for us than one which makes us appear to have yielded to force? For my part, I admit that one of the things that pleases me most is a sharp, well-conducted attack in which everything takes place with order, though also with rapidity; which never places us in the painfully embarrassing position of having to repair an awkwardness from which, on the contrary, we should have profited; which is able to preserve an appearance of violence even in those things that we grant, and skillfully flatters our two favorite passions: the glory of defense and the pleasure of defeat. I admit that this talent, which is rarer than is generally believed, has always given me pleasure, even when it has not been successful with me, and that sometimes I have given myself solely as a reward, just as in our ancient tournaments, Beauty awarded the prize of valor and skill.

But you are no longer yourself, and you act as though you were afraid of succeeding. How long have you been traveling in short stages and on side roads? When one wants to get somewhere, my friend, one uses post horses and the main road! But let us leave this subject: it annoys me all the more because it deprives me of the pleasure of seeing you. At least write to me more often than you have been doing, and keep me informed of your progress. Do you realize that you have been occupying yourself with that ridiculous adventure, and neglecting everyone, for nearly two weeks?

Speaking of neglect, you are like those people who regularly send for news of a sick friend and never ask for the reply. You ended your last letter by asking me if the Chevalier was dead. I did not reply and you were not at all concerned. Have you forgotten that my lover is your devoted friend? But have no fear: he is not dead; and if he were, it would be from excess of joy. Poor Chevalier, how tender he is! He was made for love! How keenly he feels everything! My head is in a whirl. Seriously, I have become genuinely attached to him by the perfect happiness he finds in being loved by me.

On the very day when I wrote to you that I was preparing to break off with him, how happy I made him! I was really thinking of ways to reduce him to despair when he arrived. Whether because of caprice or reason, he made a better impression on me than ever before. However, I gave him a bad reception. He was hoping to spend two hours with me before my door became open to everyone. I told him I was about to go out. He asked me where I was going and I refused to tell him. He insisted. "To a place where you won't be," I answered sharply. Fortunately for him, he was dumbfounded by this reply; for if he had said a word there would inevitably have been a scene which would have brought about the separation I had been planning. Surprised by his silence, I looked at him with no other purpose, I swear, than to see what kind of an expression he had assumed. I saw on his charming face that deep and tender sadness which, as you yourself have admitted, is so difficult to resist. The same cause produced the same effect: I was vanquished a second time. From then on my only desire was to prevent him from thinking I was at fault. "I'm going out on business," I said to him a little more gently, "and it's something that concerns you. But don't question me about it." He then recovered his power of speech, but I did not allow him to use it. "I'm in a great hurry," I went on. "Go away now, and come back this evening." He kissed my hand and left.

Immediately, to compensate him, or perhaps to compensate myself, I decided to let him become acquainted with my private little house, which he knew nothing about. I called my faithful Victoire and instructed her to tell all my other servants that I had one of my headaches and was going to bed. When I was left alone with her, I dressed myself as a chambermaid while she disguised herself as a footman. She then brought a cab to my garden gate and we left. When we reached the Temple of Love, I put on my most provocative negligee. I designed it myself and it is exquisite: it shows nothing to the eye, yet reveals everything to the imagination. I promise to give you a pattern of it for your Madame de Tourvel, when you have made her worthy of wearing it.

After these preparations, while Victoire was occupied with the other details, I read a chapter of *The Sofa*, one of Héloïse's letters, and two tales by La Fontaine, to rehearse the different tones I wished to take. Meanwhile my Chevalier came to my door with his usual eagerness. My doorkeeper refused to admit him and told him I was ill: the first incident. At the same time he gave him a note from me, but not in my handwriting, according to my prudent rule. He opened it and read, in Victoire's handwriting, "At nine o'clock sharp, on the Boulevard in front of the cafés." He went there, and a young footman whom he did not know, or whom at least he did not think he knew, for it was Victoire, came up to him and told him to send his carriage away and follow him. The whole romantic procedure excited his mind all the more, and an excited mind never does any harm. When he finally arrived, surprise and love threw him into a state of enchantment. To give him time to recover, I took him for a short walk beneath the trees, then I bought him back into the house. He saw a table set for two and a neatly made-up bed. We went into the boudoir, which was resplendent with all its adornments. There, half from premeditation and half from feeling, I put my arms around him and slipped down to his knees. "Oh, my darling," I said to him, "I reproach myself for having made you suffer from my apparent irritation in order to prepare this surprise for you, and for having veiled my heart from your gaze for a moment. Forgive those sins and let me expiate them with my love." You can imagine the effect of this little speech. The happy Chevalier lifted me up and my pardon was sealed on that same divan on which you and I so gaily, and in the same manner, sealed our eternal separation.

Since we had six hours to spend together and I was determined that the whole time should be equally delightful to him, I moderated his transports, and my tenderness was replaced by charming coquettishness. I do not think I had ever made such great efforts to please, or been so satisfied with myself. After supper I became alternately childish and sensible, playful and passionate, sometimes even licentious, and I took pleasure in considering him as a sultan in the midst of his harem, in which I was successively the different favorites. And although his repeated tributes were always received by the same woman, they were always paid to a different mistress.

Finally, at dawn, we had to part; and despite everything he said and even did to prove the contrary, his need for rest was as great as his desire to stay. When we left, as a last farewell I took the key to that happy retreat and placed it in his hand. "I acquired it only for you," I said to him, "so it's right that you should be its master: the High Priest should be in command of the temple." By this clever stratagem I forestalled any reflections he might have made about my owning a secret house, which is always suspicious. I know him well enough to be sure that he will use it only with me, and if I should want to go there without him, I still have another key. He insisted that we arrange another meeting there soon, but I still like him too much to want to use him up so quickly. One should allow oneself excesses only with those one intends to leave soon. He does not know that, but, fortunately for his happiness, I know it for both of us.

I see that it is three o'clock in the morning and that I have

written a whole volume when I meant to write only a short note.
Such is the charm of confiding friendship; because of it, you are
still the person I like best, even though it is true that the
Chevalier gives me more pleasure.

LETTER 11

~ *From Madame de Tourvel to Madame de Volanges*

August 13, 17—

Your stern letter would have frightened me, Madame, if I had
not fortunately found here more reasons for assurance than you
have given me for fear. The dangerous Monsieur de Valmont,
who is supposed to be the terror of all women, appears to have
laid down his murderous arms before entering this château. Far
from forming plans here, he has not even brought any pretensions; and the charm which even his enemies grant him has
almost disappeared here, leaving only good-natured amiability. It
is apparently the country air that has produced this miracle. In
any case, I can assure you that although he is constantly with me
and seems to like my company, he has never uttered a word that
resembled love, not one of those remarks which all men allow
themselves to make, without having, as he has, what is needed
to justify them. He never forces me into that reserve which all
self-respecting women are compelled to adopt nowadays in order
to restrain the men around them. He knows how to refrain from
abusing the gaiety he arouses. Perhaps he praises a little too
much, but he does it with such delicacy that he would accustom
modesty itself to adulation. In short, if I had a brother, I would
want him to be such as Monsieur de Valmont shows himself
here. Many women might want him to be more forward in his
attentions; I confess that I am infinitely grateful to him for
having judged me well enough not to confuse me with them.

This portrait of him is quite different from the one you have
painted for me, yet each may be a true likeness if the period is
specified. He himself admits that he has had many faults, and
others may have been falsely attributed to him. But I have met
few men who speak of virtuous women with such respect, I
might almost say enthusiasm. His conduct with regard to Madame de Merteuil is a proof of this. He often speaks of her to us,

and always with such praise and such an air of genuine attachment that I thought, until I received your letter, that what he called friendship between them was really love. I reproach myself for that rash judgment, and I was all the more to blame because he himself has often been careful to justify her. I confess that I regarded as an artifice what was actually honest sincerity on his part. I do not know, but it seems to me that a man who is capable of such constant friendship for such a worthy woman cannot be an unredeemable libertine. However, I do not know whether we owe his good conduct here to certain plans he has laid in the vicinity, as you suppose. There are a few attractive women nearby, but he seldom goes out except in the morning, and then he says he goes hunting. It is true that he almost never brings back any game, but he assures me that he is a very bad hunter. Besides, what he does when he is away from here is of little consequence to me, and if I wanted to know, it would be only in order to have one more reason for either sharing your opinion or bringing you to mine.

As for your suggestion that I make an effort to shorten his stay here, it seems extremely difficult to me to dare to ask his aunt not to have her nephew in her house, especially since she is very fond of him. Nevertheless I promise you, though only out of deference and not from necessity, that I shall take the first opportunity to make that request, either of her or of her nephew himself. As for myself, Monsieur de Tourvel knows that I intend to stay here until his return, and he would rightly be surprised if I were to change my plans for no serious reason.

This has been a long explanation, Madame, but I thought I owed it to truth to give a favorable description of Monsieur de Valmont, which he seems to need greatly in your eyes. I am no less grateful to the friendship that dictated your advice. I also owe to it the kind things you have said to me with regard to your daughter's marriage. I thank you sincerely; but no matter how great the pleasure with which I look forward to spending that time with you, I would gladly sacrifice it to my desire to know that Mademoiselle de Volanges will be happy sooner, if she can ever be happier than when she is with a mother so worthy of all her affection and respect. I share with her those two sentiments which attach me to you, and I beg you to receive kindly my assurance of them.

I have the honor of being, etc.

LETTER 12

∾   *From Cécile Volanges to the Marquise de Merteuil*

August 13, 17—

My mother is indisposed, Madame; she will not go out and I must keep her company, so I shall not have the honor of going to the opera with you. I assure you that I regret not being with you far more than I regret missing the performance. Please believe me. I like you so much! Will you tell the Chevalier Danceny that I do not have the collection of songs he mentioned to me, and that it would give me great pleasure if he would bring it to me tomorrow? If he comes today, he will be told that we are not at home, but it is because my mother does not wish to receive anyone. I hope she will be feeling better tomorrow.

I have the honor of being, etc.

LETTER 13

∾   *From the Marquise de Merteuil to Cécile Volanges*

August 13, 17—

I am very sorry, my dear, to be deprived of the pleasure of seeing you, and for the cause of that deprivation. I hope the opportunity will arise again. I shall deliver your message to the Chevalier Danceny, and I am sure he will also be very sorry to learn that your mother is ill. If she will receive me tomorrow, I shall come to keep her company. We shall attack the Chevalier de Belleroche* at piquet, and while we win his money we shall have the additional pleasure of hearing you sing with your charming teacher, to whom I shall propose it. If that is agreeable to you and your mother, I can answer for myself and my two Chevaliers. Good-by, my dear; give my regards to my dear Madame de Volanges. I kiss you tenderly.

---

*The Chevalier who is discussed in other letters by Madame de Merteuil.

LETTER 14

~ *From Cécile Volanges to Sophie Carnay*

Paris, August 14, 17—

I didn't write to you yesterday, my dear Sophie, but I assure
you that pleasure had nothing to do with it. Mama was ill, and I
stayed with her all day. When I left her and went to my room
last night, I had no heart for anything. I went to bed quickly, to
bring the day to an end; I've never spent such a long one. It's not
that I don't love Mama—I don't know what it was. I was supposed
to go to the opera with Madame de Merteuil, and the Chevalier
Danceny was going to be there. You know they're the two
people I like best. As soon as the time came when I'd have been
there too, my heart sank in spite of myself. I was disgusted with
everything, and I cried and cried, I couldn't help it. I was glad
Mama was in bed and couldn't see me. I'm sure that Chevalier
Danceny was sorry too, but he was distracted by the performance
and everyone who was there, so it was quite different.

Fortunately Mama is feeling better today, and Madame de
Merteuil will come with the Chevalier Danceny and someone
else. But she always comes very late, and it's boring to be alone
so long. It's only eleven o'clock. It's true that I must play my
harp, and then it will take some time to dress, because I want to
have my hair arranged nicely today. I think Mother Perpétue was
right when she used to say that girls become vain as soon as
they're in society. I've never wanted so much to be pretty as I
have in the past few days, and it seems to me that I'm not so
pretty as I thought; and besides, a girl is at a disadvantage when
she's with women who wear rouge. Madame de Merteuil, for
example: I can see clearly that all men think she's prettier than I
am. It doesn't bother me much because she likes me, and also
because she assures me that the Chevalier Danceny thinks I'm
prettier than she is. It was very kind of her to tell me! She even
seemed to be happy about it. I can't understand it. It's because
she likes me so much! And he! . . . Oh, how it pleased me! It
seems to me that just looking at him is enough to make a woman
pretty. I'd always be looking at him if I weren't afraid of

meeting his eyes, because every time that happens it embarrasses me terribly and almost hurts me; but it doesn't matter.

Good-by, my dear friend; I'm going to begin getting dressed. I still love you as always.

LETTER 15

~   *From the Vicomte de Valmont to the Marquise de Merteuil*

Still from the Château de ———, August 15, 17—

It is very kind of you not to abandon me to my sad fate. The life I am leading here is truly tiring because of its excessive rest and its insipid uniformity. As I read your letter and the details of your charming day, I was tempted a dozen times to invent a pretext for leaving, fly to your feet and beg you to be unfaithful with me to your Chevalier, who, after all, does not deserve his good fortune. Do you know that you have made me jealous of him? Why do you speak to me of our "eternal separation"? I adjure that oath taken in a delirium: we shall be unworthy of having taken it if we keep it. May I some day take vengeance in your arms for the involuntary resentment aroused in me by the Chevalier's good fortune! I am indignant, I admit it, when I think that without reasoning, without the slightest effort, simply by stupidly following the instinct of his heart, he has found a happiness that is beyond my reach. Oh, I shall disturb it. . . . Promise me that I shall. Are you not humiliated yourself? You have taken the trouble to deceive him, and he is happier than you. You think he is in your chains, but it is you who are in his! He sleeps calmly while you are awake for his pleasures. What more could his slave do?

As long as you are shared by several men, my fair friend, I am not at all jealous: I then see your lovers only as the successors of Alexander, incapable of holding that whole empire over which I once reigned alone. But that you should give yourself entirely to one of them! That there should be another man as happy as I! I will not tolerate it; do not expect me to. Either take me back or take a second lover; do not let an exclusive caprice betray the inviolable friendship we have sworn to each other.

It is no doubt quite enough that I should have to complain of love. As you can see, I accept your ideas and confess my wrongs. If being in love means being unable to live without the woman one desires, sacrificing one's time, pleasures and life to her, then I am really in love. I am still no closer to success. I would have nothing at all to say on the subject if I had not recently learned something which has made me reflect a great deal; I still do not know whether it gives me grounds for hope or for fear.

You know my valet, a gem for intrigue, and a real comedy-valet; as you can well imagine, my instructions to him have included falling in love with Madame de Tourvel's maid and getting her other servants drunk. The rascal is luckier than I: he has already succeeded. He has just learned that Madame de Tourvel has ordered one of her servants to make inquiries about my conduct, and even to follow my morning outings as much as he can without being seen. What is she trying to do? So even the most modest of all women dares to risk things that we ourselves would scarcely dare to try! I swear . . . But before I think of avenging myself for that feminine ruse, I must try to find a way to turn it to my advantage. So far the outings of which she is suspicious have had no object; I must give them one. It deserves all my attention, and I now leave you in order to reflect on it. Good-by, my fair friend.

LETTER 16

～ *From Cécile Volanges to Sophie Carnay*

Paris, August 19, 17—

Ah, my Sophie, now I have news! Perhaps I shouldn't tell you, but I must talk to someone; I can't help it. The Chevalier Danceny . . . I'm in such a state that I can't write, I don't know where to begin. After I told you about the lovely evening* I spent in Mama's room with him and Madame de Merteuil, I told you nothing more about him; that was because I didn't want to talk to anyone about him, but I was still thinking about him. After that evening he became sad, terribly sad, so sad that it hurt

---

*The letter in which this evening is described has not been found. We may assume that it was the evening which was proposed in Madame de Merteuil's note, and which was mentioned in the preceding letter from Cécile Volanges.

me. When I asked him why he was sad he said he wasn't, but I could see he was. Finally yesterday he was sadder than ever. He was still kind enough to sing with me as usual, but my heart ached whenever he looked at me. When we'd finished singing he went to put my harp in its case, and then when he brought me back the key he asked me to play it again that evening as soon as I was alone. I didn't suspect anything; I didn't even want to play, but he begged me so much that I said I would. He had his reasons. When I was in my room and my maid had left, I went to get my harp. In the strings I found a letter, only folded and not sealed. It was from him. Ah, if you knew what he wrote to me! Ever since I read it I've been so happy that I can't think about anything else. I reread it four times, then locked it in my writing desk. I knew it by heart; and when I was in bed I repeated it to myself so many times that I had no thought of sleeping. As soon as I closed my eyes I could see him there, telling me everything I'd just read. I didn't go to sleep till very late, and as soon as I woke up (it was still very early) I took out his letter to read it again at leisure. I took it to bed with me, and then I kissed it, as if . . . Perhaps it's wrong to kiss a letter like that, but I couldn't help it.

And now, my dear friend, although I'm very happy, I'm also terribly perplexed, because surely I shouldn't answer that letter. I know I shouldn't, and yet he's asked me to; and if I don't, I'm sure he'll go on being sad. It's very unfortunate for him! What do you advise me to do? But you know no more than I do. I'm tempted to talk to Madame de Merteuil about it. She's very fond of me. I'd like to comfort him, but I don't want to do anything wrong. We're always being told to have a kind heart, then we're forbidden to do what our heart tells us to do when it's for a man! That's not right either. Isn't a man our fellow human being as much as a woman, and even more? After all, we have a father as well as a mother, a brother as well as a sister, and a husband who stands all by himself. And yet if I did something that wasn't right, perhaps Monsieur Danceny himself wouldn't think well of me! No, I'd rather let him be sad! Besides, I still have plenty of time. Just because he wrote to me yesterday, I'm not obliged to answer him today. I'll see Madame de Merteuil this evening, and I'll tell her all about it, if I have the courage. If I do only what she says, I'll have no reason to reproach myself. And perhaps she'll tell me I can answer him a little, so he won't be sad! Oh, I'm so upset!

Good-by, my good friend. Tell me what you think.

LETTER 17

~ *From the Chevalier Danceny to Cécile Volanges*

August 18, 17—

Before I yield, Mademoiselle, to the pleasure—or shall I say the need?—of writing to you, let me begin by begging you to listen to me. I am aware that I need your indulgence in order to dare to declare my feelings to you; if I wanted only to justify them, indulgence would not be necessary. After all, what am I about to do but to show you your own work? And what have I to say to you except what has already been said by my looks, my embarrassment, my conduct and even my silence? And why should you be angered by a feeling that you yourself have brought into being? Since it arose from you, it must be worthy of being offered to you; although it is as ardent as my soul, it is also as pure as yours. Can it be a crime to have appreciated your charming face, your beguiling talents, your enchanting graces and that touching candor which adds inestimable value to qualities that are already so precious? Surely not; but one can be unhappy without being guilty, and that is the fate which lies in store for me if you refuse to accept my homage. It is the first my heart has ever offered. If I had not met you I would still be, not happy, but at peace. I have seen you; repose has fled from me, and my happiness is uncertain. Yet you are surprised by my sadness; you ask me its cause; sometimes it has even seemed to me that it grieved you. Oh, say a word and my felicity will be your handiwork! But before you speak, remember that a word can also overwhelm me with despair. It is you who must decide my destiny. You will make me eternally happy or unhappy. In what dearer hands could I place a greater trust?

I shall end, as I began, by imploring your indulgence. I have asked you to listen to me; I shall dare more: I shall dare to beg you to answer me. Your refusal would lead me to believe that you feel I have offended you, and my heart assures me that my respect is equal to my love.

P.S.—To answer me, you may use the same means by which I conveyed this letter to you; it seems to me both safe and convenient.

LETTER 18

~~   *From Cécile Volanges to Sophie Carnay*

August 20, 17—

What, Sophie! You condemn in advance what I'm going to
do! I already had enough anxieties, and now you add to them!
You say it's obvious that I shouldn't answer. It's easy for you to
talk, and besides, you don't know exactly what the situation is:
you're not here to see. I'm sure that if you were in my place,
you'd do the same. As a general rule, of course, one shouldn't
answer, and you saw from the letter I wrote to you yesterday that
I didn't want to, either; but I don't think anyone was ever in the
position I'm in now.

And I'm forced to decide all by myself, too! I expected to see
Madame de Merteuil last night, but she didn't come. Everything
is against me: it was because of her that I met him. It's nearly
always been with her that I've seen and spoken to him. Not that I
hold it against her; but she's abandoned me just when my
difficulty is greatest. Oh, I'm very much to be pitied!

And then he came here yesterday as usual! I was so upset that
I didn't dare to look at him. He couldn't talk to me because
Mama was there. I was sure he'd be angry when he saw I hadn't
written to him. I didn't know how to act. A moment later he
asked me if I wanted him to get my harp. My heart was
pounding so hard that it was all I could do to answer yes. When
he came back, it was much worse. I looked at him only for an
instant. He wasn't looking at me, but he almost seemed to be ill.
It hurt me to see him that way. He tuned my harp, and then
when he brought it to me he said, "Ah, Mademoiselle . . ."
Those two words were all he said, but he said them in a tone that
completely unnerved me. I played a prelude on my harp without
knowing what I was doing. Mama asked if we were going to
sing. He excused himself by saying he was a little ill, but I had
no excuse, so I had to sing. I wished I'd never had a voice. I
deliberately chose a song I didn't know, because I was sure I
couldn't sing anything, and everyone would have noticed that
something was wrong. Fortunately a visitor came; as soon as I

heard a carriage arrive, I stopped and asked him to take my harp back. I was afraid he'd leave, but he came back.

While Mama and the lady who'd just come were talking together, I decided to look at him again for just a moment. His eyes met mine and it was impossible for me to look away. A moment later I saw his tears begin to flow, and he had to turn away to avoid being seen. It was more than I could bear; I felt I was going to cry too. I left the room and immediately wrote in pencil on a scrap of paper, "Please don't be so sad. I promise to answer you." Surely, you can't say there was anything wrong in that; and besides, I couldn't help it. I put the piece of paper in the strings of my harp, the way he'd put his letter, then I went back into the drawing room. I felt calmer. I was anxious for the lady to go away. Fortunately she was only paying for a short visit: she left soon afterward. As soon as she was gone, I said I wanted to play my harp again and asked him to get it for me. I saw from his expression that he suspected nothing. But when he came back, oh, how happy he was! When he put my harp in front of me, he stood so that Mama couldn't see him, then he took my hand and pressed it . . . and in such a way! . . . It was only for a moment, but I can't tell you what pleasure it gave me. I drew back my hand, though, so I have no reason to feel guilty.

Now you can see, my dear friend, that I must write to him, since I gave him my promise. And I don't want to make him unhappy again, because I suffer from it more than he does. If it were for something wrong, I certainly wouldn't do it. But what harm can there be in writing, especially when it's to prevent someone from being unhappy? What troubles me is that I can't write a good letter; but he'll realize it's not my fault, and I'm sure it will please him just because it's from me.

Good-by, my dear friend. If you think I'm wrong, tell me so; but I don't think I am. Now that I'm about to begin writing my letter, my heart is beating at an incredible rate. But I must go through with it, because I promised. Good-by.

LETTER 19

~ *From Cécile Volanges to the Chevalier Danceny*

August 20, 17—

You were so sad yesterday, Monsieur, and I was so grieved by your sadness, that I allowed myself to promise to answer the letter you wrote to me. Today I feel as strongly as ever that I should not do it; but since I have promised, I shall not break my word, and that ought to convince you of the friendship I have for you. Now that you know it, I hope you will not ask me to write to you again. I also hope you will not tell anyone I have written to you, because I would surely be blamed for it, and it might cause me a great deal of sorrow. Above all, I hope that you yourself will not think badly of me: that would hurt me more than anything else. I can assure you that I would not have done this favor for anyone but you. I wish you would do me the favor of not being so sad as you have been; it takes away all the pleasure I have in seeing you. You can see, Monsieur, that I am speaking to you quite sincerely. I ask nothing better than that our friendship should last forever; but please do not write to me again.

I have the honor of being, etc.

Cécile Volanges

LETTER 20

~ *From the Marquise de Merteuil to the Vicomte de Valmont*

August 20, 17—

Ah, you rascal, you flatter me for fear I may mock you! But I shall be kind: you have written to me so many extravagant things that I am forced to forgive you for the sobriety in which you are being kept by your Madame de Tourvel. I do not think my Chevalier would be as indulgent as I am: he would be capable of not approving the renewal of our lease, and of finding nothing amusing in your wild idea. It made me laugh heartily, however, and I was sorry that I had to laugh all alone. If you had been here, I do not know how far my gaiety might have led me; but I have now had time to reflect, and I have armed myself with severity. Not that I refuse forever; but I insist on a postponement, and I am right. My vanity might become involved, and once I had been caught up in the game, it is impossible to say where it would stop. I might enchain you again, and make you forget your Madame de Tourvel; and think how scandalous it would be if I, unworthy as I am, should make you disgusted with virtue! To avoid this danger, here are my conditions.

As soon as you have possessed your pious beauty and can prove it to me, come to me and I shall be yours. But, as you know, in important matters only written proof is accepted. By this arrangement, on the one hand, I shall be a reward rather than a consolation, and that idea pleases me more; and on the other hand, your success will be all the more piquant because it will be in itself a means of infidelity. Come, come as soon as you can and bring me a token of your triumph, like those gallant knights of old who used to lay at their ladies' feet the splendid fruits of their victory. Seriously, I am curious to know what a prude will write after such a moment, and what veil she will throw over her words after having left none on her body. It is for you to see whether I have placed too high a price on myself; but I warn you that it will not be lowered. Until then, my dear Vicomte, you will forgive me if I remain faithful to my Chevalier and amuse myself by making him happy, despite the slight distress it causes you.

However, if I were less moral, I believe he would now have a dangerous rival: little Cécile Volanges. I adore that child; it is a real passion. If I am not mistaken, she will become one of our most fashionable women. I can see her little heart developing, and it is a delightful sight. She is already madly in love with her Danceny, but she does not know it yet. And although he is also very much in love, he still has the shyness of his age and does not dare to speak too openly. They both worship me. She, especially, is eager to tell me her secret. Particularly in the past few days I have seen that she is really oppressed by it, and I would have done her a great service by helping her a little; but I have not forgotten that she is only a child and I do not want to compromise myself. Danceny has spoken to me a little more clearly, but my mind is made up: I will not listen to him. As for her, I am often tempted to make her my pupil; it is a service I would like to render Gercourt. He has given me enough time, since he will be in Corsica until October. I have a notion that I shall make good use of that time, and that we shall give him a fully developed woman instead of his innocent schoolgirl. What insolent confidence on the part of that man who dares to sleep peacefully while a woman who has reason to complain of him has not yet avenged herself! If that girl were here at this moment, I do not know what I might say to her.

Good-by, Vicomte; good night and good luck; but in the name of God, make some progress! Remember that if you fail to have that woman, others will blush at having had you.

LETTER 21

~ *From the Vicomte de Valmont to the Marquise de Merteuil*

August 20, 17—

At last, my fair friend, I have taken a step forward, a large step which, although it has not led me to my goal, has at least showed me that I am on the right path, and has banished my fear that I had gone astray. I have finally declared my love, and although she has maintained a stubborn silence, I have obtained what is perhaps the least ambiguous and most flattering reply possible. But let us not anticipate; let us go back to the beginning.

You will recall that my actions were being spied upon. Well, I decided to make that scandalous procedure serve the cause of public edification, and here is what I did. I told my valet to find in the vicinity some unfortunate person who needed help. It was not a difficult mission to accomplish. Yesterday afternoon he informed me that this morning the authorities were going to seize the personal property of an entire family who could not pay their taxes. I made sure there was no girl or woman in that family whose age or appearance might cast suspicion on my act, and when I was well informed I declared at supper that I intended to go hunting the next day. Here I must do justice to my Madame de Tourvel: she no doubt regretted to some extent the orders she had given, and while she did not have the strength to overcome her curiosity, she at least had enough to oppose my desire. It would be an extremely hot day, I would run the risk of falling ill, I would kill nothing, I would tire myself in vain; and during this speech her eyes, which perhaps spoke better than she wished, showed me that she wanted me to take these bad reasons for good ones. I had no intention of giving in to them, as you may well imagine, and I also resisted a little diatribe against hunting and hunters, as well as a little cloud of ill-humor which darkened her heavenly face all evening. For a moment I was afraid her orders might be rescinded and that her delicacy might harm me. I reckoned without a woman's curiosity, so I was mistaken. My valet reassured me that same evening, and I went to bed satisfied.

I got up at dawn and left. I was scarcely fifty paces from the château when I saw my spy following me. Pretending to be hunting, I set out across the fields toward the village I wanted to reach. My only pleasure on the way was to force the rascal who was following me to run: since he did not dare to leave the roads, he often had to cover, at top speed, a distance three times as great as mine. I exercised him so much that I myself became overheated and sat down at the foot of a tree. He then had the insolence to slip behind a bush no more than twenty paces from me and sit down too! For a moment I was tempted to take a shot at him; although my gun was loaded only with bird shot, it would have given him a sufficient lesson on the dangers of curiosity. Fortunately for him, I remembered that he was useful and even necessary to my plans; this reflection saved him.

When I arrived in the village I saw a commotion. I went forward, asked questions and was told what was happening. I sent for the tax collector and, yielding to my generous compassion, I nobly paid fifty-six francs, for which five people were about to be reduced to abject poverty and despair. After this simple act you cannot imagine what a chorus of benedictions echoed around me from the spectators! What tears of gratitude flowed from the eyes of the aged head of the family and embellished his patriarchal face, which had been rendered truly hideous only a moment before by the savage imprint of despair! I was watching this spectacle when a younger peasant hurried toward me leading a woman and two children by the hand and said to them, "Let us all fall at the feet of this image of God." In a moment I was surrounded by the family prostrate at my knees. I admit my weakness; my eyes filled with tears and I felt an involuntary but delightful surge of emotion. I was surprised by the pleasure it gives one to do good; I am tempted to believe that those whom we call virtuous do not have as much merit as many are fond of attributing to them. But that as it may, I thought it only right that I should pay those poor people for the pleasure they had just given me. I handed them the ten louis I had brought with me. Their thanks began again, but with less emotion: necessity had produced the great, the true effect; the rest was merely an expression of gratitude and surprise for superfluous gifts.

Meanwhile, amid the family's wordy benedictions, I was not unlike the hero of a drama in the final scene. I must point out to you that the faithful spy was in the crowd. My purpose had been accomplished; I disengaged myself from them and went back to the château. All things considered, I congratulate myself on my stratagem. That woman is certainly worth all the pains I have taken; they will some day be my claims on her, and having thus paid for her in advance, as it were, I shall have the right to dispose of her according to my fancy, without having to reproach myself in any way.

I forgot to tell you that, in order to turn everything to my profit, I asked those good people to pray to God for the success of my plans. You will see whether their prayers have not been partly granted already. . . . But I have just been told that supper is served, and it would be too late for this letter to leave if I did not finish it until I returned to my room, so the rest will have to wait until the next post. I am sorry, because the rest is the best part. Good-by, my fair friend. You are stealing from me a moment of the pleasure of seeing her.

LETTER 22

~ *From Madame de Tourvel to Madame de Volanges*

August 20, 17—

You will no doubt be glad, Madame, to hear of an act on the part of Monsieur de Valmont which, it seems to me, is in strong contrast with all those by which he has been represented to you. It is so painful to think unfavorably of anyone, so sad to find only vices in those who could have all the qualities needed to make virtue cherished! And you are so fond of forbearance that it is rendering you a service to give you reasons for revising a judgment that was too harsh. It seems to me that Monsieur de Valmont is entitled to hope for that favor, I might almost say that justice, and this is why I think so.

This morning he went off on one of those walks which might

have led one to suspect that he was pursuing some intrigue in the vicinity, as it occurred to you that he might be. Fortunately for him, and still more fortunately for us, since it saves us from being unjust, one of my servants had to go in the same direction,* and it was through him that my reprehensible but fortunate curiosity was satisfied. He reported to us that Monsieur de Valmont, having found in the village of ———— an unfortunate family whose personal property was about to be sold because they could not pay their taxes, not only hastened to pay off the debt of those poor people, but gave them a considerable sum of money as well. My servant witnessed this virtuous act, and he also reported to me that the peasants, in talking among themselves and with him, had said that a servant, whom they described, and who my own servant thinks is Monsieur de Valmont's, made inquiries yesterday concerning those inhabitants of the village who might be in need of help. If this is true, it was not merely a passing compassion aroused by circumstances, but a deliberate plan to do good; it shows the solicitude of charity, the finest virtue of the finest souls. But whether it happened by chance or according to a plan, it was still a good and praiseworthy act, and merely listening to an account of it moved me to tears. I shall further add, still in the interest of justice, that when I spoke to him about that act, which he had not mentioned, he began by denying it, and when he finally admitted it he seemed to place so little value on it that his modesty doubled its merit.

Now tell me, my worthy friend, if Monsieur de Valmont is indeed an incorrigible libertine, if he is nothing but that, yet conducts himself in this way, what is left for decent people? What! Do the wicked share the sacred pleasure of charity with the virtuous? Would God permit a scoundrel to give an honorable family aid for which they would render thanks to His divine Providence? And could He be pleased to hear pure lips shed their blessings upon a reprobate? No, I prefer to believe that certain errors, though long-lived, are not eternal; and I cannot think that a man who does good is an enemy of virtue. Monsieur de Valmont is perhaps only one more example of the danger of bad associations. I shall end with this idea, which pleases me. If, on the one hand, it may serve to justify him in your mind, on the other, it makes more and more precious to me that friendship which unites me with you for life.

I have the honor of being, etc.

---

*Does Madame de Tourvel not dare to say that it was by her order?

P.S.—Madame de Rosemonde and I are about to go to see the honest and unfortunate family and join our belated aid to that of Monsieur de Valmont. We shall take him with us. We shall at least give those good people the pleasure of seeing their benefactor again; that, I believe, is all he has left us to do.

LETTER 23

～ *From the Vicomte de Valmont to the Marquise de Merteuil*

August 21, 17—, at four o'clock in the morning

We broke off at my return to the château; I shall continue my story from there.

I had only a short time in which to change my clothes. I went into the drawing room, where my fair lady was doing tapestry work while the local priest read the newspaper to my old aunt. I sat down near the tapestry frame. Glances that were even softer than usual, and almost caressing, soon led me to assume that the servant had already given an account of my mission. Indeed, my inquisitive beauty was unable to keep the secret she had stolen from me: without fearing to interrupt the venerable priest, even though his reading sounded like a sermon, she said, "I, too, have news to tell," and immediately related my adventure with an accuracy that honored the intelligence of her historian. You can imagine how I displayed all my modesty; but who could stop a woman when she is unknowingly praising the man she loves? And so I allowed her to continue. It was as though she were preaching the panegyric of a saint. Meanwhile I was observing, not without hope, all that was promised to love by her animated looks, her freer gestures, and especially the tone of her voice, which by an already perceptible alteration betrayed the agitation of her soul. She had scarcely finished speaking when Madame de Rosemonde said, "Come, nephew, let me embrace you!" I realized immediately that the pretty preacher could not prevent herself from being embraced also. She tried to flee, but she was soon in my arms, and far from having the strength to resist, she hardly had enough to stand. The more I observe that woman, the more desirable she seems to me. She quickly went back to her tapestry frame and seemed to everyone else to be beginning her work again; but I saw clearly that her trembling hands would not allow her to go on.

After dinner, the ladies decided to visit the unfortunate family I had so piously aided. I accompanied them. I shall spare you the boredom of that second scene of gratitude and praise. My heart, urged on by a delightful memory, hastens to the time when we returned to the château. On the way, my lovely lady, more thoughtful than usual, did not say a word. Preoccupied with trying to find some means of profiting from the day's event, I also remained silent. Only Madame de Rosemonde spoke, and received only short and rare answers from us. We must have bored her; that was my plan and it succeeded. When we got out of the carriage, she went to her room and left me alone with my fair lady in a dimly lighted drawing room—sweet darkness which emboldens timid love!

I had no difficulty in leading the conversation to where I wanted it to go. My charming preacher's fervor served me better than my own adroitness could have done. "When someone is so worthy of doing good," she said, fixing her gentle gaze on me, "how can he spend his life doing evil?" And I answered, "I deserve neither that praise nor that censure, and it is a mystery to me why, with all your intelligence, you have not yet understood me. Even though my confidence may harm me with you, you are too worthy of it for me to be able to refuse it to you. You will find the key to my conduct in a character which is unfortunately too easily influenced. Surrounded by immortal people, I imitated their vices; I may even have made it a point of pride to surpass them. Here I have fallen under the influence of virtue in the same way, and although I have no hope of being able to reach your level, I have at least tried to follow you. And perhaps the act for which you praise me today would lose all its value in your eyes if you knew its real motive!" (You can see, my fair friend, how close I was to the truth!) "It is not to me," I continued, "that those unfortunate people owe the aid I gave them. Where you see a praiseworthy act, I sought only a means of pleasing. I must tell you that I was only a weak agent of the divinity I worship." (At this point she tried to interrupt me, but I did not give her time.) "At this very moment," I added, "my secret has escaped from me only through weakness. I was determined not to reveal it to you; I found my happiness in rendering to your virtues and your charms a pure tribute of which you would always be unaware. But since I am incapable of deceiving when I have the example of candor before my eyes, I shall not have to reproach myself of a sinful dissimulation with regard to you. Do not think that I insult you by a criminal hope. I shall be unhappy, I know it; but my suffering will be dear to me because it will prove to me the intensity of my love. It is at your feet and in your bosom that I shall pour out my sorrows. There I shall draw fresh strength for suffering anew; there I shall find compassionate kindness, and I shall consider myself consoled because you have pitied me. O you whom I adore, hear me, pity me, help me!" I was by now at her knees, clasping her hands in mine; but she suddenly withdraw them and held them over her eyes with an expression of despair. "Oh, how wretched I am!" she exclaimed; then she burst into tears. Fortunately I had thrown myself into my speech so wholeheartedly that I was weeping too. I took her hands again and bathed them in my tears. This was a very necessary precaution, for she was so absorbed in her own sorrow that she would not have noticed mine if I had not found this means of bringing it to her attention. I also gained an opportunity to gaze at leisure upon her charming face, made still more beautiful by the powerful attraction of tears. I became carried away and lost my self-control to such an extent that I was tempted to take advantage of that moment.

How great is our weakness! How great is the power of circumstances when I forgot my plans and risked losing, by a premature triumph, the charm of long struggles and the details of a painful defeat; when, overcome by desire like an adolescent boy, I nearly exposed the conqueror of Madame de Tourvel to the danger of gathering as the fruit of his labors nothing but the insipid advantage of having had one more woman! Ah, I want her to yield, but I also want her to struggle! I want her to have strength enough to resist but not to conquer. I want her to savor at leisure the feeling of her weakness, and be forced to admit defeat. Let the obscure poacher kill the deer he has ambushed: the real hunter must bring it to bay. A sublime plan, is it not? But I might now be regretting that I had not followed it if chance had not come to the aid of my prudence.

We heard a noise. Someone was coming toward the drawing room. Madame de Tourvel was terrified; she leapt to her feet, took one of the candlesticks and walked out. I had to let her go. It was only a servant. As soon as I had ascertained this, I followed her. I had taken only a few steps when, whether because she recognized me or from a vague feeling of fear, I heard her quicken her pace, rush into her room and close the door behind her. I went up to it, but it was locked from inside. I did not knock, because that would have given her an opportunity to resist too easily. I had the simple and fortunate idea of looking through the keyhole, and I saw that adorable woman on her knees, bathed in tears and praying fervently! What god was she daring to invoke? Is there one who is sufficiently powerful against love? She now seeks outside help in vain: it is I who shall determine her fate.

Thinking I had done enough for one day, I also went to my room and began writing to you. I hoped to see her again at supper, but she sent word that she was indisposed and had gone to bed. Madame de Rosemonde wanted to go up to her room, but the malicious invalid claimed to have a headache which would not allow her to see anyone. As you may well imagine, I spent little time with my aunt after supper, and I, too, had a headache. When I retired to my room, I wrote Madame de Tourvel a long letter complaining of her harshness, then I went to bed, intending to give it to her this morning. I slept badly, as you can see from the date of this letter. I got up and reread my epistle. I saw that I had not been circumspect enough in it, that I showed more ardor than love, and more resentment than sadness. I ought to rewrite it, but I would have to be calmer.

I now see the first light of dawn, and I hope that the coolness which accompanies it will bring me sleep. I am going back to bed. No matter how strong Madame de Tourvel's dominion over me, I promise you that I shall never become so preoccupied with her that I do not have time to think about you a great deal.

LETTER 24

~ *From the Vicomte de Valmont to Madame de Tourvel*

August 20, 17—

In the name of pity, Madame, deign to calm the agitation of my soul! Deign to tell me what I am to hope or to fear. Placed between extreme happiness and extreme despair, I am cruelly tormented by uncertainty. Why did I speak to you? Why was I unable to resist the imperious charm which delivered my thoughts to you? When I was content to worship you in silence, I at least enjoyed my love, and that pure sentiment, which was not then troubled by the image of your sorrow, was sufficient for my happiness; but that source of happiness has become a source of despair since I saw your tears flow, since I heard that painful cry: "Oh, how wretched I am!" Madame, those words will long continue to reverberate in my heart. By what fatality does the sweetest of all sentiments arouse only fear in you? And of what are you afraid? Certainly not of sharing my feelings! I have misjudged your heart: it is not made for love. Only mine, which you constantly slander, is capable of deep feeling; yours is even insensitive to pity. If it were not, you would not have refused a word of consolation to the unfortunate man who told you of his suffering; you would not have taken yourself from his sight when looking at you was his only pleasure; you would not have made cruel sport of his anxiety by announcing that you were ill without allowing him to inquire about your condition; you would have been aware that this very night, which for you was merely twelve hours of rest, was going to be a century of torment for him.

Tell me how I have deserved this overwhelming harshness! I am not afraid to take you as my judge: what have I done except to yield to an involuntary sentiment inspired by beauty, justified by virtue, always restrained by respect, and innocently confessed through confidence rather than hope? Will you betray that confidence which you yourself seemed to allow, and to which I surrendered without reserve? No, I cannot believe it, for it would be imputing a fault to you and my heart rebels at the very idea. I disavow my reproaches: I was able to write them, but not to mean them. Ah, let me think you perfect: it is the only pleasure left to me! Prove to me that it is true by granting me your generous aid. What unfortunate person have you ever succored who needed it as much as I? Do not abandon me to the delirium into which you have plunged me: lend me your reason, since you have deprived me of mine. When you have corrected me, enlighten me in order to finish your work.

I do not wish to deceive you: you will not succeed in destroying my love; but you will teach me to control it, and by guiding my acts and dictating my speech, you will at least spare me the terrible unhappiness of displeasing you. You must dispel that agonizing fear; tell me that you forgive me, that you pity me; assure me of your indulgence. You will never have as much of it as I desire you to have; I ask only for enough to assuage my need: will you refuse it to me?

Good-by, Madame; receive the homage of my feelings with kindness; it does not diminish my respect.

LETTER 25

~ *From the Vicomte de Valmont to the Marquise de Merteuil*

Château de ———, August 22, 17—

Here is a report on yesterday's events.

At eleven o'clock I went into Madame de Rosemonde's room, and under her auspices I was taken to see the feigning invalid, who was still in bed. There was dark circles around her eyes; I hope she slept as badly as I did. When Madame de Rosemonde walked away for a moment, I took the opportunity to deliver my letter. Madame de Tourvel refused to take it, but I left it on the bed and virtuously went over to the chair in which my old aunt had sat down in order to remain with "her dear child." The letter had to be concealed to avoid a scandal. The invalid said awkwardly that she thought she was a little feverish. Madame de Rosemonde asked me to feel her pulse and praised my medical knowledge. And so my fair lady had the double vexation of having to give me her arm and knowing that her little lie was going to be discovered. I took her hand and held it in one of mine while with the other I stroked her soft, shapely arm. The malicious patient responded to nothing, and this made me say as I withdrew, "There's not the slightest agitation." I was sure her eyes would be stern and, to punish her, I did not look at them. A moment later she said she wanted to get up and we left her. She appeared at dinner, which was a gloomy meal. She announced that she would not go for a walk, by which she meant to tell me that I was not going to have a chance to speak to her. I realized that this called for a sigh and a sorrowful look; she no doubt expected it, for this was the only moment of the day when I succeeded in catching her eye. Virtuous though she is, she has her little wiles like any other woman. I found an opportunity to ask her if she would "be so kind as to inform me of my fate," and I was somewhat taken aback to hear her answer, "Yes, Monsieur, I have already written to you." I was very eager to have her letter; but whether it was another one of her wiles, or simply awkwardness or timidity, she did not give it to me until this evening, just before she went to bed. I am sending you her letter, along with the first draft of my own. Read it and judge for yourself: notice with what blatant falsity she claims not to be in love when I am sure of the contrary; and then she will complain if I deceive her later, when she is not afraid to deceive me now! My fair friend, the most adroit man can do no more than keep pace with the most sincere woman. And yet I must pretend to believe all this nonsense, and tire myself with despair, because it pleases Madame to play at severity! How can one avoid taking vengeance for such atrocities? Ah, patience! . . . But now good-by; I still have much writing to do.

Incidentally, please send me back my merciless lady's letter; she may later expect me to cherish such trifles, and I must not be caught unprepared.

I have said nothing about little Cécile Volanges; we shall talk about her at the first opportunity.

LETTER 26

~ *From Madame de Tourvel to the Vicomte de Valmont*

August 21, 17—

Surely, Monsieur, you would have received no letter from me if my foolish conduct last night had not forced me to enter into explanations with you today. Yes, I wept, I admit it; and perhaps those words which you so carefully quote actually did escape from me. Tears and words: you noticed everything; therefore everything must be explained to you.

Since I am accustomed to inspiring only honorable sentiments, to hearing only words to which I can listen without blushing, and consequently to enjoying a peace of mind which I venture to say I deserve, I do not know how to dissimulate or combat the impressions I feel. The astonishment and embarrassment into which I was thrown by your behavior, a vague fear aroused by a situation in which I ought never to have found myself, perhaps the revolting idea of seeing myself confused with women you despise, and treated as lightly as they—all these causes combined gave rise to my tears and made me say, rightly, that I was wretched. This expression, which you find so strong, would certainly have been much too weak if my tears and my words had been motivated by something else, if, rather than disapproving of sentiments which must offend me, I had been afraid of sharing them.

No, Monsieur, I am not afraid of that; if I were, I would flee a hundred leagues from you, I would go to a desert and lament the misfortune of having known you. Perhaps, despite my certainty that I do not and never shall love you, I would have done better to follow the advice of my friends and not allow you to come near me.

My only mistake was to believe that you would respect a decent woman who asked nothing better than to find you to be decent also, and to do you justice; who was defending you at the very time when you were insulting her with your criminal desires. You do not know me; no, Monsieur, you do not know me. If you did, you would never have thought that you could make your errors into a right: because you said things to me which I ought not to have heard, you considered yourself entitled to write me a letter I ought not to have read. And you ask me to "guide your acts," to "dictate your speech"! Remain silent and forget, Monsieur: that is the advice which it is my duty to give you, and your duty to follow. If you do, you will indeed have a right to my indulgence, and it will be within your power to obtain even a right to my gratitude. . . . But no, I shall ask nothing of a man who has abused my trust. You force me to fear you, perhaps to hate you. I did not wish to; I wished to see in you only the nephew of my most estimable friend; I opposed the voice of friendship to the public accusations against you. You have destroyed everything, and I foresee that you will not wish to repair anything.

I shall limit myself to telling you that your feelings offend me, that your admission of them insults me, and above all that, far from causing me to share them some day, you will force me never to see you again unless you maintain the silence on this subject which I think I have a right to expect, and even to demand of you. I am enclosing with this letter the one you wrote to me, and I hope you will be good enough to return this one to me; it would grieve me deeply if any trace were left of an event which should never have taken place. I have the honor of being, etc.

LETTER 27

~   *From Cécile Volanges to the Marquise de Merteuil*

Paris, August 23, 17—

How kind you are, Madame! How well you understood that it would be easier for me to write to you than to speak to you! What I have to tell you is very difficult; but you are my friend, are you not? Oh, yes, my very good friend! I shall try not to be afraid; and I have such a great need of you and your advice! I am terribly upset; it seems to me that everyone guesses what I am thinking, and especially when he is here I blush as soon as anyone looks at me. Yesterday, when you saw me crying, I wanted to talk to you but something held me back, and when you asked me what was wrong, my tears came against my will. I could not have said a word. If it had not been for you, my mother would have noticed, and what would have become of me then? And that is how I have been spending my life, especially since four days ago.

That was the day, Madame, yes, I am going to tell you: that was the day when the Chevalier Danceny wrote to me. Oh, I assure you that when I found his letter I had no idea what it was! But if I am not to lie, I cannot say that it did not give me great pleasure to read it; in fact, I would rather be sorry all my life than not to have received it. But I knew very well that I should not tell him so, and I can assure you that I even told him I was very angry about it. But he said he could not help it, and I believe him, because I had made up my mind not to answer him, and yet I could not help doing it. Oh, I only wrote to him once, and that was partly to tell him not to write to me again; but in spite of that he keeps writing. And since I do not answer, I see that he is sad, and that hurts me still more, so I do not know what to do, or what will become of me, and I am in a pitiful state.

Please tell me, Madame, would it be very wrong if I answered him now and then? Only until he can bring himself to stop writing to me and stay as we were before, because if this goes on I do not know what will happen to me. When I read his last letter, for example, I cried and cried, and I am sure that if I do not answer him again it will make us both very sad.

I shall send you his letter too, or a copy of it, and you can judge for yourself. You will see that he does not ask for anything wrong. However, if you think I should not answer him, I promise not to; but I think you will agree with me that it is not wrong.

While I am writing to you, Madame, let me ask you one more question: I have been told that it is wrong to love someone, but why is it? The reason I ask is that the Chevalier Danceny says it is not wrong at all, and that nearly everyone loves someone. If that is true, I do not see why I should be the only one to prevent myself from loving; or is it wrong only for unmarried girls? I once heard my mother say that Madame D—— loved Monsieur M—— and she did not sound as though she thought it was very bad; and yet I am sure she would be angry with me if she even suspected my friendship for Monsieur Danceny. She always treats me like a child, and never tells me anything. When she took me out of the convent, I thought it was because she was arranging a marriage for me, but now I do not think so, although I do not care, I assure you. But you are a good friend of hers, so perhaps you know about it, and if you do, I hope you will tell me.

This is a very long letter, Madame, but since you have allowed me to write to you I have taken this chance to tell you everything, and I count on your friendship.

I have the honor of being, etc.

LETTER 28

~ *From the Chevalier Danceny to Cécile Volanges*

Paris, August 23, 17—

And still you refuse to answer me, Mademoiselle! Nothing can sway you; and each day carries away the hope it had brought! What is this friendship you allow to exist between us if it is not even strong enough to make you sensitive to my suffering; if it leaves you cold and calm while I endure the torments of a flame I cannot extinguish; if, far from inspiring you with confidence, it is not even enough to arouse your pity? What! Your friend is suffering and you do nothing to help him! He asks only for a word and you refuse it to him! And you want him to be content with a sentiment so weak that you are afraid to repeat your assurance of it!

Yesterday you told me that you did not want to be ungrateful, but believe me, Mademoiselle, wanting to repay love with friendship is not fearing ingratitude, it is only fearing to seem ungrateful. But I no longer dare to speak to you of a feeling which can only be a burden to you if it does not affect you; I must at least keep it confined within myself until I learn to overcome it. I am aware of how difficult this task will be, and I do not conceal from myself that it will require all my strength. I shall try every means: there is one which will hurt my heart most deeply, and that is to tell myself often that yours is insensitive. I shall even try to see you less frequently; I am already seeking a plausible pretext.

What! Must I lose the sweet habit of seeing you every day? Ah, at least I shall never cease to miss it! Eternal unhappiness will be the reward of the most tender love, and it will be because you have willed it so, it will be your work! I know that I shall never recapture the happiness I am losing today; you alone were made for my heart. With what pleasure I would swear to live only for you! But you will not accept that oath; your silence tells me that your heart says nothing to you in my favor: it is both the surest proof of your indifference and the cruellest manner of informing me of it. Good-by, Mademoiselle.

I no longer dare to presume that you will answer me; love would have written eagerly, friendship with pleasure, even pity with indulgence; but pity, friendship and love are all equally foreign to your heart.

LETTER 29

〜 *From Cécile Volanges to Sophie Carnay*

August 24, 17—

I told you, Sophie, that there are cases in which one may write, and I assure you that I'm very sorry I followed your advice, because it hurt the Chevalier Danceny and me so much. What proves I was right is that Madame de Merteuil, who's a woman who surely ought to know, has finally agreed with me. I told her everything. At first she said the same thing you did, but when I explained everything to her she admitted it was quite different. She only demands that I show her all the letters I write and all the ones I receive from the Chevalier Danceny, to make sure I don't say anything I shouldn't. So my mind is now at ease. Oh, how I love Madame de Merteuil! She's so kind! And she's a very respectable woman, so nothing can be said.

Now I'm going to write to Monsieur Danceny, and how happy he's going to be! He'll be even happier than he thinks, because so far I've only spoken to him of my friendship, and he always wanted me to say my love. I think it was the same thing, but still I was afraid to say it, and he wanted me to. I told Madame de Merteuil about it; she said I was right and that one shouldn't admit loving someone until one couldn't help it any longer. I'm sure I can't help it much longer; after all, it's the same thing, and it will please him more.

Madame de Merteuil also told me she would lend me some books that talk about all this and will teach me how to behave, and also how to write better than I do. You see, she tells me all my faults, which proves she likes me. But she advised me not to say anything to Mama about those books because it would seem to be accusing her of having neglected my education, and that might make her angry. I won't say a word to her about them!

Yet it's amazing that a woman who's hardly related to me at all should take greater care of me than my mother! I'm very lucky to know her!

She also asked Mama to let her take me to the opera day after tomorrow, in her box. She told me we'd be all alone there, and we'll talk the whole time without being afraid that anyone will hear us; I like that better than the opera. We'll also talk about my marriage, because she told me it's true I'm going to be married; but we weren't able to say anything more. Isn't it surprising that Mama hasn't told me anything at all about it?

Good-by, my Sophie, I'm going to write to the Chevalier Danceny. Oh, I'm so happy!

LETTER 30

~ *From Cécile Volanges to the Chevalier Danceny*

August 24, 17—

At last, Monsieur, I have consented to write you, to assure you of my friendship, of my *love*, since otherwise you would be unhappy. You say I am not kind-hearted; I assure you that you are mistaken, and I hope that from now on you will not think so. If you were hurt because I did not write to you, do you think it did not hurt me too? It was because I would not want to do something wrong for anything in the world, and I certainly would not have even admitted my love if I could have helped it, but your sadness was too painful to me. I hope that from now on you will not be sad, and that we shall both be very happy.

I expect to have the pleasure of seeing you this evening, and that you will come early; it will never be as early as I desire. My mother is going to have supper at home, and I think she will invite you to stay. I hope you will not have another engagement, as you did day before yesterday. Was it very pleasant to have supper where you went? It must have been, because you went there quite early. . . . But let us not talk about that: now that you know I love you, I hope you will stay with me as much as you can, for I am happy only when I am with you, and I would like you to be the same.

I am very sorry that you are still sad, but it is not my fault. I shall ask for my harp as soon as you arrive, so that you can get my letter immediately. That is all I can do.

Good-by, Monsieur. I love you very much, with all my heart. The more I tell you so, the happier I am; I hope you will be happy too.

LETTER 31

~ *From the Chevalier Danceny to Cécile Volanges*

August 25, 17—

Yes, we shall surely be happy. My happiness is certain, since you love me, and yours will never end if it lasts as long as the love you have inspired in me. You love me! You are no longer afraid to assure me of your *love*! "The more you tell me so, the happier you are!" After reading that charming "I love you," written by your hand, I heard your lovely lips repeat the same admission. I saw your charming eyes gazing at me, made still more beautiful by an expression of tenderness. I received your vow to live always for me. Ah, receive my vow to devote my whole life to your happiness! Receive it and be sure that I shall never betray it.

What a happy day we spent yesterday! Oh, why does not Madame de Merteuil have secrets to tell your mother every day? Why must the exquisite memory which has taken possession of my mind be mingled with the thought of the constraint that awaits us? Why can I not constantly hold that pretty hand which has written "I love you," cover it with kisses, and thus avenge myself for your refusal of a greater favor?

Tell me, my Cécile: when your mother came back, when her presence forced us to look at each other with outward indifference, when you could no longer console me by the assurance of your love for your refusal to give me proofs of it, did you not feel any regret? Did you not say to yourself, "A kiss would have made him happier, and it is I who have denied him that happiness?" Promise me, my dearest, that at the next opportunity you will be less severe. With the aid of that promise, I shall find the courage to endure the frustrations that circumstances are preparing for us, and my cruel privations will at least be softened by the awareness that you share my regret.

Good-by, my charming Cécile: it is now time for me to go to your house. It would be impossible for me to leave you if it were not in order to go and see you again. Good-by, you whom I love so much, and whom I shall always love more!

LETTER 32

~ *From Madame de Volanges to Madame de Tourvel*

August 24, 17—

Do you really wish me, Madame, to believe in Monsieur de Valmont's virtue? I confess that I cannot bring myself to do so, and that it would be as difficult for me to consider him virtuous, on the basis of the single action you have described to me, as it would be for me to regard a man of recognized virtue as wicked after I had been told of one misdeed on his part. Mankind is not perfect in any category, in evil no more than in good. The scoundrel has his virtues, just as the decent man has his weaknesses. It seems to me particularly necessary to believe this truth because from it arises the necessity of forbearance for the wicked as well as for the good, and it preserves the latter from pride and saves the former from discouragement. You will no doubt feel that I am now failing to practice the forbearance I preach, but I see it only as a dangerous weakness when it leads us to treat the good and the wicked man in the same way. ·

I shall not allow myself to scrutinize the motives for Monsieur de Valmont's action; I am willing to believe that they are as praiseworthy as the action itself, but is it any less true that he has spent his whole life bringing dissension, disgrace and scandal to honorable families? Listen, if you wish, to the voice of the poor man he has aided, but do not let it prevent you from hearing the cries of the hundred victims he has sacrificed. Even if he were, as you say, only an example of the danger of bad associations, would it be any less dangerous to associate with him? Do you suppose him to be capable of reforming? Let us go further: let us suppose that this miracle had actually occurred; would he still not have public opinion against him, and would that not be enough to govern your conduct? God alone can absolve at the moment of repentance; He reads in our hearts. But men can judge only by actions, and no man, after he has lost the esteem of others, has a right to complain of the necessary mistrust which makes this loss so difficult to repair. Above all, my young friend, remember that if one appears to place too little value on the esteem of others, that alone is sometimes enough to make one lose it; and do not call this severity injustice, for aside from the fact that we are justified in believing that no one who has a right to claim that precious esteem will voluntarily renounce it, those who are no longer restrained by that powerful curb are actually closer to doing evil. Such would be the aspect under which you would appear if you maintained an intimate association with Monsieur de Valmont, however innocent it might be.

Alarmed by the ardor with which you defend him, I hasten to anticipate the objections I foresee. You will refer to Madame de Merteuil, who has been forgiven for her intimacy with him; you will ask me why I receive him in my house; you will tell me that, far from being rejected by decent people, he is admitted into, even sought after by what is known as good society. I believe I can answer all these objections.

First of all, Madame de Merteuil, who is indeed most estimable, has perhaps no other fault than too much confidence in her own strength; she is a skillful driver who enjoys guiding her chariot between rocks and precipices, and who is justified only by success. It is right to praise her, it would be imprudent to follow her; she herself admits this and reproaches herself for it. As she

states them; then one stands by them, not because they are sound, but to avoid going back on what one has said.

Furthermore, there is something which I am surprised that you have not noticed: in love there is nothing so difficult to write that one does not feel. I mean to write in a convincing way. One uses the same words, it is true, but one does not arrange them in the same way; or rather one arranges them, and that is enough. Reread your letter: there is an order in it which gives you away at every phrase. I am willing to believe that your Madame de Tourvel is so inexperienced that she did not notice it, but what does that matter? The letter has still failed to produce its effect. That is the defect of novels: the author makes frantic efforts to heat himself and the reader remains cold. Héloïse is the only exception, and despite the author's talent, this observation only makes me think that the story had a factual basis. It is not the same with speaking. The habit of practicing one's speech gives it feeling; facility with tears adds to it; the expression of desire in the eyes is confused with that of tenderness; finally, a less coherent speech more easily produces that air of agitation and disorder which is the true eloquence of love; and above all, the presence of the man she loves prevents a woman from reflecting and makes her want to be vanquished.

Believe me, Vicomte: since she has asked you not to write to her again, take advantage of it to repair your mistakes and wait for a chance to speak. Do you know she has more strength than I thought? Her defense is good, and if it were not for the length of her letter and the opening she has given you by her remark about gratitude, she would not have betrayed herself at all.

I think I can also draw confidence in your eventual success from the fact that she uses too many of her forces at once; I foresee that she will exhaust them in defending the word and have none left for defending the thing.

I am sending you back your two letters, and if you are wise, they will be the last until after the happy moment. If it were not so late, I would speak to you about Cécile Volanges; she is advancing rather swiftly, and I am very pleased with her. I think I shall have finished before you, and you ought to be ashamed. Good-by for today.

LETTER 34

~ *From the Vicomte de Valmont to the Marquise de Merteuil*

August 25, 17—

You speak admirably, my fair friend, but why tire yourself to prove what everyone knows? To move swiftly in love, it is better to speak than to write: that, I believe, is your entire letter. Those are the simplest elements of the art of seduction! I shall confine myself to pointing out that you make only one exception to this principle when there are actually two. To children who follow this course from timidity and surrender from ignorance, we must also add women with intellectual pretensions who enter upon it from conceit and are led into the trap by vanity. For example, I am sure that the Comtesse de B——, who readily answered my first letter, was no more in love with me than I was with her, and that she saw it only as an opportunity of writing on a subject that would do her honor.

Be that as it may, any lawyer would tell you that the principle does not apply to the case at hand, You are assuming that I have a choice between writing and speaking, and that is not true. Since the incident of the 19th, my merciless lady, who is now on the defensive, has avoided all encounters with me with an adroitness which thwarts my own. It has reached the point where, if it continues, she will force me to give serious thought to means of regaining that advantage, for I certainly do not want to be defeated by her in any respect. Even my letters are the object of a little war: not content with refusing to answer them, she also refuses to receive them. Each one requires a new ruse, which is not always successful.

You will recall the simple means I employed to deliver the first one; the second one was no more difficult. She had asked me to give her back her letter: I gave her mine instead, without her having the slightest suspicion. But whether from annoyance at having been duped, or from caprice, or even from virtue, for she will force me to believe in it, she stubbornly refused my third letter. However, I hope that the embarrassing situation in which she was nearly placed as a result of this refusal will correct her for the future.

I was not very surprised that she should refuse to take this letter, which I simply offered to her: that would have been granting something already, and I expect a longer defense. After this attempt, which was only an experiment made in passing, I placed my letter in an envelope and waited until she was getting dressed, when Madame de Rosemonde and her maid were present; I then sent it in to her by my valet, with orders to say that it was the document she had asked me for. I had correctly foreseen that she would be afraid of the scandalous explanation that would be necessitated by a refusal. She took the letter, and my ambassador, who had been instructed to watch her face and is quite a shrewd observer, perceived only a slight blush and more embarrassment than anger.

I congratulated myself, for I was sure that she would keep my letter or, if she wanted to give it back to me, that she would have to be alone with me, which would give me a chance to speak to her. An hour or so later, one of her servants came to my room and gave me, from his mistress, an envelope that was shaped differently from mine, and on which I recognized the handwriting I desired so much to see. I hurriedly opened it. . . . It contained my letter, unopened and merely folded in two. I suspect that her fear that I might be less scrupulous than she with regard to scandal made her employ that diabolical ruse.

You know me, so there is no need for me to describe my fury to you. But I had to recover my composure and seek new stratagems. Here is the only one I found.

Every morning someone goes from here to get the letters at the post office, which is about two miles from here. A closed box something like an alms box is used for this purpose; the postmaster has one key and Madame de Rosemonde has the other. Everyone puts his letters into it during the day whenever he pleases, they are taken to the post office in the evening, and in the morning someone goes to get the letters that have arrived. All the servants, those who have come with guests as well as those belonging to the household, perform this task. It was not my valet's turn, but he volunteered to go to the post office on the pretext that he had something to do nearby.

Meanwhile I wrote my letter. I disguised my handwriting for the address, and on the envelope I imitated rather well the postmark of Dijon. I chose this city because, since I was asking for the same rights as her husband, I found it more amusing to write to her from the same place, and also because she had spoken all day of her desire to receive letters from Dijon. I thought it only fair to give her that pleasure.

Once these precautions had been taken, it was easy to add my letter to the others. This expedient also gave me the advantage of being present when it was received, for it is the custom here to gather for breakfast and wait for the arrival of the mail before separating. At last it arrived.

Madame de Rosemonde opened the box. "From Dijon," she said, handing the letter to Madame de Tourvel. "It's not my husband's handwriting," she said with anxiety, quickly breaking the seal. Her first glance enlightened her, and her expression changed so radically that Madame de Rosemonde noticed it and said to her, "What's the matter?" I also went over to her and said, "Is it a terrible letter?" The pious beauty timidly kept her eyes lowered; she did not say a word, and to cover her embarrassment she pretended to peruse the letter, which she was in no condition to read. I enjoyed her agitation and did not mind pushing her a little. "Your calmer appearance," I said, "makes me hope that this letter has caused you more surprise than pain." Anger then inspired her better than prudence could have done. "It contains things which offend me," she replied, "and I am surprised that anyone could have dared to write them to me." "Who is it?" interrupted Madame de Rosemonde. "It is not signed," replied my wrathful angel, "but I have equal contempt for the letter and its writer." So saying, she tore up the audacious epistle, put the pieces in her pocket, stood up and left the room.

Despite her anger, she read my letter, and I count on her curiosity to have made her read it in full.

A detailed account of the day would take me too far. I am enclosing the first drafts of my two letters; you will know as much as I do. If you want to keep abreast of this correspondence, you must get used to deciphering my first drafts, because nothing in the world could make me endure the boredom of recopying them. Good-by, my fair friend.

LETTER 35

～ *From the Vicomte de Valmont to Madame de Tourvel*

August 21, 17—

I must obey you, Madame; I must prove to you that with all the faults you chose to attribute to me, I still have enough delicacy not to permit myself a reproach, and enough courage to impose the most painful sacrifices on myself. You order me to remain silent and forget. Very well, I shall force my love to remain silent; I shall forget, if it is possible, the cruel manner in which you have received it. No doubt my desire to please you did not give me the right to do so; and I also admit that my need of your indulgence did not entitle me to receive it. But you regard my love as an insult; you forget that if it could be a fault, you would be both its cause and its excuse. You also forget that, accustomed to opening my heart to you even when such confidence might harm me, I could no longer conceal from you the feelings which now possess me; and you regard the result of my good faith as the fruit of audacity. As a reward for the truest, most tender and respectful love, you have driven me away from you. You even speak to me of your hatred. . . . Who else would not complain of such treatment? I alone submit to it; I endure everything without a murmur; you strike and I adore you. The inconceivable power you have over me makes you the absolute mistress of my feelings; and if only my love resists you, if you cannot destroy it, that is because it is your work and not mine.

I do not ask for a change of heart which I have never presumed to expect. I have no hope of receiving even the pity I might have been led to expect by the interest you have sometimes shown in me. But I confess that I feel myself entitled to ask justice of you.

You inform me, Madame, that efforts have been made to harm me in your estimation. If you had followed the advice of your friends, you would not have allowed me to come near you: those are your words. Who are these obliging friends? Such severe and rigidly virtuous people will surely consent to be named, they would surely not want to cover themselves with an obscurity that would cause them to be confused with base slanderers; and I shall learn their names and their reproaches. You must admit, Madame, that I have a right to know both, since you have judged me by them. A criminal is not condemned without being told his crime and the names of his accusers. I ask no other favor, and I pledge myself in advance to justify myself, to force them to retract what they have said.

If I have been perhaps too contemptuous of the vain clamors of a public I care little about, the same is not true of your esteem, and when I am devoting my life to deserving it, I will not let it be taken from me with impunity. It becomes all the more precious to me since I shall no doubt owe to it that request which you are afraid to make of me, and which would give me, as you say, a right to your gratitude. Ah, far from demanding gratitude of you, I shall consider that I owe it to you if you give me an opportunity to be agreeable to you. Begin doing me greater justice by no longer leaving me in ignorance of what you desire from me. If I could guess it, I would spare you the trouble of saying it. To the pleasure of seeing you, add the happiness of serving you, and I shall have nothing but praise for your indulgence. What can be restraining you? I hope it is not the fear of a refusal; I feel I could not forgive you for that. Failing to return your letter to you was not a refusal on my part. More than you, I want it to be no longer necessary to me; but since I am accustomed to thinking of your soul as so gentle, it is only in your letter that I can find you as you wish to appear. When I desire to inspire you with tender feelings, I see in it that you would flee a hundred leagues from me rather than allow me to do so; when everything about me increases and justifies my love, your letter repeats to me that my love insults you; when I look at you and that love seems to me the supreme good, I need to read your letter in order to feel that it is only a horrible torment. You can now understand why my greatest happiness would consist in being able to return that fateful letter to you. Asking for it again would be authorizing me to stop believing what it contains; I hope you do not doubt my eagerness to return it to you.

LETTER 36

～   *From the Vicomte de Valmont to Madame de Tourvel*
     (Postmarked Dijon)

August 23, 17—

Your severity increases every day, Madame, and if I may say so, you are apparently less afraid of being unjust than of being indulgent. After having condemned me without hearing me, you must have felt that it would be easier for you not to read my justifications than to answer them. You stubbornly refuse my letters; you send them back to me with contempt. You have finally forced me to resort to trickery at the very time when my sole object is to convince you of my good faith. The necessity of defending myself which you have imposed on me will no doubt suffice to excuse the means I have employed to do so. And since the sincerity of my feelings has convinced me that it will be enough for me to make them known to you in order to justify them in your eyes, I believed I could allow myself this slight subterfuge. I also venture to believe that you will forgive me for it, and that you will not be very surprised to see that love is more ingenious in bringing itself forward than indifference is in casting it aside.

Allow my heart to reveal itself completely to you, Madame. It belongs to you, so it is right that you should know it.

When I came to Madame de Rosemonde's house I was far from foreseeing the fate that lay in store for me there. I did not know you were there; and I shall add, with my characteristic sincerity, that even if I had known it my peace of mind would not have been disturbed: not that I would not have rendered to your beauty the justice which cannot be refused to it, but since I was accustomed to feeling nothing but desires, and yielding only to those encouraged by hope, I had never know the torments of love.

You were present when Madame de Rosemonde begged me to prolong my stay here. I had already spent a day with you, yet I only yielded, or at least so I thought, to the natural and legitimate pleasure of showing regard for a respectable relative. The kind of life that was led here was certainly quite different from that to which I was accustomed; it was easy for me to conform to it, however, and without seeking to determine the cause of the change that was taking place in me, I attributed it solely to my pliable character, of which I believe I have already spoken to you.

Unfortunately (and why must it be a misfortune?), as I came to know you better, I soon realized that your captivating face, which alone had struck me at first, was the least of your assets: your heavenly soul amazed and enchanted mine. I admired your beauty, I worshiped your virtue. Without hoping to possess you, I set about trying to deserve you. In asking your indulgence for the past, I aspired to your approval for the future. I sought it in your words, I watched for it in your looks—in those looks which emitted a poison that was all the more dangerous because it was poured out unintentionally and received without mistrust.

Then I came to know love. But how far I was from complaining of it! Resolved to bury it in eternal silence, I surrendered to that exquisite emotion without fear or reserve. Each day increased its power over me. Soon the pleasure of seeing you became a need. Whenever you were absent for a moment, my heart was gripped by sadness; at the sound which announced your return, it palpitated with joy. I existed only through you and for you. And yet I can call upon you yourself as my witness: in the gaiety of playful games or in the interest of a serious conversation, did one word ever escape from me which might have betrayed the secret of my heart?

Finally the day arrived when my misfortune was to begin; and through some mysterious fatality, it was brought about by a charitable act. Yes, Madame, it was in the midst of the unfortunate family I aided that, yielding to the precious sensibility which embellishes beauty itself and enhances the value of virtue, you finally drove to utter distraction a heart that was already intoxicated by too much love. You will perhaps recall how preoccupied I was during our return. Alas, I was struggling against an inclination which I felt becoming stronger than myself.

It was after I had exhausted my strength in that unequal struggle that a chance I could not have foreseen left me alone with you. There I succumbed, I admit it. My heart was too full; I could not restrain my words or my tears. But was it a crime? and if it was, has it not been sufficiently punished by the horrible torments into which I have been plunged?

Consumed with hopeless love, I implore your pity and find only your hatred; with no other happiness than that of seeing you, my eyes seek you in spite of myself, and I tremble to meet your looks. In the painful state to which you have reduced me, I spend my days in disguising my sorrows, and my nights in giving myself up to them; while you, tranquil and peaceful, know nothing of these torments except to cause them and congratulate yourself on doing so.

I have now given you a faithful account of what you call my faults, which might perhaps more justly be called my misfortunes. Pure and sincere love, respect which has never faltered, perfect submission: such are the sentiments you have inspired in me. I would not have been afraid to offer them to God Himself. O you who are His most beautiful creation, imitate Him in His indulgence! Think of my cruel distress; think above all that since you have placed me between despair and supreme happiness, the first words you utter will decide my fate forever.

LETTER 37

~ *From Madame de Tourvel to Madame de Volanges*

August 25, 17—

I submit, Madame, to the advice your friendship has given me. Accustomed to deferring to your opinions in everything, I am also accustomed to believing that they are always based on reason. I even admit that Monsieur de Valmont must indeed be infinitely dangerous if he can pretend to be what he appears to be here, while at the same time remaining as you depict him. In any case, since you demand it, I shall send him away from me; at least I shall do my best, for things which ought to be basically simple often become complicated in form.

It still seems to me unfeasible to make that request of his aunt; it would be as ungracious to her as to him. I would also be reluctant to go away myself, for aside from the reasons I have already mentioned concerning Monsieur de Tourvel, if my departure were to upset Monsieur de Valmont, as is possible, would it not be easy for him to follow me to Paris? And would not his return, of which I would be, or at least appear to be, the cause, seem stranger than a meeting in a country house of someone who is known to be his relative and my friend?

My only resource is therefore to persuade him to leave of his own accord. I realize that this request will be difficult to make; however, since he seems to be intent on proving to me that he has more decency than is commonly supposed, I do not despair of success. I shall not be sorry to make the attempt, in fact, in order to have an opportunity to judge whether, as he often says, truly respectable women have never had and never will have any reason to complain of his conduct. If he leaves, as I desire, it will be entirely out of consideration for me, because I have no doubt that he plans to spend a large part of the autumn here. If he refuses my request and insists on staying, I shall still have time to go away myself, and I promise you that I shall.

That, I think, is all that your friendship demanded of me, Madame; I hasten to satisfy it, and to prove to you that despite the "ardor" with which I may have defended Monsieur de Valmont, I am still willing, not only to listen to, but also to follow the advice of my friends.

I have the honor of being, etc.

LETTER 38

~ *From the Marquise de Merteuil to the Vicomte de Valmont*

August 27, 17—

Your enormous packet has just arrived, my dear Vicomte. If its date is correct, I should have received it twenty-four hours sooner; in any case, if I took the time to read it I would not have time to answer it. I therefore prefer to acknowledge receipt of it and talk about something else. Not that I have anything to tell you on my own account: in autumn there is scarcely one man left in Paris who has a human face, and anyone but my Chevalier would by now have become tired of my proofs of constancy. Having nothing else to do, I amuse myself with my little Cécile Volanges, and it is about her that I wish to speak to you.

You have lost more than you think by refusing to take charge of that child. She is really delightful! She has neither character nor principles, so you can judge how pleasant and easy her company is. I do not think she will ever be noted for her sentiments, but everything about her indicates the keenest sensations. Although she is not quick-witted or cunning, she has a certain natural duplicity, if one may so describe it, which sometimes surprises even me, and which will be all the more successful since her face is the image of candor and ingenuousness. She is naturally very affectionate, and I sometimes amuse myself with this quality in her. Her little head becomes overwrought with incredible ease, and she is then all the more amusing because she knows nothing, absolutely nothing, about what she wants so much to know. She has very funny fits of impatience; she laughs, takes offense, weeps, then begs me to enlighten her with a good faith that is truly enchanting. I am really almost jealous of the man for whom that pleasure is reserved.

I do not know whether I have told you that for the past four or five days I have had the honor of being her confidante. As you can well imagine, I responded with severity at first; but as soon as I saw that she believed she had persuaded me with her bad arguments, I pretended to consider them good ones, and she is now firmly convinced that she owes her success to her eloquence: that precaution was necessary in order to avoid compromising myself. I allowed her to write and say "I love," and on that same day, unknown to her, I arranged for her to meet her Danceny in private. But he is still so foolish that he did not even get a kiss from her! Yet he writes very pretty poetry! Oh, how stupid these intellectual young men are! This one is so stupid that I am at a loss as to what to do for him, because after all I cannot stay with him to guide him!

At this point you would be very useful to me. He knows you well enough to confide in you, and we would make rapid progress if he began doing so. Hurry with your Madame de Tourvel, because I do not want Gercourt to escape. I spoke to our little girl about him yesterday, and I painted such a picture of him that she could not hate him more if she had been married to him for ten years. However, I also gave her a long lecture on conjugal fidelity; nothing equals my severity on that point. Thus I re-established with her my reputation for virtue, which might have been destroyed by too much indulgence, and at the same time I increased in her the hatred with which I want to gratify her future husband. And finally I hope that by convincing her that it is permissible for her to yield to love only in the little time she has left before she is married, I shall make her decide more quickly not to waste any of it.

Good-by, Vicomte; I am going to my dressing table, where I shall read your volume.

LETTER 39

~ *From Cécile Volanges to Sophie Carnay*

August 27, 17—

I'm sad and worried, my dear Sophie. I cried nearly all night.
It's not that I'm not very happy for the moment, but I foresee
that it won't last.

Yesterday I went to the opera with Madame de Merteuil. We
had a long talk about my marriage, and I found out nothing good
about it. It's the Comte de Gercourt that I'm going to marry, and
it's going to be in October. He's rich, he comes from a good
family, he's a colonel in the ——— Regiment. So far so good.
But first of all he's old: he's at least thirty-six! And Madame de
Merteuil says he's gloomy and stern, and that she's afraid I may
not be happy with him. I saw that she was sure of it, in fact, and
that she didn't want to say so because she didn't want to hurt
me. She talked to me almost all evening about the duties of
wives toward their husbands: she admits that Monsieur de Gercourt
is an unpleasant man, yet she says I'll have to love him. She also
told me that once I'm married I'll have to stop loving the
Chevalier Danceny. As though it were possible! Oh, I assure you
I'll always love him! I'd rather not get married. Let Monsieur de
Gercourt take care of himself, I haven't asked to have anything
to do with him. He's now in Corsica, far away from here; I wish
he'd stay there for ten years. If I weren't afraid of being sent
back to the convent, I'd tell Mama I don't want him for my
husband; but that would be even worse. I'm terribly upset. I've
never loved Monsieur Danceny as much as I do now, and when I
think that I have only a month left to be the way I am, tears
come into my eyes immediately. My only consolation is my
friendship with Madame de Merteuil. She's so kind-hearted! She
shares all my sorrows with me, and she's so charming that I
hardly think about them when I'm with her. Furthermore she's
very useful to me, because the little I know has all been learned
from her; and she's so kind that I tell her everything I think
without feeling at all ashamed. When she thinks it's not right she
scolds me sometimes, but she does it very gently, and then I kiss
her with all my heart until she stops being angry. She's at least

one person I can love as much as I want without there being anything wrong with it, and it makes me very glad. But we've agreed that I won't act as though I love her so much in front of other people, especially Mama, so that she won't suspect anything about the Chevalier Danceny. I assure you I think I'd be very happy if I could always live the way I'm living now. There's only that nasty Monsieur de Gercourt! . . . But I don't want to talk about him any more because it would make me sad again. Instead, I'm going to write to the Chevalier Danceny; I'll talk to him only about my love and not about my sorrows, because I don't want to upset him.

Good-by, my dear friend. You can see that you'd be wrong to complain, and that although I'm "busy" as you say, I still have time to love you and write to you.*

LETTER 40

~ *From the Vicomte de Valmont to the Marquise de Merteuil*

August 27, 17—

It is not enough for my heartless beauty not to answer my letters, to refuse to receive them: she now wants to deprive me of the sight of her, she demands that I go away. What will surprise you more is that I am submitting to her harshness. You will condemn me. But I did not think I ought to lose the opportunity of allowing her to give me an order, for I am convinced that a command involves a commitment, and that the illusory authority which we appear to let women take is one of the most difficult traps for them to avoid. Furthermore, the skill with which she had avoided being left alone with me had placed me in a dangerous situation which I decided I had to get out of at any cost: since I was constantly in her presence without being able to direct her attention to my love, I had reason to fear that she might eventually become accustomed to seeing me without agitation, and you know how difficult it is to alter that state of mind.

But you may be sure I did not surrender without conditions. I was even careful to make one which was impossible to grant, so

---

*The letters exchanged between Cécile Volanges and the Chevalier Danceny have been omitted because they are of little interest and report no events.

that I shall remain free to keep my word or break it, and to open a discussion, either in person or by letter, at a time when my fair lady is more pleased with me and needs me to be more pleased with her; and I would be very clumsy if I did not find a way to obtain some compensation for desisting from this claim, however indefensible it may be.

Now that I have explained my reasons to you in this long preamble, I shall begin the history of the past two days. I am enclosing, as corroborating documents, her letter and my reply to it. You must admit that few historians are as accurate as I.

You will recall the effect produced by my letter from Dijon day before yesterday; the rest of the day was very stormy. The pretty prude did not appear until dinner time, and then she announced that she had a severe headache, a pretext by which she tried to conceal one of the most violent fits of ill-humor that any woman ever had. Her face was totally transformed by it; the gentle expression that you have often seen on it had changed into a rebellious look which gave it a new beauty. I have promised myself to make use of this discovery later: I shall occasionally replace the tender mistress with the rebellious mistress.

I foresaw that the afternoon would be dreary, so, to spare myself the boredom of it, I said I had some letters to write and went to my room. I returned to the drawing room at six o'clock. Madame de Rosemonde suggested that we take a ride, and her suggestion was accepted. But just as we were about to get into the carriage, the self-styled invalid, with infernal malice, and perhaps to avenge herself for my absence, claimed that her headache had increased, and mercilessly made me endure a ride alone with my old aunt. I do not know whether my imprecations against that female demon were granted, but we found her in bed when we returned.

The next morning at breakfast she was a different woman. Her natural gentleness had returned, and I had reason to believe I had been forgiven. Breakfast was scarcely over when the gentle creature stood up indolently and went out into the park; I followed her, as you can well imagine. "What has given you this desire for walking?" I asked as I approached her. "I wrote for a long time this morning," she replied, "and my head is a little tired." "I don't suppose I'm fortunate enough," I said, "to have to reproach myself for that fatigue. . . ." "I did write to you," she said, "but I hesitate to give you my letter. It contains a request, and you have given me little reason to hope that it will be granted." "Ah, I swear that if it is possible for me . . ."

"Nothing could be easier," she interrupted, "and although you ought perhaps to grant it as a matter of justice, I consent to accept it as a favor." So saying, she gave me her letter. When I took it I also took her hand; she withdrew it, but without anger, and with more embarrassment than haste. "It's hotter than I thought," she said, "I must go back inside." And she started toward the château. I made vain efforts to persuade her to continue her walk, and I had to remind myself that we might be seen in order to prevent myself from using something more than eloquence. She returned without saying a word and I saw clearly that she had pretended to take a walk for no other purpose than to give me her letter. She went up to her room as soon as she entered the house, and I went to mine to read her letter, which you will do well to read also, along with my reply, before going any further. . . .

LETTER 41

~ *From Madame de Tourvel to the Vicomte de Valmont*

August 26, 17—

It seems to me, Monsieur, from your conduct toward me, that you are trying to increase every day the reasons I have to complain to you. Your obstinacy in wishing to speak to me constantly of a sentiment to which I will not and must not listen; the temerity with which you have abused my good faith or my timidity in order to deliver your letters to me; above all, what I do not hesitate to call the indelicate means which you employed to deliver your last one to me, without at least fearing the effect of a surprise that might have compromised me—all these things should lead me to express reproaches as sharp as they are justly deserved. However, rather than dwelling on these grievances, I shall limit myself to making a request as simple as it is just; and if I obtain it from you, I consent to forget everything.

You yourself have told me, Monsieur, that I ought not to fear a refusal; and although, by an inconsistency that is peculiar to you, this very statement was followed by the only refusal you could give me,* I am willing to believe that you will not keep the strict promise you made to me only a few days ago.

---
*See Letter 35.

I want you to be good enough to go away from me, to leave this château, where a longer stay on your part could only expose me still more to the judgment of the public, who are always quick to think ill of others, and whom you have made all too accustomed to fixing their eyes on the women who admit you into their company.

Although I had long been warned of this danger by my friends, I neglected, I even opposed their advice as long as your conduct toward me led me to believe that you did not intend to confuse me with that multitude of women who have all had reason to complain of you. Now that you are treating me like them, I can no longer remain ignorant of it; I owe it to the public, to my friends and to myself to follow this necessary course of action. I might add here that you would gain nothing by refusing my request, since I am determined to go away myself if you should insist on remaining; but I am not trying to diminish the obligation I shall have toward you for this favor, and I want you to know that you would upset my plans by forcing me to leave. Prove to me, Monsieur, that as you have so often said, decent women will never have any reason to complain of you; prove to me at least that when you have offended them you are able to make amends.

If I thought I had any need to justify my request to you, it would suffice to tell you that you have spent your whole life in making it necessary, and that it was nevertheless possible for you to avoid forcing me to make it. But let us not recall events which I wish to forget, and which force me to judge you sternly at a time when I am offering you an opportunity to deserve my gratitude. Good-by, Monsieur; your conduct will show me with what sentiments I must be, for life, your most humble, etc.

LETTER 42

~ *From the Vicomte de Valmont to Madame de Tourvel*

August 26, 17—

However harsh the conditions you impose on me, Madame, I do not refuse to fulfill them. I feel it would be impossible for me to thwart any of your desires. Having established this point, I dare to flatter myself that you will also allow me to make a few requests which will be much easier to grant than yours, but which I wish to obtain only by my perfect submission to your will.

One, which I hope will appeal to your sense of justice, is to be good enough to give me the names of my accusers; it seems to me that they have done me enough harm to give me the right to know them. The other, which I expect from your indulgence, is to be kind enough to allow me sometimes to renew the homage of a love that is going to deserve your pity more than ever.

Remember, Madame, that I hasten to obey you even when I can do so only at the cost of my happiness; I shall say more: I am doing so despite my conviction that you want me to leave only in order to spare yourself the always painful sight of the object of your injustice.

Admit, Madame, that you are less afraid of the public, who are so accustomed to respecting you that they would never dare to form an unfavorable judgment of you, than you are embarrassed by the presence of a man whom it is easier for you to punish than to blame. You are sending me away from you as one averts one's gaze from an unfortunate man one does not wish to aid.

But when absence is about to redouble my torments, to whom but to you can I address my complaints? From whom else can I expect the consolations that are going to become so necessary to me? Will you refuse them to me, when you alone are the cause of my suffering?

No doubt you will not be surprised that before I go I should be intent on justifying to you the feelings you have aroused in me, and that I should lack the courage to leave until I have received the order from your lips.

This double reason makes me request a brief conversation with you. It would be useless for us to try to replace it by letters: one writes volumes and explains badly what would be clearly understood after a quarter of an hour of conversation. You will easily find time to grant it to me, for however eager I may be to obey you, you know that Madame de Rosemonde is aware of my plan to spend part of the autumn with her, so I shall at least have to wait for a letter in order to invent a pretext for leaving.

Good-by, Madame; never has it been so painful for me to write that word as now when it forces me to think of our separation. I venture to believe that if you could imagine how it makes me suffer, you would feel some gratitude to me for my docility. At least accept, with more indulgence, the assurance and homage of the most tender and respectful love.

~ *Continuation of Letter 40, from the Vicomte de Valmont to the Marquise de Merteuil*

Let us now reason, my fair friend. You surely realize, as I do, that the scrupulous and honorable Madame de Tourvel cannot grant my first request and betray the confidence of her friends by giving me the names of my accusers; and so, by promising everything on that condition, I commit myself to nothing. But you will also realize that her refusal of this will give me a claim to obtain all the rest, and that by going away I shall gain the privilege of entering into a regular correspondence with her, by her own consent; I place little value on the meeting I have requested with her: it will have almost no other object than to accustom her in advance to not refusing me others when they become really necessary to me.

The only thing I still have to do before I go is to find out who has been turning her against me. I presume it is her priggish husband; I hope so, because aside from the fact that a conjugal prohibition is a spur to desire, I could then be sure that as soon as my fair lady consented to write to me I would have nothing more to fear from her husband, since she would already be compelled to deceive him.

But if she has a woman friend intimate enough to have her confidence, and if that friend is against me, it seems to me necessary to sow discord between them, and I expect to succeed in doing so; but first I must know with whom I am dealing.

I thought I was going to find out yesterday, but that woman does nothing like any other. We were in her apartment when a servant came to announce that dinner was served. She was just finishing her toilette, and as she hurried and made apologies I noticed that she had left the key in her writing desk; and I knew she was in the habit of leaving the key in the door of her apartment. I was thinking about it during dinner when I heard her maid come downstairs. I made up my mind immediately: I pretended to have a nosebleed and left the room. I rushed to her writing desk: I found all the drawers unlocked, but not a single letter. Yet there is no opportunity to burn them at this time of year. What does she do with the letters she receives? And she receives many of them! I neglected nothing; everything was open and I looked everywhere, but I gained nothing except the conviction that the precious collection remains in her pockets.

How can I get it out? Ever since yesterday I have been unsuccessfully trying to find a way, yet I cannot overcome my desire to find one. I regret not having the ability of a pickpocket. Should it not be part of the education of a man who pursues intrigues? Would it not be amusing to steal a rival's letter or portrait, or take something from a prude's pocket that would unmask her? But our parents have no foresight, and although I think of everything I only perceive that I am clumsy, without being able to remedy it.

In any case, I came back to the table extremely displeased. However, my fair lady calmed my ill-humor a little by the interest she appeared to take in my feigned indisposition; and I did not fail to assure her that for some time I had been suffering from violent agitations that were impairing my health. Convinced as she is that she is the cause of them, should she not consider it her duty to do her best to calm them? But although she is pious, she is not very charitable; she refuses to give any amorous alms, and it seems to me that her refusal is enough to justify my stealing them. But good-by, for even while I am writing to you I can think of nothing except those damnable letters.

LETTER 43

~ *From Madame de Tourvel to the Vicomte de Valmont*

August 27, 17—

Why do you seek to diminish my gratitude, Monsieur? Why do you wish to obey me only halfway, and to haggle, so to speak, over an honorable action? Is it not enough for you that I am aware of its value? Not only do you ask a great deal, you also ask for impossible things. If my friends have spoken to me of you, they can only have done it out of interest in me: even if they were mistaken, their intentions were good; and you want me to acknowledge this mark of attachment on their part by giving you their secret! I was wrong to mention it to you at all, and you now make me keenly aware of it. What would have been only candor with anyone else becomes a thoughtless error with you, and it would lead me to a base action if I yielded to your request. I appeal to you, to your honor: did you think I was capable of such an action? Should you have even suggested it to me? Certainly not; and I am sure that when you have given it more thought, you will not repeat that request.

Your other request, that I allow you to write to me, is no easier to grant; and if you will be just, it is not I whom you will blame. I do not wish to offend you, but with the reputation you have acquired, which by your own admission you deserve at least in part, what woman could admit being in correspondence with you? And what decent woman could bring herself to do something she knows she would have to hide?

Even so, if I were convinced that your letters would be such that I would never have reason to complain of them and could always justify myself in my own eyes for having received them, perhaps then my desire to prove to you that I am guided by reason and not by hatred would make me pass over these powerful considerations and do much more than I ought to by allowing you to write to me occasionally. If you actually desire to do so as much as you say, you will readily accept the one condition that can make me consent to it; and if you have any gratitude for what I am now doing for you, you will not delay your departure any longer.

Allow me to point out to you in this connection that you received a letter this morning and that you did not take advantage of it to announce your departure to Madame de Rosemonde, as you had promised to do. I hope that now nothing can prevent you from keeping your word. Above all, I hope that you will not wait for the conversation you have requested, which I absolutely refuse, and that instead of the order you claim to be necessary to you, you will content yourself with the entreaty I now make to you again. Good-by, Monsieur.

LETTER 44

~   *From the Vicomte de Valmont to the Marquis de Merteuil*

August 28, 17—

Share my joy, my fair friend: I am loved, I have triumphed over that rebellious heart! It is useless for it to dissimulate any longer: my fortunate adroitness has discovered its secret. Thanks to my active efforts, I now know everything that interests me. Since last night, that happy night, I have been back in my element; I have resumed my whole existence; I have unveiled a double mystery of love and iniquity: I shall enjoy one and take vengeance for the other; I shall fly from pleasure to pleasure. I am so carried away by the very thought of it that I have some difficulty in recalling my prudence, and it may also be difficult for me to put some order into the account I must write for you. However, I shall try.

Yesterday, after I had written you my letter, I received one from my heavenly prude. I am sending it to you; you will see that she gives me, with as little awkwardness as she can, permission to write to her; but she urges me to leave, and I felt I could not delay my departure too long without doing myself harm.

Tormented, however, by the desire to know who had written against me, I was still uncertain as to what I ought to do. I tried to bribe her maid: I wanted her to give me the contents of her mistress's pockets, which she could easily take at night and replace in the morning without arousing the slightest suspicion. I offered her ten louis for this small service, but she proved to be a scrupulous or timid prig who could not be vanquished by either my money or my eloquence. I was still making speeches to her when the supper bell rang. I had to leave her, only too happy that she had consented to promise secrecy, and I scarcely even counted on that, as you may well imagine.

Never have I been in a worse humor. I felt I had compromised myself, and all evening I reproached myself for my imprudent act.

When I went up to my room, not without uneasiness, I spoke to my valet, who, as a successful lover, I thought, ought to have some influence. I wanted him either to convince the maid to do what I asked of her, or at least to make certain of her discretion. But he, who usually doubts nothing, appeared to doubt the success of this undertaking, and he made a remark on the subject which astonished me by its profundity.

"You surely know better than I, Monsieur," he said, "that going to bed with a girl is only making her do what she likes; making her do what you want her to is often a very different matter."

*The rascal's good sense sometimes frightens me.**

---

*Piron, Métromanie.

"I can answer for this girl even less," he went on, "because I have reason to believe that she has another lover, and that I owe her favors only to the fact that she has nothing better to do in the country. So if it hadn't been for my zeal in your service, Monsieur, I'd have had her only once." (The man is a real treasure!) "As for secrecy, what good would it do to make her promise it, since she would risk nothing by deceiving us? Talking to her about it again would only show her still more clearly that it's important, and make her more eager to please her mistress by telling her about it."

The truth of his remarks increased my perplexity. Fortunately he was in a talkative mood, and since I needed him I let him go on. In telling me the story of his affair with the maid, he informed me, that since the room she occupies is separated from her mistress's only by a thin partition through which suspicious noises might be heard, they met in his room every night. I immediately formed my plan; I described it to him and we carried it out successfully.

I waited until two o'clock in the morning; then, as we had agreed, I went to the lovers' room with a candle in my hand, on the pretext that I had rung several times in vain. My valet, who plays his parts admirably, performed a little scene of surprise, despair and apology which I ended by sending him to heat some water I claimed to need. The scrupulous maid was all the more ashamed because the rascal, seeking to improve on my plan, had reduced her to a state of undress which the weather allowed but did not excuse.

Since I felt that the more she was humiliated the more easily I could make her do as I wished, I did not permit her to change either her situation or her attire, and after ordering my valet to wait for me in my room, I sat down beside her on the bed, which was in great disorder, and began my conversation. I needed to keep the advantage given to me by the circumstances, so I maintained a calm which would have done honor to the continence of Scipio, and without taking the slightest liberty with her, although her freshness and the occasion seemed to entitle her to expect it, I talked business with her as calmly as I might have done with a lawyer.

My conditions were that I would faithfully keep her secret provided she brought me the contents of her mistress's pockets at about the same time the following night. "Furthermore," I added, "I offered you ten louis yesterday, and I again promise them to you now. I don't wish to take advantage of your situation." She agreed to everything, as you may well believe. I then went back to my room and allowed the happy couple to make up for lost time.

I spent my own time sleeping. Since I wanted to have an excuse for not answering my fair lady's letter before I had examined her papers, which I could not do until the following night, I decided to go hunting as soon as I awoke, and I remained absent nearly all day.

She gave me a cold reception when I returned. I have reason to believe that she was somewhat irritated by my lack of eagerness to make the most of the little time I had left, especially after the gentler letter she had written me. I judge this to be the case because when Madame de Rosemonde reproached me a little for my long absence, my fair lady said rather bitterly, "Ah, let us not reproach Monsieur de Valmont for the only pleasure he can find here!" I complained of this injustice and took the opportunity to assure them that I enjoyed their company so much that I was sacrificing a very important letter I had to write. I added that since I had been unable to sleep for the past few nights, I wanted to see whether fatigue would cure my insomnia; and my looks clearly explained both the subject of my letter and the cause of my sleeplessness. I was careful all evening to maintain a gentle melancholy which seemed to be quite successful, and beneath which I had my impatience for the arrival of the hour that would finally reveal the secret which had been so stubbornly withheld from me. At last we separated, and some time later the faithful maid came to bring me the price we had agreed upon for my discretion.

Once I was in possession of this treasure, I proceeded to examine it with the prudence you have always observed in me, for it was important to put everything back in place. I first came upon two letters from her husband, a disorderly mixture of legal details and long declarations of conjugal love. I had the patience to read them through to the end, without finding a single word that referred to me. I put them back with annoyance, but my mood brightened when I found beneath my hand the carefully reassembled pieces of my famous letter from Dijon. Fortunately I decided to glance over it. Imagine my joy when I saw distinct traces of my adorable prude's tears! I must confess that I yielded to a surge of adolescent emotion and kissed that letter with a rapture of which I thought myself no longer capable. I resumed my happy search; I found all my letters arranged in order of date, and I was still more pleasantly surprised to find the first one of all, the one I thought had been returned to me by an ingrate, faithfully copied by her hand and in an altered, unsteady handwriting which showed the sweet agitation of her heart during that occupation.

So far I had been completely absorbed in love; soon it gave way to rage. Who do you think is trying to ruin me in the eyes of the woman I adore? What Fury do you suppose to be vicious enough to conceive such an abominable plot? You know her; she is your friend, your relative: Madame de Volanges! You cannot imagine what a mass of horrors that infernal shrew has written about me! It is she, she alone who has troubled that angelic woman's peace of mind; it is by her advice, by her pernicious warnings that I am forced to leave; it is to her that I am being sacrificed. Ah, her daughter must certainly be seduced! But that is not enough: she must be ruined; since that cursed woman's age protects her from my attacks, she must be struck through the object of her affection.

So she wants me to return to Paris! She is forcing me to do it! So be it; but she will lament my return. I am sorry Danceny is the hero of this adventure: he has a strain of virtue in him which will hinder us; however, he is in love and I see him often; we may be able to turn this to our advantage. But I am so carried away by my anger that I am forgetting that I owe you an account of what happened today. Let us return to it.

This morning I saw my sensitive prude again. Never had I found her more beautiful. This was inevitable: a woman's finest moment, the only one in which she can produce that intoxication of the soul which is often talked about and seldom experienced, is the moment when we are certain of her love but not of her favors; and that was precisely my situation. Perhaps her beauty was also enhanced by the thought that I was about to be deprived of the pleasure of seeing her. Finally, when the mail arrived, I was given your letter of the 27th. While I was reading it I was still hesitant as to whether I would keep my word, but then I met my fair lady's eyes and it would have been impossible for me to refuse her anything.

I therefore announced my departure. A moment later Madame de Rosemonde left us alone together; but I was still four paces from the timid beauty when she stood up with a look of terror and said, "Leave me, Monsieur, in the name of God, leave me!" This fervent prayer, which revealed her emotion, could only arouse me still more. I had already reached her and was holding her hands, which she had clasped with a most touching expression. I was beginning to utter tender complaints when a hostile demon brought back Madame de Rosemonde. My apprehensive prude, who indeed had some reason to be alarmed, took the opportunity to leave.

However, I offered her my hand and she accepted it. Auguring well from this gentleness, which she had not shown for a long time, I began my complaints again and tried to press her hand. At first she tried to withdraw it, but when I insisted more earnestly she yielded with fairly good grace, though without responding to either my gesture or my words. When we reached the door of her apartment, I tried to kiss her hand before letting go of it. Her defense was vigorous at first, but a "Remember that I'm leaving," spoken very tenderly, made it awkward and inadequate. Scarcely had the kiss been given when her hand recovered enough strength to escape, and she went into her apartment, where her maid was waiting. Here ends my story.

Since I presume that tomorrow you will be at the house of the Maréchale de ————, where I shall surely not go to meet you, and since I also presume that during our first conversation we shall have more than one matter to discuss, notably that of little Cécile Volanges, which I am keeping well in mind, I have decided to let this letter precede me. Long though it is already, I shall not end it until just before I send it to the post office, for at the point I have now reached, everything may depend on an opportunity; I shall now leave you and go to watch for it.

P.S. (Eight o'clock in the evening.)—Nothing new; not the slightest moment of freedom; deliberate efforts to avoid it. However, at least as much sadness as decency allowed. One development which may not be unimportant is that Madame de Rosemonde has asked me to convey an invitation to Madame de Volanges to come and spend some time with her in the country.

Good-by, my fair friend, until tomorrow or the day after at the latest.

LETTER 45

~ *From Madame de Tourvel to Madame de Volanges*

August 29, 17—

Monsieur de Valmont left this morning, Madame; you seemed to desire his departure so much that I thought I ought to inform you of it. Madame de Rosemonde misses her nephew very much, and it must be admitted that his company is pleasant. She spent the entire morning talking to me about him with the sensibility you know so well; she never tired of praising him. I felt I owed her the kindness of listening without contradicting her, especially since I had to admit that she was right on so many points. I also felt that I was to blame for her separation from him, and I have no hope of being able to compensate her for the pleasure of which I have deprived her. As you know, I have little natural gaiety, and the kind of life we are going to lead here will do nothing to increase it.

If I had not taken your advice as my guide, I would be afraid I had acted rather thoughtlessly, for I was truly afflicted by my worthy friend's sorrow; I was so deeply touched by it that I would readily have mingled my tears with hers.

We are now living in the hope that you will accept the invitation to come and spend some time here which Monsieur de Valmont is to extend to you on behalf of Madame de Rosemonde. I hope you have no doubt of the pleasure it will give me to see you here; and indeed you owe us that compensation. I shall be very happy to have that opportunity of becoming sooner acquainted with Mademoiselle de Volanges, and of being in a position to convince you more and more of my respectful sentiments, etc.

LETTER 46

~ *From the Chevalier Danceny to Cécile Volanges*

August 29, 17—

What has happened to you, my adorable Cécile? What can have caused such a sudden and cruel change in you? What has become of your vows never to change? Only yesterday you repeated them with so much pleasure! What can have made you forget them today? However much I examine myself, I cannot find the cause in me, and it is horrible for me to have to seek it in you. Ah, you are certainly neither fickle nor deceitful! Even in this moment of despair, I will not allow my soul to be blighted by any insulting suspicions. Yet by what fatality are you no longer the same? No, cruel one, you are no longer the same! The tender Cécile, the Cécile I adore, would not have avoided my eyes, would not have thwarted the lucky chance that placed me near her; or if some reason I cannot conceive had forced her to treat me so harshly, she would at least have deigned to inform me of it.

Ah, you do not know, you will never know, my Cécile, how much you made me suffer today, how much I am still suffering at this moment! Do you think I can live if you have ceased to love me? And yet when I asked you for a word, one word, to dispel my fears, instead of answering, you pretended to be afraid of being overheard; and you immediately created that obstacle, which had not existed till then, by the place you chose in the circle. When, forced to leave you, I asked you at what time I could see you tomorrow, you pretended not to know, and I had to learn it from Madame de Volanges. And so that moment I desire so much, which ought to bring me closer to you, will arouse nothing but anxiety in me tomorrow, and the pleasure of seeing you, hitherto so dear to my heart, will be replaced by the fear of being unwelcome.

I already feel that fear holding me back, and I dare not speak to you of my love. That "I love you" which I was so fond of repeating when I could hear it repeated to me in return, that sweet assurance which sufficed for my happiness, now offers me, if you have changed, only the image of an eternal despair. But I cannot believe that this talisman of love has lost all its power, and I still try to make use of it.* Yes, my Cécile, I love you. Repeat with me that expression of my happiness. Remember that you have accustomed me to hearing it, and that if you deprive me of it you will be condemning me to a torment which, like my love, will end only with my life.

LETTER 47

~ *From the Vicomte de Valmont to the Marquise de Merteuil*

P——, August 30, 17—

I shall not see you today, my fair friend, and here are my reasons, which I beg you to accept with indulgence.

Instead of returning directly yesterday, I stopped at the château of the Comtesse de ———, which was almost on my route, and asked to have dinner with her. I did not arrive in Paris until seven o'clock, and I went to the opera, where I hoped you might be.

---

*This sentence will be meaningless to those who have never had occasion to feel the value of a word or an expression consecrated by love.

When the performance was over, I went to pay a visit to my lovely young friends backstage. I found my former love Emilie in the midst of a large circle of admirers, women as well as men, whom she had invited to supper that evening at P——. As soon as I appeared I was also invited, by acclamation. The invitation was seconded, in halting Dutch French, by a short, fat individual whom I recognized as the true hero of the feast. I accepted.

I learned on the way that the house to which we were going was the price which that grotesque figure had agreed to pay for Emilie's favors, and that the supper was going to be a veritable wedding feast. The little man was beside himself with joy in expectation of the happiness that was about to be his; he seemed to be so satisfied with it that he made me want to disturb it, which I did.

The only difficulty I encountered was in persuading Emilie, who was made a little scrupulous by the burgomaster's wealth. After some hesitation, however, she agreed to my plan, which was to fill that beer-barrel with wine and thus put him out of action for the whole night.

The sublime idea we had formed of a Dutch drinker made us employ all known methods. We succeeded so well that by the end of the meal he no longer had strength enough to hold his glass, but the helpful Emilie and I continued to vie with each other in filling him up. Finally he fell under the table in such a state of intoxication that it ought to last a week. We then decided to send him back to Paris; since he had not kept his carriage, I had him loaded into mine, and I remained in his place. I received the congratulations of the company, who withdrew soon afterward, leaving me master of the battlefield. This amusing prank, and perhaps also my long retirement, made me find Emilie so desirable that I promised to stay with her until the Dutchman's resurrection.

I granted her that favor in return for her obligingness in serving as a desk on which to write to my fair prude; I found it amusing to send her a letter written in bed, almost in a girl's arms, even interrupted for a complete infidelity, and in which I gave her an exact account of my situation and my conduct. Emilie laughed wildly when she read it, and I hope it will make you laugh too.

Since my letter must be postmarked from Paris, I am sending it to you. I have left it open; please read it, seal it and have it posted. Be sure not to use your own seal, or any amorous emblem; use only a head. Good-by, my fair friend.

P.S.—I re-open my letter; I have persuaded Emilie to go to the

Italian Opera. . . . I shall make use of the time to go to see you. I shall be there at six o'clock at the latest; and if it suits you, we shall go to see Madame de Volanges together at seven. It would not be decent for me to delay the invitation I have to give her on behalf of Madame de Rosemonde; also, I shall be glad to see her little daughter.

Good-by, my lovely lady. I want to take such pleasure in embracing you that the Chevalier can be jealous of it.

LETTER 48

~ *From the Vicomte de Valmont to Madame de Tourvel (Postmarked Paris, written at P——)*

August 30, 17—

After a turbulent night during which I did not close my eyes, after having alternated ceaselessly between the agitation of a consuming ardor and the complete annihilation of all the faculties of my soul, I now come to you, Madame, to seek the calm I need but do not yet expect to enjoy. Indeed, the situation in which I find myself as I write to you makes me more keenly aware than ever of the irresistible power of love; it is difficult for me to preserve enough control over myself to put my thoughts in some semblance of order, and I already foresee that I shall not finish this letter without being forced to interrupt it. Oh, may I not hope that you will some day share the agitation I am now experiencing? I venture to believe that if you knew it well you would not be entirely insensitive to it. Believe me, Madame, cold tranquillity, the sleep of the soul and the image of death do not lead to happiness; only active passions can do so, and despite the torments you inflict on me, I believe I can assure you without hesitation that at this moment I am happier than you. In vain do you overwhelm me with your disheartening severity: it does not prevent me from abandoning myself wholly to love, or from forgetting, in the rapture it gives me, the despair into which you have plunged me. It is thus that I wish to avenge myself for the exile to which you have condemned me. Never have I had so much pleasure in writing to you, never have I felt such sweet yet powerful emotion while engaged in that occupation. Everything seems to increase my rapture: the air I breathe is burning with voluptuous delight, the very table on which I am writing, and which has never been used for that purpose before, has become for me the sacred altar of love. How much it will be embellished in my eyes! I shall have recorded on it my vow to love you forever! I beg you to excuse the disorder of my senses. Perhaps I ought to abandon myself less to emotions you do not share. I must leave you for a short time to quell an agitation which is increasing at every moment, and is rapidly becoming uncontrollable.

I return to you, Madame, and I shall always return to you with the same eagerness. Yet the feeling of happiness has fled from me and has been replaced by that of cruel privation. Of what use is it for me to speak to you of my feelings if I seek in vain the means of convincing you? After so many repeated efforts, strength and confidence both abandon me. If I again recall the pleasures of love, it is only to feel more keenly my regret at being deprived of them. I see no resource for me except your indulgence, and at this moment I feel all too strongly how much I need it in order to hope to obtain it. However, never has my love been more respectful, never should it have offended you less; I venture to say that it is such that the sternest virtue ought not to fear it; but I myself am afraid to speak to you any longer of the distress I feel. Knowing that she who causes it does not share it, I must not abuse her kindness; and it would be doing so to spend any more time in recalling that painful image to you. I shall take time only to beg you to answer me, and never to doubt the truth of my feelings.

LETTER 49

～ *From Cécile Volanges to the Chevalier Danceny*

August 31, 17—

Without being fickle or deceitful, Monsieur, it is sufficient for me to be enlightened as to my conduct in order to feel the necessity of changing it; I have promised this sacrifice to God, until I can offer Him that of my feelings for you, which are made still more criminal by your religious condition.* I know it will

---

*Cécile Volanges mistakenly believes that the Chevalier Danceny has already taken the religious vows of the Knights of Malta. (Translator's note.)

cause me great pain, and I shall not hide the fact that since day before yesterday I have cried every time I have thought of you. But I hope that God will grant me the grace of giving me the strength I shall need to forget you, as I ask of Him morning and evening. I count on your friendship and your honor to prevent you from seeking to shake the good resolution which has been inspired in me, and which I am trying to maintain. I therefore ask you to be kind enough not to write to me any more, especially since I warn you that I will not answer you again, and that you would force me to tell my mother everything that has happened, which would completely deprive me of the pleasure of seeing you.

I shall nevertheless remain as strongly attached to you as I can without doing anything wrong, and I wish you every kind of happiness with all my heart. I am sure you will now love me less, and perhaps you will soon love someone else more than me. But that will be one more penance for the wrong I did by giving you my heart, which I ought to give only to God and to my husband, when I have one. I hope that divine mercy will take pity on my weakness and send me no more sorrow than I can endure.

Good-by, Monsieur; I can assure you that if I were permitted to love someone, I would never love anyone but you. But that is all I can tell you, and it is perhaps more than I ought to say.

LETTER 50

～ *From Madame de Tourvel to the Vicomte de Valmont*

September 1, 17—

Is it thus, Monsieur, that you fulfill the conditions under which I consented to receive letters from you occasionally? And can I "have no reason to complain" when you speak to me of nothing except a sentiment to which I would still be afraid to yield even if I could do so without failing in all my duties?

Moreover, if I needed new reasons for retaining that salutary fear, it seems to me that I could find them in your last letter. At the very moment when you think you are vindicating love, what are you actually doing except showing me its fearful storms? Who could wish for a happiness that is bought at the price of reason, and whose fleeting pleasures are at least followed by regret, if not remorse?

Habit must have by now lessened the effect of that dangerous delirium on you, and yet are not you yourself obliged to admit that it sometimes becomes stronger than you, and are you not the first to complain of the involuntary agitation it causes in you? What frightful ravages would it not cause in a fresh and sensitive heart, which would increase its power still more by the greatness of the sacrifices it would have to make to it?

You believe, Monsieur, or you pretend to believe, that love leads to happiness; but I am so firmly convinced that it would make me unhappy that I wish I could never hear its name mentioned. It seems to me that merely speaking of it disturbs one's peace of mind, and it is as much from inclination as from duty that I beg you to keep silent about it.

After all, this request must now be quite easy for you to grant. Now that you are back in Paris, you will find many opportunities to forget a sentiment which perhaps owed its origin only to your habit of occupying yourself with such objects, and its strength only to the dullness of country life. Are you not in the same place where you used to see me with such indifference? Can you take a single step there without encountering an example of the ease with which you can change? And are you not surrounded there by women who are all more gracious than I, and have more rights to your homage? I do not have the vanity for which my sex is reproached; still less do I have that false modesty which is only a refinement of pride: it is in good faith that I tell you here that I have very few means of pleasing; and even if I had them all, I would not consider them sufficient to hold you. Asking you not to concern yourself with me any more is therefore asking you to do what you have already done in the past, and what you would surely do again within a short time if I asked you to do the opposite.

This truth, which I do not lose sight of, would in itself be a sufficiently strong reason for not wishing to listen to you. I have a thousand others; but without entering into a long discussion, I shall confine myself to asking you, as I have already done, to cease speaking to me of a sentiment to which I must not even listen, much less respond.

~ PART TWO ~

LETTER 51

~ *From the Marquise de Merteuil to the Vicomte de Valmont*

September 2, 17—

Really, Vicomte, you are unbearable. You treat me as lightly as though I were your mistress. What! You are to see Danceny tomorrow morning, you know how important it is that I speak to you first, yet you blithely keep me waiting for you all day while you run off I know not where! Because of you I arrived "indecently" late at Madame de Volanges' house, and all the old women said I was "incredible." I had to flatter them all evening to appease them, for old women must not be angered: it is they who make the reputations of young women.

It is now one o'clock in the morning and instead of going to bed, as I am dying to do, I must write you a long letter which will increase my sleepiness by the boredom it will cause me. It is lucky for you that I do not have time to reprimand you more thoroughly. Do not let that make you think I have forgiven you; it is only that I am pressed for time. Listen to me, I must hurry.

If you are at all adroit, you ought to obtain Danceny's confidence tomorrow. This is a favorable time for him to confide in you: he is unhappy. The little girl has gone to confession; she told everything, like a child, and since then she has been so tormented by fear of the devil that she is determined to break off with Danceny entirely. She has told me about her little scruples with an animation which revealed how overwrought she was. She sowed me her farewell letter: it is a real sermon. She babbled for an hour without saying one sensible word. But she embarrassed me nevertheless, because I certainly could not risk speaking freely to such an unruly girl.

However, in the midst of all her chatter I gathered that she still loves Danceny as much as ever; I even noticed one of those stratagems which love never fails to devise, and by which she is rather amusingly deceived. Tormented by the desire to think about her lover, and by the fear of damning herself if she does, she has hit upon the idea of praying God to make her forget him, and since she renews this prayer at every moment of the day, it enables her to think about him constantly.

With someone more experienced than Danceny, this little incident might have been more favorable than unfavorable, but he is such a Céladon* that if we do not help him it will take him so long to overcome the slightest obstacles that we shall not have time to carry out our plan.

You are quite right: it is a pity, and I am sorry as you are that he is the hero of this adventure. But you have no right to complain: what is done is done, and it is your fault. I asked to see his reply**; it is pitiful. He sets forth endless arguments to prove to her that an involuntary sentiment cannot be a crime—as though it did not cease to be involuntary as soon as one ceases to combat it! This idea is so simple that it even occurred to the little girl. He complains of his unhappiness in a rather touching manner, but his sorrow is so gentle, and appears to be so deep and sincere, that it seems impossible to me that a woman who finds an opportunity of driving a man to such despair, and with so little danger, should not be tempted to gratify her fancy to do so. Finally he explains to her that he is not a monk, as she thought he was; and that is unquestionably the best thing he has done, for if one were to go so far as to indulge in monastic love, the Knights of Malta would certainly not deserve preference.

Be that as it may, instead of wasting my time on arguments that would have compromised me and might not have convinced her, I approved of her decision to break off with him; but I told her that it was more courteous in such cases to state one's reasons in person rather than writing them, and that it was also customary to return the letters and any other trifles one had received; and, while thus appearing to share her views, I made her decide to grant him an interview. We planned it immediately, and I undertook to persuade her mother to go out without her. The decisive moment will come tomorrow afternoon. Danceny

---

*A sentimental, platonic lover in *L'Astrée*, a novel by Honoré d'Urfé. (Translator's note.)

**This letter has not been found.

has already been informed; but for God's sake, if you find an opportunity, convince that handsome swain that he must not be so languishing, and tell him, since he must be told everything, that the real way to overcome scruples is to leave those who have them with nothing to lose.

Finally, to prevent a repetition of that ridiculous scene, I raised doubts in her mind about the discretion of confessors, and I assure you that she is now paying for the fright she gave me by her own fright at the idea that her confessor may go to her mother and tell her everything. I hope that after I have talked with her once or twice more she will give up that habit of recounting all her follies to anyone who will listen.*

Good-by, Vicomte; take charge of Danceny and lead him. It would be shameful if we could not do what we wanted to do with two children. If we find it more difficult than we thought, stimulate your zeal with the thought that she is Madame de Volanges' daughter, and I shall stimulate mine by recalling that she is Gercourt's future wife. Good-by.

LETTER 52

～   *From the Vicomte de Valmont to Madame de Tourvel*

September 3, 17——

You forbid me, Madame, to speak to you of my love; but where shall I find the courage I need to obey you? Wholly absorbed in a sentiment which ought to be so sweet but which you make so cruel, languishing in the exile to which you have condemned me, living only on privations and regrets, racked by torments that are all the more painful because they constantly remind me of your indifference, must I now lose the only consolation I have left? And can I have any other than occasionally opening to you a soul which you fill with turmoil and bitterness? Will you avert your gaze to avoid seeing the tears you cause to flow? Will you refuse even the homage of the sacrifices

---

*No doubt the reader has long since guessed from Madame de Merteuil's morals how little she respected religion. This whole paragraph would have been omitted had it not been for the belief that, in showing effects, one should not neglect to show their causes as well.

you demand? Would it not be worthier of you, of your virtuous and gentle soul, to pity a wretched man, who suffers only because of you, than to increase his suffering still more by a prohibition than is both unjust and harsh?

You claim to fear love and you will not see that you alone cause the evils of which you accuse it. Yes, it is certainly a painful sentiment when the person who inspires it does not share it; but where is happiness to be found if not in reciprocal love? Tender friendship, sweet confidence, the only confidence that is without reserve, heightened pleasures, enchanting hope, delightful memories—where else can they be found but in love? You slander it, you who need only cease refusing yourself to it in order to enjoy all the goods it offers you; and I forget my sorrows in order to defend it.

You also force me to defend myself, for while I devote my life to worshipping you, you spend yours in finding fault with me. You already suppose me to be fickle and deceitful, and by an unfair use of certain errors which I myself confessed to you, you deliberately confuse what I was in the past with what I am now. Not content with having plunged me into the torment of living far from you, you augment it with cruel banter about pleasures to which, as you well know, you have made me completely insensitive. You believe neither my promises nor my vows, but I can still offer you one guarantee of which you will not be suspicious: it is yourself. I ask you only to question yourself in good faith; if you do not believe in my love, if you doubt for a moment that you alone reign over my soul, if you are not certain that you have captured my heart, which was indeed too inconstant in the past, I consent to bear the consequences of that error: I shall suffer from it, but I shall make no appeal; but if, on the contrary, doing justice to us both, you are obliged to admit to yourself that you have no rival and never will have one, cease forcing me, I beg you, to combat vain figments of your imagination, and leave me at least the consolation of knowing that you no longer doubt a sentiment which will not and cannot end before my life. Allow me, Madame, to beg you to give a definite answer to this part of my letter.

But if I abandon that period of my life which seems to harm me so cruelly in your eyes, it is not because I lack reasons with which to defend it if necessary.

After all, what did I do except fail to resist the whirlpool into which I had been thrown? I entered society young and inexperienced, I was passed from hand to hand, so to speak, by women who all hastened to forestall, by their wantonness, reflections which they felt would have to be unfavorable to them—was it for me to show the example of a resistance that was not opposed to me? Or should I have punished myself for a moment of error, which had often been provoked, by a constancy that would surely have been useless, and would have been regarded only as ridiculous? What else can excuse a shameful choice except a quick repudiation!

But I can affirm that that intoxication of the senses, perhaps even that delirium of vanity, did not reach my heart. It was born for love: intrigues could distract it, but were not sufficient to occupy it. I was surrounded by seductive but contemptible women, none of whom reached my heart. I was offered pleasures, I sought virtues. Finally I myself believed I was inconstant, because I was delicate and sensitive.

It was when I saw you that I was enlightened: I soon recognized that the charm of love was based on qualities of the soul, that they alone could cause its excess and justify it. I felt that it was equally impossible for me not to love you and to love any woman but you.

Such, Madame, is the heart to which you fear to entrust yourself, and whose fate you must decide; but whatever the destiny you reserve for it, you will change nothing in the sentiments that attach it to you: they are as unalterable as the virtues that gave birth to them.

LETTER 53

~ *From the Vicomte de Valmont to the Marquise de Merteuil*

September 3, 17—, in the evening

I have seen Danceny, but he confided in me only partially; he was particularly obstinate in concealing little Cécile Volanges's name. He spoke of her as a very virtuous and even rather pious woman. Aside from that, he gave me a fairly accurate account of his adventure, especially the last episode. I stirred him up as much as I could, and I jested a great deal about his delicacy and his scruples, but he seems to be attached to them and I cannot answer for him. However, I shall be able to tell you more after tomorrow. I am taking him to Versailles then, and I shall carefully scrutinize him on the way.

The meeting that is supposed to have occurred today also gives me some hope: perhaps everything took place to our satisfaction, and perhaps all we have to do now is to draw out an admission of it and gather proofs. This task will be easier for you than for me, because the little girl is more confiding, or, what comes to the same thing, more talkative than her discreet Danceny. However, I shall do my best.

Good-by, my fair friend; I am in a great hurry; I shall see you neither this evening nor tomorrow. If you find out anything, write me a note for my return. I shall surely come back to Paris to sleep.

LETTER 54

～ *From the Marquise de Merteuil to the Vicomte de Valmont*

September 4, 17—

Oh, that Danceny! With him, how can there be anything to find out? If he has told you anything, he was boasting. I do not know anyone so stupid in love, and I reproach myself more and more for the kindness we have shown him. Do you know I almost compromised myself because of him? And it was utterly useless! Oh, I shall take vengeance, I promise!

When I came yesterday for Madame de Volanges, she did not want to go out: she felt indisposed. It took all my eloquence to persuade her, and I was afraid Danceny was going to arrive before we left, which would have been all the more awkward because Madame de Volanges had told him the day before that she would not be at home. Her daughter and I were on pins and needles. We finally left, and Cécile squeezed my hand so affectionately when she told me good-by that in spite of her plan to break off with Danceny, which she still sincerely believed she was going to carry out, I foresaw wondrous results from the evening.

I had not reached the end of my anxieties. We had not been with Madame de ———— for more than half an hour when Madame de Volanges became truly and seriously ill. She naturally wanted to go home, and I was all the more opposed to it because I was afraid that if we surprised the two young people together, as there was every reason to believe we would, my earnest efforts to persuade Madame de Volanges to go out might become suspicious to her. I began to alarm her about her health, which is fortunately not difficult to do, and I kept her for an hour and a half without consenting to take her home, pretending to fear that the motion of the carriage would be dangerous for her. From the shame-faced expression I observed on arriving, I admit that I hoped my efforts had at least not been wasted.

My desire to learn what had happened made me stay with Madame de Volanges, who went to bed immediately; and after having supper at her bedside, we left her very early, on the pretext that she needed rest, and went into her daughter's room. Cécile did everything I expected of her: scruples forgotten, new vows of love forever, etc., etc. In short, she did her part with good grace. But that fool Danceny did not advance one inch beyond the point where he had been before. One need have no fear of quarreling with *him*—the reconciliation will not be dangerous!

However, Cécile says he wanted more, but that she was able to defend herself. I am willing to bet that she is either boasting or making an excuse: I made almost certain of it for myself. I took it into my head to find out what kind of a defense she was capable of, and by leading her on from one remark to the next, I, a mere woman, aroused her to such a point . . . In short, you may take my word for it that never was anyone more likely to succumb to an attack on the senses. She is really charming, that dear little girl! She deserves a different lover; she will at least have a good friend, for I am becoming sincerely attached to her. I have promised to develop her, and I believe I shall keep my word. I have often felt the need of having a woman in my confidence, and I would rather have her than any other; but I can do nothing with her until she is . . . what she must be; and that is one more reason for being angry with Danceny.

Good-by, Vicomte; do not come to see me tomorrow, unless you come in the morning. I have given in to the Chevalier's entreaties for an evening in my private little house.

LETTER 55

~ *From Cécile Volanges to Sophie Carnay*

September 4, 17—

You were right, my dear Sophie; your prophecies are more successful than your advice. As you predicted, Danceny has proved to be stronger than you, my confessor and myself, and we are now exactly where we were before. Oh, I'm not sorry! And if you scold me, it will be because you don't know what pleasure there is in loving Danceny. It's easy for you to say what ought to be done, there's nothing to prevent you from saying it; but if you'd felt how much it hurts to see the sorrow of someone you love, how his joy becomes yours, and how hard it is to say no when you want to say yes, you wouldn't be surprised by anything. I felt it, very keenly, and I don't understand it yet. Do you think, for example, that I can see Danceny cry without crying myself? I assure you it's impossible for me; and when he's happy, I'm as happy as he is. You can say whatever you like: words don't change the way things are, and I'm sure what I say is true.

I'd like to see you in my place. . . . No, I don't mean that, because I certainly wouldn't want to change places with anyone. But I wish you were also in love with someone, not only because you'd understand me better and scold me less, but also because you'd be happier, or rather only then would you begin to be happy.

Our amusements, our laughter, all those things were only childish games; nothing is left of them once they are past. But love! Ah, love . . . A word, a look, only to know he's there: that's happiness! When I see Danceny, I want nothing else; when I don't see him, I want nothing but him. I don't know how it happens, but it's as though everything that pleases me is like him. When he's not with me, I think about him, and when I can think about him completely, without being distracted, when I'm all alone, for example, I'm happy again. I close my eyes and immediately I seem to see him; I remember something he said and I seem to hear him. It makes me sigh, and then I feel a flame, an agitation. . . . I can't sit still. It's like a torment, and that torment gives me indescribable pleasure.

I even think that when you're in love it also extends to friendship. My friendship for you hasn't changed, though: it's still the same as it was in the convent; I'm talking about what I feel for Madame de Merteuil. It seems to me that I love her more like Danceny than like you, and sometimes I wish she were he. It may be because it's not a childhood friendship like ours; or perhaps it's because I see them together so often that it makes me confuse them. Anyway, one thing is certain: between the two of them they make me very happy; and after all, I don't think there's anything very wrong in what I'm doing, so I ask nothing more than to remain as I am. The thought of my marriage is the only thing that makes me sad, because if Monsieur de Gercourt is the way I've been told he is, and I don't doubt it, I don't know what will become of me. Good-by, my Sophie; I love you as tenderly as ever.

LETTER 56

~ *From Madame de Tourvel to the Vicomte de Valmont*

September 5, 17—

What good would it do you to receive the reply you have asked of me, Monsieur? Would not believing in your sentiments be one more reason for fearing them? And without either attacking or defending their sincerity, it is not enough for me, and should it not be enough for you, to know that I will not and must not respond to them?

Suppose you really loved me (and it is only to avoid returning to the subject that I consent to this supposition), would the obstacles that separate us be any less insurmountable? And would I have anything to do except to wish that you would soon overcome your love, and above all to help you to do so to the best of my ability by hastening to deprive you of all hope? You yourself admit that "it is a painful sentiment when the person who inspires it does not share it." You know very well that it is impossible for me to share it; and even if that misfortune were to befall me, I would be all the more to be pitied, without your being any happier. I hope you esteem me enough not to doubt it for a moment. I therefore beg you to cease your efforts to trouble a heart to which tranquillity is so necessary; do not force me to regret having known you.

Since I am cherished and esteemed by a husband whom I love and respect, my duties and my pleasures meet in the same person. I am happy, as I should be. If there are keener pleasures, I do not desire them, I do not want to know them. Is there any sweeter pleasure than to be at peace with oneself, to spend only tranquil days, to go to sleep without agitation and awaken without remorse? What you call happiness is only a tumult of the senses, a storm of the passions which is frightening to watch, even from the shore. How could I brave these tempests? How could I dare to embark upon a sea covered with the debris of countless thousands of shipwrecks? And with whom? No, Monsieur, I shall remain on land; I cherish the bonds that attach me to it. I would not break them if I could, and if I did not have them I would hasten to acquire them.

Why do you cling to my steps? Why do you persist in following me? Your letters, which were supposed to be rare, arrive in rapid succession. They were supposed to be sober, and you speak to me of nothing in them except your mad love. You press the idea of you upon me, more than you did yourself. Removed from my presence in one form, you reappear in another. When I ask you to cease saying certain things, you say them again in another way. You take pleasure in embarrassing me with specious reasoning, and you evade my arguments. I will not answer you again. . . . How you treat the women you have seduced! With what contempt you speak of them! I am willing to believe that some of them deserve it, but are they all so contemptible? Ah, no doubt they are, since they betrayed their duties to yield to a criminal love! At that moment they lost everything, even the respect of the man for whom they sacrificed everything. It is a just punishment, but the mere idea of it makes me shudder. But after all, what does it matter to me? Why should I concern myself with them or with you? What right have you to trouble my tranquillity? Leave me in peace, do not see me again, stop writing to me, I beg you; I demand it. This letter is the last you will receive from me.

LETTER 57

~ *From the Vicomte de Valmont to the Marquise de Merteuil*

September 5, 17—

I found your letter yesterday on my return. Your anger thoroughly delighted me. You could not resent Danceny's shortcomings more bitterly if they concerned you directly. It is no doubt from vengeance that you are accustoming his beloved to committing little infidelities; you are a very bad influence! Yes, you are charming, and I am not surprised that she should oppose less resistance to you than to Danceny.

At last I know him inside out, that fine romantic hero! He no longer has any secrets to withhold from me. I told him repeatedly that virtuous love was the supreme good, that one sentiment was worth more than ten intrigues, and that I myself was in love and timid, until finally he found my way of thinking in such close agreement with his own that, in his enchantment with my candor, he told me everything and swore friendship to me without reserve. However, this has not furthered our plan.

First of all, it became clear to me that he has the idea that an unmarried girl deserves to be treated with much more deference than a woman, since she has more to lose. He feels that nothing can justify a man in placing a girl under the necessity of either marrying him or living in dishonor when she is infinitely richer than he, as is true in his case. The mother's confidence, the daughter's candor—everything intimidates and restrains him. The difficulty would not be to combat his arguments, however true they may be. With a little adroitness and the help of passion, they could be overcome, especially since they lend themselves to ridicule and we would have the authority of custom on our side. But what makes it impossible to obtain a hold on him is that he is happy as he is. If first loves appear in general to be more virtuous and, as is commonly said, purer, and if they are at least slower in their progress, it is not, as many think, because of delicacy or timidity: it is because the heart, surprised by an unknown feeling, hesitates at each step, so to speak, to enjoy the charm it feels, and because this charm has such power over a fresh heart that it occupies it to such an extent that it forgets every other pleasure. This is so true that a libertine in love—if a libertine can be in love—becomes from that moment onward less eager for sensual pleasure; and there is only a difference of degree between Danceny's conduct with Cécile Volanges and my conduct with the prudish Madame de Tourvel.

To become inflamed, our young man would have had to encounter more obstacles; and above all he should have had more mystery, for mystery leads to boldness. I am not far from thinking that you have harmed us in serving him so well; your conduct would have been excellent with an experienced man who had only desires, but you might have foreseen that for a virtuous young man in love, the greatest value of a woman's favors is that they are the proof of her love, and that consequently the more certain he is of being loved, the less enterprising he will be. What is to be done now? I have no idea; but I have no hope that the girl will be taken before her marriage, and I am afraid all our efforts will have been wasted. I am sorry, but I can see no help for it.

While I am discoursing here, you are doing something better with your Chevalier, which reminds me that you have promised me an infidelity in my favor: I have your promise in writing, and I do not intend to make it a "La Châtre note."* I admit that it has not yet fallen due, but it would be magnanimous of you not to wait till then; and for my part I shall give you credit for the interest. What do you say to that, my fair friend? Are you not tired of your constancy? Is your Chevalier so wonderful? Give me a chance to make you admit that if you attributed any merit to him, it was only because you had forgotten me.

Good-by, my fair friend; I kiss you as I desire you, and I defy all the Chevalier's kisses to have as much ardor.

---

*Before going off to the army, the Marquis de La Châtre made his mistress, the celebrated Ninon de Lenclos, give him a written promise to be faithful to him. She lost no time in breaking it. In the course of doing so, she laughed and exclaimed, "Ah, what a good note La Châtre has!" The expression "a La Châtre note" soon came to designate any worthless promise. (Translator's note.)

LETTER 58

~ *From the Vicomte de Valmont to Madame de Tourvel*

September 7, 17—

How have I deserved your reproaches, Madame, and the anger you show toward me? The most fervent yet respectful attachment, the most complete submission to your slightest wishes: there, in a few words, is the story of my feelings and my conduct. Overwhelmed by the afflictions of an unhappy love, I had no other consolation than that of seeing you; you ordered me to deprive myself of it and I obeyed without a murmur. As a reward for this sacrifice you allowed me to write to you, and now you wish to deny me that one pleasure. Shall I let it be taken from me without trying to defend it? No, certainly not. Ah, how could it not be dear to my heart? It is the only pleasure left for me, and it comes to me from you.

You say my letters are too frequent! Please bear in mind that during the ten days my exile has lasted I have not spent one moment without thinking of you, and yet you have received only two letters from me. You say I speak to you of nothing except my love in them. But what am I to say, if not what I think? All I could do was to weaken my expression of it, and you can believe me when I tell you that I have let you see only what it has been impossible for me to hide. You end your letter by threatening never to answer me again. Thus you are not content with your harsh treatment of a man who prefers you to all else and respects you even more than he loves you: you also wish to augment it with scorn! And why these threats and this anger? What need do you have of them? Are you not sure of being obeyed, even when your orders are unjust? Is it not impossible for me to thwart any of your desires, and have I not already proved it? But will you abuse your power over me? After making me unhappy, after becoming unjust, will it be easy for you to enjoy that peace of mind which you say is so necessary to you? Will you never say to yourself, "He placed his fate in my hands and I made him wretched; he implored my aid and I looked at him without pity"? Do you know how far my despair can go? No.

To calculate my misery, you would have to know how much I love you, and you do not know my heart.

To what are you sacrificing me? To illusory fears. And who arouses them in you? A man who worships you, a trustworthy man over whom you will never cease to have absolute power. What do you fear, what can you fear, from a sentiment which you will always be able to direct as you please? But your imagination creates monsters, and you attribute the terror they cause you to love. With a little confidence, those phantoms will vanish.

A wise man has said that fears can nearly always be dispelled by delving into their causes.* This truth is particularly applicable to love. Love, and your fears will vanish. Instead of the things that frighten you, you will find a delightful sentiment, a tender and submissive lover; and all your days, permeated with happiness, will leave you no other regret than that of having wasted some of them in indifference. Since recognizing my errors and beginning to exist only for love, I myself regret the time I thought I had spent in pleasure, and I feel that it is for you alone to make me happy. But I beg you not to let the pleasure I find in writing to you be disturbed by the fear of displeasing you. I do not wish to disobey you, but I am at your knees, imploring the happiness you would take away from me, the only happiness you have left me, and I cry out to you: Hear my prayers and see my tears! Ah, Madame, will you refuse me?

LETTER 59

~ *From the Vicomte de Valmont to the Marquise de Merteuil*

September 8, 17—

Tell me, if you know, what Danceny means by this drivel. What has happened to him, and what has he lost? Has his fair lady become irritated by his everlasting respect? In fairness to her, I must admit that anyone would be irritated by less. What shall I say to him when I meet him this afternoon as he has requested, and as I have agreed to do without knowing exactly

---

*This is believed to be Rousseau in *Emile*, but the quotation is not accurate, and Valmont's application of it is quite false; and then, had Madame de Tourvel read *Emile*?

why? I have no intention of wasting my time in listening to his complaints if it is not going to be of any use to us. Amorous lamentations are not good to listen to except in recitatives or ariettas. So tell me what the situation is and what I am to do, otherwise I shall desert my post to avoid the boredom I foresee. May I have a talk with you this morning? If you are "engaged," at least write me a note and give me the cues for my part.

Where were you yesterday? I can no longer manage to see you. There was really no point in keeping me in Paris this month. Make up your mind, because the Comtesse de B—— has just sent me a pressing invitation to come to see her in the country, and, as she writes amusingly, her husband "has the finest woods* in the world, which he carefully preserves for the pleasure of his friends." As you know, I have certain rights to those woods, and I shall go to pay them another visit if I am not useful to you. Good-by; bear in mind that Danceny is coming to see me at four o'clock.

LETTER 60

~   *From the Chevalier Danceny to the Vicomte de Valmont (Enclosed in the preceding letter)*

September 8, 17—

Ah, Monsieur, I am in despair, I have lost everything! I dare not confide to paper the secret of my grief, but I need to pour it out to a faithful and trustworthy friend. At what time may I see you and come to you for consolation and advice? I was so happy the day I opened my soul to you! What a difference now! Everything has changed for me. What I suffer on my own account is the least part of my torment: my anxiety for someone far dearer to me than myself, that is what I cannot endure! More fortunate than I, you can see her, and I count on your friendship to assure me that you will do so. But first I must see you and tell you what has happened. You will pity me and help me; you are my only hope. You are sensitive, you know what love is, and you are the only one in whom I can confide; do not refuse me your aid.

Bois: the word can also mean "antlers" and is sometimes used in referring to a cuckold's horns, hence Valmont's amusement. (Translator's note.)

Good-by, Monsieur; my pain is relieved only by the thought that I still have a friend like you. Please let me know at what time I may see you. If it is not this morning, I would like it to be early this afternoon.

LETTER 61

~ *From Cécile Volanges to Sophie Carnay*

September 7, 17—

My dear Sophie, pity your Cécile, your poor Cécile: she's terribly unhappy! Mama knows everything. I can't imagine how she could have suspected anything, yet she's discovered everything. She seemed a little cross last night, but I didn't pay much attention to it. In fact, while we were waiting for her game to end, I talked very gaily with Madame de Merteuil, who'd come here for supper, and we talked a great deal about Danceny. But I don't think we could have been overheard. I went up to my room as soon as she left.

I was undressing when Mama came in, sent my maid away and asked me for the key to my writing desk. Her tone made me tremble so much that I could hardly stand up. At first I pretended I couldn't find it, but finally I had to obey her. The first drawer she opened was the very one that contained the Chevalier Danceny's letters. I was so upset when she asked me what they were that I could only answer that they were nothing, but when I saw her begin reading the first one I had just enough time to get to a chair before I felt so ill that I fainted. As soon as I recovered, my mother, who'd called in my maid, told me to go to bed and walked out. She took all of Danceny's letters with her. I shudder each time I think that I'm gong to have to appear before her again. I cried all night.

I'm now writing to you at dawn, in the hope that Joséphine will come. If I can talk to her alone, I'll ask her to deliver a little note that I'm going to write to Madame de Merteuil; if not, I'll put it in your letter, and I hope you'll do me the favor of sending it to her as though it were from you. She's the only one who can give me any consolation. At least we'll talk about him, because I have no hope of ever seeing him again. I'm so unhappy! Perhaps she'll be kind enough to give him a letter. I don't dare to count on Joséphine for that, much less my maid, because she may have been the one who told my mother I had some letters in my writing desk.

I'll end this letter now because I want to have time to write to Madame de Merteuil, and also to Danceny, so that my letter will be ready if she's willing to take it. After that, I'll go back to bed and stay there till my maid comes in. I'll say I'm ill to avoid going to see Mama. It will hardly be a lie: I'm certainly suffering more than if I had a fever. My eyes are burning from having cried so long, and I have a weight on my stomach that makes it hard for me to breathe. When I think that I'll never see Danceny again, I wish I were dead. Good-by, my dear Sophie. I can't tell you any more; my tears are suffocating me.

(Note: Cécile Volanges's letter to the Marquise has been omitted, because it contained the same facts as the above letter, with fewer details. The letter to the Chevalier Danceny has not been found: the reason for this will be seen in Letter 63, from Madame de Merteuil to the Vicomte.)

LETTER 62

~ *From Madame de Volanges to the Chevalier Danceny*

September 7, 17—

After having abused a mother's confidence and a child's innocence, Monsieur, you will surely not be surprised to learn that you will no longer be received in a house where you have responded to the proofs of the most sincere friendship by violating all the rules of decent behavior. I prefer to ask you never to come here again, instead of giving orders that you are not to be admitted, which would compromise us all through the remarks the servants would be sure to make. I have a right to hope that you will not force me to resort to that. I warn you also that if you ever make the slightest attempt to maintain my daughter in the aberration into which you have plunged her, an austere and eternal retirement will remove her from your pursuit. It is for you to see, Monsieur, whether you will have as little fear of causing her misfortune as you have had of attempting to cause her dishonor. As for myself, my choice is already made, and I have informed her of it.

You will find enclosed a packet of your letters. I expect you to send me all of my daughter's letters in exchange, and to cooperate in leaving no trace of an event which can never be recalled by me without indignation, by her without shame, and by you without remorse. I have the honor of being, etc.

LETTER 63

~ *From the Marquise de Merteuil to the Vicomte de Valmont*

September 9, 17—

Yes, indeed, I shall explain Danceny's note to you. The event which made him write it is my handiwork, and I believe it is my masterpiece. I have not wasted my time since your last letter. Like the Athenian architect, I said, "What he has said, I will do."

So that fine romantic hero needed obstacles! He was falling asleep in his felicity! Oh, he can count on me: I shall give him plenty to keep him busy! And if I am not mistaken, his sleep will no longer be peaceful. He had to be taught the value of time, and I venture to say that he now regrets the time he has wasted. You said he also needed more mystery; well, he will no longer lack it. I have one good point: I need only to be shown my mistakes and I do not rest until I have corrected them completely. Let me tell you what I have done.

When I came home day before yesterday morning, I read your letter; I found it enlightening. Convinced that you had quite clearly pointed out the cause of the difficulty, I devoted all my attention to finding a way to remove it. However, I began by going to bed, for the indefatigable Chevalier had not let me sleep for a moment, and I thought I was sleepy; but not at all: I was entirley preoccupied with Danceny, and my desire to draw him from his indolence or punish him for it did not allow me to close my eyes. It was not until I had thoroughly worked out my plan that I was able to sleep for two hours.

That evening I went to see Madame de Volanges, and, in accordance with my plan, I confided to her that I felt sure there was a dangerous relationship between Danceny and her daughter. Madame de Volanges, so clear-sighted against you, was so blind in this matter that at first she replied that I was surely mistaken, that her daughter was only a child, etc., etc. I could not tell her everything I knew, but I referred to looks and words "which alarmed my virtue and my friendship"; in short, I spoke almost as well as a pious prude could have done. To strike the decisive blow, I went so far as to say that I thought I had seen a letter given and received. "That reminds me," I added, "that one day she opened a drawer of her writing desk in front of me, and I saw a thick bundle of papers which she is no doubt keeping. Do you know whether she corresponds frequently with anyone?" At this point Madame de Volanges's face changed and I saw tears in her eyes. "I thank you, my worthy friend," she said to me, pressing my hand, "and I shall find out the truth."

After this conversation, which was too short to seem suspicious, I went over to Cécile. I left her soon afterward to ask her mother not to compromise me with her daughter, which she promised all the more willingly because I pointed out to her how fortunate it would be if the child should come to have enough confidence in me to open her heart to me and place me in a position to give her "my wise advice." I do not doubt that she will keep her promise, because I am sure she wants to impress her daughter with her perspicacity. This enabled me to maintain my tone of friendship with Cécile without appearing deceitful in Madame de Volanges' eyes, which I wanted to avoid. I also gained the future advantage of being with Cécile as long and as secretly as I wish, without ever offending her mother.

I exploited this advantage that same evening: when I had finished my game of cards, I took Cécile into a corner and started a conversation about Danceny, a subject on which she could talk forever. I amused myself by exciting her with the idea of the pleasure she would have in seeing him the next day; there is no kind of folly I did not make her say. I had to give her back in hope what I was taking away from her in reality; furthermore, all this will make her feel the blow more acutely, and I am convinced that the more she has suffered, the more eager she will be to compensate herself for it at the first opportunity. And it is good to accustom to great emotions those whom one has destined to great adventures.

After all, can she not pay with a few tears for the pleasure of having her Danceny? She is mad about him? Well, I promise her she will have him, and even that she would not have had him without this storm. It is a bad dream from which it will be delightful to awaken. On the whole, it seems to me that she ought to be grateful to me; and while I may have helped her with a certain malice, one must have one's amusements.

*Fools were placed on earth for our little pleasure.**

I finally, left, highly pleased with myself. "Animated by obstacles," I said to myself, "Danceny is either going to redouble his love, in which case I shall serve him with all my power, or else, if he is nothing but a fool, as I am sometimes tempted to believe, he will be in despair and consider himself defeated; in that case I shall at least have taken vengeance on him to the best of my ability, and so doing I shall have increased Madame de Volanges' respect for me, her daughter's friendship, and the confidence of both. As for Gercourt, who is my primary concern, I shall be either very unlucky or very inept if, having placed myself in control of his wife's mind as I am now and shall be even more, I do not find countless ways of making him what I want him to be." I went to bed with these pleasant thoughts, so I slept well and woke up late.

When I awoke, I found two notes, one from Madame de Volanges and one from her daughter, and I could not help laughing when I found this same sentence, word for word, in both of them: "It is only from you that I can expect any consolation." Is it not amusing to console for and against, and to be the sole agent of two directly opposed interests? I am now like the Divinity, receiving the conflicting prayers of blind mortals and changing nothing in my immutable decrees. However, I discarded that august role for a time to assume that of consoling angel, and, in accordance with the percept, I went to visit my friends in their affliction.

I began with the mother; I found her in the depths of a sorrow which already avenges you to some extent for the setbacks she caused you with your fair prude. Everything succeeded perfectly; my only worry was that she might take advantage of that moment to gain her daughter's confidence, which would have been easy to do by using the language of gentleness and friendship with her, and by giving an appearance and tone of indulgent affection to the counsels of reason. Fortunately she armed herself with severity and conducted herself so badly that she deserved my applause. It is true that she nearly upset all our plans by her decision to send her daughter back to the convent, but I parried

---

*Gresset: *Le Méchant*, a comedy.

that blow and persuaded her merely to threaten to do so in case Danceny should continue his efforts; I did this in order to force them both into the circumspection which I consider necessary for success.

I then went to the daughter. You cannot imagine how much sorrow increases her beauty! If she becomes at all coquettish, I guarantee you that she will weep often; this time, however, her tears had no ulterior motive. . . . Struck by this new charm which I had never seen in her before, and which I was very glad to observe, at first I gave her only clumsy consolations that increased her sorrow more than they soothed it, and in this way I brought her to the point of actually choking. She was no longer weeping, and for a moment I was afraid of convulsions. I advised her to go to bed, which she agreed to do. I acted as her maid; she had not dressed, and soon her hair fell loosely over her shoulders and her completely uncovered breasts. I kissed her; she abandoned herself in my arms, and soon her tears began flowing freely again. My God, how beautiful she was! If Mary Magdalene was like that, she must have been much more dangerous as a penitent than as a sinner.

When the grief-stricken beauty was in bed. I began to console her in good faith. First I allayed her fear of the convent. I kindled a hope in her of being able to see Danceny in secret. I sat down on the bed and said, "If he were here . . ." Then, embroidering on that theme, I led her from one diversion to another until she forgot her affliction. We would have parted perfectly satisfied with each other if she had not tried to give me a letter for Danceny, which I steadfastly refused to accept. Here are my reasons; I am sure you will approve of them.

First of all, it would have meant compromising myself with Danceny; and although this was the only reason I could give to her, there were many others between you and me. Would it not have been jeopardizing the fruits of my labors to give our young people such an easy way of soothing their pain? And I would not be sorry to force them to involve a few servants in this adventure, for if it turns out well, as I hope it will, it must become known immediately after her marriage, and there are few more certain means of spreading the news of it; or if by some miracle the servants do not talk, we ourselves shall talk, and it will be more convenient to blame them for the indiscretion.

So you must give Danceny this idea today; and since I am not sure of Cécile's maid, whom she herself seems to mistrust, send him to my own faithful Victoire. I shall make sure that she succeeds. This idea pleases me all the more because the confidence will be useful only to us and not to them: for I have not yet reached the end of my story.

While I was refusing to take her letter, I was afraid that at any moment she might ask me to send it by the city postal service, which I could scarcely have refused to do. Fortunately, whether from agitation or from ignorance, or because the letter meant less to her than the reply, which she could not have received in that way, she said nothing to me about it; but, to prevent this idea from occurring to her, or at least to prevent her from making use of it, I made up my mind immediately: when I went back to her mother, I persuaded her to take her daughter away for some time, to take her to the country. . . . And where? Is your heart not pounding with joy? To the house of your aunt, of old Madame de Rosemonde. She is to write to her about it today. Thus it is now permissible for you to return to your prude, for she will no longer be able to use the objection of the scandal that would arise from being alone with you; and, thanks to my efforts, Madame de Volanges herself will repair the harm she has done you.

But listen to me and do not concern yourself with your own affairs so eagerly that you lose sight of this one; remember that I have an interest in it. I want you to make yourself the two young people's correspondent and advisor. Tell Danceny about the journey and offer him your services. Admit no difficulty except that of delivering your letter of credit to Cécile, then remove that obstacle immediately by telling him about my maid. There is no doubt that he will accept; and as the reward of your efforts you will have the confidence of a fresh young heart, which is always interesting. Poor girl! How she will blush when she hands you her first letter! Really, this role of confidant, against which prejudices have arisen, seems to me a very pleasant diversion when one is occupied elsewhere, as you will be.

The outcome of this intrigue will depend on you. Choose the right time to bring the actors together. The country offers countless means, and Danceny will certainly be ready to go there at your first signal. A night, a disguise, a window . . . who knows? But if the little girl returns in the same state in which she left, I shall lay the blame on you. If you feel that she needs any encouragement from me, let me know. After the lesson I have given her about the danger of keeping letters, I think I may now write to her without fear; and I still plan to make her my pupil.

I think I have forgotten to tell you that her suspicions about the betrayal of her correspondence first fell upon her maid, and that I then directed them to her confessor. I thus killed two birds with one stone.

Good-by, Vicomte; I have been writing to you for a long time and my dinner has been delayed by it, but my letter has been dictated by self-esteem and friendship, and they are both loquacious. However, you will have it by three o'clock, and that is all you need.

Complain of me now if you dare, and go to visit the Comte de B——'s woods if you are tempted to. You say he keeps them for his friends' pleasure! He must be everybody's friend! But good-by, I am hungry.

LETTER 64

~ *From the Chevalier Danceny to Madame de Volanges (First draft; enclosed with Letter 66, from the Vicomte to the Marquise)*

September 9, 17—

Without seeking to justify my conduct, Madame, and without complaining of yours, I can only be grieved by an event which has brought sorrow to three people, all of whom are worthy of a happier fate. I feel the chagrin of being its cause even more acutely than that of being its victim. Since yesterday I have repeatedly tried to have the honor of replying to you, without finding the strength to do so. Yet I have so many things to say to you that I must now make a serious effort, and if this letter has little order and coherence, you must be sufficiently aware of the painfulness of my situation to grand me some indulgence.

To begin with, allow me to protest against the first phrase of your letter. I dare to assert that I have abused neither your confidence nor Mademoiselle de Volanges's innocence; I have respected both in all my actions. Only my actions were under my control, and if you hold me responsible for an involuntary sentiment, I shall not be afraid to say that the sentiment inspired in me by your daughter is such that, while it may displease you, it cannot offend you. In this matter, which touches me more deeply than I can tell you, I want only you as my judge, and my letters as my witnesses.

You forbid me to come to your house in the future, and I shall certainly yield to any orders you may wish to give me, but will not my total and sudden absence give as much occasion to the gossip you want to avoid as the order not to admit me to your house which, for that very reason, you did not want to give to your servants? I shall insist on this point all the more because it is of greater importance to Mademoiselle de Volanges than to me. I beg you to weigh everything carefully, and not to allow your severity to impair your prudence. Convinced that your decisions will be determined only by your daughter's welfare, I shall await new orders from you.

However, if you should permit me to call on you periodically, I promise, Madame (and you can count on my promise), not to abuse those occasions by trying to speak to Mademoiselle de Volanges in private, or to deliver any letters to her. My fear of anything that might endanger her reputation imposes this sacrifice on me; and the happiness of seeing her sometimes will compensate me for it.

This part of my letter is the only answer I can give to what you have told me about the fate which you hold in store for Mademoiselle de Volanges, and which you wish to make dependent upon my conduct. To promise you more would be to deceive you. A vile seducer can adapt his plans to circumstances and make allowances for events, but the love that animates me permits me only two sentiments: courage and constancy.

How could I ever consent to be forgotten by Mademoiselle de Volanges, or to forget her myself? No, no, never! I shall remain faithful to her; she has received my oath to do so, and I renew it today. Excuse me, Madame, I have allowed myself to be carried away; I must return.

I have still another subject to discuss with you: that of the letters you ask me to send you. I am truly pained to add a refusal to the wrongs you already attribute to me, but listen to my reasons, I beg you, and remember, in order to appreciate them, that my only consolation for the misfortune of having lost your friendship is the hope of keeping your esteem.

Mademoiselle de Volanges's letters, always so precious to me, have now become much more so. They are all I have left; they alone still recall to me a sentiment which makes all the charm of my life. And yet you may believe me when I tell you that I would not hesitate for a moment to sacrifice them to you, and that my regret at being deprived of them would yield to my desire to prove my respectful deference to you, were it not for the fact that I am restrained by powerful considerations which you yourself, I am sure, will not be able to condemn.

It is true that you have Mademoiselle de Volanges's secret; but permit me to say that I have reason to believe that it was the result of a surprisal, not of confidence. I do not presume to condemn an act which was authorized, perhaps, by maternal solicitude. I respect your rights, but they do not go so far as to relieve me of my duties. The most sacred of all is never to betray a confidence that has been placed in us. I would be failing in that duty if I were to expose to the eyes of another the secrets of a heart which wished to unveil them only to mine. If your daughter consents to confide them to you, let her speak; her letters are useless to you. If, however, she wishes to keep her secrets within herself, you will surely not expect me to reveal them to you.

As for the silence in which you wish this event to remain buried, have no fear, Madame: in everything that concerns Mademoiselle de Volanges, I can defy even the heart of a mother. To relieve you of all anxiety, I have provided for all eventualities. The precious packet which had previously been marked, "Papers to be burned" is now marked, "Papers belonging to Madame de Volanges." This should also prove to you that my refusal is not motivated by the fear that you would find in those letters any sentiment of which you might personally have reason to complain.

This is a very long letter, Madame, but it will not be long enough if it leaves you with the slightest doubt of the honesty of my sentiments, my sincere regret at having displeased you, and the profound respect with which I have the honor of being, etc.

LETTER 65

~ *From the Chevalier Danceny to Cécile Volanges (Sent open to the Marquis de Merteuil in Letter 66, from the Vicomte)*

September 9, 17—

Oh, my Cécile, what will become of us? What god will save us from the misfortunes that threaten us? May love at least give us the courage to endure them! How can I describe my surprise and despair when I saw my letters and read Madame de Volanges's note? Who could have betrayed us? Whom do you suspect? Can it be that you did something imprudent? What are you doing now? What have you been told? I would like to know everything and I know nothing. Perhaps you yourself know nothing more than I.

I am sending you your mother's note and a copy of my reply. I hope you will approve of what I have said to her. I also need your approval of the steps I have taken since that fateful event; the purpose of them all has been to hear from you and to let you hear from me, and—who knows?—perhaps to see you again, and more freely than ever.

Can you imagine, my Cécile, the pleasure it would give us to be together again, to be able to swear eternal love again, and to see in each other's eyes, to feel in our souls, that that vow was not deceptive? What sorrows would not be obliterated by such a sweet moment? Well, I have hopes of seeing it occur, and I owe them to those same steps which I beg you to approve. What am I saying? I owe them to the consoling care of the most affectionate friend in the world, and my only request is that you will allow him to be your friend also.

Perhaps I ought not to have given your confidence without your permission, but I have unhappiness and necessity as my excuse. It was love that guided me, and it is now love that implores your indulgence and asks you to forgive a necessary confidence without which we might have remained separated forever.* You know the friend of whom I am speaking; he is the friend of the woman you love most. He is the Vicomte de Valmont.

My purpose in going to him was at first to ask him to persuade Madame de Merteuil to deliver a letter to you. He did not believe this would be successful; but while he does not wish to rely on Madame de Merteuil, he answers for her maid, who has certain obligations to him. She will deliver this letter to you, and you may give her your reply.

This assistance will be of little use to us if, as Monsieur de Valmont believes, you are going to the country immediately. But in that case he himself will help us. The woman to whose house you are going is his relative. He will take advantage of this pretext to go there when you do, and our correspondence will pass through his hands. He even assures me that if you will do as

---

*Danceny's statement is not accurate. He had already confided in Monsieur de Valmont before this event. See Letter 57.

he says, he will arrange for us to see each other without any risk of compromising you.

And now, my Cécile, if you love me, if you pity my unhappiness, if, as I hope, you share my regrets, will you refuse your confidence to a man who will be our guardian angel? If it were not for him, I would be reduced to the despair of not even being able to soften the sorrows I cause you. They will end, I hope; but promise me, my dearest, that you will not yield to them too much, that you will not let them overwhelm you. The thought of your pain is an unbearable torture to me. I would give my life to make you happy! You know that very well. May the certainty of being adored bring some consolation to your soul! Mine needs your assurance that you forgive love for the pain it is making you suffer.

Good-by, my Cécile; good-by, my dearest.

LETTER 66

~ *From the Vicomte de Valmont to the Marquise de Merteuil*

September 9, 17—

When you read the two enclosed letters, my fair friend, you will see whether I have carried out our plan well. Although they are both dated today, they were written yesterday, in my house and before my eyes; the one written to the little girl says everything we could wish. One can only bow to the profundity of your views if they are judged by the success of your acts. Danceny is aflame, and I am sure that at the first opportunity you will no longer have any reason to reproach him. If his guileless beauty will be docile, everything will be over within a short time after his arrival in the country; I have a hundred means already prepared. Thanks to your efforts, I am now definitely "Danceny's friend"; all he lacks now is to be a "Prince."*

He is still very young, that Danceny! Would you believe that I was never able to persuade him to promise Madame de Volanges that he would give up his love? As though it were difficult to make a promise when one has already decided not to keep it! "That would be deceitful," he kept repeating. An edifying compunction, especially when he wants to seduce her daughter!

---

*Allusion to a passage in a poem by Monsieur de Voltaire.

That is how all men are! They are all equally unscrupulous in their schemes, and if they have any weakness in carrying them out, they call it integrity.

It is your responsibility to prevent Madame de Volanges from being alarmed by the little indiscretions our young man has allowed himself in his letter; preserve us from the convent. Try also to make her give up her request for her daughter's letters. First of all, he will not return them; he does not want to, and I agree with him: here love and reason are in harmony. I have read those letters, I have swallowed their boredom. They may become useful. Let me explain.

Despite all our prudence, there may be a scandal. That would prevent the marriage and wreck all our plans for Gercourt, would it not? But since, on my own account, I want to take vengeance on the mother, in that case I reserve for myself the task of dishonoring the daughter. By carefully choosing from that correspondence and producing only part of it, it could be made to appear that the little girl had taken all the first steps and had absolutely thrown herself at him. Some of the letters might even compromise the mother, and would at least "sully" her with unforgivable negligence. I realize that the scrupulous Danceny would rebel at first, but since he would be personally attacked, I think he could be overcome. There is only one chance in a thousand that luck will turn that way, but we must provide for every possibility.

Good-by, my fair friend; it would be very kind of you to come to the Maréchale de ———'s house for supper tomorrow; I was unable to refuse.

I do not suppose there is any need to urge you to keep my country plans a secret from Madame de Volanges; she would soon have plans of her own to stay in Paris, whereas once she has arrived, she will not leave the next day; and if she gives us only a week, I will answer for everything.

LETTER 67

~ *From Madame de Tourvel to the Vicomte de Valmont*

September 9, 17—

I did not want to answer you again, Monsieur, and perhaps the embarrassment I now feel is in itself a proof that I should not do so. However, I do not want to leave you any reason for complaint against me; I want to convince you that I have done everything I could for you.

You say I gave you permission to write to me. I agree, but when you remind me of that permission do you think I forget the conditions on which it was given to you? If I had adhered to them as much as you have violated them, do you think you would have received a single reply from me? Yet this is the third one; and when you do everything that is required to make me break off this correspondence, it is I who concern myself with means of maintaining it. There is one, but it is the only one; and if you refuse to accept it, you will be proving to me, no matter what you may say, how little this correspondence means to you.

Abandon a language to which I cannot and will not listen; renounce a sentiment which offends and frightens me, and to which, perhaps, you ought to be less attached when you reflect that it is the obstacle that separates us. Is it the only sentiment of which you are capable? Will love have the additional fault, in my eyes, of excluding friendship? Will you yourself have the fault of not wishing to have as a friend the woman in whom you have desired more tender feelings? I am unwilling to think so: that humiliating idea would disgust me and turn me against you forever.

In offering you my friendship, Monsieur, I give you all that is mine, all that is at my disposal. What more can you desire? To yield to that gentle sentiment, so well suited to my heart, I await only your assent and the promise I demand of you: that this friendship will suffice for your happiness. I shall forget everything that has been said to me, and I shall count on you to justify my choice.

You see my frankness: you should regard it as proof of my confidence. It will depend only on you to increase it still more; but I warn you that the first word of love will destroy it forever and bring back all my fears, and above all that it will be for me the signal for eternal silence toward you.

If, as you say, you have "recognized your errors," would you not prefer to be the object of a virtuous woman's friendship, rather than that of a guilty woman's remorse? Good-by, Monsieur; you will understand that after having spoken thus, I can say nothing more until you have replied to me.

LETTER 68

~   *From the Vicomte de Valmont to Madame de Tourvel*

September 10, 17—

How can I reply to your last letter, Madame? How can I dare to be sincere when it may ruin me with you? But I must do so nevertheless, and I shall have the courage I need. I tell myself repeatedly that it is better to deserve you than to obtain you; and even if you should refuse me a happiness which I shall constantly desire, I must at least prove to you that my heart is worthy of it.

What a pity that, as you say, I have "recognized my errors"! With what transports of joy I would have read that same letter to which I now fear to reply! You speak to me in it with "frankness," you express your "confidence" in me, and you offer me your "friendship": what treasures, Madame, and how I regret not being able to take advantage of them! Why am I no longer the same?

If I were, if I had only an ordinary inclination for you, that slight inclination which is nowadays called love, and which is only the child of seduction and pleasure, I would hasten to turn everything I could obtain to my advantage. With little delicacy concerning means, as long as they led to success, I would encourage your frankness because of my need to guess your thoughts; I would desire your confidence for the purpose of betraying it; I would accept your friendship in the hope of leading it astray. . . . Does this picture frighten you, Madame? Well, it would be my portrait if I told you that I consented to be nothing but your friend. . . .

What! Could I consent to share with anyone a sentiment that emanates from your soul? If I ever say so, cease to believe me. From that moment on, I shall be seeking to deceive you. I may still desire you, but I shall certainly have stopped loving you.

It is not that charming friendship, sweet confidence and sympathetic friendship are without value in my eyes. . . . But love, true love, the kind you inspire, combining all those sentiments and giving them more vigor, cannot lend itself, like them, to that tranquillity, that coldness of the soul which allows comparisons, which even tolerates preferences. No, Madame, I shall not be your friend; I shall love you with the most tender, most ardent, yet most respectful love. You may drive it to despair, but you cannot destroy it.

By what right do you presume to dispose of a heart whose homage you refuse? By what refinement of cruelty do you envy me even the happiness of loving you? That happiness is mine, it is independent of you; I will defend it. While it is the source of my torments, it is also their remedy.

No, once again, no. Persist in your cruel refusals, but leave me my love. You delight in making me unhappy: well, so be it! Try to weary my courage, I shall at least force you to decide my fate; and some day, perhaps, you will do me more justice. Not that I have any hope of ever making you responsive to my feelings; but without being persuaded, you will be convinced, and you will say to yourself, "I misjudged him."

I shall go further: you are being unjust to yourself. To know you without loving you and to love you without being constant are both equally impossible; and despite the modesty that adorns you, it must be easier for you to complain of the sentiments you inspire than to be surprised by them. As for myself, my only merit is having been able to appreciate you, and I will not lose it. Far from accepting your insidious offers, I renew at your feet my vow to love your forever.

LETTER 69

~ *From Cécile Volanges to the Chevalier Danceny (Written in pencil and copied by Danceny)*

September 10, 17—

You ask me what I am doing: I love you, and I weep. My mother has stopped speaking to me; she has taken away my paper, pens and ink; I am using a pencil which fortunately was left to me, and I am writing to you on a piece of your letter. I must approve of everything you have done; I love you too much not to use every possible means of hearing from you and letting you hear from me. I did not like Monsieur de Valmont and I did not think he was such a good friend of yours, but I shall try to accustom myself to him and like him because of you. I do not know who betrayed us; it can only have been my maid or my confessor. I am very unhappy: we are leaving for the country tomorrow, I do not know for how long. Oh, never to see you again! I have no more space. Good-by; try to read this. These words written in pencil will perhaps fade away, but never the sentiments engraved in my heart.

LETTER 70

~ *From the Vicomte de Valmont to the Marquise de Merteuil*

September 11, 17—

I have an important warning to give you, dear friend. As you know, I had supper yesterday at the Maréchale de ———'s house. Your name was mentioned and I said, not all the good things I think about you, but all those I do not think. Everyone appeared to agree with me and the conversation was languishing, as it always does when we say nothing but good of other people, when a contradictor arose: it was Prévan.

"God forbid," he said, standing up, "that I should ever doubt Madame de Merteuil's good behavior, but I dare to think that she owes it more to her agility than to her principles. It is perhaps more difficult to follow her than to please her. Since in running after a woman one almost never fails to meet others on the way, and since, all things considered, these other women may be as good as she is, or even better, some men are distracted by a new inclination, while others stop from weariness; and Madame de Merteuil has perhaps had to defend herself less than any other woman in Paris. For my part," he added, encouraged by the smiles of several women, "I shall not believe in her virtue until I have killed six horses in paying court to her."

This bad joke was successful, like all those based on vilification. During the laughter it aroused, Prévan sat down again and the general conversation changed. But the two Comtesses de P—, who were sitting beside our skeptic, engaged him in a private conversation which I was fortunately able to overhear.

He accepted their challenge to inspire your tenderness and gave his promise to tell everything; and of all the promises that might be given in this adventure, that would surely be the one most scrupulously kept. But you are now forewarned, and you know the proverb.

It remains for me to tell you that this Prévan, whom you do not know, is extremely charming and still more adroit. If you have sometimes heard me say the opposite, it is only because I do not like him, because I enjoy thwarting his successes, and because I am aware of the weight my opinion carries with at least thirty of our most fashionable women.

In this way I prevented him for a long time from appearing on what we call the great stage; and he performed wonders without adding anything to his reputation. But the sensation stirred up by his triple adventure turned all eyes on him. This gave him the confidence he had previously lacked, and made him truly formidable. In short, he is now the only man, perhaps, whom I would be afraid of meeting on my path, and aside from your own interests, you would do me a real service by inflicting some sort of ridicule on him along the way. I leave him in good hands, and I hope he will be a ruined man by the time I come back.

In return, I promise to bring your pupil's adventure to a successful conclusion, and to concern myself with her as much as with my fair prude.

The latter has just sent me a plan of capitulation. Her whole letter manifests a desire to be deceived. It would be impossible to offer a more convenient and commonplace method. She wants me to be her friend. But I like new and difficult methods, and I have no intention of letting her off so easily; after all the trouble I have taken with her, I will certainly not settle for an ordinary seduction.

On the contrary, my plan is to make her keenly aware of the value and extent of each sacrifice she makes for me, not to lead her so swiftly that remorse cannot follow her, to make her virtue expire in slow agony, to keep her attention constantly fixed on that distressing spectacle, and to grant her the happiness of having me in her arms only after I have forced her to cease concealing her desire for it. After all, I am not worth much if I am not worth the trouble of asking for me. And could I take a milder vengeance on a haughty woman who seems ashamed to admit that she adores me?

So I refused her precious friendship and held fast to my title of lover. Since I do not overlook the fact that obtaining this title, while it may at first sight seem to be merely a quibble over words, is nevertheless of genuine importance, I wrote my letter with great care and tried to fill it with that disorder which is the only means of depicting sentiment. I talked as nonsensically as possible, for without nonsense there is no tenderness; and that, I believe, is the reason why women are so superior to us in writing love letters.

I ended mine with a bit of flattery, and that is another result of my profound observations. After a woman's heart has been exercised for some time, it needs rest, and I have noticed that flattery is the softest pillow that can be offered to any woman.

Good-by, my fair friend. I am leaving tomorrow. If you have any orders to give me for the Comtesse de ———, I shall stop at her house, at least for dinner. I am sorry to leave without seeing you. Send me your sublime instructions and aid me with your wise advice at this decisive time.

Above all, resist Prévan; and may I some day be able to compensate you for that sacrifice! Good-by.

LETTER 71

~ *From the Vicomte de Valmont to the Marquise de Merteuil*

Château de ———, September 13, 17—

My scatterbrained valet has left my portfolio in Paris! The letters from my prude and those from Danceny to Cécile Volanges were all left behind, and I need them all. He is about to go back to repair his stupid blunder, and while he is saddling his horse I shall tell you the story of last night; for I beg you to believe that I am not wasting my time.

The adventure in itself was of little importance: it was only a revival with the Vicomtesse de M——. But it interested me by its details. Moreover, I am glad to be able to show you that if I have a talent for ruining women, I have an equal talent, when I wish, for saving them. The most difficult or amusing course is always the one I take, and I do not reproach myself for a good deed, provided it challenges or amuses me.

I found the Vicomtesse here, and when she joined her entreaties to the others' insistance that I spend the night in the château, I said to her, "Very well, I consent on condition that I spend it with you." "That's impossible," she replied: "Vressac is here." I had made my offer only out of courtesy, but the word "impossible'' provoked me, as usual. I felt humiliated at being sacrificed to Vressac, and I resolved not to tolerate it: I insisted.

The circumstances were not favorable. Vressac has foolishly aroused the Vicomte's suspicion, so the Vicomtesse can no longer receive him in her own house, and they had arranged this visit to the good Comtesse for the purpose of stealing a few nights together. At first the Vicomte even showed his irritation at finding him here, but since his passion for hunting is still greater than his jealousy, he stayed nevertheless. The Comtesse, who is still the same as you have always known her, gave the wife a room on the main hall, then lodged the husband on one side and the lover on the other and left them to arrange matters for themselves. The evil destiny of both men decreed that I should be given a room across the hall.

That same day, that is, yesterday, Vressac, who is doing his best to ingratiate himself with the Vicomte, as you may well imagine, went hunting with him despite his dislike of hunting, expecting to console himself at night in the wife's arms for the boredom the husband inflicted on him all day. But I felt he would need rest, so I set about persuading his mistress to give him time for it.

I succeeded: she agreed to quarrel with him for having gone hunting, which he had consented to do, of course, only for her sake. A worse pretext could not have been found, but she possesses to a supreme degree that talent, common to all women, of substituting ill-humor for reason and never being so difficult to appease as when she is in the wrong. Moreover, it was not a convenient time for explanations; and since I wanted only one night, I agreed that they should be reconciled the next day.

And so she treated Vressac coldly when he returned. He asked the reason; she started a quarrel with him. He tried to justify himself. Her husband, who was present, served as a pretext for breaking off the conversation. Finally he took advantage of a moment when her husband was absent to ask her to listen to him that night. It was then that the Vicomtesse became sublime. She expressed indignation at the audacity of men who, because they have received a woman's favors, think they have a right to abuse her kindness even when she has reason to complain of them. Then, having changed the subject by this skillful maneuver, she spoke of delicacy and sentiment so eloquently that Vressac was reduced to silence and confusion, and even I was tempted to think she was right; for I must tell you that, as a friend of both, I was present during this conversation.

Finally she declared emphatically that she would not add the fatigue of love to that of hunting, and that she would reproach herself if she troubled such sweet pleasures. At this point her husband came back. The wretched Vressac, no longer free to answer her, addressed himself to me; after giving me a lengthy exposition of his arguments, which I knew as well as he did, he begged me to speak to the Vicomtesse, and I promised to do so. I did indeed speak to her, but it was to thank her, set the time of our rendezvous and decide how it was to take place.

She told me that since her room was between her husband's and her lover's, she had thought it more prudent to go to Vressac than to have him come to her, and that since my room was across the hall from hers, she thought it would also be safer for her to come to me. She said she would come as soon as her maid had left her alone, and that I had only to leave my door ajar and wait for her.

Everything took place as we had agreed; she came into my room at about one o'clock in the morning, "in the simple attire of a beauty just torn from her sleep."*

Since I have no vanity, I shall not dwell on the details of the night; but you know me, and I was satisfied with myself.

At dawn we had to part. Here is where the interest begins. The absent-minded Vicomtesse thought she had left her door ajar, but we found it locked, with the key inside. You cannot imagine the expression of despair with which she immediately said to me, "Oh, I'm ruined!" You must admit that it would have been amusing to leave her in that situation, but could I allow a woman to be ruined for me without being ruined by me? And should I have let myself be dominated by circumstances, like the common run of men? I had to find a solution. What would you have done, my fair friend? Here is what I did, and it succeeded.

I soon saw that the door in question could be broken in, though with a great deal of noise. I therefore persuaded the Vicomtesse, not without difficulty, to give loud screams of terror such as "Thief!" "Murder!" etc. We agreed that at the first scream I would break open the door and she would run to her bed. You would not believe how long it took me to make her do it, even after she had given her consent. But she had to go through with it, and at the first kick the door gave way.

She did well not to waste any time, for the Vicomte and Vressac appeared in the hall at the same moment, and her maid also came running into her room.

---

*Racine, tragedy of *Britannicus*.

I was the only one with a cool head, and I took advantage of it to extinguish a night-lamp that was still burning, and to throw it on the floor, for you must realize how ridiculous it would have been to feign that wild terror with a light in the room. I then reprimanded the husband and the lover for sleeping so soundly and assured them that the screams which had brought me running from my room, and my efforts to break open the door, had lasted at least five minutes.

The Vicomtesse, who had recovered her courage in her bed, seconded me well enough and swore by all the gods that there was a thief in her room; she declared with more sincerity that she had never been so frightened in her life. We were looking everywhere and finding nothing when I pointed to the overturned night-lamp and concluded that a rat had no doubt caused the damage and her terror. My opinion was unanimously accepted and, after a few hackneyed jests about rats, the Vicomte was the first to go back to his room and his bed, asking his wife to have quieter rats in the future.

When Vressac was left alone with us, he went over to the Vicomtesse and told her tenderly that it had been a vengeance of love, to which she replied, looking at me, "Then love must have been very angry, because it was an impressive vengeance. But," she added, "I'm exhausted and I want to sleep."

I was in a magnanimous mood, so before we separated I pleaded Vressac's cause and brought about a reconciliation. The two lovers kissed, then I was kissed in turn by each of them. I no longer had any interest in the Vicomtesse's kisses, but I admit that Vressac's gave me pleasure. After I had received his lengthy thanks, each of us went back to his own bed.

If you find this story amusing, I do not ask you to keep it secret. Now that I have had my amusement, it is only fair that the public should have its turn. For the moment I am speaking only of the story; perhaps we shall soon say as much of the heroine.

Good-by; my valet has been waiting for an hour. I shall only take time enough to send you a kiss and urge you to be on your guard against Prévan.

LETTER 72

~   *From the Chevalier Danceny to Cécile Volanges (Not delivered until the 14th)*

September 11, 17—

Oh, my Cécile, how I envy Valmont's fate! He will see you tomorrow. He will deliver this letter to you; and I, languishing far from you, shall continue to drag out my painful existence between regrets and suffering. Pity me for my sorrows, my dearest, and pity me still more for your own: it is against them that my courage fails me.

How terrible it is for me to cause your unhappiness! If it had not been for me, you would now be happy and tranquil. Do you forgive me? Tell me, oh, tell me that you forgive me! Tell me also that you love me, that you will always love me. I must have you repeat it to me—not that I doubt it, but it seems to me that the more certain I am of it, the sweeter it is to hear it said. You love me, do you not? Yes, you love me with all your soul. I have not forgotten that those were the last words I heard you speak. How I gathered them into my heart! How deeply they engraved themselves in it! And with what joy it responded to them!

Alas, in that moment of happiness I was far from foreseeing the terrible fate that lay in store before us. Let us think, my Cécile, of how to soften it. If I am to believe my friend, it can be done if you will only give him the confidence he deserves.

I confess that I was pained by the unfavorable idea you seem to have of him. I recognized your mother's prejudices in it. It was out of deference to them that I neglected for some time that truly kind man who is doing everything for me, who is working to unite us after your mother has separated us. I beg you, my dearest, to take a more favorable view of him. Remember that he is my friend, that he wants to be yours, that he can give me back the happiness of seeing you. If these reasons do not make you change your mind, my Cécile, you do not love me as much as I love you, you do not love me as much as you used to. Ah, if you should ever love me less! . . . But no, my Cécile's heart belongs to me, it is mine for life; and although I must fear the sorrows of an unfortunate love, her constancy will at least save me from the torments of a betrayed love.

Good-by, my charming Cécile; remember that I am suffering, and that it is within your power to make me happy, perfectly happy. Listen to the prayer of my heart, and receive the most tender kisses of love.

LETTER 73

~ *From the Vicomte de Valmont to Cécile Volanges*
(Enclosed with the preceding letter)

Château de ———, September 14, 17—

The friend who serves you learned that you had nothing with which to write, and he has already provided for that need. In the antechamber of the apartment you occupy, under the large wardrobe on the left, you will find a supply of paper, pens and ink. He will replenish it whenever you wish, and it seems to him that you can leave it in the same place if you do not find a safer one.

He asks you not to be offended if he appears to pay no attention to you in company, and to regard you as only a child. This conduct seems to him necessary in order to create the confidence he needs, and to be able to work more effectively for his friend's happiness and yours. He will try to arrange opportunities to speak to you when he has something to say or give to you, and he hopes to succeed if you give him your earnest assistance.

He also advises you to give him back each of the letters you will receive, in order to reduce the risks of compromising yourself.

He ends by assuring you that if you will give him your confidence, he will make every effort to soften the persecution which a cruel mother is inflicting on two people, one of whom is already his best friend, while the other seems to him worthy of the most tender interest.

LETTER 74

~ *From the Marquise de Merteuil to the Vicomte de Valmont*

September 15, 17—

Since when have you been so easily frightened, my friend? Is this Prévan really so formidable? But see how simple and modest I am: I have often met that proud conqueror, and I have scarcely even looked at him! It took nothing less than your letter to make me pay attention to him. I made amends for my injustice yesterday. He was at the opera, almost opposite me, and I observed him carefully. He is at least handsome, very handsome: fine, delicate features! He must look even better from close up. And you say he wants to have me! He will certainly do me honor and give me pleasure. Seriously, I have taken a fancy to him, and I here confide to you that I have made the first moves. I do not know if they will succeed. Here is what happened.

As we were leaving the opera, he was only two steps away from me when, in a loud voice, I agreed to meet the Marquise de ———— for supper at the Maréchale's house on Friday. I think that is the only house where I can see him. I have no doubt that he heard me. . . . What if the ingrate does not come? Tell me, do you think he will? Do you know that if he does not, I shall be annoyed all evening? You can see that he will not find so much difficulty in "following me," and what will surprise you more is that he will find still less in "pleasing me." You say he wants to kill six horses in paying court to me! Oh, I shall save the lives of those horses! I would never have the patience to wait so long. You know it is against my principles to make a man languish once I have made up my mind, and I have made it up for him.

Yes, you must admit that it is a pleasure to talk reason to me! Has your "important warning" not been a great success! But what else can you expect? I have been vegetating for so long! It has been over six weeks since I last allowed myself a diversion. This one has presented itself: can I refuse it? Is its subject not worth the trouble? Could there be a more agreeable one, in any sense of the word?

You yourself are forced to do him justice; you do more than praise him: you are jealous of him. Well, I shall judge between you; but first I must gather the evidence, and that is what I intend to do. I shall be an honest judge, and you will both be weighed in the same balance. As for you, I already have all the evidence I need: your case has been thoroughly investigated. Is it not fair that I should now concern myself with your opponent? Come, yield with good grace; and, to begin with, please tell me about the triple adventure of which he is the hero. You speak of it as though I knew it as well as my own name, yet I had never heard a word about it before. It apparently happened while I was in Geneva, and your jealousy must have prevented you from writing to me about it. Rectify that injustice immediately; remember that "nothing concerning him is foreign to me." It does seem to me that people were still talking about it when I returned, but I was occupied with other things, and I seldom listen to stories of that kind unless they have just occurred.

Even if what I ask of you should annoy you a little, is it not the least you owe me for my efforts on your behalf? Did they not bring you back to your Madame de Tourvel when your foolishness had separated you from her? And was it not I who gave you the means of taking vengeance for Madame de Volanges's bitter zeal? You have complained so often of the time you wasted in going off to seek your adventures! You now have them close at hand. Love, hatred: you have only to choose, they both sleep under the same roof; and, doubling your existence, you can caress with one hand and strike with the other.

It is also to me that you owe your adventure with the Vicomtesse. I am quite pleased about it; but, as you say, it must be talked about, for if the occasion led you, as I can well understand, to prefer secrecy to scandal for the moment, it must nevertheless be admitted that she did not deserve such chivalrous conduct.

Moreover, I have reason to complain of her. The Chevalier de Belleroche considers her prettier than I like, and for many reasons I would be glad to have a pretext for breaking off relations with her; and there is no more convenient one than being able to say, "One can no longer see that woman."

Good-by, Vicomte; remember that in your position time is precious: I shall devote mine to Prévan's happiness.

LETTER 75

~   *From Cécile Volanges to Sophie Carney*

Château de ———, September 14, 17—
*(Note: In this letter, Cécile Volanges relates in great detail
everything that concerns her in the events which the reader has
seen in Letter 59 and those following. This repetition has been
omitted. She finally speaks of the Vicomte de Valmont and
expresses herself as follows:)*

. . . I assure you he's an extraordinary man. Mama says many
bad things about him, but the Chevalier Danceny speaks very
well of him, and I think he's right. I've never seen such a clever
man. When he gave me Danceny's letter we were in a room full
of people and nobody saw anything. It's true I was very frightened, because he hadn't told me about anything, but from now
on I'll be prepared. I understood very well how he wanted me to
go about giving him my answer. It's easy to understand things
with him because his looks say anything he wants. I don't know
how he does it. In the note I told you about he said he'd seem
not to pay any attention to me in front of Mama, and it's true: he
doesn't even seem to know I exist, yet whenever I seek his eyes
I'm sure to meet them immediately.

There's a good friend of Mama's here whom I didn't know
before and who also seems to dislike Monsieur de Valmont, even
though he's very attentive to her. I'm afraid he'll soon become
so bored with the life we lead here that he'll go back to Paris; that
would be a great pity. He must have a very kind heart to have
come here just to help his friend and me! I'd like to tell him how
grateful I am, but I don't know how to go about speaking to him,
and if I did find an opportunity I'd be so shy that I might not
know what to say to him.

Madame de Merteuil is the only one with whom I can speak
freely, when I talk about my love. I tell you everything, but I
might be embarrassed even with you if we were talking together
in person. With Danceny himself I've often felt, in spite of
myself, a certain fear that prevented me from saying everything I
was thinking. I'm angry with myself for it now, and I'd give

anything in the world for a chance to tell him once, just once, how much I love him. Monsieur de Valmont has promised me that if I follow his instructions he'll arrange an opportunity for us to see each other again. I'll do whatever he says, but I can't believe it's possible.

Good-by, my dear friend, I have no more space.*

LETTER 76

~ *From the Vicomte de Valmont to the Marquise de Merteuil*

Château de ————, September 17, 17—

Either your letter is a joke which I do not understand, or else you were in a very dangerous delirium when you wrote it. If I did not know you so well, my fair friend, I would be really very frightened; and no matter what you may say, I am not frightened too easily.

I have read and reread your letter without being able to come to any conclusion, for it is impossible to take it in the obvious sense it seems to present. What do you mean to say?

Is it only that it was unnecessary for me to take so many precautions against such an innocuous enemy? But in that case you might be mistaken. Prévan is really charming, more charming than you think; and above all, he has the very useful talent of arousing great interest in his love by his skill in talking about it in company and in front of everyone, making use of the first conversation he finds. There are few women who then avoid the trap of replying to him, because they all have pretensions to subtlety and none of them wants to miss a chance to show it; and as you well know, a woman who consents to talk about love soon ends by feeling it, or at least by acting as though she did. By this method, which he has really perfected, he has the further advantage of often calling the woman herself as witness to her defeat. This is something I have seen for myself.

I had been given only a second-hand account of the secret, for I have never been on close terms with Prévan; in any case, there

---

*Mademoiselle de Volanges began confiding in someone else a short time later, as will be seen in subsequent letters. This collection will therefore not include any of those she continued to write to her friend in the convent: they would tell the reader nothing.

were six of us, and the Comtesse de P——, who considered herself quite cunning, and actually did appear, to those who did not share the secret, to be carrying on a general conversation, told us in great detail how she had given herself to Prévan and everything that had happened between them. She related this with such confidence that she was undismayed by a fit of laughter which came over all six of us at once; and I shall always remember that when one of us tried to excuse himself by pretending to doubt what she was saying, or rather what she seemed to be saying, she gravely replied that she was sure none of us knew as much about the matter as she did, and she did not even hesitate to turn to Prévan and ask him if she had been mistaken in a single word.

And so I had reason to believe him to be dangerous for everyone; but for you, Marquise, was it not enough that he was "handsome, very handsome," as you yourself have said. Or that he should make one of those attacks on you which you sometimes choose to reward for no other reason than that you find them to be skillfully carried out? Or that you should have thought it amusing to give in to him for some other reason? Or . . . What can I say? Can I guess the countless whims which govern a woman's mind, and by which alone you still share the mentality of your sex? Now that you have been warned of the danger, I do not doubt that you will easily avoid it; but still you had to be warned of it. Let me now return to my text: What do you mean?

If it is a joke about Prévan, besides the fact that it is a very long one, it was wasted on me: it is in society that some sort of ridicule must be inflicted on him, and I repeat my request to you on that subject.

Ah, I think I have the key to the enigma! Your letter is a prophecy, not of what you will do, but of what he will believe you ready to do at the time of the fall you are preparing for him. I approve of that plan; however, it will require great caution. You know as well as I that, so far as the public is concerned, to have a man or to receive his attentions is exactly the same thing, unless the man is a fool, which Prévan is not, far from it. If he can gain only an appearance, he will boast and the matter will be settled. Nearly everyone will be either foolish enough to believe it or malicious enough to pretend to believe it. What will be your resources? Yes, I am frightened. Not that I doubt your adroitness, but it is the best swimmers who drown.

I do not think I am more stupid than others; I have found a

hundred, a thousand ways to dishonor a woman, but whenever I have tried to think of how she might save herself from them, I have never seen the slightest possibility. Your conduct is a masterpiece, my fair friend, yet it has seemed to me dozens of times that even you were saved more by luck than by skill.

But after all, perhaps I am seeking a reason where there is none. I am surprised to find that for the past hour I have been treating seriously what is surely nothing but a joke on your part. You are going to laugh at me! Well, so be it; but hurry, and let us talk of something else. Something else! I am mistaken: it is always the same thing, always women to be had or ruined, and often both.

As you have quite rightly pointed out, I have here the possibility of accomplishing both, though not with the same ease. I foresee that vengeance will be swifter than love. Little Cécile has already surrendered, I will answer for it; she is now awaiting only an opportunity, and I guarantee to provide one. But it is not the same with Madame de Tourvel: that woman is maddening, I do not understand her; I have a hundred proofs of her love, but a thousand of her resistance, and to tell the truth, I am afraid she may escape from me.

The first effect produced by my return made my hopes rise. As you have probably guessed, I wanted to be able to judge it for myself, so, to make sure of seeing her first reactions, I sent no one on ahead of me, and I timed my journey so that I would arrive while everyone was at table. I dropped from the sky like a god in the final scene of an opera.

Having made enough noise on entering to turn all eyes toward me, I saw at a single glance the joy of my old aunt, the annoyance of Madame de Volanges, and the disconcerted pleasure of her daughter. My fair lady was sitting with her back to the door. Engaged in cutting something at that moment, she did not even turn her head, but when I addressed Madame de Rosemonde, at the first word my pious beauty recognized my voice and a cry escaped from her in which I thought I discerned more love than surprise and alarm. I had by now come far enough forward to see her face: the tumult of her soul and the struggle between her ideas and her feelings were painted on it in a dozen different ways. I sat down beside her; she knew absolutely nothing of what she was doing or saying. She tried to go on eating; it was impossible. Finally, less than a quarter of an hour later, her embarrassment and her pleasure became too strong for her and she could think of nothing better than to ask permission to leave the table. She hurried out into the park, on the pretext that she needed some fresh air. Madame de Volanges offered to accompany her, but the tender prude refused; she was no doubt too happy to have an excuse to be alone and abandon herself without constraint to the sweet agitation of her heart!

I shortened dinner as much as I could. Dessert had scarcely been served when that infernal Volanges woman, apparently goaded by her need to do me harm, rose from her place to go and find my charming invalid; but I had foreseen this plan and I foiled it. I pretended to take this one movement for a general withdrawal: I stood up at the same time, and little Cécile and the local priest followed this double example, so that Madame de Rosemonde found herself alone at the table with the old Commandeur de T——, and they both decided to leave too. So we all went out to rejoin my fair lady, whom we found in the grove near the château; and since she needed solitude and not a walk, she was just as glad to come back with us as to have us stay with her.

As soon as I was sure that Madame de Volanges would have no opportunity of speaking to her alone, I turned my attention to carrying out your orders and began to concern myself with your pupil's interests. Immediately after coffee, I went up to my room and also went into the others' rooms, to reconnoiter the terrain. I made arrangements to provide for Cécile's correspondence; after this first good deed, I wrote her a note informing her of it and asking for her confidence. I enclosed my note with Danceny's letter and returned to the drawing room. I found my fair lady stretched out on a chaise longue in a pose of delightful abandon.

In awakening my desires, this sight animated my gaze; I felt that it must be tender and pressing, and I placed myself in such a way as to be able to make use of it. Its first effect was to make my heavenly prude lower her big, modest eyes. I contemplated her angelic face for some time, then I ran my eyes over her whole body, taking pleasure in trying to discern its curves beneath a light but still troublesome garment. After desending from her head to her feet, I returned from her feet to her head. . . . My fair friend, those gentle eyes were staring at me! They were immediately lowered again; but, wishing to favor their return, I looked away. Then there was established between us that tacit agreement, the first treaty of timid love, which, to satisfy the need to see each other, allows looks to follow one another until it is time for them to mingle.

Convinced that she was completely absorbed in this new

pleasure, I took it upon myself to watch over our common safety; but after ascertaining that a rather lively conversation was saving us from being noticed by the rest of the company, I tried to make her eyes speak their language openly. For this purpose I first surprised a few looks, but with so much reserve that her modesty could not be alarmed; and to put my timid beauty more at ease, I appeared to be as embarrassed as she was. Little by little, our eyes grew accustomed to meeting, then remained together for a long time; finally they stopped turning away altogether and I saw in hers that soft languor which is the happy signal of love and desire. But it was only for a moment; she soon recovered herself and, not without a certain shame, changed her bearing and her gaze.

Not wishing to leave her any doubt that I had noticed her various movements, I leapt to my feet and asked her in a tone of alarm if she felt ill. Everyone immediately came over and surrounded her. I let them all pass in front of me; and since Cécile, who was doing tapestry work near a window, needed a little time to leave her frame, I seized the opportunity to give her Danceny's letter.

I was a short distance away from her; I tossed the letter into her lap. She had no idea what to do with it. You would have laughed to see her look of surprise and perplexity; I did not laugh, however, for I was afraid that all her awkwardness might betray us. But an emphatic glance and gesture finally made her understand that she had to put the letter in her pocket.

The rest of the day was uninteresting. What has happened since then may lead to events that will please you, at least insofar as your pupil is concerned; but it is better to spend one's time in carrying out plans than in relating them. Besides, this is the eighth page I have written, so good-by.

You have no doubt already assumed, without my telling you, that Cécile has replied to Danceny.* I have also received a reply from my fair lady, to whom I wrote on the day after my arrival. I am enclosing both these letters. Read them or not, as you please, because this endless drivel, which has already ceased to amuse me very much, must be quite dull for anyone not directly concerned.

Once more, good-by. I still love you very much; but if you speak to me about Prévan, please do it in such a way that I can understand you.

---

*This letter has not been found.

LETTER 77

~⌣~ *From the Vicomte de Valmont to Madame de Tourvel*

September 15, 17—

What can be the origin, Madame, of the cruel persistence with which you avoid me? How can it be that the most tender zeal on my part elicits nothing from you except conduct that would scarcely be permissible toward a man of whom you had the strongest reasons to complain? What! Love brought me back to your feet, and then when a fortunate chance placed me beside you, you preferred to pretend to be ill and alarm your friends, rather than consent to remain near me! How often yesterday did you turn away your eyes to deprive me of the favor of a look? And if for one moment I was able to see less severity in your eyes, that moment was so short that you seemed to have wished less to let me enjoy it than to make me aware of what I was losing by being deprived of it.

That, I venture to say, is not the treatment which love deserves or friendship would allow itself to inflict; yet you know that I am animated by one of those two sentiments, and it seems to me that I was entitled to believe that you did not refuse me the other. What have I done to lose that precious friendship of which you must have considered me worthy, since you were willing to offer it to me? Can I have harmed myself by my confidence in you? Are you punishing me for my frankness? Are you not at least afraid of abusing them both? Was it not to you, as my friend, that I entrusted the secret of my heart? Was it not with you alone that I felt obliged to refuse conditions which I had only to accept in order to give myself the opportunity of failing to abide by them, or perhaps of misusing them to my advantage? Do you wish to force me, by your undeserved harshness, to believe that I had only to deceive you in order to obtain more indulgence?

I do not regret having followed a line of conduct which I owed to you and to myself; but by what fatality does each priaseworthy action become the signal for a new misfortune for me?

It was after I had earned the only praise you have yet deigned to give to my conduct that, for the first time, I had to suffer from the misfortune of having displeased you. It was after I had proved my perfect submission to you by depriving myself of the happiness of seeing you, solely to reassure your delicacy, that you wanted to break off all correspondence with me, and deprive me even of the love which alone had given you the right to do so. And it is after I have spoken to you with a sincerity which even the interests of my love could not weaken that you now avoid me as though I were a dangerous seducer whose treachery you had recognized.

Will you never tire of being unjust? At least tell me what new transgressions on my part have driven you to such severity, and do not refuse to give me the orders you wish me to follow; having committed myself to carrying them out, is it too presumptuous of me to ask to know what they are?

LETTER 78

~ *From Madame de Tourvel to the Vicomte de Valmont*

September 16, 17—

You seem to be surprised by my conduct, Monsieur, and you are not far from calling me to account for it as though you had a right to condemn it. I confess I would have thought I had more reason than you for surprise and complaint; but since the refusal contained in your last reply, I have adopted the course of enclosing myself in an indifference which no longer leaves any occasion for observations or reproaches. However, since you ask me to enlighten you, and since, thank Heaven, I feel nothing in me which might prevent me from doing so, I am willing to enter into explanations with you once again.

Anyone who read your letters would think me unjust or capricious. I think I deserve that no one should have that idea of me, and it seems to me that you had less reason to hold it than anyone else. You no doubt felt that by compelling me to justify myself, you would be forcing me to recall everything that has happened between us. Apparently you thought you could not fail to gain by such an examination. As for myself, since I do not think I have anything to lose by it, at least in your eyes, I am not afraid to undertake it. Perhaps it is actually the only means of determining which of us has a right to complain of the other.

I believe you will admit, Monsieur, that from the day of your arrival at this château your reputation at least entitled me to maintain a certain reserve with you, and that, without fear of being accused of excessive prudery, I could have confined myself to expressing nothing but cold politeness. You yourself would have treated me with indulgence, and you would have considered it only natural that such an inexperienced woman should lack even the merit necessary to appreciate your own. That would surely have been the prudent course; and I shall not conceal from you that it would have been all the easier for me to follow since when Madame de Rosemonde came to inform me of your arrival I had to recall my friendship for her, and hers for you, in order not to let her see how much that news annoyed me.

I readily admit that at first you showed yourself in a more favorable light than I had imagined; but you will admit in your turn that it did not last long, and that you soon wearied of a constraint for which you apparently did not consider yourself sufficiently compensated by the favorable idea it had made me form of you.

It was then that, abusing my good faith and confidence, you dared to speak to me of a sentiment which you knew would offend me. And while you did nothing but seek to worsen your wrongs by multiplying them, I was trying to enable myself to forget them by offering you an opportunity to make amends for them, at least in part. My request was so just that even you did not feel you could refuse it; but you turned my indulgence into a right and took advantage of it to ask me for a permission which no doubt I ought not to have granted, but which you obtained nevertheless. Conditions were attached to it: you observed none of them; and your correspondence was such that each one of your letters made it my duty not to reply. It was at the very time when your obstinacy compelled me to send you away from me that, with an obligingness that was perhaps reprehensible, I tried the one means which might allow me to bring you back; but of what value is a virtuous sentiment in your eyes? You scorn friendship; and in your mad intoxication, counting sufferings and shame as nothing, you seek only pleasures and victims.

You are as unreliable in your behavior as you are inconsequential in your reproaches; you forget your promises, or rather you amuse yourself by breaking them. After having consented to go away from me, you have come back here without my invitation, without regard for my entreaties or my reasons, without even being considerate enough to notify me beforehand. You were not afraid to expose me to a surprise whose effect, though surely quite simple, might have been misinterpreted by those around me. After causing this embarrassment, far from trying to distract attention from it or to dispel it, you seemed to make every effort to increase it. You sat down next to me at table; a slight indisposition forced me to leave before the others, and instead of respecting my solitude, you caused everyone to come and disturb it. When we returned to the drawing room, whenever I took a step I found you beside me; whenever I said a word it was always you who answered me. The most insignificant remark became a pretext for you to return to a conversation which I did not wish to hear, which might even have compromised me: for after all, Monsieur, no matter how clever you may be, if I am able to understand something, I think others may be able to understand it also.

Having thus forced me into immobility and silence, you nevertheless continued to pursue me; I could not raise my eyes without encountering yours. I was constantly obliged to look away; and, with incomprehensible indiscretion, you fixed the eyes of the entire company on me at a time when I would have liked to escape even my own attention.

And you complain of my conduct! You are surprised by my eagerness to avoid you! Ah, condemn my indulgence instead, and be surprised that I did not leave as soon as you arrived! Perhaps I ought to have left; and you will force me to take that extreme but necessary course if you do not cease your offensive pursuit. No, I have not forgotten, I shall never forget what I owe to myself, what I owe to the bonds which I have formed and which I respect and cherish; and I beg you to believe that if I ever found myself reduced to the unfortunate choice of sacrificing them or sacrificing myself, I would not hesitate for an instant. Good-by, Monsieur.

LETTER 79

~ *From the Vicomte de Valmont to the Marquise de Merteuil*

September 18, 17—

I intended to go hunting this morning, but the weather is abominable. I have nothing to read except a new novel that would bore even a schoolgirl. It will be at least two hours until breakfast, so despite my long letter yesterday I am going to talk to you again. I am sure I shall not bore you, for I am going to speak to you about the "very handsome" Prévan. How can you not have heard of his famous adventure, the one which separated the "inseparables"? I am willing to bet that the first word will bring it back to your mind. However, here it is, since you want to hear it.

You will recall that everyone in Paris was surprised that three women, all pretty, all possessing the same talents, and all able to advance the same claims, should have remained intimately united from the time of their entry into society. At first their extreme timidity was thought to be the reason, but they were soon sharing the attentions of a large circle of admirers, and were made aware of their value by the eager efforts that were made to please them, yet their union became all the stronger, and it seemed that the triumph of one was always the triumph of the two others. It was hoped that the advent of love would at least create some rivalry. Our gallants vied with one another for the honor of being the apple of discord, and even I would have entered the competition if the great favor to which the Comtesse de ——— rose at that same time had allowed me to be unfaithful to her before obtaining the acquiescence I was seeking.

Meanwhile our three beauties, in the same carnival, made their choice as though in concert; and far from arousing the storms that had been expected, it only made their friendship more interesting by giving them the additional pleasure of confiding in one another.

The crowd of rejected suitors then joined the crowd of jealous women, and this scandalous constancy was submitted to public censure. Some claimed that in this society of "inseparables" (as they were then named), the fundamental law was common ownership of property, and that it applied even to love; others said that while the three lovers were free of male rivals, they were not free of female ones; still others went so far as to say that they had been accepted only out of concern for decency, and had been given merely an honorary title.

These rumors, true or false, did not have the expected effect. On the contrary, the three couples felt that they would be lost if they separated at that time; they decided to weather the storm. The public, who weary of everything, soon wearied of a fruitless satire. Carried away by their natural frivolity, they turned to other matters; then, coming back to this one, with their usual inconsistency they changed censure into praise. Since everything ere is subject to fashion, enthusiasm spread; it was reaching ever pitch when Prévan undertook to verify these wonders and acquire definite information about them for himself and the public.

He therefore sought out these models of perfection. He easily gained admittance into their society and considered this a good sign. He was well aware that happy people are not so easily accessible. And true enough, he soon saw that their much-vaunted happiness was, like that of kings, more envied than desirable. He observed that these so-called inseparables were beginning to seek outside pleasures and even distractions. From this he concluded that the bonds of love or friendship were already slackened or broken, and that only those of vanity and habit still had any strength.

Meanwhile the women, held together by necessity, maintained among themselves the appearance of the same intimacy; but the men, freer in their conduct, were beginning to find duties to fulfill or business matters to deal with; they still complained of them, but no longer avoided them. There were few evenings when the full contingent was present.

This behavior on their part was profitable to the assiduous Prévan, who, naturally placed beside the forsaken lady of the day, was able to offer alternately, according to circumstances, the same homage to each of the three friends. He knew very well that he would be lost if he made a choice among them, for the woman he singled out would be intimidated by the idea of being the first to be unfaithful, the wounded vanity of the two others would make them enemies of the new lover, and they would not fail to oppose him with the severity of lofty principles; and finally jealousy would be sure to revive the attentions of a rival who might still be dangerous. Everything would have become an obstacle, but everything became easy in his triple undertaking: each women was indulgent because it was to her interest, each man because he thought it was not.

Prévan, who at that time had only one woman to sacrifice, was fortunate enough to have her acquire a certain renown. Her position as a foreigner, and a great prince's advances which she had artfully rejected, had fixed the attention of the court and the city on her; her lover shared this honor and turned it to his advantage with his new mistresses. The only difficulty lay in carrying on these three intrigues simultaneously, for their progress was necessarily regulated by the slowest. I have been told by one of his confidants that his greatest problem was to stop one of them which was ready to come to fruition nearly two weeks before the others.

At last the great day arrived. Prévan, who had obtained the acquiescence of all three, was already in command of the proceedings, and he directed them as you will see. Of the three husbands, one was absent, another was going to leave at dawn the next day, and the third was in town. The inseparable friends were to have supper in the house of the future widow; but the new master did not allow the three lovers to be invited. On the morning of that day, he divided the letters he had received from his mistress into three packets. In one he enclosed the portrait she had given him, in another a monogram containing their intertwined initials which she had painted herself, and in the third a lock of her hair. Each woman received a third of the sacrifice under the impression that it was complete and agreed in exchange to send her lover a letter informing him in forthright terms that she was breaking off with him.

It was a great deal; yet it was not enough. The woman whose husband was in town was free only during the day: it was agreed that a feigned indisposition would excuse her from going to supper at her friend's house, and that the whole evening would be Prévan's; the night was granted by the one whose husband was absent; and dawn, when her husband was to leave, was designated as the hour of love by the third.

Prévan, who overlooks nothing, then hurried to his fair foreigner, brought with him and created the ill-humor he needed, and did not leave until he had provoked a quarrel which assured him of twenty-four hours of freedom. Having thus made all his arrangements, he went home, intending to take a little rest; but other affairs were awaiting him there.

The letters received by the three lovers had immediately enlightened them: each one had no doubt that he had been sacrificed to Prévan, and their resentment at having been duped was added to the irritation of being abandoned. All three of them, without having communicated with one another, but as though acting in concert, had resolved to demand satisfaction from their favored rival.

He therefore found the three challenges waiting for him when he came home. He accepted them honorably, but since he wished to lose neither the pleasures not the glory of his adventure, he set the encounters for the following morning, all three of the same time and place, at one of the gates of the Bois de Boulogne.

When evening came, he set out on the course he had laid

down for himself and ran all three races with equal success; or at least he later boasted that each of his new mistresses had received three demonstrations of his love. Here, as you will surely realize, the story lacks proof; all the impartial historian can do is point out to the skeptical reader that excited vanity and imagination can achieve wonders, and that furthermore the morning which was to follow that brilliant night seemed to be such as to remove all concern for the future. In any case, the following facts are more certain.

Prévan arrived punctually at the meeting place he had designated. He found his three rivals, each somewhat surprised to see the others there, and perhaps already partially consoled by having learned that he had companions in misfortune. Prévan greeted them with casual affability and made the following little speech, which was faithfully reported to me:

"Gentlemen, on finding yourselves gathered here, you have no doubt guessed that all three of you have the same reason for complaint against me. I am ready to give you satisfaction. Let fate decide which one of you will be the first to attempt a vengeance to which you are all equally entitled. I have not brought a second or witnesses. I had none for the offense; I ask none for the reparation." Then, yielding to his propensity for gambling, he added, "I know that one seldom wins on three consecutive cards; but no matter what fate may hold in store for me, one has always lived long enough if one has had time to acquire the love of women and the esteem of men."

While his astonished adversaries looked at one another in silence, and while their delicacy was perhaps calculating that such a triple combat would not be an even match, Prévan went on: "I shall not conceal the fact that the night I have just spent has cruelly tired me. It would be generous of you to allow me to restore my strength. I have given orders for a breakfast to be kept ready here; do me the honor of accepting it. Let us have breakfast together and, above all, gaily. We may fight for such trifles, but I do not think we should let them spoil our good humor."

The breakfast was accepted. Never, I was told, had Prévan been more charming. He was clever enough to avoid humiliating any of his rivals, to convince them that any of them could easily have achieved the same success, and to make them confess that they would not have missed the opportunity any more than he had. Once these facts had been admitted, all hostility vanished; before the meal was over, it had been repeated a dozen times that such women did not deserve to be fought for by honorable men. This idea brought on cordiality, which was strenghtened by wine, and soon it was not enough to have cast aside all rancor: they swore friendship to one another without reserve.

Prévan was no doubt as pleased with this result as with the other, but he did not want to lose any of his celebrity, so, skillfully adapting his plans to the circumstances, he said to the three offended lovers, "Now that you have realized that you ought to take vengeance not against me, but against your faithless mistresses, let me offer you an opportunity of doing so. I already feel, like you, a grievance which I shall soon share, for if each of you has been unable to hold one of them, how can I hope to hold all three? Your quarrel will become mine. Accept my invitation to supper this evening in my private house, and I hope to delay your vengeance no longer." They asked him to explain, but he replied in the tone of superiority which the circumstances authorized him to assume, "Gentlemen, I think I have proved to you that I have some ability in carrying out plans; rely on me." They all consented; and after embracing their new friend they separated until that evening, awaiting the result of his promises.

Prévan returned to Paris without wasting any time and, in accordance with custom, went to visit his new conquests. All three of them agreed to come to his house that evening to have supper alone with him. Two of them were somewhat reluctant, but what is there left to refuse on the morning after? He arranged for their arrivals at one-hour intervals, the time he needed for his plan. After these preparations, he went off to notify the three other conspirators, and all four gaily went to wait for their victims.

They heard the first one arrive. Prévan went to meet her alone, received her with an air of eagerness and led her to the sanctuary of which she thought herself the divinity; he then disappeared on some slight pretext and immediately sent in the outraged lover to take his place.

As you may well imagine, the confusion of a woman not yet accustomed to adventures made it easy to triumph over her at that moment; every reproach that was not made was counted as an act of grace, and the fugitive slave, delivered into the hands of her former master, was all too happy to submit to her first bondage again in the hope of being pardoned. The peace treaty was ratified in a more solitary place, and the empty stage was occupied by the other actors in turn, in a similar manner and with the same ending.

Each woman, however, still thought herself to be the only one involved. Their astonishment and embarrassment increased when all three couples gathered for supper; but their discomposure reached its peak when Prévan reappeared among them and was cruel enough to give the three faithless women apologies which revealed their secret and clearly showed them the full extent to which they had been duped.

However, they sat down to table and gradually regained their composure. The men were expansive, the women submissive. They all had hatred in their hearts, but their words were none the less tender; gaiety awakened desire, which in return lent it new charms. This astonishing orgy lasted till morning. When they separated, the women must have thought they had been forgiven, but the men, who had kept their resentment, broke off with them the next day in a way that eliminated all possibility of reconciliation; and, not content with leaving their fickle mistresses, they completed their vengeance by making their adventure public. One of the women has been in a convent ever since, and the two others are still languishing in exile on their country estates.

Such is Prévan's story; it is for you to decide whether you wish to add to his glory and harness yourself to his triumphal chariot. Your letter has really made me uneasy, and I am impatiently awaiting a wiser and clearer answer to the last letter I wrote you.

Good-by, my fair friend; beware of the amusing or whimsical ideas that always beguile you too easily. Remember that in the course you are pursuing, intelligence is not enough, and that one imprudent act may become an irreparable misfortune. Allow prudent friendship sometimes to be the guide of your pleasures.

Good-by. I still love you as much as if you were reasonable.

LETTER 80

~ *From the Chevalier Danceny to Cécile Volanges*

Paris, September 18, 17—

Cécile, my dear Cécile, when will the time come for us to see each other again? What can teach me to live away from you? What will give me the strength and courage to do it? Never, no, never shall I be able to endure this fatal absence. Every day adds to my unhappiness—and I see no end to it! Valmont, who promised me help and consolations, is now neglecting me, and has perhaps forgotten me. He is near the object of his love; he no longer knows how one suffers when one is removed from it. When he sent me your last letter he did not write to me, yet it is he who must tell me when and how I shall be able to see you. Has he nothing to tell me? You yourself do not speak to me of it; can it be that you no longer share my desire for it? Oh, Cécile, Cécile, I am so unhappy! I love you more than ever, but that love which is the charm of my life is now becoming its torment.

No, I cannot go on living this way, I must see you, I must, if only for a moment. Each time I get up I say to myself, "I shall not see her." When I go to bed I say, "I have not seen her." My long, long days do not have one moment of happiness. Everything is privation, regret, despair; and all these pains come to me from where I expected all my pleasures! Add these deadly sufferings to my anxiety about yours and you will have some idea of my situation. I think about you constantly, and never without apprehension. If I see you afflicted and unhappy, I suffer from all your sorrows; if I see you tranquil and consoled, my own sorrows redouble. I find unhappiness everywhere.

Ah, it was different when we both lived in the same place! All was pleasure then. The certainty of seeing you embellished even your absence; the time I had to spend away from you brought me nearer to you as it passed. The use I made of it was never alien to you. If I cultivated some talent, I hoped to please you more. Even when the distractions of society took me away from you, I was not separated from you. At the theater I tried to guess what would have pleased you; concerts reminded me of your talents and our sweet occupations. In company and during walks, I seized upon the slightest resemblance. I compared you with everyone, and you had the advantage everywhere. Each moment of the day was marked by a new homage, each evening I laid the tribute of it at your feet.

What is left for me now? Painful regrets, unending privations, and a slight hope which is being diminished by Valmont's silence, and changed into anxiety by yours. We are separated by only ten leagues, and that distance, so easy to cross, has become for me an insurmountable obstacle! And when I implore my friend and my beloved to help me overcome it, they both remain cold and calm! Far from aiding me, they do not even answer me.

What has become of Valmont's active friendship? Above all, what has become of your tender feelings, which used to make you so ingenious in finding ways for us to see each other every day? I remember that sometimes, though still desiring it, I was forced to sacrifice it to certain considerations, to duties. What did you say to me then? With how many pretexts did you oppose my reasons? And remember, my Cécile, that my reasons always yielded to your desires. I do not claim it as a merit; I did not even have the merit of sacrifice. I was eager to grant what you wanted to obtain. But now it is I who am asking, and what is my request? To see you for a moment, to give and receive once again the vow of an eternal love. Is it no longer your happiness as it is mine? I reject that heartrending thought which would climax my misfortunes. You love me, you will always love me; I believe it, I am sure of it, I shall never doubt it; but my situation is terrible and I cannot endure it much longer. Good-by, Cécile.

LETTER 81

~⁓   *From the Marquise de Merteuil to the Vicomte de Valmont*

September 20, 17—

How I pity you for your fears! How clearly they show my superiority over you! And you want to teach me, to guide me? Ah, my poor Valmont, what a great distance there still is between you and me! No, all the pride of your sex would not be enough to bridge the gap that separates us. Because you could not carry out my plans, you judge them to be impossible! It well befits you, you proud, weak creature, to try to measure my means and judge my resources! Really, Vicomte, your advice has put me in a bad temper, and I cannot conceal it from you.

I do not object when, to mask your incredible awkwardness with regard to your Madame de Tourvel, you present to me as a triumph the fact that for a moment you disconcerted that timid woman who loves you. When you tell me you obtained a look from her, a single look, I smile indulgently. I am also willing to be indulgent when, realizing in spite of yourself the worthlessness of your conduct, you hope to hide it from my attention by gratifying me with an account of your sublime effort in bringing together two children who were dying to see each other and who, let me point out in passing, owed the ardor of that desire to me alone. And finally, when you take these brilliant actions as a pretext for pompously telling me that "it is better to spend one's time in carrying out plans than in relating them," your vanity does not harm me and I forgive you for it. But when you believe that I need your prudence, that I would go astray if I did not defer to your opinions, and that I ought to sacrifice a pleasure, a caprice to them, then, Vicomte, you have drawn too much pride from the confidence I have been willing to place in you!

What have you done that I have not surpassed a thousand times? You have seduced, even ruined, many women; but what difficulties did you have to overcome, what obstacles did you have to surmount? Where was there any merit that was truly yours? A handsome face, the result of pure chance; social graces, which are nearly always given by experience; wit, it is true, but it could be replaced by ordinary drawing-room chatter if necessary; a rather praiseworthy impudence, although it may be due solely to the case of your first successes—those, if I am not mistaken, are all your resources, for as to the celebrity you have been able to acquire, I do not think you will expect me to place a great deal of value on the art of creating or seizing the opportunity of a scandal.

As for prudence and shrewdness, I am not speaking of myself, but what woman would not have more than you? Even your Madame de Tourvel leads you like a child!

Believe me, Vicomte, one seldom acquires qualities one can do without. Fighting without risk, you necessarily act without caution. For you mean, defeats are only so many fewer victories. In that unequal battle, our good fortune is not to lose, and your misfortune is not to win. Even if I were to grant you as many talents as we have, how much more we would still have to surpass you through our necessity of making constant use of them!

Let us suppose that you show as much skill in conquering us as we do in defending ourselves or in yielding: you will at least admit that your skill becomes useless to you after you have succeeded. Concerned solely with your new inclination, you plunge into it without fear or reserve; its duration does not matter to you.

Those bonds reciprocally given and received, to speak the jargon of love, can be tightened or broken by you alone, as you choose; and we are all too happy if, in your fickleness, you prefer secrecy to publicity and content yourselves with a humiliating abandonment without making the idol of one day the victim of the next!

But if an unfortunate woman is the first to feel the weight of her chain, what risks must she run if she tries to escape from it, or even dares to lift it? She trembles as she attempts to rid herself of the man whom her heart repels with effort. If he persists in staying, she must yield to fear what she granted to love: "Her arms still open when her heart is closed." She must untie with prudence and skill those same bonds which you would have broken. At the mercy of her enemy, she is without resource if he is without magnanimity; and how can she expect it of him when, though he is sometimes praised for having it, he is never blamed for lacking it?

You will surely not deny these truths which are so obvious that they have become commonplace. But if you have seen me controlling events and opinions and making those formidable men and playthings of my whims, depriving some of the will, others of the power to harm me; if, following my changing inclinations, I have been able to capture and then reject "those dethroned tyrants who have become my slaves"*; and if, amid those frequent upheavals, my reputation has remained pure, have you not been forced to conclude that I was born to avenge my sex and dominate yours, and that I have been able to devise methods that were unknown to anyone but me?

Ah, keep your advice and your fears for those delirious women who claim to be "women of feeling"; whose feverish imagination would make one think nature had placed their senses in their heads; who, never having reflected, constantly confuse love with a lover; who, in their foolish illusions, believe that the man with whom they have sought pleasure is the sole depository of it; and who, being truly superstitious, give the priest the respect and faith which ought to be given only to the divinity.

Fear also for those women who, more vain than prudent, do not know how to consent to being abandoned when necessary.

Tremble above all for those women, active in their idleness, whom you call "sensitive," and of whom love takes possession so easily and so powerfully; who feel a need to devote themselves to it even when they do not enjoy it; who, abandoning themselves without reserve to the ferment of their ideas, give

---

*It is not known whether this line and the earlier one—"Her arms still open when her heart is closed"—are quotations from known works or whether they are part of Madame de Merteuil's prose. One might be led to believe so by the multitude of faults of this kind that are found in all the letters of this correspondence. Only those of the Chevalier Danceny are free of them; perhaps, since he sometimes concerned himself with poetry, his more practiced ear allowed him to avoid this defect more easily.

birth through them to those sweet letters which are so dangerous to write, and do not hesitate to confide those proofs of their weakness to the man who causes them—heedless women who cannot see their future enemy in their present lover!

But what have I in common with those rash women? When have you ever seen me depart from the rules I have laid down for myself, and violate my principles? I call them my principles and I do so deliberately, for they are not, like those of other women, given at random, received without examination and followed from habit; they are the fruit of my profound reflections; I have created them, and I can say that I am my own work.

Having entered society when I was still an unmarried girl, at a time when my condition imposed silence and inaction upon me, I took the opportunity to observe and reflect. While others thought me foolish or absent-minded because I paid little attention to the things they were eager to tell me, I carefully noted those they tried to hide from me.

This useful curiosity, which served to instruct me, also taught me to dissimulate: often forced to hide the objects of my attention from the eyes of those around me, I tried to direct my own eyes as I wished; I then learned to assume at will that distracted look which you have praised so often. Encouraged by this first success, I sought to control the various movements of my face in the same way. If I felt sorrow, I did my best to take on an expression of serenity, even of joy; I carried my zeal so far as to inflict voluntary pain on myself and try to maintain an expression of pleasure at the same time. I worked on myself with the same care and greater effort to suppress the manifestations of any unexpected joy. It was thus that I was able to acquire that control of my features by which I have sometimes seen you so astonished.

I was still very young and almost without interest, but my thoughts were all I had of my own, and I was indignant that anyone should be able to take them away from me, or discover them against my will. Armed with these first weapons, I tried using them. Not content with no longer letting anyone see into me, I took pleasure in showing myself under various guises. Sure of my gestures, I carefully observed my words; I regulated them both according to circumstances, or even only according to my whims. From then on, my way of thinking was for myself alone, and I showed only what it was useful for me to let others see.

This work on myself fixed my attention on the expression and character of faces, and this in turn gave me that penetrating glance which, although experience has taught me not to trust it entirely, has seldom deceived me.

By the time I was fifteen I already had the talents to which most of our politicians owe their reputations, yet I had not gone beyond the rudiments of the knowledge and skill I wanted to acquire.

Like all young girls, of course, I tried to learn about love and its pleasures; but I had never gone to a convent school, I had no close friends, and I was carefully watched by a vigilant mother, so I had only vague ideas which I could not clarify. Even nature, which I have since had every reason to be satisfied with, had not yet given me any indications. It was as though it were working in silence to perfect the result of its labors. My head alone was in a ferment; I wanted knowledge, not pleasure. My desire to learn suggested the means to me.

I realized that the only man with whom I could talk about this subject without compromising myself was my confessor. I made up my mind immediately. I overcame my little shame and, boasting of a sin I had not committed, I accused myself of having done "everything that women do." That was my expression, but when I used it I did not really know what I meant by it. My hopes were neither entirely disappointed nor entirely fulfilled; the fear of betraying myself prevented me from obtaining the information I wanted, but the good father presented the evil to me as so extreme that I thought the pleasure must be very great, and my desire to know about it was succeeded by a desire to experience it.

I do not know where that desire might have led me, and since I was then totally lacking in experience, a single opportunity would have ruined me. Fortunately for me, my mother told me a few days later that I was going to be married; the certainty of knowing immediately extinguished my curiosity, and I was still a virgin when I came into Monsieur de Merteuil's arms.

I confidently awaited the moment that would enlighten me, and I had to make a conscious effort to show embarrassment and apprehension. I viewed that first night, which is usually thought to be either so cruel or so sweet, as merely an opportunity for experience; I carefully noted both pleasure and pain, and I saw nothing in those various sensations except facts to be gathered and meditated upon.

This kind of study soon began to please me; but, faithful to my principles, and realizing, perhaps by instinct, that no one should be further from my confidence than my husband, I resolved, from the sole fact that I was responsive, to show myself to him as impassive. This apparent coldness was later the unshakable foundation of his blind confidence in me; to it I joined, as the result of further reflection, the air of thoughtlessness that befitted my age, and he never thought me so childish as when I was deceiving him most audaciously.

I confess that at first, however, I allowed myself to be carried away by the whirlwind of society, and I plunged wholeheartedly into its futile distractions. But several months later, when Monsieur de Mertueil had taken me to his dreary country estate, fear of boredom brought back my taste for study; finding myself surrounded by people whose position was so far removed from mine that it placed me above all suspicion, I took the opportunity to broaden the range of my experience. It was there that I became fully convinced that love, which is praised as the cause of our pleasures, is at most only the pretext for them.

Monsieur de Merteuil's illness interrupted these pleasant activities. I had to accompany him back to Paris, where he went for aid. He died, as you know, a short time later. Although, on the whole, I had no reason to complain of him, I was nevertheless keenly aware of the value of the freedom my widowhood was going to give me, and I promised myself to make good use of it.

My mother expected me to enter a convent or come back to live with her. I refused to do either, and all I granted to decency was to return to that same country estate, where I still had a few more observations to make.

I strengthened them with the support of reading; but do not think it was all of the kind you suppose. I studied our manners and morals in novels, our opinions in philosophers; I even read the sternest moralists to learn what they demanded of us, and thus I ascertained what one could do, what one should think, and how one ought to appear. Once I had settled these three points, only the last one presented some difficulties in practice; I hoped to overcome them and I meditated on the means of doing so.

I began to be bored with my rustic pleasures, which had too little variety for my active mind. I felt a need for coquetry which reconciled me with love; I wanted not to feel it, but to arouse and feign it. It was in vain that I had read and been told that this sentiment could not be feigned: I saw that to do so it was sufficient to combine the mind of an author with the talent of an actor. I practiced both, perhaps with some success; but instead of seeking the vain applause of the theater, I resolved to employ for my happiness what others sacrificed to vanity.

I spent a year in these different occupations. My mourning then allowed me to reappear in society. I returned to Paris with my great plans; I had not foreseen the first obstacle I encountered there.

My long solitude and my austere retirement had given me a veneer of prudery which frightened our most charming men: they stayed away from me and left me in the clutches of a crowd of bores who all wanted to marry me. I had no difficulty in refusing them, but several of my refusals displeased my family, and these domestic annoyances took up the time I had promised myself to use so charmingly. I was therefore obliged, in order to attract one kind of men and repel the other, to display a few indiscretions and employ as much care in damaging my reputation as I had expected to employ in preserving it. I easily succeeded, as you may well believe. But since I was not carried away by any passion, I did only what I judged to be necessary, and prudently measured the doses of my thoughtlessness.

As soon as I had achieved my purpose, I reversed my direction and gave the honor of my improvement to some of those women who, unable to make any claims to attractiveness, fall back on claims to merit and virtue. This was a move that proved to be more valuable to me than I had hoped. The grateful matrons made themselves my defenders, and their blind zeal for what they called their handiwork was so great that whenever anyone ventured to make the slightest remark about me, the entire prudish faction raised an outcry of scandal and insult. The same means also gave me the support of our women with pretensions, who, convinced that I had given up all thought of pursuing the same course as themselves, chose me as the object of their praises whenever they wanted to prove that they did not speak ill of everyone.

Meanwhile, my preceding conduct had brought back the lovers. To remain on good terms with them as well as with the faithful ladies who had become my protectors, I showed myself as a woman who was responsive yet difficult to please, and whose extreme delicacy gave her weapons against love.

I then began to display on the great stage of society the talents I had given myself. My first concern was to acquire the reputation of being invincible. For this purpose, I pretended to accept the attentions only of those men who did not please me. I employed them usefully in procuring for myself the honors of resistance while I yielded without fear to the lover of my choice. But my feigned timidity never allowed him to accompany me in public, and thus the attention of others was always directed toward my rejected admirers.

You know how quickly I make up my mind: that is because I have observed that it is nearly always the preliminary attentions which reveal a woman's secret. No matter what one does, the tone is never the same after success as before. This difference does not escape an attentive observer, and I have found it less dangerous to be mistaken in my choice than to let it be discovered. In this way I also gain the advantage of eliminating the appearances by which alone we can be judged.

These precautions, added to that of never writing, of never giving any proof of my defeat, might seem to be excessive, yet they have never seemed sufficient to me. Having descended into my own heart, I studied the hearts of others in it. I saw that there is no one who does not have a secret that it is important for him not to reveal. This is a truth which Antiquity seems to have known better than we, and of which the story of Samson may be an ingenious symbolic representation. Like Delilah, I have always used my power to discover that important secret. How many modern Samsons there are whose hair I keep between the blades of my scissors! I have ceased to fear them; they are the only men I have sometimes allowed myself to humiliate, I have been more flexible with the others; I have procured their discretion by the art of making them unfaithful in order to avoid seeming fickle to them, by feigned friendship, apparent confidence, a few generous actions, and the flattering idea, which each one of them has preserved, of having been my only lover. Finally, when I have foreseen breaking off and these means have failed me, I have been able to smother in advance, beneath ridicule or calumny, any credence those dangerous men might have obtained.

You see me constantly practicing what I am now telling you, yet you doubt my prudence! Remember the time when you made your first advances to me: no other man's attentions had ever flattered me so much; I desired you even before I had seen you. I had been captivated by your reputation and it seemed to me that I needed you for my glory; I was eager to come to grips with you. It was the only one of my inclinations that ever held sway over me for a moment. But if you had wanted to ruin me, what means would you have found? Idle talk which leaves no trace behind it and which would have been made suspect by your reputation itself, and a series of improbable facts, an accurate account of which would have sounded like a badly written novel. It is true that since then I have revealed all my secrets to you, but you know the interests that unite us, and whether it is I who ought to be accused of imprudence.*

Since I am now giving you an account of my conduct, I shall do it with exactitude. I can already hear you telling me that I am at the mercy of my maid, and it is true that, while she does not know the secret of my feelings, she does know that of my actions. You once spoke to me about her and I answered only that I was sure of her; the proof that this reply was sufficient for your peace of mind is that you have since confided some rather dangerous secrets to her of your own accord. But now that Prévan has upset you and made you lose your head, I no longer expect you simply to take my word for anything. I must therefore enlighten you.

First of all, that girl's mother was my wet nurse, and that bond, which does not seem to us a bond at all, is not without strength for people of her class. Furthermore, I have her secret, and something still better. She was once the victim of an amorous folly and would have been ruined if I had not saved her. Her parents, bristling with honor, were determined to do nothing less than to have her locked up. They addressed themselves to me. I saw at a glance how useful their anger could be to me. I expressed approval of it and solicited the order, which I obtained. Then I suddenly advocated clemency and persuaded her parents to grant it. Making use of my influence with the old Minister, I made them all consent to leave the order in my hands, with the power to prevent or request its execution, according to whether or not I saw any merit in the girl's future conduct. So she knows that I control her fate; and even if, against all possibility, those powerful considerations should fail to restrain her, is it not obvious that the disclosure of her conduct and the actual carrying out of her punishment would soon remove all credibility from her statements?

To these precautions, which I call fundamental, are added countless others adapted to specific places and situations, which reflection and habit have made me devise when necessary. To describe them in detail would be tedious, but the practice of them is important, and you must take the trouble to gather them from the whole of my conduct if you wish to know them.

Can you suppose that after having made so many efforts I

---

*It will be seen later, in Letter 152, not what Monsieur de Valmont's secret was, but more or less to what category it belonged, and the reader will understand that no further information could be given on the subject.

shall not enjoy the fruits of them? That after having raised myself above other women I shall consent to crawl like them between rashness and timidity? That I could ever be so afraid of a man as to see safety only in flight? No, Vicomte, never. I must conquer or perish. As for Prévan, I want to have him and I shall have him; he wants to tell it and he will not tell it: that, in a few words, is our whole story. Good-by.

LETTER 82

~ *From Cécile Volanges to the Chevalier Danceny*

Château de ————, September 21, 17—

How your letter has hurt me! And to think that I was so impatient to receive it! I hoped to find consolation in it and now my sorrow is greater than ever. I cried when I read it; I do not reproach you for that: I have cried many times because of you, without being hurt. But this time it was not the same.

What do you mean when you say that your love is becoming a torment for you, that you cannot live this way or endure your situation any longer? Do you mean that you are going to stop loving me because it is not so agreeable as before? It seems to me that I am no happier than you, quite the contrary; and yet I only love you all the more. If Monsieur de Valmont has not written to you, it is not my fault. I have not been able to ask him to, because I have not been alone with him and we have agreed that we shall never speak to each other in front of other people— and that is for you, so that he can sooner do what you want. I am not saying that I do not want it also, and you should be sure that I do; but what do you expect me to do? If you think it is so easy, find a way to do it, I ask nothing better.

Do you think it is very pleasant for me to be scolded every day by my mother, who never used to say anything to me? It is now worse than if I were in the convent. I had been consoling myself by remembering that it was for your sake, and there were even times when I felt happy about it; but when I see that you are angry too, and for nothing that is my fault, I feel more upset than I have ever been by anything else that has happened to me so far.

Merely receiving your letters is a problem, and if Monsieur de Valmont were not as kind and clever as he is, I would not know what to do; and it is even harder to write to you. All morning I do not dare to do it, because my mother is nearby and keeps coming into my room at every moment. Sometimes I can do it in the afternoon when I am supposed to be singing or playing my harp, but even then I must interrupt my letter at every line so the others can hear that I'm practicing. Fortunately my maid sometimes goes to sleep in the evening and I tell her I do not mind going to bed alone, so that she will go away and leave me a light. And then I must get under my bed curtains so that no light can be seen, and I must listen for the slightest sound so that I can hide everything in my bed if anyone comes. I wish you were here to see! You would see that I must be very much in love to do all this. Anyway, it is true that I am doing everything I can, and that I wish I could do more.

Certainly I do not refuse to tell you I love you and that I shall always love you; I have never said it more wholeheartedly, and you are angry! Yet you assured me before I had said it to you that it would be enough to make you happy. You cannot deny it: it is in your letters. Although I no longer have them, I remember it as well as when I used to read them every day. And because we are now apart, you think differently! But perhaps our separation will not last forever. Oh, how unhappy I am! And it is because of you!

Speaking of your letters, I hope you have kept the ones my mother took away from me and sent back to you. There will surely come a time when I shall be under less constraint than I am now, and I want you to give them all back to me then. How happy I shall be when I can keep them forever without anyone's having a word to say about it! For the time being, I give them back to Monsieur de Valmont, because the risk would be too great otherwise; even so, I never give one back to him without feeling pain.

Good-by, my dearest. I love you with all my heart. I shall love you all my life. I hope you are no longer upset now; if I were sure of it, I would not be upset either. Write to me as soon as you can, because I feel I shall be sad till then.

LETTER 83

~ *From the Vicomte de Valmont to Madame de Tourvel*

Château de ———, September 23, 17—

I beg you, Madame, let us resume the conversation that was so unfortunately interrupted! Let me finish proving to you how much I differ from the odious picture of me that has been presented to you; above all, let me again enjoy that gracious confidence you were beginning to show in me! What charm you impart to virtue! How you embellish all honorable sentiments and make me cherish them! Ah, that is your true charm! It is the strongest of all, and the only one that is both powerful and respectable.

Seeing you is enough to make one desire to please you; hearing you in company is enough to make that desire grow stronger. But someone who has the happiness of knowing you better, who can sometimes read in your soul, soon yields to a nobler enthusiasm and, imbued with venerations as well as love, worships in you the image of all the virtues. I was perhaps created to love and follow them more than others, and after certain errors had led me away from them, it was you who brought me back to them and made me feel all their charm again. Will you treat this new love as though it were a crime? Will you condemn your own work? Would you reproach yourself for the interest you might take in it? What evil can you fear from such a pure sentiment? And what sweetness would there not be in savoring it?

My love frightens you: you find it violent, unrestrained! Temper it by a gentler love; do not refuse the power I offer you. I swear never to escape from it, and I venture to believe that it would not be entirely without benefit for virtue. What sacrifice could seem painful to me if I were sure your heart would appreciate it? What man is wretched enough not to be able to enjoy the privations he imposes on himself, not to prefer a granted word or look to all the pleasures he might steal or take by surprise? You thought I was such a man, and you feared me! Ah, why does your happiness not depend on me! How I would avenge myself on you by making you happy! But that sweet power is not produced by sterile friendship; it belongs only to love.

That word intimidates you! And why? A more tender attachment, a stronger union, a single thought, the same happiness and the same sorrows—what is there in all that which is foreign to your soul? Yet such is love! Such at least is the love that you inspire and I feel. It is that love which calculates without self-interest and is able to appreciate actions according to their merit rather than their value; it is the inexhaustible treasure of sensitive souls; everything becomes precious when done by it or for it.

Is there anything frightening in these truths that are so easy to grasp and so sweet to practice? What fears can be aroused in you by a sensitive man to whom love allows no other happiness than yours? That is now my only wish; I will sacrifice anything to fulfill it, except the sentiment that inspires it. Consent to share that sentiment and you will govern it as you choose. But let us not allow it to divide us any longer when it ought to unite us. If the friendship you have offered me is not a vain word, if, as you told me yesterday, it is the sweetest sentiment your soul knows, then let it stipulate the terms between us, I shall not reject its authority. But if friendship is to be the judge of love, then it must give love a hearing; a refusal to listen to it would be an injustice, and friendship is not unjust.

A second interview will have no more drawbacks than the first; chance can again supply the opportunity, and you yourself can choose the time. I am willing to believe that I am wrong; would you not rather reform me than combat me, and do you doubt my docility? If that unwelcome third person had not interrupted us, I might have accepted your opinion entirely by now—who knows how far your power can go?

Shall I tell you that I am sometimes afraid of that invincible power to which I yield without daring to calculate it, of that irresistible charm which makes you the ruler of all my thoughts and actions? Alas, perhaps it is I who ought to dread the interview I am asking of you! Afterward, perhaps, I shall find myself chained by my promises and reduced to burning with a love which I feel can never be extinguished, without even daring to implore your aid! Ah, Madame, I beg you not to abuse your power! But if they will make you happier, and if they will make me appear worthier of you, then what pains will not be softened by these consoling ideas! Yes, I know: in speaking to you again I shall be giving you stronger weapons against me, and submitting more completely to your will. It is easier for me to defend myself against your letters: the words are the same, but you are not there to give them strength. But the pleasure of hearing you makes me brave the danger of it; at least I shall have the happiness of having done everything for you, even against myself, and my sacrifices will become an act of homage. I shall be all too happy to prove to you in a thousand ways, just as I feel it in a thousand ways, that, not excepting myself, you are and always will be what is dearest to my heart.

LETTER 84

～ *From the Vicomte de Valmont to Cécile Volanges*

September 24, 17—

You saw how we were thwarted yesterday. All day long I was unable to give you the letter I had for you. I do not know whether I shall find an opportunity today. I am afraid of compromising you by showing more zeal than adroitness, and I would never forgive myself for an imprudence that would be so disastrous to you and would drive my friend to despair by making you eternally unhappy. Yet I know the impatience of love; I realize how painful it must be for you, in your situation, to experience any delay in the only consolation you can enjoy at this time. In my efforts to find ways of eliminating the obstacles, I have devised a plan which will be easy to carry out if you will carefully do your part.

I believe I have noticed that the key to your bedroom door which opens onto the corridor is always on your mother's mantelpiece. You will surely understand that everything would become easy if we had that key; lacking it, however, I shall procure you one like it which will replace it. To do so, I need only have the original key in my possession for an hour or two. You should easily find an opportunity to take it, and so that its absence will not be noticed I am enclosing one of my own which is so similar that the difference cannot be seen unless it is tried in the lock, which will not be done. However, you must be sure to put a faded blue ribbon on it like the one that is on yours.

You must try to have that key tomorrow or the day after at breakfast time, because it will be easier for you to give it to me then, and because it can be returned to its place before evening, when your mother might pay more attention to it. I shall be able to give it back to you at dinner time if we carry out our plan correctly.

As you know, when we go from the drawing room to the dining room, Madame de Rosemonde is always the last to leave. I shall give her my arm. You will have only to leave your tapestry frame slowly, or drop something, so that you can stay behind; you will then be able to take the key, which I shall hold behind me. As soon as you have taken it, you must not neglect to rejoin my old aunt and say a few affectionate things to her. If you should happen to drop the key, do not be disconcerted: I shall pretend that it was I who dropped it, and I answer for everything.

This little deceit is justified by your mother's lack of confidence in me and her harsh treatment of you. It is also the only way for you to go on receiving Danceny's letters and sending him yours. All others are too dangerous and might irreparably ruin you both, so my prudent friendship would reproach me if I continued to use any of them.

When we have the key, we shall still have to take precautions against the sound of the door of the lock, but they will be quite easy. Under the same wardrobe where I hid your paper, you will find some oil and a feather. You occasionally go to your room at times when you are alone there; you must oil the lock and the hinges at one of those times. The only thing you must guard against is leaving oil stains that could be used as evidence. You must also wait until night has come, because if this is done with the intelligence of which you are capable, there will be no trace of it the next morning.

However, if it is noticed, do not hesitate to say that it was done by the floor polisher of the château. In this case you must specify the time and even what he said to you: such as, for example, that he takes this precaution against rust for all locks that are not used. For you must realize that it is not likely that you would witness such an operation without asking the reason for it. It is these little details which give plausibility, and plausibility makes a lie safe by preventing any desire to investigate it.

After you have read this letter, please read it again with great care: first, because one must know well what one wishes to do well, and then in order to make sure I have not omitted anything. I am unaccustomed to using trickery on my own account, so I have little experience with it; it required nothing less than my keen friendship for Danceny, and the interest you have inspired in me, to make me use these means, however innocent they may be. I hate anything that looks like deceit; such is my character. But your misfortunes have touched me so deeply that I will try anything to soften them.

You will readily understand that once this communication has been established between us, it will be much easier for me to procure you the meeting with Danceny which he desires. But do not tell him about all this yet; you would only increase his impatience, and the time to satisfy it has not quite arrived. I think you ought to soothe it rather than to intensify it; I rely on your delicacy. Good-by, my fair pupil; for you are my pupil. Love your teacher a little, and above all, be docile with him: you will find it to your advantage. I am working for your happiness, and you may be sure that I shall find my own in it.

LETTER 85

~ *From the Marquise de Merteuil to the Vicomte de Valmont*

Paris, September 25, 17—, at
seven o'clock in the evening

At last your mind will be at rest and above all you will do me justice. Listen, and never again confuse me with other women. I have ended my adventure with Prévan: *ended,* do you understand what that means? You will now judge whether he or I can boast. The story will not be as amusing as the action has been, but it would be unjust if you, who have done nothing but reason well or badly about this affair, were to receive as much pleasure from it as I, who have devoted my time and effort to it.

However, if you have some bold action to attempt, some great enterprise in which that formidable rival seems dangerous to you, come back to Paris. He has left the field open to you, at least for some time; and perhaps he will never recover from the blow I have given him.

How lucky you are to have me as your friend! I am your good fairy. When you were languishing far from the beauty who had captivated you, I said a word and you found yourself with her again. When you wished to avenge yourself on a woman who was harming you, I pointed out the place to strike and delivered her to your discretion. Finally, when you wanted to eliminate dangerous competitor, you appealed to me and I granted your request. Really, if you do not spend the rest of your life thanking me, you are an ingrate.

I shall now return to my adventure and take it from the beginning. The rendezvous agreed upon so loudly as I was leaving the opera* was overhead as I had hoped. Prévan went to the Maréchale's house, and when she obligingly told him she was glad to see him come to her at-home days twice in succession, he was careful to reply that since Tuesday night he had canceled all sorts of engagements in order to be free for that evening. A word to the wise is sufficient! However, since I wanted to know with more certainty whether or not I was the real object of that flattering eagerness, I decided to force my new admirer to choose between me and his dominant passion. I declared that I was not going to gamble; he in turn found countless reasons for not gambling, and my first triumph was over a game of cards.

I seized upon the Bishop of ———— for my conversation. I chose him because of his acquaintance with the hero of the day, for whom I wanted to make it easy to approach me. I was also glad to have a respectable witness who could testify to my conduct and speech if necessary. This arrangement succeeded.

After the usual vague remarks, Prévan soon made himself master of the conversation and successively tried different tones to see which one would please me. I refused that of sentiment, as not believing in it; I stopped his gaiety by my seriousness, because it seemed to me too light for a beginning; he fell back on delicate friendship, and it was under that commonplace flat that we began our reciprocal attack.

When it was time for supper, the bishop did not go downstairs; Prévan therefore gave me his arm and was naturally seated beside me at table. I must be fair: he showed great skill in keeping up our private conversation while appearing to be concerned only with the general conversation, which he seemed to be maintaining almost unaided. During dessert, someone mentioned a new play that was going to be performed at the Théâtre-Français the following Monday. I expressed some regret at not having my box. He offered me his and at first I refused it, as is customary. To this he replied rather amusingly that I had not understood him, that he would certainly not sacrifice his box to someone he did not know, but that he was simply informing me that the Maréchale would be free to use it.

---

*See Letter 74.

When we returned to the drawing room he naturally asked for a seat in the box. The Maréchale, who treats him with great kindness, promised it to him "if he were good." He took the opportunity to launch into one of those converstations with double meaning for which you have praised his talent. He knelt before her like an obedient child, he said, and on the pretext of asking for her opinion and advice, he said many flattering and rather tender things which it was easy for me to apply to myself. Since several people had not returned to their card games after supper, the conversation was more general and less interesting, but our eyes spoke a great deal. I say our eyes, but I should have said his, because mine expressed only one thing: surprise. He must have thought I was amazed and deeply concerned with the prodigious impression he was making on me. I think I left him extremely satisfied, and I was no less pleased.

The following Monday I went to the theater as we had agreed. Despite your literary curiosity, I can tell you nothing about the play except that it was a failure and that Prévan had a wonderful talent for seductive conversation: that was all I learned. I regretted seeing the evening about to end, for it had really pleased me greatly. To prolong it, I invited the Maréchale to come to my house for supper, and this gave me a pretext for extending the same invitation to the charming seducer, who only asked for time enough to hurry to the Comtesses de P——* and break off his appointment with them. This name brought back all my anger: I saw clearly that he was going to begin confiding in them. I recalled your wise advice and promised myself . . . to pursue the adventure, sure that I would cure him of his dangerous indiscretion.

Since he was a stranger among my guests, who were not numerous that evening, he owed me the customary attentions, so when we went to supper he offered me his arm. In taking it, I deliberately made my hand quiver slightly, and as we were walking I breathed rapidly and kept my eyes lowered. He noticed this perfectly, and the traitor immediately changed his tone and bearing. He had been gallant: he now became tender. His words were almost the same as before, because circumstances would not have allowed him to speak otherwise; but his looks became less sparkling and more caressing, the inflection of his voice was softer, and his smile was no longer one of shrewdness but of contentment. Finally, in his talk he gradually extinguished the

*See Letter 70.

fire of his sallies, and wit gave way to delicacy. I ask you, how could you have done any better?

For my part, I became so distracted that the others were forced to notice it, and when I was reproached for it I was skillful enough to defend myself clumsily and give Prévan a quick but timid and disconcerted glance that was well suited to making him think that my only fear was that he might guess the cause of my agitation.

After supper, while the good Maréchale was telling one of those stories she always tells, I placed myself on my ottoman in the attitude of abandon which results from a tender reverie. I was not sorry that Prévan should see me like that, and he honored me with a very particular attention. You may be sure that my timid glances did not dare to seek my conqueror's eyes, but when I directed them toward him in a humbler way they soon told me that I was obtaining the effect I wanted to produce. I still had to convince him that I shared it, so when the Maréchale announced that she was leaving, I cried out in a soft, tender voice. "Oh! I was so comfortable here!" I got up, but before taking leave of her I asked her plans, to give myself a pretext for telling mine and making it known that I would stay home two days later. Then everyone left.

I began to reflect. I had no doubt that Prévan would keep the veiled appointment I had made with him, that he would come early enough to find me alone, and that the attack would be sharp; but I was also sure that in view of my reputation he would not treat me with that lightness which men of any experience at all employ only with women who have had many adventures or those who are completely uninitiated; and I saw my success as certain if he spoke the word "love," and above all if he tried to make me say it to him.

How convenient it is to deal with you "men of principles"! Sometimes a bungling lover disconcerts a woman by his shyness, or embarrasses her with his fiery raptures; it is a fever which, like any other, has its chills and flashes of heat, and sometimes varies in its symptoms. But your methodical advance is so easy to foresee! The arrival, the bearing, the tone, the words—I knew everything the day before. I shall therefore not describe our conversation; you can easily imagine what it was like. Let me point out to you that in my feigned defense I helped him as much as I could: embarrassment, to give him time to talk; poor arguments, to be refuted; fear and mistrust, to bring forth his protestations; and that constant refrain on his part: "I ask only one word of you"; and that silence on my part which seemed to make him wait for it only in order to make him desire it more; and through all this a hand taken a hundred times, always withdrawn and never refused. One could spend an entire day in this way; we spent one deadly hour. We might still be there if we had not heard a carriage come into my courtyard. This fortunate mishap naturally made his entreaties more urgent. Seeing that I was now safe from any sudden attack, I prepared myself by a long sigh and granted the precious word. The first visitor was announced, and within a short time there was a rather numerous company.

Prévan asked if he might come the next morning and I consented; but, careful to defend myself, I ordered my maid to remain in my bedroom during his entire visit. As you know, from there one can see everything that takes place in my dressing room, which was where I received him. Free in our conversation, and both having the same desire, we were soon in agreement; but we had to rid ourselves of our bothersome spectator, and I was all prepared for him when he broached that subject.

After giving him a fanciful account of my life at home, I easily convinced him that we would never find a moment of freedom, that the brief freedom we had enjoyed the day before was almost a miracle, and that a repetition of it would be too dangerous, since someone might come into my drawing room at any time. I did not fail to add that all those customs had become established because until then they had never hindered me, and at the same time I insisted on the impossibility of changing them without compromising myself in the eyes of my servants. He tried looking sad, showing irritation and telling me my love was feeble; you can guess how much all that touched me! But, wishing to strike the decisive blow, I called on my tears to help me. It was exactly like the scene in *Zaïre* in which Orosmane says, "Zaïre, you are weeping." The power that Prévan thought he had over me, and the hope he had conceived of being able to ruin me as he wished, replaced all of Orosmane's love in this case.

When this dramatic performance was over, we returned to our arrangements. Since daytime was out of the question, we considered the night; but my doorkeeper became an insurmountable obstacle, and I would not allow Prévan to try to bribe him. He suggested the small door to my garden; but I had foreseen that, and I invented a dog which, though calm and silent during the day, was a real demon at night. The ease with which I entered nto all these details made him bolder, so he finally proposed the most ridiculous expedient, and that was the one I accepted.

First of all he said that his servant was as trustworthy as himself, and in this he did not deceive me, because one was no more trustworthy than the other. I was to give a large supper party at my house; he would be there, and would unhurriedly leave alone. His adroit accomplice would call the carriage, and Prévan, instead of getting into it, would nimbly slip away. His coachman would be unable to notice that he was not in the carriage; thus everyone would think he had gone, yet he would still be in my house. The next step was to see whether he could get to my bedroom. I confess that at first I had difficulty in finding weak objections to this plan so that he could destroy them; he replied to them with examples. According to him, nothing was more common than this method: he himself had used it often; it was, in fact, the one he used more often than any other, since it was the least dangerous.

Subdued by this unimpeachable authority, I candidly admitted that I did have a concealed staircase which ended very close to my boudoir. I told him I could leave the key in the lock and that he could lock himself in and wait without much risk until my maids had gone. And then, to make my consent more plausible, I withdrew it a moment later and agreed to give it again only on condition that he would guarantee perfect obedience and good behavior—ah, such good behavior! In short, I was willing to prove my love to him, but not to satisfy his.

I forgot to tell you that he was to leave by the little garden gate. He had only to wait till dawn, when the watchdog would no longer say a word. Not a soul passes at that hour, and the servants are all sound asleep. If you are surprised by this mass of absurd reasoning, it is because you are forgetting our mutual situation. What need was there to reason better? He asked nothing better than that the whole thing should become known, and I was sure it would not. The time was set for two days later.

Notice that the affair had been arranged without anyone's having seen Prévan alone with me. I had met him at supper in a friend's house; he offered her his box for a new play, and I accepted a seat in it. I invited her to supper during the play and in front of Prévan: it was almost impossible for me not to offer him the same invitation. He accepted it, and two days later he paid me the visit demanded by custom. It is true that he came to see me the next morning; but aside from the fact that morning visits are no longer of any consequence, I could have considered this one improper if I had so chosen. Indeed, I placed him in the category of my more distant acquaintances by sending him a written invitation to a formal ceremony. Like Annette, I could say, "But that was all!"

When the fateful day arrived, the day when I was to lose my virtue and my reputation, I gave my instructions to my faithful Victoire, and she carried them out as you will soon see.

Evening came. There were already many people with me when Prévan was announced. I received him with a marked politeness which showed how far I was from being on close terms with him, and I placed him in the Maréchale's group, since it was through her that I had made his acquaintance. The evening produced nothing except a short note which my discreet admirer managed to hand me, and which I burned in accordance with my custom. In it he informed me that I could count on him, and these essential words were surrounded by all the parasitic words about love, happiness, etc., which are never missing on such occasions.

At midnight, when the card games were over, I suggested a short *macédoine*.* I had the double intention of facilitating Prévan's departure while at the same time making the others notice it, which they could not fail to do, considering his reputation as a gambler. I was also glad that they should be able to remember, if necessary, that I had not been in a hurry to remain alone.

The game lasted longer than I had thought. The devil tempted me, and I succumbed to a desire to go and console the impatient prisoner. I was on my way to my ruin when it occurred to me that once I had yielded to him completely, I would no longer have sufficient power over him to keep him in the costume of decency that was necessary to my plan. I had the strength to resist. I turned back and, not without ill-humor, resumed my place in that everlasting game. It finally ended, however, and everyone left. I rang for my maids, quickly undressed and sent them away immediately.

Can you see me, Vicomte, in my light attire, walking timidly and cautiously, and opening the door to my conqueror with a faltering hand? He saw me and acted with the speed of lightning. What shall I tell you? I was conquered, completely conquered, before I was able to say a word to stop him or defend

---

*There may be some readers who do not know that a *macédoine* is a group of several games of chance among which each player has the right to choose when it is his turn to deal. It is one of the inventions of the age.

myself. He then wanted to place himself in a more comfortable situation, better suited to the circumstances. He cursed his clothes which, he said, kept him away from me; he wanted to combat me with equal weapons. But my extreme shyness opposed this plan, and my tender caresses did not leave him time to carry it out. He became concerned with other matters.

His rights were doubled and his pretensions returned; but then I said to him, "Listen to me: up to this point you will have a pleasant story to tell the two Comtesses de P—— and a thousand others; but I am curious to know how you will relate the end of the adventure." As I said this, I rang the bell with all my might. This time it was my turn, and my action was quicker than his words. He had only began to stammer when I heard Victoire running toward me and calling the servants she had kept in her room as I had ordered. I then said loudly, in my queenly tone, "Go, Monsieur, and never appear before me again," whereupon my servants all came into the room at once.

Poor Prévan lost his head: thinking he saw an ambush in what was actually no more than a joke, he rushed for his sword. This was a mistake, because my brave and vigorous footman seized him and threw him to the floor. I admit that I had a moment of mortal fear. I cried out to my servants to stop, and ordered them to let him go free, merely making sure that he left my house. They obeyed me, but with much grumbling; they were indignant that anyone should have dared to show disrespect for "their virtuous mistress." They all accompanied the unfortunate Chevalier, with loud cries of outrage, as I wished. Only Victoire stayed behind, and during this time we repaired the disorder of my bed.

My servants came back upstairs in as great a tumult as ever, and I, "still in the grip of my agitation," asked them by what good fortune they had still been awake. Victoire then told me that she had invited two of her friends to supper, that the others had stayed up in her room; in short, everything we had agreed upon beforehand. I thanked them all and sent them away, after ordering one of them to bring my doctor immediately. It seemed to me that I was entitled to fear the effects of my "terrible shock," and it was a certain means of causing the news to circulate and attract attention.

The doctor came, pitied me a great deal and ordered me to rest. And I ordered Victoire to go out early in the morning and gossip in the neighborhood.

Everything succeeded so well that before noon, and as soon as

I was ready to receive vistors, my devout neighbor came to my bedside and asked me to tell her the truth and the details of my horrible adventure. I was forced to spend an hour with her lamenting the corruption of our times. Then I received from the Maréchale the note I am enclosing in this letter. Finally, before five o'clock, to my great surprise I saw M——* arrive. He had come, he said, to apologize to me for the fact that an officer in his corps had shown such great disrespect for me. He had not learned of it until he was dining with the Maréchale, and he had immediately sent Prévan an order to report to prison. I asked that he be pardoned and my request was refused. I then decided that, as an accomplice, I ought to share the punishment by keeping myself imprisoned in my house, so I announced that I was indisposed and would receive no more visitors.

You owe this long letter to my solitude. I shall also write one to Madame de Volanges, who will surely read it in public; you will then hear this story as it ought to be told.

I forgot to tell you that Belleroche is beside himself with indignation and is determined to fight a duel with Prévan. Poor boy! Fortunately I shall have time to calm him. Meanwhile, I am going to rest, because my mind is weary from writing. Goodby, Vicomte.

LETTER 86

～ *From the Maréchale de —— to the Marquise de Merteuil*
• *(Note enclosed in the preceding letter)*

Paris, September 25, 17—

Good heavens, Madame, what is this I hear! Is it possible that little Prévan should commit such an abomination? And against you, too! The things one is exposed to! Are we no longer safe even in our own houses? Really, such things are a consolation for being old. But I shall never be consoled for being partly the cause of your having received such a monster in your house. I promise you that if what I have been told is true, he will never set foot in my house again; and all decent people will treat him in the same way if they act as they should.

---

*The commander of the corps in which Monsieur de Prévan was serving.

I have been told that you were in a distressing state, and I am worried about your health. Please let me have some news of your dear self, or have one of your maids do it if you cannot. I ask only for a few words to put my mind at rest. I would have hurried to see you this morning if it had not been for my baths, which my doctor will not allow me to interrupt; and this afternoon I must go to Versailles about that affair of my nephew's.

Good-by, my dear Madame; you may count on my sincere friendship as long as I live.

LETTER 87

~ *From the Marquise de Merteuil to Madame de Volanges*

Paris, September 26, 17—

I am writing to you in bed, my dear, good friend. A most unpleasant and unforeseeable event has made me ill with shock and sorrow. Not that I have anything at all with which to reproach myself, but it is always painful for a respectable woman, one who has preserved the modesty that befits her sex, to have public attention directed upon her. I would give anything in the world to have been able to avoid that unfortunate incident, and I still do not know whether I shall not decide to go to the country and wait there until it has been forgotten. Here is what happened.

At the Maréchale de ———'s house I met a Monsieur de Prévan, whom you surely know by name, and whom I did not know otherwise. But since he was in that house, it seems to me that I was justified in assuming him to be a decent man. He is quite handsome, and he appeared to be not lacking in intelligence. Chance and the boredom of gambling left me the only woman between him and the Bishop of ——— which everyone else was playing cards. The three of us talked until supper time. At table, someone spoke of a new play, which gave him an opportunity to offer his box to the Maréchale. She accepted it, and it was agreed that I was to have a seat in it. The play was performed last Monday, at the Théâtre-Français. Since the Maréchale was coming to my house for supper afterward, I invited him to accompany her, which he did. Two days later he paid me a visit which was spent entirely in polite conversation, and during which nothing unusual occurred. The next day he came to see me in the morning; this seemed a little improper to me, but I felt that, rather than making him aware of it by the manner in which I received him, it would be better to notify him by an act of politeness that we were not on such close terms as he seemed to believe. For that purpose I sent him, that same day, a very austere and formal invitation to a supper party I gave day before yesterday. I did not speak to him more than three times all evening, and he left as soon as he had finished his game of cards. You will agree that so far nothing could have seemed less likely to lead to an adventure. After the card games there was a *macédoine* which lasted until nearly two o'clock. Finally I went to bed.

At least half an hour after my maids had gone, I heard a noise in my room. I opened the curtains of my bed with great fear and saw a man coming in through the door that leads to my boudoir. I cried out, and in the glow of my night-light I recognized Monsieur de Prévan, who, with incredible effrontery, told me not to be alarmed, that he would explain the mystery of his conduct, and that he begged me not to make any noise. He lit a candle as he spoke. I was so shocked that I could not speak. I think his calm, relaxed manner petrified me still more. But I saw what his "mystery" was as soon as he had said his first few words, and my only answer, of course, was to pull my bell cord.

By an amazing stroke of good fortune, all the men from the servants' hall had been staying up in the room of one of my maids and were not yet in bed. As my maid was coming up the stairs, she heard me speaking with great animation; she became frightened and called the others. You can imagine what a scene there was! My servants were furious, and for a moment I thought my footman was going to kill Prévan. I admit that at the time I was glad to have them all present, but, looking back on it now, I wish that only my maid had come: she would have been enough, and I might have avoided the scandal which now distresses me.

Instead, the tumult awoke the neighbors, the servants related the story, and since yesterday it has been the talk of Paris. Monsieur de Prévan is in prison by order of the commander of his corps, who had the decency to come to see me, to apologize, he said. Prévan's imprisonment will increase the talk, but I was unable to have him pardoned. The city and the court have left inquiries at my door, which I have closed to everyone. The few people I have seen have told me that justice is being done to me, and that public indignation against Monsieur de Prévan is running high. He certainly deserves it, but that does not remove the unplesantness of the incident.

Furthermore, he surely has some friends, and any friends of his must be malicious—who knows, who can know what they will invent to harm me? How unfortunate a young woman is! She has accomplished nothing when she has made herself safe from gossip; she must still silence slander.

Please tell me what you would have done and what you would do in my place; tell me everything you think. It has always been from you that I have received the sweetest consolations and the wisest advice, and it if from you that I like best to receive them.

Good-by, my dear and good friend; you know the sentiments which attach me to you forever. I kiss your charming daughter.

∿ PART THREE ∿

∿ *From Cécile Volanges to the Vicomte de Valmont*

September 26, 17—

Despite all the pleasure it gives me, Monsieur, to receive letters from the Chevalier Danceny, and although I wish no less than he does that we could see each other again without anyone's being able to prevent it, I have not dared to do what you suggest. First of all, it is too dangerous: the key you want me to put in place of the other one does indeed look like it, but there is still some difference between them, and my mother looks at everything and notices everything. Furthermore, although the key has not been used since we have been here, it would take only one stroke of bad luck to ruin me forever. And then it seems very wrong to me, making a double key like that! It is true that it would be you who would have the kindness to do it, but even so, if it were found out I would still have to take the blame for it, since it would be for me that you had done it. Anyway, I tried twice to take the key; it would certainly be quite easy if it were something else, but for some reason I began to tremble and I never had the courage to do it. So I think it is better to leave things as they are.

If you still have the kindness to be as obliging as you have been so far, you will always find a way to give me a letter. It would have been easy for us even with the last one if you had not unfortunately turned around rather quickly at a certain moment. I realize that you cannot think about this all the time as I do, but I prefer to have more patience and not run such great risks. I am sure Monsieur Danceny would say the same thing,

179

because whenever he wanted something that upset me too much, he always consented to do without it.

I shall give you at the same time as this letter, Monsieur, your own letter, Monsieur Danceny's, and your key. I am none the less grateful to you for all your kindnesses, and I beg you to continue them. It is true that I am very unhappy, and if it were not for you I would be much more so; but after all, she is my mother and I must be patient. And provided Monsieur Danceny still loves me and you do not abandon me, a happier time may come.

I have the honor of being, Monsieur, with much gratitude, your most humble and most obedient servant.

LETTER 89

~   *From the Vicomte de Valmont to the Chevalier Danceny*

Château de ———, September 26, 17—

If your affairs do not always move so swiftly as you would like, my friend, you must not place all the blame on me. I have more than one obstacle to overcome here. Madame de Volanges's vigilance and severity are not alone: your young friend also has these qualities, and she sometimes opposes me with them. Whether from coldness or timidity, she does not always follow my advice, yet I think I know better than she what ought to be done.

I have found a simple, convenient and safe means of delivering your letters to her, and even of later facilitating the interviews you desire, but I cannot persuade her to use it. This afflicts me all the more because I see no other way of bringing you together, and even with your correspondence I am constantly afraid of compromising all three of us. You may be sure that I do not want to run that risk or expose either of you to it.

Yet it would truly grieve me if your young friend's lack of confidence in me should prevent me from being useful to you. Perhaps you would do well to write to her about it. Consider what you wish to do; the decision is yours alone, for it is not enough simply to serve one's friends: they must be served in the manner they choose. It might also be another way of making sure of her feelings for you, because a woman who keeps a will of her own does not love as much as she says.

Not that I suspect your beloved of inconstancy; but she is very young and very much afraid of her mother, who, as you know, seeks only to harm you; and perhaps it would be dangerous to let too much time pass without making her concern herself with you. However, do not become too alarmed by what I am telling you here. I have no real reason for mistrust; it is only the solicitude of friendship.

I do not write to you at greater length because I also have some affairs on my own account. I have not advanced as far as you have, but my love is as great, and that is a consolation. Even if I do not succeed for myself, I shall feel that I have employed my time well if I can be useful to you. Good-by, my friend.

LETTER 90

~ *From Madame de Tourvel to the Vicomte de Valmont*

September 27, 17—

I sincerely hope, Monsieur, that this letter will not cause you any pain, or, if it does, that it will at least be softened by the pain I feel in writing to you. You must know me well enough by now to be quite sure that it is not my intention to hurt you; and you, no doubt, would not want to plunge me into eternal despair. I beg you, then, in the name of the tender friendship I have promised you, in the name even of those sentiments, perhaps more intense but certainly no more sincere, which you have for me, to stop forcing me to see you. Please leave, and until you do, let us particularly avoid those private and too dangerous conversations in which, through some incredible power, I spend all my time listening to things I ought not to hear, without ever being able to tell you what I want to say.

Only yesterday, when you came to join me in the park, my sole intention was to tell you what I am now writing to you, and yet what did I do except to concern myself with your love . . . with your love, to which I must not respond! Oh, I beg you, leave me!

Do not be afraid that your absence will ever alter my feelings for you: how could I succeed in overcoming them when I no longer even have the courage to combat them? As you can see, I am telling you everything; I am less afraid of admitting my weakness than of succumbing to it. But while I have lost control of my feelings, I will regain control of my actions; yes, I am determined to retain it, even at the cost of my life.

Alas, it was not long ago that I felt quite sure that I would never have to engage in such combats. I was glad of it, and perhaps I gloried in it too much. Heaven has punished, cruelly punished my pride; but, full of mercy at the very moment when it strikes, it has warned me again before my fall, and I would be doubly guilty if I continued to lack prudence when I already know that I have no more strength.

You have told me a hundred times that you would not want a happiness bought by my tears. Ah, let us talk no more about happiness, but let me recover some tranquillity!

In granting my request, what new rights will you not acquire over my heart? And since they will be founded on virtue, I shall not have to defend myself against them. What pleasure I shall take in my gratitude! I shall owe to you the sweetness of savoring a delightful sentiment without remorse. But now, on the contrary, I am frightened by my feelings and thoughts, and I am as afraid to think about you as about myself. The very idea of you terrifies me: When I cannot avoid it, I combat it; I do not drive it away, but I repel it.

Would it not be better for both of us to end this state of agitation and anxiety? You, whose sensitive soul has remained a friend of virtue even in the midst of its errors, will be considerate of my painful situation, you will not reject my prayer! These violent agitations will be replaced by a sweeter but no less tender interest; then, breathing through your kindness, I shall cherish my existence, and I shall say in the joy of my heart, "This calm I feel is a gift from my friend."

In submitting to a few slight privations, which I do not impose on you, but which I ask of you, do you think you will be paying too high a price for the cessation of my torments? Ah, if I could make you happy merely by consenting to be unhappy, believe me, I would not hesitate for a moment. But to become guilty . . . No! No, my friend, I would rather die a thousand deaths.

Already assailed by shame, on the eve of remorse, I dread others and myself; I blush in company, and I shudder in solitude; I am living a life of sorrow; I shall have no tranquillity without your consent. My most praiseworthy resolutions are not sufficient to reassure me; I made this one yesterday, yet I spent last night in tears.

Consider your friend, the woman you love, abashed and supplicating, asking you for rest and innocence. Alas, if it had not been for you, would she ever have been reduced to that humiliating request? I do not reproach you: I myself am all too aware of how difficult it is to resist an imperious sentiment. A moan is not a complaint. Do from generosity what I am doing from duty, and to all the sentiments you have inspired in me, I shall add that of eternal gratitude. Good-by, good-by, Monsieur.

LETTER 91

~ *From the Vicomte de Valmont to Madame de Tourvel*

September 27, 17—, in the evening

Your letter has thrown me into consternation, Madame, and I still do not know how to reply to it. Certainly if a choice must be made between your unhappiness and mine, it is for me to sacrifice myself, and I do not hesitate. But it seems to me that such an important matter deserves to be discussed and made clear, and how can that be done if we are never to see or speak to each other again?

What! When we are united by the sweetest sentiments, will a vain terror suffice to separate us, perhaps forever? Tender friendship and ardent love will demand their right in vain: their voices will not be heard. And why? What is this pressing danger which threatens you? Ah, believe me: such fears, so lightly conceived, are already, it seems to me, strong enough reasons for confidence.

Allow me to tell you that I see in this the traces of the unfavorable impressions you have been given of me. A woman does not tremble when she is with a man she esteems; above all, she does not send away a man she had judged to be worthy of a certain friendship: it is only a dangerous man whom she fears and avoids.

Yet who was ever more respectful and submissive than I? Already, as you can see, I am restraining myself in my language: I no longer allow myself to use those words which are so sweet and so dear to my heart, and which it has not ceased murmuring to you in secret. I am no longer the faithful and unhappy lover receiving the advice and consolations of a tender and sensitive friend: I am the accused before his judge, the slave before his master. These new titles no doubt impose new duties; I promise to fulfill them all. Listen to me, and if you condemn me I shall accept your judgment and leave. I promise more: if you prefer that despotism which judges without hearing, if you feel in yourself the courage to be unjust, you have only to command and I shall still obey.

But let me hear your judgement or your command from your own lips. Perhaps you will ask why. If so, you know little about love and my heart! It is nothing to see you once more? Even if you fill my soul with despair, perhaps a consoling look will save me from succumbing to it. And if I must renounce the love and friendship for which alone I exist, at least you will see your work and your pity will be left to me. It seems to me that even if I do not deserve that slight favor, I am prepared to pay so dearly for it that I have a right to hope it will be granted.

What! Are you going to send me away from you? You are willing to have us become strangers to each other! What am I saying? You desire it! And while you assure me that absence will not alter your sentiments, you hasten my departure so that you can work more easily to destroy them.

You already speak to me of replacing them by gratitude. The sentiment that you would grant to a stranger for the slightest service, even to an enemy for ceasing to harm you—that is what you are offering to me! And you want my heart to be content with it! Question your own heart: if your lover or your friend should one day speak to you of his gratitude, would you not say to him indignantly, "Leave me, you are ungrateful!"

I shall stop at this point and appeal to your indulgence. Forgive the expression of a grief that you have created: it will not impair my complete submission. But in my turn I beg you, in the name of those sweet sentiments to which you yourself appeal, not to refuse to hear me; and at least from pity for the mortal distress into which you have plunged me, do not delay your consent. Good-by, Madame.

LETTER 92

~ *From the Chevalier Danceny to the Vicomte de Valmont*

Paris, September 27, 17—

Oh, my friend, your letter has frozen me with terror! Cécile . . .
Oh, God! It is possible? Cécile no longer loves me. Yes, I
see that horrible truth through the veil your friendship has cast
over it. You wish to prepare me to receive that mortal blow; I
thank you for your efforts, but can love be deceived? It antici-
pates what concerns it; it is not informed of its fate, it senses it. I
no longer have any doubt about mine; you can speak to me
frankly, and I beg you to do so. Tell me everything: what gave
birth to your suspicions and what confirmed them. The slightest
details are precious. Above all, try to remember exactly what she
said. One word in place of another can change a whole sentence;
the same word sometimes has two meanings. . . . You may be
mistaken—alas, I am still trying to delude myself! What did she
say to you? Does she reproach me for anything? Does she not at
least defend herself for her wrongs? I ought to have foreseen this
change because of the difficulties which for some time she has
been finding in everything. Love does not recognize so many
obstacles.

What should I do? What do you advise me? Should I try to see
her? Is that impossible? Absence is so cruel, so destructive. . . .
And she has refused a way to see me! You do not say what it
was; if it was really too dangerous, she knows very well that I do
not want her to risk too much, but I also know your prudence
and, to my misfortune, I cannot help believing in it.

What am I to do now? How can I write to her? If I let her see
my suspicions, they may hurt her; and if they are unjust, could I
ever forgive myself for having distressed her? To hide them from
her would be to deceive her, and I cannot dissimulate with her.

Oh, if only she knew how much I am suffering, my pain
would touch her! I know she is sensitive; she has a very kind
heart, and I have countless proofs of her love. Too much timidity, a certain embarrassment—she is so young! And her mother
treats her with such severity! I am going to write to her; I shall
control myself, I shall ask her only to rely on you entirely. Even

if she still refuses, at least she cannot be angered by my request; and perhaps she will consent.

I send you a thousand apologies, my friend, for her and for myself. I assure you that she realizes the value of your efforts, and that she is grateful for them. It is only timidity on her part, not mistrust. Be indulgent; that is the finest trait of friendship. Yours is very precious to me and I do not know how to show my appreciation for everything you are doing for me. Good-by, I am going to write to her immediately.

I feel all my fears returning; who would ever have believed that it would some day be difficult for me to write to her! Alas, only yesterday it was my sweetest pleasure.

Good-by, my friend; continue your efforts, and pity me greatly.

LETTER 93

～　*From the Chevalier Danceny to Cécile Volanges*
(Enclosed with the preceding letter)

Paris, September 27, 17—

I cannot conceal from you the sorrow it gave me to learn from Valmont how little confidence you still have in him. You know he is my friend and that he is the only person who can bring us together: I thought those qualifications would be sufficient for you; I see with pain that I was mistaken. May I at least hope that you will tell me your reasons? Will you still find difficulties to prevent you from doing so? But unless you explain it to me, I cannot guess the mystery of your conduct. I do not dare to suspect your love, and no doubt you would not dare to betray mine. Ah, Cécile! . . .

It is really true that you have refused a means of seeing me, a means that is simple, convenient and safe?* Is that how you love me? A short absence has greatly changed your feelings. But why deceive me? Why tell me you still love me, that you love me more than ever? In destroying your love, has your mother also destroyed your candor? If she has at least left you a little pity, you will not be unmoved when you learn of the horrible torments you are causing me. Ah, my suffering would be less if I were dying!

---

*Danceny does not know what this means was: he is merely repeating Valmont's expression.

Tell me, is your heart closed to me forever? Have you completely forgotten me? Thanks to your refusal, I know neither when you will hear my complaints nor when you will reply to them. Valmont's friendship had assured our correspondence, but you did not want it, you found it difficult, you preferred that our letters should be rare. No, I shall no longer believe in love, in good faith. What can I believe, if Cécile has deceived me?

Please answer me: is it true that you have stopped loving me? No, that is impossible, you are deluding yourself, you are slandering your own heart. A passing fear, a moment of discouragement which love soon drove away—that was all, was it not, my Cécile? Yes, surely that was all, and I am wrong to accuse you. How happy I would be to be wrong! How I would love to make tender apologies to you, to make amends for this moment of injustice by an eternity of love!

Cécile, Cécile, have pity on me! Consent to see me, take any means of doing it! See what absence produces: fears, suspicions, perhaps coldness! One look, one word and we shall be happy. But can I still speak of happiness? Perhaps it is lost to me, lost forever. Tormented by fear, cruelly pressed between unjust suspicions and the still more painful truth, I cannot fix my attention on any thought, I conserve only enough existence to suffer and to love you. Ah, Cécile, you alone have the right to make life dear to me! I expect from the first word you utter either the return of happiness or the certainty of eternal despair.

LETTER 94

~ *From Cécile Volanges to the Chevalier Danceny*

Château de ———, September 28, 17—

I understand nothing about your letter except the pain it causes me. What has Monsieur de Valmont told you, and what can have made you believe I do not love you? It might be fortunate for me, because I would surely be less tormented; and it is very hard, when I love you as I do, to see that you always think I am wrong, and that instead of consoling me, it is always you who cause me the pains which grieve me most. You think I deceive you and tell you things that are not so! You have a fine idea of me! But if I were as deceitful as you accuse me of being, what could I hope to gain from it? Certainly if I no longer loved you I would only have to say it and everyone would praise me for it; but unfortunately my love is stronger than I am—and it has to be for someone who is not at all grateful to me for it!

What have I done to make you so angry? I did not dare to take a key because I was afraid my mother would notice it, and I knew that my unhappiness would then be even greater, and yours too, because of me. Besides, it seemed wrong to me. But it was only Monsieur de Valmont who talked to me about it; I could not know whether you wanted it or not, since you knew nothing about it. Now that I know you want it, do I refuse to take that key? I shall take it tomorrow, and then we shall see what else you will have to say.

Although Monsieur de Valmont is your friend, I think I love you at least as much as he does, yet it is always he who is right, and I am always wrong. I assure you I am very angry. You do not care, because you know I am quickly pacified; but if I had the key now and could see you whenever I wanted, I assure you I would not want to if you acted like this. I prefer to have my sorrow come to me from myself, rather than from you. Decide what you want to do.

If you were willing, we would love each other so much! And at least we would have no sorrows except those inflicted on us by others! I assure you that if I were free to do as I pleased, you would never have any reason to complain of me; but if you do not believe me, we shall always be very unhappy, and it will not be my fault. I hope we shall soon be able to see each other, and that we shall then have no more occasions for hurting each other as we do now.

If I had been able to foresee this, I would have taken the key immediately; but really, I thought I was doing right. So please do not be angry with me. Do not be sad, either, and always love me as much as I love you: then I shall be very happy. Good-by, my dearest.

LETTER 95

~⌇   *From Cécile Volanges to the Vicomte de Valmont*

September 28, 17—

Please be so kind, Monsieur, as to give me back that key you gave me to put in place of the other one; since everyone wants me to do it, I must consent.

I do not know why you told Monsieur Danceny I had stopped loving him. I do not think I have ever given you any reason to think so. It has hurt him very much, and me too. I know you are his friend, but that is no reason to make him sad, or me either. You would do me a great favor if you would tell him it is not true the next time you write to him, and that you are sure of it, for it is in you that he has the most confidence, and when I have said something and am not believed, I do not know what to do.

As for the key, do not worry: I clearly remember everything you told me in your letter. However, if you still have it, and if you will give it to me at the same time as the key, I promise to pay close attention to it. If you can do it tomorrow when we are going to dinner, I shall give you the other key at breakfast day after tomorrow, and you can give it back to me in the same way as the first one. I hope it will not take any longer, so that there will be less risk of my mother's noticing it.

And then, once you have that key, please be so kind as to use it to take my letters also; in that way, Monsieur Danceny will hear from me more often. It is true that it will be more convenient than now, but at first it frightened me too much. I beg you to excuse me, and I hope you will continue to be as obliging as you have been in the past. I shall always be grateful to you for it.

I have the honor of being, Monsieur, your most humble and most obedient servant.

LETTER 96

~ *From the Vicomte de Valmont to the Marquise de Merteuil*

Château de ———, October 1, 17—

I am willing to bet that every day since your adventure you have been expecting my compliments and praise. I do not doubt that my long silence has somewhat annoyed you, but I have always thought that when there was nothing more than praise to give to a woman, one could take her for granted and concern oneself with something else. However, I thank you on my own account and congratulate you on yours. To make you perfectly happy, I am even willing to admit that this time you have surpassed my expectations. After that, let us see if I have at least partly fulfilled yours.

It is not about Madame de Tourvel that I want to talk to you: her excessively slow progress displeases you. You like only completed affairs. Drawn-out scenes bore you; yet I had never before known the pleasure I now savor in this supposed slowness.

Yes, I like to see, to contemplate that prudent woman who, without realizing it, is moving along a path which allows no return, and whose steep, dangerous slope pulls her onward in spite of herself, and forces her to follow me. Terrified by the risks she is running, she would like to stop, yet cannot hold herself back. Her efforts and skill may make her steps shorter, but each step must still be followed by another. Sometimes, not daring to look at the danger, she closes her eyes, lets herself go and abandons herself to my attentions. More often a new fear revives her efforts: in mortal terror, she again tries to go back; she exhausts her strength in laboriously climbing a short distance, and soon a magic power places her still nearer to the danger she had tried to escape. Then, having no one but me to guide and support her, without thinking of reproaching me for her inevitable fall, she begs me to delay it. Fervent prayers, humble supplications: everything that mortals, in their fear, offer to the divinity, I receive from her—and you want me to be deaf to her entreaties, to destroy the worship she gives me, and to throw her down with the power she invokes to support her! Ah, at least leave me time to watch those touching combats between love and virture.

That same spectacle makes you hurry eagerly to the theater, and you applaud it wildly: do you think it is any less fascinating in reality? You listen with enthusiasm to the sentiments of a pure and tender soul which dreads the happiness it desires and does not cease to defend itself even when it has ceased to resist: should they be without value only for the man who has given rise to them? Yet such are the delightful enjoyments which that heavenly woman offers me every day, and you reproach me for savoring their sweetness! The time will come all too soon when, degraded by her fall, she will be only an ordinary woman to me.

But in speaking to you of her I am forgetting that I did not want to speak of her. I do not know what power attaches me to her, constantly brings me back to her, even when I am dishonoring her. Let us put aside the dangerous idea of her; let me become myself again to deal with a more amusing subject. I am referring to your pupil, who has become mine, and I hope that here you will recognize me.

For several days I had been better treated by my tender prude and, being therefore less concerned with her, I had noticed that little Cécile Volanges is indeed very pretty; and I decided that, while it is foolish to be in love with her as Danceny is, it might be equally foolish for me not to seek with her the distraction that my solitude had made necessary. Also, it seemed to me that I ought to pay myself for my efforts on her behalf; furthermore, I remembered that you had offered her to me before Danceny could pretend to any rights over her, and I left that I was entitled to make a few claims on a property which he possessed only through my refusal and abandonment. These wise reflections were fortified by her pretty face, her fresh mouth, her childish air, even her awkwardness. I resolved to act on them, and the enterprise was crowned with success.

You are already trying to decide by what means I supplanted her cherished lover so soon, and what method of seduction is suited to that age and inexperience. Save yourself the trouble: I used none. While you were skillfully wielding the weapons of your sex and triumphing by subtlety, I was restoring man's inalienable rights and conquering by authority. Sure of seizing my prey if I could come within reach of her, I needed a ruse only to approach her, and the one I used scarcely deserves the name.

I took advantage of the first letter I received from Danceny for his beloved, and after notifying her of it by the signal we had agreed upon, instead of using my skill to give it to her, I used it to avoid finding any way of doing so. I pretended to share the impatience I had created, and after causing the difficulty I pointed out its solution.

The young lady's room has a door opening onto the hall, but her mother had naturally taken the key to it. The only problem was to gain possession of it. Nothing could have been easier to carry out; I guaranteed to have another one like it if I could have it at my disposal for only two hours. Then everything—correspondence, conversations, nocturnal meetings—would become convenient and safe. But would you believe it? The timid child became frightened and refused. Other men would have been disheartened by this; I saw it only as an opportunity for a more piquant pleasure. I wrote a letter to Danceny complaining of her refusal, and I succeeded so well that our foolish young man did not rest until he had demanded and obtained his timorous sweetheart's consent to grant my request and abandon herself entirely to my discretion.

I confess that I was glad to have changed roles in this way, and to have the young man do for me what he expected me to do for him. This idea doubled the value of the adventure in my eyes, so I hastened to use the precious key as soon as I had it. This was last night.

After making sure that everything was quiet in the château, armed with my dark lantern and in the attire suited to the hour and required by the circumstances, I paid my first visit to your pupil. I had had everything prepared (and by the girl herself) for my being able to enter noiselessly. She had just fallen asleep, and was sleeping as one does at that age, so I went all the way to her bed without awakening her. At first I was tempted to go further and try to pass for a dream, but, fearing the effect of surprise and the noise it involves, I preferred to awaken the pretty sleeper cautiously, and I succeeded in preventing the cry I had dreaded.

After calming her first fears I ventured to take a few liberties, since I had not come there to talk. Apparently she had not been well informed in her convent about the various perils to which timid innocence is exposed, and everything it has to guard in order not to be taken by surprise, for in concentrating all her attention on defending herself against a kiss, which was only a false attack, she left everything else without defense—how could I fail to take advantage of that! I changed my tactics and immediately took up my position. At this point we were both nearly lost: she became terrified and tried to scream in earnest; but fortunately her voice was smothered by tears. She had also tried to reach her bell cord, but I deftly caught her arm in time.

"What are you trying to do: ruin yourself forever?" I said to her. "What does it matter to me if someone comes? Do you think you can convince anyone that I am not here by your wish? Who else but you could have made it possible for me to come here? And are you willing to explain the use of this key which I have received from you, which could have been given to me by no one else?" This little speech calmed neither her grief nor her anger, but it did make her more submissive. I do not know if I had the tone of eloquence; it is at least certain that I did not have its gestures. One hand occupied by force and the other by love: what orator could pretend to grace in such a situation? If you imagine it clearly, you will admit that it was at least favorable to attack; but I understand nothing about anything, and, as you say, the simplest woman, even a schoolgirl, leads me like a child.

Despite all her distress, she realized that she had to adopt some course of action and come to terms with me. Since her entreaties left me unmoved, she had to resort to offers. You no doubt think I sold my important position dearly; no, I promised everything for a kiss. It is true that once I had taken the kiss I did not keep my promise; but I had good reasons. Had we specified whether it was to be given or taken? After a great deal of bargaining, we agreed on a second kiss, and it was stated that this one would be received. When I had guided her timid arms around my body and held her more amorously in one of mine, the sweet kiss was received, and well received, so perfectly that love itself could not have done better.

Such good faith deserved a reward, so I immediately granted her request. I withdrew my hand, but somehow I found myself in its place. You assume that I was here very eager and active, do you not? Not at all. I have taken a liking to slowness, as I have told you. When one is certain of arriving, why hasten the journey?

Seriously, I was glad to observe for once the power of opportunity, and here I found it divested of all extraneous aid. Yet it had to combat love, and love supported by modesty or shame and fortified above all by the great anger I had aroused. Opportunity was alone, but it was there, always offered, always present, and love was absent.

To make sure of my observations, I deliberately used no more force than she could combat. However, if my charming adversary abused my leniency and made ready to escape, I restrained her by the same fear whose fortunate effects I had already noted. Finally, without any further efforts on my part, she forgot her vows and yielded at first, then consented. Not that tears and reproaches did not return together after this first moment; I do not know whether they were real or feigned, but, as always happens, they ceased as soon as I set about giving her new reasons for them. In short, after weakness followed by reproaches, and reproaches followed by weakness, we did not part until we were satisfied with each other and had agreed on a rendezvous for this evening.

I did not go back to my room until dawn. I was in great need of rest and sleep, but I sacrificed them both to my desire to be present at breakfast this morning. I am passionately fond of watching reactions and expressions the next morning. You cannot imagine what they were like this time. There was such embarrassment in her demeanor! She had such difficulty in walking! She kept her eyes lowered, and they were so big, with such dark rings around them! That round face had grown much longer! Nothing could have been more amusing. And for the first time her mother, alarmed by this extreme change, showed tender interest in her! And Madame de Tourvel bustled around her with great concern! Ah, those attentions are only lent; the day will come when they can be returned to her, and that day is not far off. Good-by, my fair friend.

LETTER 97

~ *From Cécile Volanges to the Marquise de Merteuil*

Château de ———, October 1, 17—

Oh, how distressed I am, Madame! How unhappy I am! Who will console me in my sorrow? Who will advise me in my difficulty? That Monsieur de Valmont . . . and Danceny! No, the thought of Danceny fills me with despair. . . . How can I describe it? How can I tell you? I do not know how to go about it. Yet my heart is full. . . . I must talk to someone, and you are the only one in whom I can, in whom I dare to confide. You have been so kind to me! But do not be kind to me now, I am not worthy of it. How can I say it? I do not want your kindness. Everyone here has shown great interest in me today. . . . They all increased my sorrow. I was so keenly aware that I did not deserve it! Scold me instead, give me a good scolding, because I am very guilty; but afterward, save me. If you do not have the kindness to advise me, I shall die of sorrow.

So let me tell you. . . . My hand trembles, as you can see; I can hardly write, I feel my cheeks aflame. . . . Ah, it is the red of shame! Well, I shall endure it; it will be the first punishment of my sin. Yes, I shall tell you everything.

First you must know that Monsieur de Valmont, who had been giving me Monsieur Danceny's letters, suddenly decided it was too difficult and wanted to have a key to my room. I can assure you I did not want to do it, but he wrote to Danceny about it, and Danceny wanted me to do it too, and it hurts me so much to refuse him anything, especially since my absence has been making him unhappy, that I finally gave in. I did not foresee the misfortune that would come from it.

Last night Monsieur de Valmont used the key to come into my room while I was asleep. It was so unexpected that I was very frightened when he woke me up, but since he spoke to me immediately, I recognized him and did not scream; and then it occurred to me at first that he might have come to give me a letter from Danceny. It was far from that. A short time later he tried to kiss me, and while I was defending myself, as was only natural, he managed to do something I would not have let him do for anything in the world. . . . But he wanted a kiss before he would stop. I had to consent, because what could I do? I had tried to call someone, but besides the fact that I was unable to, he had told me that if anyone came he would throw all the blame on me, and I knew it would be easy for him to do, because of the key. After the kiss he did not withdraw. He wanted another one, and I did not know what there was about it, but it made me all upset, and afterward it was even worse than before. Oh, it was very wrong! Then after that. . . . You will excuse me for not telling you the rest; but I am as unhappy as anyone can be.

What I blame myself most for, and yet I must talk to you about it, is that I am afraid I did not defend myself as much as I could have. I do not know how it happened. I certainly do not love Monsieur de Valmont, quite the contrary; but there were times when it was as though I did love him. . . . That did not prevent me from still saying no to him, as you may well suppose; but I realized that I was not acting the way I spoke, and it was as though I could not help it. Besides, I was terribly upset! If it is always so difficult to defend oneself, it must take a lot of practice! It is true that Monsieur de Valmont has a way of talking that makes it impossible to answer him. And then, would you believe it? When he went away it was as if I were sorry to see him go, and I was weak enough to consent to his coming back this evening: that grieves me more than all the rest.

Oh, in spite of that, I promise you I shall prevent him from coming! As soon as he was gone I realized how wrong I had been to consent. I cried all the rest of the time. I was especially sorry about Danceny! Every time I thought about him, my tears increased until they nearly choked me, and I went on thinking about him anyway. . . . And even now you can see the effects: my paper is all wet. No, I shall never be consoled, if only because of him. . . . Finally I was utterly exhausted, but I could not sleep for one minute. And when I got up this morning and looked at myself in the mirror, I was frightened to see how much I had changed.

My mother noticed it as soon as she saw me, and she asked me what was wrong. I began crying again. I thought she was going to scold me, and it might have hurt me less, but no: she spoke to me gently! I did not deserve it. She told me not to grieve so much. She did not know the reason for my grief. She said it would make me ill! There are times when I wish I were dead. I could not endure it. I threw myself into her arms, sobbing, and I said to her, ''Oh, Mama, your daughter is very unhappy!'' She could not help crying a little. And that only increased my sorrow. Fortunately she did not ask me why I was so unhappy; I would not have known what to tell her.

I beg you, Madame, to write to me as soon as you can and tell me what I ought to do, for I do not have the courage to think about anything and I can do nothing but grieve. Please send me your letter by Monsieur de Valmont, but if you write to him at the same time, please do not tell him that I have told you anything.

I have the honor of being, Madame, always with great friendship, your must humble and obedient servant. . . .

I do not dare to sign this letter.

LETTER 98

~   *From Madame de Volanges to the Marquise de Merteuil*

Château de ———, October 2, 17—

Only a few days ago, my charming friend, you asked me for consolation and advice: today it is my turn, and I make the same request of you as you made of me. I am truly in great distress, and I am afraid I may not have taken the best means of avoiding the sorrows I feel.

My daughter is the cause of my anxiety. Ever since my departure I had seen her always sad and despondent, but I had been expecting it and I had armed my heart with severity I judged to be necessary. I hoped that absence and distractions would soon destroy a love which I regarded as an error of childhood rather than as a real passion. However, far from having gained anything by our stay here, I have seen her sinking further and further into a dangerous melancholy, and I am seriously afraid that her health may be impaired. Particularly in the past few days, she has been changing visibly. Yesterday, especially, I was struck by her appearance, and everyone here was really alarmed.

What convinces me that she is deeply affected is that I now see her ready to overcome the shyness she has always had with me. Yesterday morning when I merely asked if she was ill, she threw herself into my arms and told me she was very unhappy; and she was sobbing! I cannot tell you how much she pained me; tears came into my eyes immediately, and I scarcely had time to turn away to prevent her from seeing them. Fortunately I was prudent enough not to ask her any questions and she did not dare to tell me anything more; but it is clear that it is her unfortunate passion which is tormenting her.

What shall I do if this continues? Shall I make my daughter unhappy forever? Shall I turn against her the most precious qualities of the soul: sensibility and constancy? Is it for that that I am her mother? And if I smother the natural sentiment which makes us wish the happiness of our children; if I regard as a weakness what I believe to be, on the contrary, the most sacred of our duties; if I force her choice, shall I not have to answer for the disastrous results it may have? What a use to make of maternal authority: to place one's daughter between crime and unhappiness!

My friend, I shall not imitate what I have so often condemned. To be sure, I tried to make a choice for my daughter; in doing so, I was only aiding her with my experience: I was fulfilling a duty, not exercising a right. But I would be betraying a duty if I were to dispose of her without regard for an inclination which I was unable to prevent from arising, and whose extent and duration neither she nor I can know. No, I shall not have her marry one man and love another, and I prefer to compromise my authority rather than her virtue.

I therefore think that I shall follow the wisest course and withdraw the commitment I have made to Monsieur de Gercourt. You have just seen my reasons; it seems to me that they must prevail over my promises. I shall go further and say that, in the present state of things, to fulfill my commitment would really be to break it. After all, if I owe it to my daughter not to reveal her secret to Monsieur de Gercourt, I at least owe it to him not to abuse the ignorance in which I am leaving him, and to do for him everything he himself would do if he were fully informed. Shall I unscrupulously betray him when he has placed his trust in my good faith? When he has honored me by choosing me as his second mother, shall I deceive him in the choice he wishes to make of the mother of his children? These true reflections, which I cannot reject, alarm me more than I can tell you.

With the misfortunes they make me dread, I compare my daughter, happy with the husband her heart has chosen, knowing her duties only by the pleasure she finds in fulfilling them; my son-in-law equally satisfied and congratulating himself in his choice every day; each of them finding happiness only in the happiness of the other, and the happiness of both uniting to increase my own. Should the hope of such a delightful future be sacrificed to vain considerations? And what are those which restrain me? Only material interests. What advantage would it be for my daughter to have been born rich if she must be the slave of wealth?

I admit that Monsieur de Gercourt is perhaps a better match than I could have hoped for my daughter; I even admit that I was extremely flattered by his choice of her. But after all, Danceny is from an equally good family, he yields nothing to Monsieur de Gercourt in the way of personal qualities, and he has over him the advantage of loving and being loved. He is not rich, it is true, but is not my daughter rich enough for them both? Why should I deprive her of the sweet satisfaction of enriching the man she loves?

Those marriages which are well calculated rather than well matched, which are called "suitable marriages," and in which each partner is indeed well suited to the other in everything except tastes and character—are they not the most fertile source of those violent scandals which are becoming more frequent every day? I prefer to delay; at least I shall have time to study my daughter, whom I do not know. I feel that I have the courage to cause her a momentary sorrow if it will bring her a more solid happiness; but it is not in my heart to risk plunging her into lifelong despair.

Those are the ideas which torment me, my dear friend, and on which I request your advice. Such stern matters contrast sharply with your charming gaiety and scarcely seem in keeping with your age; but your reason is so far in advance of your age! Your friendship will aid your prudence, and I do not fear that either will be refused to the maternal solicitude which implores them.

Good-by, my charming friend; never doubt the sincerity of my sentiments.

LETTER 99

﹏ *From the Vicomte de Valmont to the Marquise de Merteuil*

Château de ———, October 2, 17—, in the evening

More little events, my fair friend, but only scenes, not actions, so arm yourself with patience. Take a great deal of it, in fact, for while my Madame de Tourvel is advancing with such small steps, your pupil is retreating, and that is much worse. Well, I have the good sense to be amused by such trifles. I am really becoming quite accustomed to my stay here, and I can say that I have not had one moment of boredom in my old aunt's gloomy château. Do I not have enjoyments, privations, hope and uncertainty? What more does one have on a greater stage? Spectators? Give me time, they will not be lacking! Although they do not see me in action, I shall show them my work when it is completed; they will then have only to admire and applaud. Yes, they will applaud, for I can at last predict with certainty the time of my austere prude's downfall. This evening I witnessed the death agony of her virtue. Sweet weakness will soon reign in its place. I fix the time no later than our next private meeting. But I can already hear you crying out against my pride. I announce my victory, I boast of it in advance! There, there, calm yourself! To prove my modesty to you, I am going to begin with the story of my defeat.

Your pupil is truly a ridiculous little person! She is only a child and ought to be treated as such; one would be showing leniency toward her if she were only made to stand in a corner! Would you believe that after what happened between us night before last, after the friendly way we parted yesterday morning, when I tried to return to her room last night, as she agreed, I found the door locked from inside? What do you think of that? Such childishness sometimes occurs on the day before, but on the day after! . . . Is it not amusing?

At first, however, I did not laugh at it; never before had I felt so strongly the domination of my character. I had certainly gone to that rendezvous without pleasure, solely as a matter of procedure. My bed, which I needed greatly, seemed to me for the moment preferable to anyone else's, and I had left it with regret.

Yet no sooner did I encounter an obstacle than I was eager to overcome it. I was particularly humiliated at having been taken in by a child. I withdrew in great irritation, and, having decided to have nothing more to do with that stupid child or her affairs, I immediately wrote her a note which I intended to give her today, and in which I evaluated her at her true worth. But, as the saying goes, sleep brings wisdom: this morning I felt that since I had no choice of distractions here, I had to keep this one, so I tore up my severe note. Looking back on the incident, I am amazed that I should even have considered ending an adventure before acquiring the means of ruining its heroine. Where might we not be led by our first impulses? Happy are those who, like you, my fair friend, have trained themselves never to give in to them! In short, I postponed my vengeance; I made that sacrifice to your plans for Gercourt.

Now that I am no longer angry, I see your pupil's conduct only as ridiculous. I would like to know what she hopes to gain by it! I cannot fathom it; if it is only to defend herself, she has begun a little late. Some day she will have to tell me the answer to this enigma! I want very much to know it. Was it only that she was tired? That might actually be so, for no doubt she does not yet know that the arrows of love, like Achilles' lance, carry with them the remedy for the wounds they inflict. But no, after seeing the little grimaces she wore all day I am willing to bet that repentance has entered into it . . . something . . . something like virtue . . . Virtue! It is out of place in her. Let her leave it to the woman who was truly born for it, the only woman who is able to make it attractive, who might even make one love it! . . . Forgive me, my fair friend, but it was this very evening that the scene I am about to relate to you took place between Madame de Tourvel and me, and I still feel some emotion from it. I need to make an effort to distract myself from the impression it made on me; it was to help myself do so, in fact, that I began writing to you. You must make allowances for this first moment.

For several days Madame de Tourvel and I have been in agreement with regard to our sentiments; we were no longer disputing about anything except words. It was still "her friendship" which responded to "my love," but that conventional language did not basically alter things, and if we had remained on those terms I might have advanced less swiftly, but no less surely. Already there was no longer any question of sending me away, as she wanted to do at first; and as for our daily conversations, I devote my efforts to offering her the opportunity, and she devotes hers to seizing it.

Since our little meetings usually take place when we are out walking, today's terrible weather left me without hope. I was really annoyed by it; I did not foresee how much I was to gain from that mishap.

Being unable to go out for a walk, the others began playing cards as soon as they left the table, and since I play very little and am no longer necessary, I went up to my room at that time, with no other plan than to wait until the game was nearly over.

I was on my way to rejoin the company when I saw my charming lady going into her room. Whether from imprudence or weakness, she said to me in her gentle voice, "Where are you going? There is no one in the drawing room?" I needed nothing more, as you may well believe, to make me try to enter her room; I met with less resistance than I had expected. It is true that I took the precaution of beginning the conversation at the door, and in a casual tone; but as soon as we were inside I brought up the real topic and "spoke of my love to my beloved." Her first answer, though simple, seemed rather expressive to me: "Oh! Let's not talk about that here!" And she was trembling. Poor woman! She sees herself dying.

But she was wrong to be afraid. Some time ago, sure of succeeding one day or another, and seeing her use up so much strength in futile combats, I had decided to save my own strength and wait without effort until she surrendered from weariness. You will understand that I must have a complete triumph in this case, and that I want to owe nothing to opportunity. It was in accordance with this plan, and to enable myself to be pressing without committing myself too far, that I returned to the word "love," which she had so stubbornly refused; sure that she had no doubts about my ardor, I tried a more tender tone. Her refusal no longer irritated me, it afflicted me; did not my sensitive friend owe me some consolation?

While she was consoling me, her hand remained in mine; her pretty body leaned on my arm, and we were extremely close to each other. You have surely noticed how, in this situation, as the defense weakens, requests and refusals take place at closer range; how the head turns away and the eyes are lowered, while words, always spoken in a weak voice, become rare and broken. These precious symptoms unmistakably announce the consent of the soul, but it has seldom passed to the senses yet. In fact, I think it is always dangerous to make any definite attempt then, because that state of abandonment is never without a very sweet pleasure, so that a woman cannot be forced to leave it without producing an ill-humor which invariably strengthens her defense.

But in this case prudence was all the more necessary to me because I had good reason to be apprehensive of the fear which this forgetfulness of herself would not fail to arouse in my tender dreamer. So I did not even demand that the avowal I was requesting be spoken: a look would be sufficient; one look and I would be happy.

My fair friend, those beautiful eyes were raised to mine, those heavenly lips even said, "Yes! I . . ." But suddenly her eyes were dimmed, her voice failed, and that adorable woman fell into my arms. Scarcely had I received her when she tore herself away from me with convulsive strength and, wild-eyed, raising her hands to heaven, she cried out, "God! Oh, my God, save me!" And immediately, quicker than lightning, she fell to her knees ten paces away from me. I could hear that she was almost choking. I went toward her to help her, but she took my hands and, bathing them in tears, sometimes even embracing my knees, she said, "Yes, it will be you, it will be you who will save me! You do not want me to die! Leave me, save me, leave me, in the name of God, leave me!" And these incoherent words escaped from her painfully, through her redoubled sobs. Meanwhile she was holding me so tightly that I could not have gone away. Finally I gathered my strength and lifted her in my arms. Her tears ceased at the same moment; she stopped speaking, all her limbs stiffened, and this storm was succeeded by violent convulsions.

I confess that I was deeply moved, and I think I would have consented to her request even if circumstances had not forced me to. In any case, after giving her some assistance I left her as she begged me to do, and I am glad I did. Already I have almost received my reward for it.

I expected that, as on the day of my first declaration, she would not show herself all evening. But at about eight o'clock she came down to the drawing room and merely announced to the company that she had been extremely indisposed. Her face was downcast, her voice was weak and her bearing was stiff; but her eyes were gentle, and they were often fixed on me. When her refusal to play cards obliged me to take her place, she sat down beside me. During supper she remained alone in the drawing room. When I returned with the others, I thought I noticed that she had been crying. To make sure, I told her it seemed to me that she had again been suffering from her indisposition, to which she obligingly replied, "That illness doesn't go as quickly as it comes!" Finally, when we retired, I gave her my hand, and at the door of her room she pressed it strongly. It is true that there seemed to be something involuntary in this movement, but so much the better: it is one more proof of my domination.

I am willing to bet that she is now delighted to have reached this point: she has paid the price of her pleasure and she now has only to enjoy it! Perhaps while I am writing to you she is already thinking about that sweet idea! And even if, on the contrary, she is thinking about a new plan of defense, do we not know very well what becomes of all such plans? I ask you, can it be any later than our next private meeting? I fully expect her to make some difficulties in granting it, but once the first step has been taken, these austere prudes are unable to stop. Their love is a real explosion; resistance gives it greater strength. My own shy and pious prude would run after me if I stopped running after her.

In short, my fair friend, I shall soon come to call on you to keep your word. You have no doubt not forgotten what you have promised me after my success: an infidelity to your Chevalier. Are you ready? For my part, I desire it as much as if we had never known each other. Or perhaps knowing you is a reason for desiring it all the more: "I am just, not gallant."*

It will also be my first infidelity to my solemn conquest, and I promise you that I shall make use of the first pretext to absent myself from her for twenty-four hours. That will be her punishment for having kept me away from you so long. Do you realize that I have been occupied with this adventure for over two months? Yes, two months and three days. It is true that I am counting tomorrow, since it will not be really consummated until then. That reminds me that Madame de B—— resisted for three whole months. I am glad to see that forthright coquetry has more defense than austere virtue.

Good-by, my fair friend; I must leave you, because it is very late. This letter has led me further than I expected, but since I am sending someone to Paris tomorrow, I wanted to take advantage of it to let you share your friend's joy one day sooner.

*Voltaire: *Nanine*.

LETTER 100

∼   *From the Vicomte de Valmont to the Marquise de Merteuil*

Château de ———, October 3, 17—

My friend, I have been taken in, betrayed, ruined: Madame de Tourvel has gone. She has gone, and I did not know it! I was not there to oppose her departure, to reproach her for her infamous betrayal! Ah, do not believe that I would have let her go! She would have stayed; yes, she would have stayed, even if I had had to use violence. But in my credulous confidence I was sleeping peacefully; I was sleeping and the thunderbolt fell upon me. No, I understand nothing about her departure; I must give up trying to understand women.

When I remember yesterday! . . . What am I saying? Only last night! Those gentle eyes, that tender voice, that pressure on my hand! And during that time she was planning to run away from me! Oh, women, women! And you complain if you are deceived! Yes, every treachery we employ is stolen from you.

What pleasure I shall have in avenging myself! I shall find that treacherous woman again; I shall regain my power over her. If love was enough to make me find means for it, what will it not do when it is aided by vengeance? I shall see her at my knees again, trembling and bathed in tears, crying out to me for mercy in her deceitful voice; and I shall be without pity.

What is she doing now? What is she thinking? Perhaps she is congratulating herself on having deceived me and, faithful to the tastes of her sex, finding that this is the sweetest pleasure of all. The spirit of ruse has effortlessly achieved what vaunted virtue was unable to do. What a fool I was! I feared her chastity when I should have feared her bad faith!

And I am forced to swallow my resentment! I dare to show only tender sorrow when my heart is filled with rage! I see myself reduced to imploring a rebellious woman who has eluded my domination! Ought I to be so humiliated? And by whom? By a timid woman without experience in combat. Of what use is it to me to have established myself in her heart, to have inflamed her with all the fires of love, to have stirred her senses to fever pitch, if she is now tranquil in her retreat, if she can now take more pride in her flight than I in my victories? And shall I endure it? My friend, you do not believe it; you cannot have such a humiliating idea of me!

But what fatality attaches me to that woman? Are there not a hundred others who desire my attentions? Will they not be eager to respond to them? Even if none of them is worth as much as she, am I not offered sweet enough pleasures by the attraction of variety, the charm of new conquests and the glory of their number? Why run after a pleasure which eludes us and neglect those which present themselves to us? Ah, why? . . . I do not know, but I feel it strongly.

There will be no happiness or rest for me until I possess that woman whom I hate and love with equal fury. My fate will be intolerable to me until I am in control of hers. Then, tranquil and satisfied, I shall see her, in her turn, shaken by the storms that now agitate me, and I shall stir up a thousand others as well. Hope and fear, mistrust and confidence, all the evils invented by hatred, all the goods granted by love: I want them to fill her heart, to follow one another in it at my will. That time will come. . . . But what work still remains! How close I was to it yesterday, and how far I am from it today! How can I bring it closer? I do not dare to take any steps; I feel that I must be calmer before making my decision, and my blood is now boiling in my veins.

What redoubles my torment is the composure with which everyone here answers my questions about that event, about its cause, about all its extraordinary aspects. . . . No one knows anything, no one wants to know anything; they would scarcely even have mentioned it if I had been willing to talk about something else. When I learned the news this morning, I hurried to Madame de Rosemonde, who told me with the coldness of her age that it was the natural result of the indisposition Madame de Tourvel had felt yesterday, that she had been afraid of an illness, and that she had preferred to be in her own home. It seems quite simple to her; she would have done the same, she told me—as though there could be anything in common between them, between a woman who might as well die now and the woman who is the charm and torment of my life!

Madame de Volanges, whom I at first suspected of being an accomplice, seems to be upset only at not having been consulted in the matter. I admit that I am glad she did not have the pleasure of harming me. It proves to me that she does not have Madame de Tourvel's confidence as much as I feared, which means that I have one less enemy. How happy she would be if she knew Madame de Tourvel had fled from me! How puffed up with pride she would have been if it had been done at her advice! How her self-importance would have redoubled! My God, how I hate her! Oh, I shall resume my affair with her daughter! I want to work on her as I please, so I think I shall stay here some time; at least that is what I have been inclined to do by the few reflections I have been able to make.

Do you not think that after such a vigorous action my ingrate must dread my presence? If it has occurred to her that I might follow her, she will surely give orders that I am not to be admitted into her house, and I do not want to let her become accustomed to using that means any more than I want to suffer the humiliation of it. On the contrary, I prefer to inform her that I am staying here. I shall even beg her to come back, and when she is fully convinced of my absence I shall come to her house; we shall see how she reacts to that meeting with me. I ought to delay it to increase its effect, and I do not yet know whether I shall have the patience: I have opened my mouth a dozen times today to call for my horses. But I shall make an effort to control myself: I promise to stay here until your reply arrives; I only ask you, my fair friend, not to keep me waiting for it.

What would annoy me most would be not to know what is happening; but my servant, who is in Paris, has a right to some access to her maid: he will be able to help me. I am sending him instructions and money. I am taking the liberty of enclosing both in this letter; please send them to him by one of your servants, with orders to give them to him in person. That precaution is necessary because the scoundrel has a habit of never receiving letters from me when they tell him to do something that strikes him as bothersome, and for the moment he does not seem to be as enamored of his conquest as I would like him to be.

Good-by, my fair friend; if any good ideas occur to you, any ways of hastening my progress, tell me about them. I have experienced more than once how useful your friendship can be to me, and I am now experiencing it once again, for I have felt calmer since I began writing to you: at least I am talking to someone who understands me, and not to the automata with whom I have been vegetating since this morning. Really, the longer I live, the more I am tempted to believe that you and I are the only people in the world who are worth anything.

LETTER 101

~ *From the Vicomte de Valmont to Azolan, his valet*
    (Enclosed in the preceding letter)

Château de ———, October 3, 17—

You must be an imbecile not to have known when you left this morning that Madame de Tourvel was leaving also, or not to have told me about it if you did know. What good does it do for you to spend my money getting drunk with the footmen, and to make yourself agreeable to the maids during the time you should be giving to my service, if I am no better informed of what is taking place? But such are your negligences! I warn you that if there is one more in this affair, it will be your last in my service.

You must tell me everything about Madame de Tourvel: the state of her health; whether she sleeps well; if she is sad or cheerful; if she goes out often, and whom she visits; if she receives company at home, and who comes to see her; how she spends her time; whether she is irritable with her maids, particularly the one she brought here; what she does when she is alone; if, when she reads, she continues steadily or stops to daydream now and then; and the same when she writes. Be sure to become friendly with the servant who takes her letters to the post office. Offer to perform that duty for him often, and when he accepts, mail only those letters which seem unimportant to you, and send the others to me, especially those addressed to Madame de Volanges, if there are any.

Arrange to go on being your Julie's lover for some time yet. If she has another, as you thought, make her agree to share herself; and do not let yourself be carried away by ridiculous squeamishness: you will be in the same position as many others who are worth much more than you. However, if your second becomes too bothersome, if you see, for example, that he takes up too much of Julie's time during the day and that she is therefore with her mistress less often, find some means of making him go away; or pick a quarrel with him: do not fear the consequences, I shall support you. Whatever you do, do not leave that house. It is by constant attention that one sees everything, and sees clearly. If one of the servants should happen to be dismissed, apply for his position, saying that you are no longer in my service, and that you have left me in order to seek a quieter and more orderly house. Try to get yourself accepted. I shall keep you in my service nevertheless; it will be the same as it was with the Duchesse de ———, and later Madame de Tourvel will reward you in the same way.

If you had enough adroitness and zeal, these instructions would be sufficient, but to make up for your lack of both, I am sending you some money. The enclosed note authorizes you, as you will see, to draw five hundred francs from my agent; for I do not doubt that you are penniless. Use as much of this sum as will be necessary to persuade Julie to establish a correspondence with me. The rest will serve to buy drinks for the servants. Try as much as possible to have this take place in the doorkeeper's quarters, so that he will be glad to see you come. But do not forget that I intend to pay for your services, not your pleasures.

Accustom Julie to observing and reporting everything, even things that seem to her only trivial details. It will be better for her to write ten useless sentences than to omit a single interesting one; and often what appears to be unimportant is not so. Since I must be informed immediately if something happens which you think deserves attention, as soon as you have read this letter tell Philippe to take the errand horse, go to ———* and stay there until further orders, he will be a relay in case one is needed. For ordinary correspondence the post will be sufficient.

Be careful not to lose this letter. Reread it every day, to make sure you have not forgotten anything and that you still have it. In short, do everything that one ought to do when one is honored by my confidence. You know that if I am satisfied with you, you will be equally satisfied with me.

LETTER 102

~ *From Madame de Tourvel to Madame de Rosemonde*

October 3, 17—, at one o'clock in the morning

You will be greatly surprised, Madame, to learn that I have left your house so suddenly. My action will seem most extraordi-

—————
*A village halfway between Paris and Madame de Rosemonde's château.

nary to you; but your surprise will be still greater when you know the reasons for it! Perhaps you will feel that in confiding them to you, I am not respecting the tranquillity necessary to your age, that I am even departing from the sentiments of veneration to which you are entitled on so many accounts. Ah, forgive me, Madame, but my heart is oppressed; it needs to pour out its grief to a friend who is both gentle and prudent, and what other friend than you could it choose? Consider me as your child. Show me the kindness of a mother; I implore it. Perhaps my feelings for you give me some right to it.

Where is the time when, wholly absorbed in those praiseworthy feelings, I knew nothing of those which arouse in the soul the mortal turmoil I now feel, and take away the strength to combat them at the same time as they impose the duty of doing so? Ah, this fateful visit has ruined me! . . .

How shall I tell you? I am in love, yes, I am madly in love. Alas, that word which I have just written for the first time, that word so often requested without being obtained—I would give my life for the sweetness of being able to say it only once to the man who inspires it, yet I must constantly refuse it! He will still doubt my feelings; he will think he has reason to complain of them. I am so unhappy! Why is it not as easy for him to read in my heart as to reign over it? Yes, my suffering would be less if he knew how great it is; but even you, whom I am telling about it, can have only a weak idea of it.

In a few moments I am going to flee from him and hurt him deeply. While he thinks himself still close to me, I shall already be far from him; at the hour when I used to see him every day, I shall be in a place where he has never been, and where I must not allow him to come. All my preparations have been made; everything is here, before my eyes; I cannot rest them on anything that does not announce my cruel departure. Everything is ready, except myself! . . . The more my heart refuses this departure, the more it proves to me the necessity of submitting to it.

And I shall certainly submit to it; it is better to die than to live in guilt. I feel that I am already too guilty; I have saved only my chastity: my virtue has vanished. I hesitate to confess it, but I am indebted only to his magnanimity for what I have left. Intoxicated with the pleasure of seeing and hearing him, and with the greater happiness of being able to make him happy, I was helpless and without strength; I scarcely had enough to combat, I no longer had any to resist; I shuddered at my danger without being able to flee from it. Then he saw my distress and took pity on me. How could I not cherish him? I owe him much more than my life.

Ah, if in staying near him I had to tremble only for my life, do not think that I would ever consent to leave him! What is life to me without him? Would I not be all too glad to lose it? I am doomed to make him and myself unhappy forever; to dare neither to complain nor to console him; to defend myself every day against him and against myself; to turn my efforts to causing him sorrow, when I would like to devote them all to his happiness—is not living in this way the same as dying a thousand deaths? Such will be my fate; but I shall endure it, I shall have the courage. Receive my oath to it, you whom I choose as my mother!

Receive also my oath never to conceal any of my actions from you; receive it, I beg you; I ask it of you as an aid I need: thus committed to telling you everything, I shall become accustomed to thinking of myself as being always in your presence. Your virtue will replace mine. Surely I shall never consent to blush before your eyes; restrained by that powerful curb, I shall cherish in you the indulgent friend in whom my weakness confides, and at the same time I shall honor the guardian angel who will save me from shame.

Having to make this request is already sufficient shame. It is the inevitable result of my presumptuous self-confidence! Why was I not sooner afraid of that inclination I felt growing within me? Why did I flatter myself that I could control it or overcome it at will? Fool that I was! How little I knew about love! If I had opposed it more carefully, it might have gained less power over me! Perhaps this departure would not then have been necessary; or even if I had submitted to this painful course, I might have been able to avoid breaking off entirely a relationship which it would have sufficed to make less frequent. But to lose everything at once! . . . And forever! Oh, my friend . . . But even as I write to you I stray into criminal wishes! Ah, I must leave! May these involuntary errors at least be expiated by my sacrifices.

Good-by, my estimable friend; love me as your daughter, adopt me as such; and have no doubt that, despite my weakness, I would rather die than make myself unworthy of your choice.

LETTER 103

~ *From Madame de Rosemonde to Madame de Tourvel*

Château de ———, October 3, 17—

I was, my dear beauty, more distressed by your departure than surprised by its cause; long experience and the interest you inspire were enough to enlighten me as to the state of your heart; and, to be frank with you, your letter told me nothing, or almost nothing, that I did not know already. If it had been my only source of information, I would still not know with whom you are in love, for in speaking to me of *him* the whole time, you did not write his name once. But it was not necessary; I know very well who he is. I noticed it only because I remembered that that has always been the style of love. I see that it is still the same as in the past.

I scarcely thought I would ever find myself obliged to return to memories so far away from me and so foreign to my age, yet since yesterday I have really given a great deal of attention to them, because of my desire to find something in them which might be useful to you. But what can I do except to admire and pity you? I praise the wise decision you have made; but it frightens me because I conclude that you have judged it to be necessary, and when a woman has reached that point it is very difficult for her to stay away from the man to whom her heart is constantly drawing her nearer.

But do not be discouraged. Nothing should be impossible for your fine soul; and even if some day you should have the misfortune to succumb (God forbid!), believe me, my dear beauty, you can at least keep for yourself the consolation of having fought with all your strength. And then, what human wisdom cannot do, divine grace brings to pass when it pleases. Perhaps you are about to receive its aid; and your virtue, tried in these agonizing combats, will emerge purer and more radiant than ever. Hope that you will receive tomorrow the strength you do not have today. Do not look forward to it in order to rest on it, but in order to encourage yourself to use all the strength you have now.

Although I must leave to Providence the task of aiding you in a danger against which I can do nothing, I shall nevertheless support and comfort you as much as I can. I shall not relieve your pain, but I shall share it. For that purpose I shall be glad to have you confide in me. I feel that your heart must need to unburden itself. I open my own to you; age has not yet chilled it to the point of being insensitive to friendship. You will find it always ready to receive you. It will be a poor relief for your suffering, but at least you will not weep alone; and when that unfortunate love gains too much power over you and forces you to speak of it, it will be better to speak of it with me than with *him*. Now I am speaking as you do; I do not think either of us can ever bring herself to name him; but we understand each other.

I do not know whether I am doing right to tell you that he seemed to be keenly affected by your departure; it would perhaps be wiser not to mention this to you, but I do not like that wisdom which grieves one's friends. However, I am forced not to speak of him at greater length. My failing sight and trembling hand do not permit me long letters when I must write them myself.

And so good-by, my dear beauty; good-by, my sweet child; yes, I gladly adopt you as my daughter, and you have everything needed to make the pride and pleasure of a mother.

LETTER 104

~ *From the Marquise de Merteuil to Madame de Volanges*

Paris, October 4, 17—

Really, my dear and good friend, it was difficult for me to restrain my pride when I read your letter. You honor me with your complete confidence! You even go so far as to ask my advice! Ah, I am very fortunate if I deserve that favorable opinion on your part, if I do not owe it only to the bias of friendship. But no matter what its basis may be, it is no less precious to my heart; and having obtained it is in my eyes only one more reason for making greater efforts to deserve it. I shall therefore (but without presuming to give you advice) freely set forth my way of thinking. I mistrust it because it differs from yours, but you will judge my reasons when I have given them to you, and if you condemn them I accept your judgment in advance. I shall at least have the wisdom not to think myself wiser than you.

However, if in this one instance my opinion should be preferable to yours, the cause must be sought in the illusions of maternal love. Since that sentiment is praiseworthy, it must be present in you. Indeed, it is clearly recognizable in the decision you are tempted to make! It is thus that, if you sometimes err, it is always in the choice of virtues.

It seems to me that prudence is the virtue that ought to be preferred when we are determining the fate of others, particularly when it is to be determined by a sacred and indissoluble bond like that of marriage. It is then that an equally wise and tender mother should, as you say so well, aid her daughter with her experience. Now I ask you, what does she have to do in that case if not to distinguish, for her daughter, between what is pleasing and what is proper?

Would it not be debasing maternal authority, would it not be annihilating it, to subordinate it to a frivolous inclination whose illusory power is felt only by those who fear it, and vanishes as soon as it is despised? For my part, I confess that I have never believed in those overwhelming, irresistible passions which seem to be so widely accepted as the general excuse for our dissoluteness. I do not understand how an inclination which is born one moment and dies the next can have more strength than the inalterable principles of purity, decency and modesty; nor do I understand how a woman who betrays them can be justified by what she calls her passion, any more than a thief could be justified by the passion for money, or a murderer by that of vengeance.

What woman can say that she has never had to struggle? But I have always tried to convince myself that the will to resist was enough to make resistance possible, and so far, at least, my experience has confirmed my opinion. What would virtue be without the duties it imposes? Its worship is in our sacrifices, its reward is in our hearts. These truths can be denied only by those who have an interest in disregarding them, and who, already depraved, hope to create a momentary illusion by trying to justify their bad conduct by bad reasons.

But can this be feared from a simple and timid child, a child born of you, and whose pure, modest upbringing can only have strenghtened her natural goodness? Yet it is to that fear, which I dare to call humiliating for your daughter, that you want to sacrifice the advantageous marriage your prudence has arranged for her! I am very fond of Danceny, and for a long time, as you know, I have seen little of Monsieur de Gercourt; but my friendship for the one and my indifference to the other do not prevent me from being aware of the enormous difference between them as prospective husbands.

Their birth is equal, I agree; but one has no fortune and the other's is so great that even without good birth it would have sufficed to lead him anywhere. I admit that money does not make happiness; but it must also be admitted that it greatly facilitates it. Mademoiselle de Volanges is, as you say, rich enough for two; however, the income of sixty thousand francs which she will enjoy would not be very great if she bore the name of Danceny and had to establish and maintain a household in keeping with it. We are no longer in the days of Madame de Sévigné. Luxury absorbs everything; we condemn it, but we must imitate it, and the superfluous eventually deprives us of the necessary.

As for the personal qualities to which you attach great importance, and with good reason, Monsieur de Gercourt is certainly irreproachable in that respect, and he has already proved it. I like to believe, and I do believe, that Danceny yields to him in nothing; but are we equally sure of him? It is true that so far he appears to be free of the faults of his age, and that despite the tone of our times he shows a taste for good society which allows one to augur well of him; but who knows whether he does not owe this apparent respectability to the mediocrity of his fortune? Although a man may fear to be dishonest or licentious, it takes money to be a gambler or a libertine, and he may still be attracted to certain vices even when he dreads their excesses. In short, Danceny would not be the first man who had frequented good society solely because he could do nothing better.

I am not saying (God forbid!) that I believe all this of him; but there would always be that risk, and think of how you would have to blame yourself if the outcome were unfortunate! What would you reply to your daughter if she said to you, "Mother, I was young and inexperienced; I was carried away by an error that was pardonable at my age; but heaven, which had foreseen my weakness, had given me a wise mother to remedy it and protect me from it. Why, then, did you forget your prudence and consent to my misfortune? Was it for me to choose a husband when I knew nothing about marriage? Even if I had wanted to, would it not have been your duty to oppose me? But I never had that foolish desire. Perfectly willing to obey you, I awaited your choice with respectful resignation; I never departed from the submission I owed to you, and yet I am now enduring the punishment that ought to befall only rebellious children. Ah, your weakness has ruined me. . . .'' Perhaps her respect would stifle these complaints, but maternal love would sense them, and even though her tears were concealed from you, they would nevertheless flow upon your heart. Where would you then seek consolation? Would it be in that mad love against which you should have protected her, and by which, on the contrary, you had allowed yourself to be led astray?

I do not know, my dear friend, whether I have too strong a prejudice against that passion, but I consider it dangerous, even in marriage. Not that I object to that sweet and honorable sentiment which may arise to embellish the conjugal bond and soften, as it were, the duties it imposes; but the bond should not be formed by such a sentiment; a lifetime choice should not be made on the basis of a momentary illusion. After all, in order to choose we ought to compare, and how can we compare when we are entirely preoccupied with a single person, when we cannot know him, since we are plunged into rapture and blindness.

I have, of course, known a number of women afflicted with this dangerous illness, and some of them have confided in me. From what they say, it would seem that each one of them is in love with a man who is perfect in every way; but those illusory perfections exist only in their imagination. Their feverish minds dream of nothing but charms and virtues, and they lavishly bestow them on the man of their choice, covering him with godlike raiment that is often worn by an abject model; but in any case, no sooner have they dressed him in it than they are duped by their own handiwork and prostrate themselves to worship it.

Either your daughter does not love Danceny or she is experiencing that same illusion; it is common to them both, if their love is mutual. Thus your reason for uniting them forever is reduced to the certainty that they do not and cannot know each other. "But," you may say, "do Monsieur de Gercourt and my daughter know each other any better?" No, they do not; but at least they do not delude each other: they are merely ignorant of each other. What occurs in that case between a husband and wife, whom I assume to be virtuous? Each studies the other, is circumspect with him, seeks and soon perceives what must be yielded to his tastes and wishes for their mutual contentment. These slight sacrifices are made without pain because they are reciprocal and have been foreseen. They soon create mutual good will, and habit, which strengthens all inclinations it does not destroy, gradually gives rise to that sweet friendship and tender confidence which, joined to esteem, form what seems to me the real and solid happiness of marriage.

The illusions of love my be sweeter, but who does not know that they are also less durable? And what dangers are brought by the moment that destroys them! It is then that the slightest defects seem offensive and intolerable, by their contrast with the idea of perfection which had misled the two lovers before their marriage. Yet each thinks that only the other has changed, and that he himself still has all the qualities that were attributed to him in a moment of error. He is surprised to see that he no longer exercises the attraction he has ceased to feel; he is humiliated by this: wounded vanity embitters the mind, increases faults, produces ill-humor and gives birth to hatred; and frivolous pleasures are finally paid for by long misfortunes.

Such, my dear friend, is my way of thinking with regard to the subject that now concerns us; I am not defending it, I am merely setting it forth: it is for you to decide. But if you persist in your opinion, I ask you to let me know the reasons that will have prevailed over mine. I shall be glad to be enlightened by you, and above all I shall be glad to be reassured as to the fate of your charming daughter, whose happiness I ardently desire, because of my friendship for her as well as that which unites me to you for life.

LETTER 105

~   *From the Marquise de Merteuil to Cécile Volanges*

Paris, October 4, 17—

Well, my child, you are now overcome with anger and shame, and Monsieur de Valmont is a very wicked man, is he not? What! He dares to treat you as the woman he loves best! He has taught you what you were dying to know! Such conduct is indeed unforgivable. And for your part, you wanted to keep your chastity for your beloved (who does not abuse it); you cherish only the pains of love, not its pleasures! It would take nothing more to make you an excellent character in a novel. Passion, misfortune, virtue above all—so many beautiful things! It is true that one is sometimes bored in such radiant surroundings, but one has the satisfaction of inflicting equal boredom on others.

Poor little girl, how she is to be pitied! She had dark rings around her eyes the next morning! And what will you say when it is your lover's eyes that are haggard? Yours will not always be thus, my fair angel: all men are not Valmonts. And then to be afraid to raise those eyes! Oh, you were quite right: everyone would have read your adventure in them! But if that were always so, believe me, our women and even our girls would have more modest gazes.

Despite the praises I am forced to give you, as you see, it must still be admitted that you failed in what would have been your master stroke: to tell your mother everything. You began so well! You had already thrown yourself into her arms, you were sobbing, she was weeping also: what a touching scene! And what a pity not to have completed it! Your tender mother would have been delighted to aid your virtue by shutting you up in a convent for the rest of your life, and there you could have loved Danceny as much as you liked, without rivals and without sin; you could have indulged your despair at leisure, and Valmont would certainly not have come to trouble your sorrow with annoying pleasures.

Seriously, how is it possible, at the age of fifteen, to be as childish as you are? You are right to say that you do not deserve my kindness. Yet I would like to be your friend: you may need one with your mother you have, and the husband she wants to give you! But if you do not grow up a little more, what is to be done with you? What hope is there if what usually develops a girl's understanding takes yours away instead?

If you could force yourself to reason for a moment, you would soon realize that, rather than complaining, you ought to be glad. But you are ashamed, and that troubles you! Well, you can put your mind at rest: the shame of love is like its pain: it comes only once. It may still be feigned later, but it is no longer felt. But the pleasure remains, and that is certainly something. In fact I seem to discern through your chatter that you might count it for a great deal. Come now, be honest. That agitation which prevented you from "acting the way you spoke," which made you find it "so difficult to defend yourself," which made you feel "as though you were sorry" to see Valmont go—did it come from shame, or was it caused by pleasure? And his "way of talking that makes it impossible to answer him"—might it not come from his way of acting? Ah, little girl, you are lying, and lying to your friend! That is not right. But let us say no more about it.

What would be a pleasure for anyone, and might be nothing more than that, becomes in your situation a real stroke of good fortune. Placed between a mother by whom it is important for you to be loved and a young man by whom you want to be loved forever, how can you not see that the only way to achieve those opposite ends is to occupy yourself with a third party? Diverted by your new adventure, you will give your mother the impression that you are sacrificing an inclination that displeases her out of deference to her, and at the same time you will be acquiring with Danceny the honor of long resistance. While constantly assuring him of your love, you will not grant him the final proof of it. He will credit your virtue with these refusals, which are not at all painful in your situation. He may complain of them, but he will love you all the more, and in order to gain the double merit of sacrificing love in your mother's eyes and resisting it in Danceny's, you will have only to enjoy its pleasures. How many women have lost their reputation who would have carefully preserved it if they had been able to do so in such a way!

Does not this course which I am proposing to you seem the most reasonable as well as the most agreeable? Do you know what you have gained by the one you have followed so far? Your mother has attributed your increase of sadness to an increase of love, she is outraged by it, and she is waiting only to be more certain of it before punishing you for it. She has just written to me; she will try everything to make you admit it yourself. She says she may go so far as to propose Danceny to you as your husband in order to make you speak. If you let yourself be misled by that deceitful tenderness and reply according to your heart, you will soon be shut up in a convent for a long time, perhaps forever, and you will be able to weep for your blind credulity at leisure.

You must use another ruse to combat the one she wants to use against you. Begin by showing less sadness, by making her believe you are thinking less about Danceny. She will be all the more easily convinced of it because it is the usual effect of absence, and she will be all the more pleased with you because she will see it as an opportunity to congratulate herself on her prudence, which suggested that means to her. But if she still has some doubt and insists on testing you by speaking to you of marriage, withdraw into complete submission, as a wellborn girl should. After all, what will you be risking? For what one does with a husband, one is as good as another, and the most disagreeable husband is still less bothersome than a mother.

Once she is more pleased with you, your mother will finally conclude your marriage. Then, freer in your actions, you will be able to leave Valmont and take Danceny, or even keep them both, as you choose. For remember this: your Danceny is amiable, but he is one of those men whom one can have whenever and as long as one wishes, so you need not worry about him. It is not the same with Valmont: he is difficult to keep and dangerous to leave. With him you need great adroitness or, failing that, great docility. But also you will be very fortunate if you can succeed in attaching him to you as a friend. He will immediately place you in the first rank of our fashionable women. That is how one acquires prominence in the world, not by blushing and weeping, as you did when your nuns made you eat your dinner kneeling.

If you are wise, you will try to become reconciled with Valmont, who must be very angry with you; and since we must be able to make up for our foolish mistakes, do not be afraid to make advances to him: you will soon learn that if men make the first advances to us, we are nearly always obliged to make the next ones. You have a pretext for them: you must not keep this letter, and I insist that you give it to Valmont as soon as you have read it. However, do not forget to reseal it first. You must be allowed all the merit of the step you will take with regard to him: it must not seem to have been suggested to you; and there is no one in the world except you with whom I am friendly enough to speak as I am now doing.

Good-by, my beautiful angel; follow my advice, and you will let me know whether or not you are glad you did.

P.S.—By the way, I was forgetting. . . . One word more. Try to be more careful with your style. You still write like a child. I can see why: it is because you say everything you think, and nothing you do not think. That is all very well between you and me, who should have nothing to hide from each other, but not with everyone! Especially not with Danceny! You would always seem like a little fool. You must realize that when you write to someone it is for him and not for you, so you must try to say less what you are thinking than what will please him more.

Good-by, my heart; I kiss you instead of scolding you, in the hope that you will be more sensible.

LETTER 106

~ *From the Marquise de Merteuil to the Vicomte de Valmont*

Paris, October 4, 17—

Wonderful, Vicomte! This time I love you madly! Moreover, after the first of your two letters the second one was to be expected, so it did not surprise me; and while you were already proud of your future success, while you were soliciting your reward for it and asking me if I was ready, I saw clearly that I had no need to hurry. Yes, I give you my word that as I read your fine account of that tender scene which had so "deeply moved" you, and as I saw your restraint, worthy of the best days of knighthood, I said to myself a dozen times, "He's failed!"

But it could not have been otherwise. What do you expect a poor woman to do when she surrenders and is not taken? In such a case she must at least save her honor, and that is what your Madame de Tourvel has done. I see that the course she has taken is really not ineffective, and I intend to use it on my own account at the next fairly serious opportunity that occurs; but I assure you that if the man for whom I make the effort does not take advantage of it any better than you have done, he can certainly give up all hope of ever succeeding with me.

So you are now absolutely reduced to nothing! And between two women, one of whom had already reached the day after, while the other asked nothing better than to do the same! You will think I am boasting and say that it is easy to prophesy after the event, but I can swear to you that I expected it. The truth is that you really do not have the genius of your conditon; you know only what you have learned, and you invent nothing, so as soon as circumstances no longer fit into your usual formulas and you are forced to leave the beaten path, you are as bewildered as a schoolboy. A childish reaction on the part of one woman, and a return of prudishness on the part of the other, are enough to disconcert you because they are not encountered every day, and you can neither forestall nor remedy them. Ah, Vicomte, Vicomte! You are teaching me not to judge men by their successes, and soon one will have to say of you, "He was brave on such and such a day." And when you have piled stupidity upon stupidity, you come to me! It would seem that I had nothing to do except to correct your mistakes. It is true that that would be enough to keep me busy.

In any case, one of those two adventures was undertaken against my will, so I shall take no part in it; as for the other, since you began it partly out of consideration for me, I shall make it my business. The letter I am enclosing, which you will read first, then give to your little Cécile, is more than sufficient to bring her back to you; but please devote some attention to her, and let us make her the despair of both her mother and Gercourt. There is no reason to be afraid of giving her an overdose. I see clearly that she will not be frightened; and once our plans for her have been carried out, she will become whatever she can.

I have lost all interest in her. For a time I thought of at least making her a subordinate intriguer and taking her to play secondary parts under me, but I now see that she is not suitable material. She has a foolish ingenuousness that has resisted even the medicine you have administered, which scarcely ever fails. In my opinion, it is the most dangerous malady a woman can have. It particularly indicates a weakness of character which is nearly always incurable and stands in the way of everything, so that if we were to devote our efforts to training this little girl for intrigue, we would only make her a loose woman. I know of nothing so abject as those women who are wanton through stupidity, who yield without knowing how or why, solely because they are attacked and do not know how to resist. Such women are nothing but pleasure machines.

You will tell me that we have only to make her into one of them, and that that will be enough for our plans. True enough, but let us not forget that everyone soon comes to know the springs and levers of those machines, so that in order to make use of this one without danger, we must hurry, stop in time, then break it. We shall have no difficulty in finding ways of getting rid of her, and Gercourt will always have her shut up in a convent whenever we choose. After all, when he can no longer doubt his humiliation, when it has become thoroughly public and notorious, what will it matter to us if he avenges himself, as long as he is not consoled? What I am saying about the husband, you no doubt think about the mother; so it is as good as done.

This course, which I believe to be the best, and which I have decided to take, has made me lead the young lady rather swiftly, as you will see from my letter. This makes it very important not to leave anything in her hands which might compromise us;

please give it your attention. Once this precaution has been taken, I will answer for her state of mind; the rest is your affair. If, however, we see afterward that her ingenuousness is being cured, we shall still have time to change our plans. Soon or later we shall have to concern ourselves with what we are going to do; in no case will our efforts be wasted.

But do you know that my own efforts were nearly wasted, and that Gercourt's lucky star nearly won out over my prudence? Madame de Volanges had a moment of maternal weakness and wanted to give her daughter to Danceny! That was the meaning of the more tender interest you noticed "the next morning." It is again you who would have been the cause of that magnificent turn of events! Fortunately the tender mother wrote to me about it, and I hope my reply will make her lose interest in the idea. I talked to her so much about virtue, and above all I flattered her so much, that she will surely feel that I am right.

I am sorry I did not have time to make a copy of my letter, so that I could edify you on the austerity of my morals. You would have seen how I despise women who are so depraved as to have a lover! It is so convenient to be a rigid moralist in words! It harms only others and never hinders us in the least. . . . And then I am not unaware that the good lady had her little weaknesses in her younger days the same as anyone else, and I was not sorry to humiliate her, at least in her conscience; that consoled me a little for the praise I gave her against my own conscience. It was thus that in the same letter, the idea of harming Gercourt gave me the courage to speak well of him.

Good-by, Vicomte; I strongly approve of your decision to stay where you are for some time longer. I have no means of hastening your advance, but I invite you to relieve your boredom with our common pupil. As for what concerns me, despite your polite summons you can see that you must still wait; and you will surely admit that it is not my fault.

LETTER 107

～ *From Azolan to the Vicomte de Valmont*

Paris, October 5, 17—,
at eleven o'clock in the evening

Monsieur,

In accordance with your orders, as soon as I received your letter I went to Monsieur Bertrand, who gave me five hundred francs as you had instructed him to do. I had told Philippe to leave immediately, as you wrote in your letter, and he had no money, so I asked for forty francs more for him, but your agent would not give it to me. He said he had no order for it from you. I had to give Philippe the money myself, and I hope you will be kind enough to take it into account.

He left last night. I told him to stay in the inn so he can be found if he is needed.

Immediately afterward I went to Madame de Tourvel's house to see Mademoiselle Julie, but she was out and I only talked to La Fleur. I could not find out anything from him because since his arrival he had been in the house only at meal times. All the serving has been done by the second footman and, as you know, I was not acquainted with him. But I began today.

I went back this morning and Mademoiselle Julie seemed glad to see me. I asked her why her mistress had come back, but she said she knew nothing about it, and I think she was telling the truth. I reproached her for not having told me she was going and she said she had not known about it until that same evening, when she went to help Madame to bed; so she spent the whole night packing, and the poor girl got less than two hours of sleep. She did not leave her mistress's room till after one o'clock, and her mistress was just beginning to write then.

As she was leaving the next morning, Madame de Tourvel gave a letter to the doorkeeper of the château. Mademoiselle Julie does not know who it was for. She says it may have been for you, Monsieur, but you have not mentioned it to me.

During the whole journey, Madame had a big hood over her face, so it could not be seen, but Mademoiselle Julie is almost sure she cried often. She did not say a word all the way and would not stop at ————,* as she had done when she was coming to the château. That did not please Mademoiselle Julie, because she had not had any breakfast. But, as I told her, masters are masters.

Madame went to bed as soon as she arrived, but she stayed there only two hours. When she got up, she sent for her doorkeeper and told him not to let anyone come in. She did not get dressed. She sat down to dinner, but she ate only a little soup, then left immediately. Her coffee was brought to her in her room, and Mademoiselle Julie went in at the same time. She found her mistress putting away some papers in her writing desk and saw that they were letters. I would bet they were from you, Monsieur, and of the three letters that came in the afternoon, there was one she still had in front of her all evening! I am sure it was another one from you. But then why did she go away like that? It amazes me! But you must know more about it, and it is none of my business.

Madame de Tourvel went to her library in the afternoon, took two books and brought them to her boudoir, but Mademoiselle Julie says she read them less than a quarter of an hour all day, and that she did nothing but read that letter and daydream with her head on her hand. Since I thought you would be glad to know what those books were, and since Mademoiselle Julie did not know, today I said I wanted to look over the library and had myself taken there. There were empty spaces for only two books: one was the second volume of *Christian Thoughts* and the other was the first volume of a book called *Clarissa*. I am writing it exactly as I saw it; perhaps you will know what it is.

Madame had no supper last night; she only drank some tea.

She rang early this morning, asked for her horses immediately, and before nine o'clock she went to the Feuillants, where she heard Mass. She wanted to go to confession, but her confessor was gone and he will not be back for a week or ten days. I thought it would be good to tell you this.

She came home and had breakfast, then began writing and did not stop till nearly one o'clock. I soon found a chance to do what you wanted most: it was I who took the letters to the post office. There was no letter for Madame de Volanges, but I am sending you one that was for Monsieur de Tourvel; it seemed to me that it ought to be the most important. There was also one for Madame de Rosemonde, but I thought you could always see it

---

*The same village halfway between Paris and the château.

whenever you wanted to, so I let it go. Besides, you will know everything, because Madame de Tourvel writes to you too. From now on I can get all the letters you want, because it is nearly always Mademoiselle Julie who gives them to the servants, and she has told me that out of friendship for me, and also for you, she will be glad to do what I want.

She would not even take the money I offered her, but I think you will want to give her some little present. If you do, and if you will leave it to me, I can easily find out what she would like.

I hope you will not think I have shown any negligence in serving you, Monsieur, and I want very much to defend myself against your reproaches. If I did not know that Madame de Tourvel was leaving, it was because of my zeal for your service, which made me leave at three o'clock in the morning. That was why I did not see Mademoiselle Julie the night before as usual, since I slept in the roadside inn so as not to wake up anyone in the château.

As for your reproach that I am often without money, first of all it is because I like to keep myself well dressed, as you can see; and then I must uphold the honor of the clothes I wear. I know I ought to save a little for the future, but I entrust myself entirely to your generosity, for you are a good master.

As for entering Madame de Tourvel's service while remaining in yours, I hope you will not demand it of me, Monsieur. It was very different with the duchess; but I will not wear livery, and a magistrate's livery at that, after having had the honor of being your valet. In everything else, Monsieur, you may dispose of the man who has the honor of being, with as much respect as affection, your most humble servant.

                                                            Roux Azolan

LETTER 108

～   *From Madame de Tourvel to Madame de Rosemonde*

                                        Paris, October 5, 17—
Oh, my indulgent mother, how grateful I am to you, and how much I needed your letter! I read it over and over again, I could not tear myself away from it. I owe to it the only less painful moments I have spent since my departure. How kind you are! I

now know that wisdom and virtue can sympathize with weakness! You pity my sufferings! Ah, if you knew them! . . . They are terrible. I thought I had endured the pains of love, but the inexpressible torment, the torment that must be experienced in order to have any idea of it, is to be separated from the object of one's love, and separated forever! . . . Yes, the pain that overwhelms me today will return tomorrow, and the day after, and every day for the rest of my life! Dear God, I am still so young, I still have so long to suffer!

I am the creator of my own unhappiness, I tear my heart with my own hands, and while I suffer these unbearable pains, I am constantly aware that I can end them with a word, and that that word is a crime! Ah, my friend! . . .

When I took the painful step of going away from him, I hoped that absence would increase my courage and strength. How mistaken I was! It seems, on the contrary, that it has completed their destruction. I had more to combat, it is true; but even while I was resisting, all was not privation. At least I saw him sometimes, and often, though not daring to look at him, I felt his gaze on me. Yes, my friend, I felt it, it seemed to warm my soul; and without passing through my eyes, it nevertheless reached my heart. Now that I am plunged into cruel solitude, isolated from everything that is dear to me, alone with my misfortune, every moment of my sad existence is marked by tears, and nothing softens their bitterness; no consolation is mingled with my sacrifices, and those I have made so far serve only to increase the painfulness of those I still have to make.

Only yesterday I felt this very keenly. Among the letters brought to me, there was one from him; I distinguished it from the others when the servant was still two paces away from me. I stood up involuntarily; I was trembling, it was difficult for me to hide my emotion, and that state was not without pleasure. As soon as I was alone again a moment later, that deceptive pleasure vanished and left me only with one more sacrifice to make. How could I allow myself to open that letter, even though I was dying to read it? Through the fatality that pursues me, the consolations which seem to be offered to me actually do nothing but impose new privations on me, and these are made still more cruel by the thought that Monsieur de Valmont shares them.

There it is at last, that name which is constantly in my mind, and which I had such difficulty in writing. I was truly alarmed by the mild reproach you addressed to me on that subject. I beg you to believe that no false shame has impaired my confidence in you; and why should I be afraid to name him? I blush for my feelings, not for the man who causes them! Who could be worthier of inspiring them? Yet for some reason his name does not come naturally to my pen, and this time also I had to reflect before writing it. But let me return to him.

You tell me that he seemed "keenly affected by my departure." What has he done? What has he said? Has he spoken of returning to Paris? I beg you to dissuade him from it as much as you can. If he has judged me rightly, he must not be angry with me for what I have done, but he must also be aware that my decision is irrevocable. One of my greatest torments is not knowing what he thinks. I still have his letter here . . . but you will surely agree with me that I must not open it.

It is only through you, my indulgent friend, that I can avoid being entirely separated from him. I do not wish to abuse your kindness; I understand perfectly that your letters cannot be long; but you will not refuse two words to your child: one to sustain her courage, the other to console her for it. Good-by, my estimable friend.

LETTER 109

~ *From Cécile Volanges to the Marquise de Merteuil*

Château de ———, October 10, 17—

It was only today, Madame, that I gave Monsieur de Valmont the letter you did me the honor of writing to me. I kept it for four days, even though I was often afraid it might be found; but I hid it very carefully, and I locked myself in to read it whenever my sorrow returned.

I see now that what I thought was such a great misfortune is hardly a misfortune at all, and I must admit there is great pleasure in it, so I have almost completely stopped being sad about it. Only the thought of Danceny still torments me sometimes. But there are already plenty of times when I do not think about him at all! And also Monsieur de Valmont is very nice!

I made up with him two days ago. It was very easy for me, because I had said only a few words when he told me that if I had something to say to him he would come to my room that night, and all I had to do was answer that I was willing. And then when he came he seemed no more angry than if I had never done anything to him. He only scolded me afterward, and then very gently, and in such a way . . . Just like you; which proved to me that he had great friendship for me too.

I cannot tell you how many funny things he told me that I would never have believed, especially about my mother. I would appreciate it if you would tell me whether it is all true. One thing is certain: I could not help laughing. Once, in fact, I laughed so loudly that we were both frightened, because my mother might have heard me; and if she had come to see what was happening, what would have become of me? This time she would surely have sent me back to the convent!

Since we must be careful, and since, as Monsieur de Valmont himself says, he would not risk compromising me for anything in the world, we agreed that in the future he would only come to unlock my door, and that we would go to his room. I have nothing to fear there; I went there last night, and as I write this letter I am waiting for him to come again. Now, Madame, I hope you will not scold me any more.

But there is one thing in your letter that surprised me: it is what you say about Danceny and Monsieur de Valmont after I am married. It seems to me that one day at the opera you told me the opposite, that once I was married I could no longer love anyone but my husband, and that I would even have to forget Danceny. Perhaps I misunderstood, and I hope I did, because as things are now I no longer dread my marriage. I am even looking forward to it, because I shall have more freedom, and I hope that I can then arrange things so that I shall think only of Danceny. I feel that I shall never be happy with anyone but him, for the thought of him still torments me and I am happy only when I can stop thinking about him, which is very difficult; and I become unhappy again as soon as I think about him.

What consoles me a little is that you assure me he will love me all the more; but are you really sure? . . . Oh, yes, you would not want to deceive me! Still, though, it is odd that I should be in love with Danceny, while it is Monsieur de Valmont who . . . But, as you say, it may be a stroke of good fortune! In any case, we shall see.

I do not understand too clearly what you say about my way of writing. It seems to me that Danceny likes my letters the way they are. But I know very well that I must not tell him anything about what is happening with Monsieur de Valmont, so you have no reason to be afraid.

My mother has not yet said anything to me about my marriage, but do not worry: I promise you I shall lie to her when she does talk to me about it, since she will be doing it only to trap me.

Good-by, my very good friend; I thank you very much, and I promise you that I shall never forget all the kindness you have shown me. I must stop now because it is nearly one o'clock and Monsieur de Valmont should be here soon.

LETTER 110

~ *From the Vicomte de Valmont to the Marquise de Merteuil*

Château de ———, October 11, 17—

"Powers of heaven, I had a soul for sorrow: give me one for bliss!"* It is, I believe, the tender Saint-Preux who expresses himself thus. Better endowed than he, I possess both existences at once. Yes, my friend, I am at the same time very happy and very unhappy; and since you have my entire confidence, I owe you the double account of my pains and of my pleasures.

I shall begin by telling you that my ungrateful prude is still treating me harshly. She has already sent back four of my letters. Perhaps I am wrong to say four of them, for having guessed after the first return that it would be followed by many others, and not wishing to waste my time, I adopted the course of expressing my complaints in commonplace phrases and not writing any date, so since the second time it has always been the same letter going back and forth; I only change the envelope. If some day my fair lady relents, as fair ladies usually do, if only from weariness, she will finally keep the letter, and it will then be time for me to find out how things stand. As you can see, with this new kind of correspondence, I cannot be perfectly informed.

I have, however, discovered that the fickle lady has changed her confidante; at least I have ascertained that since her departure from the château no letter has come from her for Madame de Volanges, while two have come for old Rosemonde. Since the latter has not even mentioned them to us, and since she no longer opens her mouth about "her dear beauty," whom she used to talk about all the time, I have concluded that it is she who now

---

La Nouvelle Héloïse.

enjoys her confidence. I presume that this great revolution was produced by a need to talk about me, and also by a little twinge of shame at the thought of opening her heart to Madame de Volanges with regard to a sentiment she had disavowed so long. I am afraid the change has been to my disadvantage, for the older women get, the more harsh and severe they become. The first would have said worse things about me, but the second will say worse things about love, and my sensitive prude is much more afraid of the sentiment than of the person.

The only way for me to find out precisely what is taking place is, as you can see, to intercept that clandestine correspondence. I have already given my valet orders to that effect, and I am awaiting their execution from day to day. Until then, I can only act at random, so for the past week I have been vainly going over all the known methods, all those in novels and in my secret memoirs; I have not found a single one which suits either the circumstances of the adventure or the character of its heroine. The difficulty would not be to get into her house, even at night, or even to drug her and make her a new Clarissa; but after two months of toil and trouble, how could I resort to means that are alien to me? How could I slavishly follow in the footsteps of others, and triumph without glory? No, she shall not have "the pleasures of vice and the honors of virtue."* It is not enough for me to possess her: I want her to give herself to me. For that, I must not only get into her house but come there with her consent; I must find her alone and with the intention of listening to me; and above all I must close her eyes to the danger, for if she sees it she will either surmount it or die. But the more clearly I realize what must be done, the more difficult it seems to me, and at the risk of making you laugh at me again I shall admit to you that my perplexity grows as I continue to think about it.

My head would be spinning, I think, if it were not for the pleasant diversions given to me by our common pupil; I owe it to her that I still have something to do besides writing elegies.

Would you believe that the little girl was so frightened that three whole days went by before your letter had produced its entire effect? There you see how a single false idea can spoil the best natural temperament!

It was not until Saturday that she began hovering around me and stammered a few words to me; and even then they were spoken so softly, and were so stifled by shame, that it was

---

*La Nouvelle Héloïse.

impossible to understand them. But the blush they caused enabled me to guess their meaning. Till then I had stood on my pride; but, softened by such an amusing repentance, I graciously promised to pay a visit to the pretty penitent that same evening, and this favor was received with all the gratitude that was owed to such a great kindness.

Since I never lose sight of either your plans or mine, I decided to take this opportunity to find out exactly what the child is worth, and also to accelerate her education. But to carry on this work with greater freedom, I needed to change the place of our meetings, for the mere closet which separates her room from her mother's could not inspire her with enough confidence to allow her to display herself at ease. I therefore promised myself to make some noise "innocently" which would frighten her enough to make her decide to take a safer refuge in the future; she spared me that trouble too.

She laughs easily; and to stimulate her gaiety I related to her, during our intermissions, all the scandalous adventures that came into my mind; and to make them more interesting, and hold her attention better, I attributed them all to her mother, thus amusing myself by adorning her with vices and ridicule.

It was not without reason that I made this choice: it encouraged my timid schoolgirl more than anything else, and at the same time I inspired her with profound contempt for her mother. I have long noticed that while it is not always necessary to use this method for seducing a girl, it is indispensable, and often the most efficacious method of all, if one wants to make her depraved, for a girl who does not respect her mother does not respect herself; this is a moral truth which I consider so useful that I was glad to furnish an example in support of the precept.

Meanwhile your pupil, who was not thinking of morality, was choking with laughter every few moments, and finally she almost laughed aloud. I had no difficulty in making her believe that she had made "a terrible noise." I feigned great alarm, which she easily shared. To make her remember it better, I did not allow pleasure to reappear, and I left her three hours earlier than usual; and so, when we parted, we agreed that from then on we would meet in my room.

I have received her there twice, and in that short space of time the pupil has become almost as learned as the teacher. Yes, I have truly taught her everything, including extreme obligingness! I have omitted only precautions.

Occupied thus all night, I gain the advantage of sleeping a

large part of the day; since the present company in the château has nothing that attracts me, I appear in the drawing room no more than an hour each day. Today I even decided to eat in my room, and from now on I intend to leave it only for short walks. This odd behavior is supposedly due to my health. I have declared that I was "overcome with vapors," and also that I had a slight fever. The only symptom I maintain is that of speaking in a slow, lifeless voice. As for the change in my face, rely on your pupil for that. "Love will see to it."*

I spend my leisure in thinking of ways to regain the advantages I have lost over my ungrateful prude, and also in composing a kind of catechism of debauchery for the use of my pupil. I amuse myself by calling everything by its technical name, and I laugh in advance at the interesting conversation this will produce between her and Gercourt on their wedding night. Nothing could be more amusing than the ingenuousness with which she already uses the little she knows of that language! She does not imagine that anyone could speak otherwise. That child is really delightful! The contrast between her artless candor and her shameless language is most effective; and I do not know why, but only strange things please me now.

Perhaps I am plunging into this too deeply, since I am using up all my time and endangering my health; but I hope that my feigned illness, besides saving me from the boredom of the drawing room, will also be of some use to me with the austere prude, whose ferocious virtue is allied with gentle sensitivity. I do not doubt that she has already been informed of this great event, and I am eager to learn what she thinks of it, especially since I am willing to bet that she will not fail to attribute the honor of it to herself. I shall regulate the state of my health according to the impression it makes on her.

And now, my fair friend, you know as much about my affairs as I do myself. I hope that I shall soon have more interesting news to tell you, and I beg you to believe that, in the pleasure to which I am looking forward, I count for a great deal the reward I am expecting from you.

---

*Régnard, *Folies Amoureuses*.

LETTER 111

~ *From the Comte de Gercourt to Madame de Volanges*

Bastia, October 10, 17—

It seems, Madame, that everything in this country will be tranquil, and we are daily expecting permission to return to France. I hope you will not doubt that I still have the same eagerness to return and form the bond that will unite me with you and Mademoiselle de Volanges. However, my cousin the Duc de ————, to whom, as you know, I have many obligations, has just informed me that he is being recalled from Naples. He writes to me that he intends to pass through Rome and see, on the way, the part of Italy with which he is not yet acquainted. He has invited me to accompany him on this journey, which will last for six weeks or two months. I shall not conceal from you that it would be agreeable for me to take advantage of this opportunity, since I am aware that once I am married it will be difficult for me to take time for any journeys other than those required by my service. Also, it might be better to postpone the marriage until winter, since all my relatives cannot be gathered in Paris until then, particularly the Marquis de ————, to whom I owe the hope of being related to you. Despite these considerations, my plans in this matter will be completely subordinated to yours; if you prefer your original arrangements, I am ready to give up mine. I ask you only to let me know your intentions as soon as possible. I shall await your reply here, and it alone will determine my conduct.

I am with respect, Madame, and with all the sentiments that befit a son, your most humble, etc.

The Comte de Gercourt

LETTER 112

~~ *From Madame de Rosemonde to Madame de Tourvel (Dictated)*

Château de ———, October 14, 17—

I have just now received, my dear beauty, your letter of the eleventh,* and the gentle reproaches it contains. Confess that you would have liked to reproach me more, and that if you had not recalled that you were "my daughter," you would have really scolded me. Yet you would have been very unjust! It was the desire and the hope of being able to reply to you myself that made me put it off each day, and, as you can see, even now I am forced to borrow my maid's hand. My unfortunate rheumatism has returned; it has settled in my right arm this time, and I am absolutely one-armed. That is what it is like, young and fresh as you are, to have such an old friend! You suffer from her infirmities.

As soon as my pain gives me a little respite, I intend to talk to you at length. For the moment, I shall tell you only that I have received your two letters, that they would have redoubled my tender friendship for you if that had been possible, and that I shall never cease to be keenly interested in everything that concerns you.

My nephew is also a little indisposed, but without danger or any cause for alarm; it is only a slight ailment which, it seems to me, affects his mood more than his health. We scarcely see him any more.

His retirement and your departure have not made our little company more cheerful. Young Cécile, especially, misses you terribly, and yawns all day long. Particularly in the past few days, she has been doing us the honor of falling fast asleep after dinner.

Good-by, my dear beauty; I shall always be your good friend, your mother, even your sister, if my great age permitted me that title. In short, I am attached to you by all the most tender sentiments.

Signed: Adélaïde, for Madame de Rosemonde

---

*This letter has not been found.

LETTER 113

~ *From the Marquise de Merteuil to the Vicomte de Valmont*

Paris, October 15, 17—

I think I ought to warn you, Vicomte, that people in Paris are beginning to talk about you, that your absence is noticed, and that its cause has already been guessed. Last night I was present at a large supper party where it was positively stated that you were being retained in the village by a romantic and unfortunate love. Joy immediately appeared on the faces of all the men who envy your successes, and of all the women you have neglected. If you take my advice, you will not let these dangerous rumors become established: you will return at once and destroy them by your presence.

Remember that once you have allowed the loss of the idea that you are irresistible, you will soon find that you are in fact resisted more easily, and that your rivals will also lose their respect for you and dare to compete with you, for who among them does not believe himself to be stronger than virtue? Remember above all that in the multitude of women whom you have flaunted, all those you have not had will try to undeceive the public, while the others will try to deceive it. In short, you must expect to be rated perhaps as far below your true worth as you have so far been rated above it.

Come back, Vicomte, and do not sacrifice your reputation to a childish whim. You have done all we wanted with little Cécile, and as for your Madame de Tourvel, you will obviously not satisfy your fancy for her by remaining ten leagues away from her. Do you think she will come to find you? Perhaps she has already stopped thinking about you, or thinks about you only to congratulate herself on having humiliated you. Here, at least, you will be able to find some opportunity of making a brilliant reappearance, and you need it; and even if you persist in your ridiculous adventure, I do not see how your return could hinder it—quite the contrary.

If your Madame de Tourvel "adores you," as you have told me so often and proved to me so little, her only consolation, her sole pleasure, must now be to talk about you and to know what you are doing, what you are saying, what you are thinking, and even the slightest details of everything that concerns you. Such trifles gain value in proportion to the privations one endures. They are like crumbs of bread that fall from a rich man's table: he scorns them, but the poor man avidly gathers them and is nourished by them. Poor Madame de Tourvel is now receiving all those crumbs, and the more of them she has, the less eager she will be to indulge her appetite for the rest.

Furthermore, since you know her confidante you cannot doubt that each letter from her contains at least a little sermon and everything she considers likely to "strengthen her chastity and fortify her virtue,"* so why should you give resources for defense to one and means of harming you to the other?

Not that I am at all in agreement with you when you say that her change of confidantes is to your disadvantage: first of all, Madame de Volanges hates you, and hatred is always more ingenious and clear-sighted than friendship. All of your old aunt's virtue will never make her speak ill of her dear nephew for one moment; for virtue also has its weaknesses. And then your fears are based on an utterly false observation.

It is not true that "the older women get, the more harsh and severe they become." It is between the ages of forty and fifty that the despair of seeing their faces become wrinkled, and the rage of feeling themselves obliged to abandon pretensions and pleasures to which they are still strongly attached, make nearly all women shrewish and strait-laced. They need that long interval in which to make that great sacrifice; but once it has been made, they all fall into two classes.

The more numerous, that of women who never had anything in their favor except beauty and youth, sink into idiotic apathy and emerge from it only to play cards and perform a few devotional practices. They are always boring, often grumbling, sometimes a little cantankerous, but seldom spiteful. It cannot be said that they are either severe or not severe: without ideas and without existence, they repeat, indifferently and without understanding, everything they hear, and in themselves they remain absolute nonentities.

The other class, much smaller but really precious, is that of women who, having had character and having not neglected to nourish their reason, are able to create an existence for themselves when that of nature fails them, and adopt the course of

---

*On ne s'Avise Jamais de Tout! Comedy!

embellishing their minds as they formerly embellished their faces. They usually have very sound judgment and minds that are solid, gay and gracious. They replace seductive charms by engaging kindness, and also by a sprightliness whose charm increases with age; it is thus that, to some extent, they succeed in bringing themselves closer to youth by making themselves loved by it. But then, far from being "harsh and severe," they are inclined perhaps a little too strongly toward laxity by their habit of indulgence, by their long reflections on human weakness, and especially by the memories of their youth, through which alone they still cling to life.

I realized early in life how useful the support of old women could be, so I have always sought them out, and I can tell you that I have met several to whom I returned as much from inclination as from self-interest. I shall stop here, for now that you become inflamed so quickly and so morally, I would be afraid you might suddenly fall in love with your old aunt and bury yourself with her in the tomb in which you have already been living for so long. I shall therefore go on to other matters.

Despite your apparent enchantment with your little pupil, I cannot believe that she plays any part in your plans. You found her close at hand and you took her: well done! But it cannot be a real inclination. It is not really even a complete enjoyment: you possess only her body! I am not speaking of her heart, which I am sure you care nothing about; but you do not even occupy her head. I do not know if you are aware of it, but I have proof of it in her latest letter to me*; I am sending it to you so that you can judge for yourself. Notice that when she writes about you it is always "Monsieur de Valmont," that all her ideas, even those you have engendered in her, invariably lead her to Danceny, and that she never calls him "Monsieur," but simply "Danceny." In that way she distinguishes him from all others; even though she gives herself to you, she speaks familiarly only of him. If such a conquest seems "delightful" to you, if the pleasures it gives you captivate you, then you are certainly modest and easy to please! I am quite willing for you to keep her, it is part of my plan; but it seems to me that it is not worth troubling yourself for a quarter of an hour, that you should also have some power over her and not permit her, for example, to return to Danceny until you have made her forget him a little more.

Before I cease to concern myself with you and turn to myself,

*See Letter 109.

I want to tell you that the method of feigned illness which you tell me you have adopted is well known and thoroughly worn out. Really, Vicomte, you are not inventive. I sometimes repeat myself also, as you will soon see; but I try to make up for it by the details, and above all I am justified by success. I am going to attempt to achieve one more, and undertake a new adventure. I admit that it will not have the merit of difficulty, but at least it will be a diversion, and I am dying of boredom.

I do not know why, but since my adventure with Prévan, Belleroche has become unbearable to me. He has so greatly increased his attentions, tenderness and "veneration" that I can no longer endure it. At first his anger seemed amusing to me; I still had to calm it, however, for he would have compromised me if I had let him continue, and there was no way of making him listen to reason. I therefore decided to show him more love in order to overcome him more easily; but he took it seriously, and ever since then he has been wearying me with his everlasting enchantment. I have particularly noticed the insulting confidence he has in me, and the assurance with which he regards me as his forever. I am really humiliated by it. He must not value me very highly if he considers himself good enough to hold me! And he recently told me he would always be the only man I had ever loved! Ah, I needed all my prudence to restrain myself from undeceiving him then and there by telling him the true facts of the matter! What an amusing gentleman to be claiming exclusive rights! I admit he is well built and has a fairly handsome face; but on the whole he is only an unskilled laborer in love. The time has come: we must separate.

I have already been trying for two weeks, and I have successively employed coldness, caprice, ill-humor and quarrels, but the tenacious individual does not let go so easily. I must use more violent means, so I am taking him to my country house. We are leaving day after tomorrow. We shall be accompanied only by a few people who are disinterested and not very clear-sighted, so we shall have almost as much freedom there as if we were alone. I shall overload him so heavily with love and caresses, and we shall live so exclusively for each other, that I am willing to bet that he will be even more eager than I for the end of our stay in the country, to which he is now looking forward with such great happiness; and if he does not come back more bored with me than I am with him, you have my permission to tell me that I know no more than you.

The pretext for this little retirement is to concern myself

seriously with my great lawsuit, which will finally come up for judgment early this winter. I am glad of it, for it is really unpleasant to have one's entire fortune held in suspense this way. Not that I am worried about the outcome: first of all, I am in the right, all my lawyers assure me of that; and even if I were not, I would be a hopeless bungler if I could not win a lawsuit in which my only adversaries are little girls and their old guardian. However, since nothing must be neglected in such an important matter, I shall in fact have two lawyers with me. Does it not sound like a gay journey to you? But if it enables me to win my lawsuit and lose Belleroche, I shall consider the time well spent.

And now, Vicomte, can you imagine who his successor is going to be? I give you a hundred guesses. But no, I am forgetting that you never guess anything, so I shall tell you: it is Danceny. You are astonished, are you not? After all, I am not yet reduced to educating children! But this one deserves to be an exception: he has only the graces of youth, not its frivolity. His great reserve in company is well suited to keeping away all suspicion, and it makes him all the more charming when he abandons it in private. Not that I have yet had any private conversations with him on my own account: I am still only his confidante; but beneath that veil of friendship I think I can see that he has a strong inclination toward me, and I feel that I am acquiring one toward him. It would be a great pity if so much intelligence and delicacy were to be sacrificed and stupefied with that idiotic little Volanges girl! I hope he is mistaken in thinking he loves her: she is so far from deserving him! It is not that I am jealous of her; but it would be a crime, and I want to save him from it. So I beg you, Vicomte, to see to it that he cannot rejoin "his Cécile" (as he still has the bad habit of calling her). A first infatuation always has more power than one thinks, and I would not be sure of anything if he saw her again now, especially during my absence. When I return I shall take charge of everything, and I guarantee the result.

For a time I thought of taking the young man with me, but then I sacrificed the idea to my usual prudence; besides, I would have been afraid he might notice something between Belleroche and me, and I would be in despair if he had the slightest notion of what is going on. I want at least to offer myself to his imagination as pure and untarnished: that is, as a woman ought to be in order to be truly worthy of him.

LETTER 114

～ *From Madame de Tourvel to Madame de Rosemonde*

Paris, October 16, 17—

My dear friend, I am giving in to my keen anxiety: without knowing whether or not you will be in a condition to answer me, I cannot help questioning you. Monsieur de Valmont's condition, which you describe as being "without danger," does not leave me as untroubled as you seem to be. It is not rare that melancholy and aversion to company are advance symptoms of some serious illness; the sufferings of the body, like those of the mind, make one desire solitude, and we often reproach someone with ill-humor when we should only pity his afflictions.

It seems to me that Monsieur de Valmont should at least consult someone. Why is it that, being ill yourself, you do not have a doctor with you? I saw mine this morning, and I shall not conceal from you that I consulted him indirectly about Monsieur de Valmont. He is of the opinion that with people who are naturally active, that kind of sudden apathy should never be neglected, and he also told me that illnesses do not yield to treatment unless it is begun in time. Why take that risk with someone who is so dear to you?

What redoubles my anxiety is that I have not received a letter from him for four days. Are you deceiving me about his condition? Why has he suddenly stopped writing to me? If it were merely the result of my persistence in sending back his letters, I think he would have done so sooner. In any case, although I do not believe in presentiments, for the past few days I have been in the grip of a sadness which frightens me. Perhaps I am on the threshold of the greatest of misfortunes!

You cannot imagine, and I am ashamed to tell you, how much it grieves me not to receive those letters even though I refused to read them. I was at least sure that he was thinking about me, and I saw something that came from him! I did not open those letters, but I wept when I looked at them; the tears I shed then were gentler and easier, and they alone partially relieved the distress that has overwhelmed me since my return. I beg you, my indulgent friend, to write to me yourself as soon as you can; and in the meantime, please have your maid send me news of you and of him every day.

I see that I have scarcely said a word about you; but you know my feelings, my attachment without reserve, my tender gratitude for your compassionate friendship; you will forgive my agitation, my mortal grief, and the terrible torment of having to dread evils of which I am perhaps the cause. Dear God, that agonizing idea pursues me and tears my heart! I lacked that misfortune, and I feel that I was born to endure them all.

Good-by, my dear friend; love me, pity me. Shall I have a letter from you today?

LETTER 115

~ *From the Vicomte de Valmont to the Marquise de Merteuil*

Château de ———, October 19, 17—

It is amazing, my fair friend, how easily people cease to understand each other as soon as they are apart. As long as I was with you, we always had the same feelings, the same way of looking at things; but now, because I have not seen you for nearly three months, we no longer have the same opinion about anything. Which of us is wrong? You would surely not hesitate over the answer, but I, being wiser, or more polite, shall not decide. I shall only reply to your letter and continue to inform you of what I have been doing.

First of all, let me thank you for notifying me of the rumors that are circulating about me; but I am not yet disturbed by them: I feel certain that I shall soon be able to put an end to them. Do not worry: when I reappear in society I shall be more celebrated and worthier of you than ever.

I hope I shall be given some credit for my adventure with little Cécile, which you seem to consider trivial, as though it were nothing to have taken a young girl away from her beloved in one evening, and then to have made use of her as much as I wanted, without further ado, as though she were my property, obtaining things from her which one does not even dare to demand of all women who make their living by being obliging, and all this without disturbing her tender love in any way, without making her inconstant or even unfaithful (for it is true that I do not occupy her mind!), so that when my whim has passed, I shall return her to Danceny's arms, so to speak, without her having noticed anything. Is that such an ordinary achievement? And then, believe me, once she has left my hands, the principles I am giving her will continue to develop, and I predict that the timid pupil will soon make great progress which will honor her teacher.

However, if the public prefers the heroic mode, I shall point to Madame de Tourvel, that often cited model of all the virtues, respected even by our greatest libertines to such an extent that they had lost all thought of attacking her! I shall show her forgetting her duties and her virtue, sacrificing her reputation and two years of purity, to run after the happiness of pleasing me, to intoxicate herself with the happiness of loving me, considering herself sufficiently rewarded for all her sacrifices by a word or a look, which she will not always obtain. I shall do more: I shall leave her; and if I know that kind of woman, I shall have no successor. She will resist the need for consolation, the habit of pleasure, even the desire for vengeance. In short, she will have existed only for me; and however long her course may be, I alone shall have begun and ended it. Once I have achieved this triumph, I shall say to my rivals, "Behold my work, and try to find its equal in our time!"

You may ask me why I am now so confident. For the past week I have known all my fair lady's secrets; she has not given them to me: I have intercepted them. Two letters from her to Madame de Rosemonde have told me all I needed to know, and I shall read the others only from curiosity. To succeed, I need only to come into her presence; I have already devised a plan for doing so, and I shall begin carrying it out immediately.

You are curious, are you not? But no, to punish you for not believing in my inventiveness, I shall not tell you my plan. Really, you deserve to be deprived of my confidence, at least in this adventure; indeed, if it were not for the sweet reward you have promised me for success in it, I would not speak to you of it again. You can see that I am angry. However, in the hope that you will mend your ways, I am willing to go no further than that slight punishment, and, returning to indulgence, I shall forget my great projects for a moment to discuss yours with you.

So you are now in the country, which is as boring as sentiment and as dreary as faithfulness! And poor Belleroche! Not content with making him drink the water of forgetfulness, you want to drown him in it! How is he feeling? Is he bearing up well under the nausea of love? I wish it would only make him more attached to you: I am curious to see what more efficacious remedy you would then use. I pity you for being obliged to resort to this one. Only once in my life have I made love as a matter of procedure. I certainly had a good reason, since it was with the Comtesse de ———, and yet when I was in her arms I was tempted a dozen times to say, "Madame, I renounce the position I have been soliciting; allow me to withdraw from the one I now occupy." Thus, of all the women I have had, she is the only one I really enjoy slandering.

As for your reason, to tell you the truth, I find it supremely ridiculous. You are right to believe that I would never have guessed Belleroche's successor. What! It is for Danceny that you are going to all that trouble? Leave him to adore "his virtuous Cécile" and do not compromise yourself in those childish games. Let schoolboys develop themselves with chambermaids, or play "innocent little games" with schoolgirls. Why should you burden yourself with a novice who will not know either how to take you or how to leave you, and with whom you will have to do everything? I tell you seriously that I disapprove of your choice, and however secret it may remain, it will humiliate you at least in my eyes and in your conscience.

You say that you are acquiring a strong inclination toward him—come, come, you are surely wrong, and I think I have found the cause of your error. Your fine disgust with Belleroche came to you in a time of scarcity, and since Paris offered you no choice, your mind, always too quick, fixed itself upon the first object you encountered. But remember that when you return you can choose among a thousand; and if you dread falling into inaction if you delay, let me offer to help you while away the time.

Between now and your arrival, my great affairs will be settled in one way or another, and certainly neither Cécile nor even Madame de Tourvel will then occupy me so much that I cannot be with you as much as you wish. Perhaps then I shall already have returned the little girl to her discreet Danceny. Although I do not agree, no matter what you say, that this is not a captivating enjoyment, my plan is that for the rest of her life she shall have an idea of me that is superior to her idea of any other man, so I have been proceeding with her at a pace which I could not sustain for long without damaging my health, and already I am no longer attached to her by anything except the concern one ought to have for family matters. . . .

You do not understand me? What I mean is that I am waiting

for a second period to confirm my hope and assure me that I have fully succeeded in my plans. Yes, my fair friend, I already have a first indication that my pupil's husband will not run the risk of dying without issue, and that in the future the head of the House of Gercourt will be only a younger son of the House of Valmont. But let me finish as I please this adventure which I undertook only at your request. Bear in mind that you will take away all its piquancy if you make Danceny unfaithful. And consider that in offering myself to you as his representative, I have, it seems to me, some rights to the preference.

I count on it so much that I have not hesitated to hinder your plans by assisting in increasing the discreet Danceny's tender passion for the first and worthy object of his choice. Last night I found your pupil engaged in writing to him; after having disturbed her in this sweet occupation to lead her into another that was still sweeter, I asked to see her letter. Since I found it cold and constrained, I pointed out to her that this was not the way to console him, and I persuaded her to write him another letter which I dictated to her. In it, imitating her chatter as best I could, I tried to nourish his love with a more certain hope. She was overjoyed, she said, to find herself speaking so well, and from now on I shall be in charge of her correspondence. What shall I not have done for that Danceny! I shall have been his friend, his confidant, his rival and his sweetheart! And I am now rendering him the further service of saving him from your dangerous bonds. Yes, they are dangerous, for to possess you and then lose you is to pay for a moment of happiness with an eternity of regret.

Good-by, my fair friend; have the courage to dispatch Belleroche as soon as you can. Forget Danceny and prepare to receive and give once again the delightful pleasures of our first intimacy.

P.S.—I congratulate you on the forthcoming settlement of your great lawsuit. I shall be very glad if that happy event takes place under my reign.

LETTER 116

~ *From the Chevalier Danceny to Cécile Volanges*

Paris, October 17, 17—

Madame de Merteuil left this morning for the country; thus, my charming Cécile, I am now deprived of the only pleasure that was left to me in your absence: that of talking about you to your friend and mine. For some time she has allowed me to give her that title, and I have done so all the more eagerly because it seems to draw me closer to you. How gracious she is! And what flattering charm she is able to give to friendship! That sweet sentiment seems to be embellished and strengthened in her by all that she refuses to love. If you only knew how fond she is of you, and how it pleases her to hear me talk about you! . . . That is no doubt what attaches me so strongly to her. What happiness it is for me to be able to live only for the two of you, to pass constantly from the delights of love to the sweetness of friendship, to devote my whole life to them, to be, as it were, the meeting point of your mutual attachment, and always to feel that in occupying myself with the happiness of one, I shall also be working for the happiness of the other! Love that adorable woman, my charming friend, love her very much. Give still greater value to my attachment to her by sharing it. Since I have begun to savor the charm of friendship, I want you to experience it also. It seems to me that I only half enjoy those pleasures which I do not share with you. Yes, my Cécile, I would like to surround your heart with all the sweetest sentiments, I would like its every movement to give you a sensation of happiness, and even then I would not think I could give you back more than a part of the felicity I owed to you.

Why must these charming plans be nothing but a figment of my imagination, while reality offers me nothing but painful privations whose end is still not in sight? I see clearly that I must abandon the hope you gave me of being able to see you in the country. My only consolation is to convince myself that it is not possible for you. And you neglect to tell me so, to lament it with me! Already my complaints about it have twice remained unanswered. Ah, Cécile, Cécile, I believe that you love me with all the faculties of your soul, but your soul is not aflame as mine is! How I wish it were for me to overcome the obstacles, that it were my interests which had to be safeguarded instead of yours! I could soon prove to you that nothing is impossible for love.

Nor do you tell me when this cruel absence is to end. Here, at least, I might see you. Your charming glances would revive my downcast soul, their touching expression would give reassurance to my heart, which sometimes needs it. Forgive me, my Cécile: this fear is not a suspicion. I believe in your love, in your constancy. Ah, I would be too wretched if I doubted them! But there are so many obstacles, and they are continually renewed! I am sad, my dearest, very sad. Madame de Merteuil's departure seems to have renewed my awareness of all my misfortunes.

Good-by, my Cécile; good-by, my beloved. Remember that I am in pain, and that only you can restore my happiness.

LETTER 117

~ *From Cécile Volanges to the Chevalier Danceny (Dictated by Valmont)*

Château de ———, October 18, 17—

Do you think, my good friend, that I need to be scolded in order to be sad when I know that you are in pain? And do you doubt that I suffer as much as you from all your sorrows? I share even those which I cause voluntarily, and I have one more than you when I see that you do not do me justice. Oh, that is not right! I can see what it is that makes you angry: it is that I did not answer your question the last two times you asked me if you could come here; but is that answer so easy to give? Do you think I do not know that what you want is very wrong? Yet if I already had such difficulty in refusing you from a distance, what would it be like if you were here? And then I would be unhappy all my life for having wanted to console you for a moment.

I have nothing to hide from you; here are my reasons: judge them for yourself. I might have done what you want if it had not been for the fact that Monsieur de Gercourt, who is the cause of all our sorrow, will not arrive as soon as we expected, as I have already told you; and since my mother has begun to show much more friendship for me, while I am treating her as affectionately as I can, who knows what I may be able to obtain from her? And would it not be much better if we could be happy without my having to reproach myself for anything? If I am to believe what I have often been told, a man always loves his wife less if he has loved her too much before she became his wife. That fear holds me back even more than all the rest. Are you not sure of my heart, and will there not always be time?

Listen to me: I promise you that if I cannot avoid the misfortune of marrying Monsieur de Gercourt, whom I already hate so much before knowing him, nothing will hold me back from giving myself to you as much as I can, and even before everything. Since I care only about being loved by you, and you will see that if I do wrong it will not be my fault, nothing else matters to me as long as you promise me that you will always love me as much as you do now. But till then, let me go on as I am, and do not ask me to do something I have good reasons for not doing, although it grieves me to refuse it to you.

I also wish Monsieur de Valmont would not be so pressing for you: it only makes me sadder than ever. Oh, you have a very good friend in him, I assure you! He does everything just as you would do it yourself. But good-by, my dearest; it was very late when I began writing to you, and I have spent part of the night doing it. I shall now go to bed and make up for lost time. I kiss you, but do not scold me again.

LETTER 118

~ *From the Chevalier Danceny to the Marquise de Merteuil*

Paris, October 19, 17—

If I believe my calendar, my adorable friend, you have been gone for only two days; but if I believe my heart, it has been two centuries. Now you yourself have told me that one must always believe one's heart, so it is surely time for you to return, and all your business must be more than finished. How do you expect me to be interested in your lawsuit if, whether it is lost or won, I must still pay the costs by the boredom of your absence? Oh, how I would like to quarrel! And how sad it is, with such a fine reason for ill-humor, not to have a right to show it!

Yet is it not a real infidelity, a barbarous betrayal, to leave your friend far from you, after you have made him unable to do without your presence? You may consult your lawyers all you like, they will not find you any justification for such misconduct; besides, lawyers only give reasons, and reasons are insufficient to reply to sentiments.

As for me, after hearing you tell me so often that reason required you to make this journey, I have been completely turned against reason. I will never listen to it again, not even when it tells me to forget you. Yet that reason is very reasonable; and actually it would not be so difficult to do as you might believe. It would suffice merely to lose the habit of always thinking about you, and I assure you that nothing here would remind me of you.

Our prettiest women, those who are said to be the most attractive, are still so far from you that they could give only a very weak idea of you. I even believe that with practiced eyes, the more one thought at first that they resembled you, the greater difference one would find later; whatever they may do, and however much they may put into it everything they know, they always lack being you, and that is where the whole charm lies. Unfortunately, when the days are long and I am idle, I dream, I make castles in Spain, I create a fantasy; gradually my imagination becomes impassioned: I want to embellish my work, I bring together everything that is attractive, I finally reach perfection; and as soon as I have done so, the portrait brings me back to the model, and I am amazed to see that I have only been thinking of you.

At this very moment I am again the dupe of a similar error. You may believe that I began writing to you because I wanted to think about you. Not at all: it was to distract myself from you. I had a hundred things to say to you of which you were not the object, and which, as you know, concern me deeply; yet it is from them that I have been distracted. Since when does the charm of friendship distract from that of love? Ah, if I looked more closely I might have to reproach myself a little! . . . Enough! I must forget that slight transgression for fear of falling into it again; and may my friend herself know nothing of it.

So why are you not here to answer me, to bring me back if I go astray, to speak to me of my Cécile, to increase, if that is possible, the happiness I feel in loving her by the sweet idea that it is your friend whom I love? Yes, I admit that the love she inspires in me has become still more precious to me since you have allowed me to confide it to you. I love to open my heart to you, to occupy yours with my sentiments, to entrust them to it without reserve! I seem to cherish them more when you deign to receive them; and then I look at you and say to myself, "All my happiness is enclosed in her."

I have nothing new to tell you about my situation. The last letter I received from *her* increases and assures my hope, but still retards it. However, her motives are so tender and virtuous that I can neither blame her for them nor complain of them. Perhaps you do not understand too well what I am telling you; but why are you not here? Although one says everything to one's friend, one does not dare to write everything. The secrets of love, especially, are so delicate that we cannot let them leave us in that way on their good faith. If we sometimes allow them to go out, we must at least not lose sight of them; we must, as it were, see them enter their new refuge. Ah, come back, my adorable friend! You can see that your return is necessary. Either forget the "countless reasons" which detain you where you are, or teach me how to live where you are not.

I have the honor of being, etc.

LETTER 119

～ *From Madame de Rosemonde to Madame de Tourvel*

Château de ———, October 20, 17—

Although I am still suffering a great deal, my dear beauty, I am trying to write to you myself, so that I can speak to you of what interests you. My nephew is still misanthropic. He regularly sends for news of me every day, but not once has he come in person, even though I have asked him to do so; I therefore see no more of him than if he were in Paris. I did meet him this morning, however, in a place where I scarcely expected to see him. It was in my chapel, where I had gone for the first time since my painful indisposition. I learned today that for the past four days he has been going regularly to hear Mass. God grant that it will last!

When I entered, he came up to me and affectionately congratulated me on the improved state of my health. Since Mass was beginning, I cut short the conversation, expecting to resume it later; but he disappeared before I could join him. I shall not conceal from you that I found him a little changed. But, my dear beauty, do not make me regret my confidence in your reason by becoming unduly alarmed; and above all, do not doubt that I would rather distress you than deceive you.

If my nephew continues to avoid me, as soon as I am feeling better I shall go to see him in his room and try to discover the cause of his singular conduct, which I believe you have something to do with. I must leave you now, since I can no longer move my fingers; and then if Adélaïde knew that I have been writing, she would scold me all evening. Good-by, my dear beauty.

LETTER 120

~ *From the Vicomte de Valmont to Father Anselme (a Cistercian monk in the monastery on the Rue Saint-Honoré)*

Château de ———, October 22, 17—

I do not have the honor of being known by you, Monsieur, but I know the complete confidence which Madame de Tourvel has in you, and I also know how worthily it is placed. I therefore feel that I can address myself to you without indiscretion to obtain an essential service which is truly worthy of your holy ministry, and in which Madame de Tourvel's interest is joined with mine.

I have in my possession certain important papers which concern her, which cannot be entrusted to anyone else, and which I must not and will not give to anyone but her in person. I have no way of informing her of this, because reasons which you may have learned from her, but which I do not feel I have a right to tell you, have led her to refuse all communication with me. I now freely admit that I cannot blame her for this decision, since she could not foresee certain events; I myself was far from expecting them, and they could have been brought about only by the more than human force which I am forced to recognize in them.

I therefore beg you, Monsieur, to be so kind as to inform her of my new resolutions and to ask her to grant me a private interview in which I can at least partially atone for my sins by my apologies and, as a last sacrifice, obliterate in her eyes the only existing traces of an error or a transgression which had made me guilty with regard to her.

Only after this preliminary expiation shall I dare to lay at your feet the humiliating admission of my long deviations from virtue

FEDERAL RESERVE NOTE

THE UNITED STATES OF AMERICA

THIS NOTE IS LEGAL TENDER
FOR ALL DEBTS, PUBLIC AND PRIVATE

WASHINGTON, D.C.

E 00324265 L

B 586

5 5

5 5

B₁

E 00324265 L

SERIES
1988
A

WASHINGTON

ONE DOLLAR

The United States
Treasurer of the United States

Secretary of the Treasury

and implore your mediation for a reconciliation that is still more important, and unfortunately more difficult. May I hope, Monsieur, that you will not refuse me such necessary and precious aid, and that you will deign to support my weakness and guide my steps in a new path which I ardently desire to follow, but which I blush to admit that I do not yet know?

I await your reply with the impatience of a repentance that desires to make reparations, and I beg you to believe that I am, with as much gratitude as veneration,

Your most humble, etc.

P.S.—I authorize you, Monsieur, if you should see fit, to show this letter in its entirety to Madame de Tourvel, whom I shall respect for the rest of my life, and whom I shall never cease to honor as the woman heaven employed to bring back my soul to virtue through the touching spectacle of hers.

LETTER 121

~ *From the Marquise de Merteuil to the Chevalier Danceny*

Château de ———, October 22, 17—

I have received your letter, my too young friend; but before thanking you I must scold you, and I warn you that if you do not mend your ways you will not have another reply from me. If you take my advice, you will abandon that tone of flattery which is nothing but jargon when it is not an expression of love. Is that the style of friendship? No, my friend, each sentiment has a language that is suited to it, and to use another is to disguise the thought one is expressing. I know very well that our little women understand nothing of what is said to them unless it is translated, so to speak, into that customary jargon; but I confess that I thought I was justified in expecting you to distinguish me from them. I am really annoyed, and perhaps more than I should be, that you should have misjudged me so badly.

You will therefore find in my letter only what is lacking in yours: frankness and simplicity. I shall tell you, for example, that it would give me great pleasure to see you, and that I am sorry to be only with people who bore me, instead of people who please me; but you translate that same statement thus: "Teach me how to live where you are not." I suppose that when you are with your Cécile you will not be able to live unless I am there too! What a pity! And you feel that she suffers from the same lack as those women who "always lack being me"! But that is where you are led by a language which, because of the abuse that is made of it nowadays, is even lower than the jargon of compliments, and is becoming a mere social convention in which no one believes any more than in "your most humble servant."

My friend, when you write to me, let it be to tell me your way of thinking and feeling, and not to send me phrases which I can find, without your help, more or less well expressed in any current novel. I hope you will not be angered by what I have said to you, even if you should see a certain ill-humor in it, for I do not deny that I am annoyed; but to avoid even the appearance of the defect for which I am reproaching you, I shall not tell you that my ill-humor may be slightly increased by your absence. It seems to me that, on the whole, you are more interesting than a lawsuit and two lawyers, perhaps even more than the "attentive" Belleroche.

You can see that instead of lamenting my absence, you ought to be glad of it, for I have never given you such a fine compliment before. I think I am being influenced by your example, and that I am tempted to flatter you too; but no, I prefer to maintain my frankness: it alone assures me of my tender friendship and the interest it inspires in me. It is very pleasant to have a young friend whose heart is occupied elsewhere. That is not the viewpoint of all women, but it is mine. It seems to me that we yield with more pleasure to a sentiment from which we have nothing to fear, so with you I have assumed, rather early, perhaps, the role of confidante. But you fall in love with such young girls that you have made me realize for the first time that I am beginning to grow old! You do well to prepare a long career of constancy for yourself in this way, and I hope with all my heart that it will be reciprocal.

You are right to defer to the "tender and virtuous motives" which, you tell me, are "retarding your happiness." A long defense is the only merit left to women who do not always resist; and, in the case of anyone except a child like your Cécile, I would consider it unpardonable not to be able to avoid a danger of which she has been sufficiently warned by the avowal she has made of her love. You men have no idea of what virtue is and of what it costs to sacrifice it! But if a woman reasons a little, she must know that, aside from the wrong she commits, a weakness is for her the greatest of misfortunes, and I cannot imagine how any woman ever allows it to befall her when she can give it a moment's reflection.

Do not combat this idea, for it is principally what attaches me to you. You will save me from the dangers of love; and although I have so far been able to defend myself from them without you, I consent to be grateful to you, and I shall like you more and better for it.

With this thought I leave you, my dear Chevalier, and I pray God to keep you in His holy care.

LETTER 122

~ *From Madame de Rosemonde to Madame de Tourvel*

Château de ——, October 25, 17—

I had hoped, my charming daughter, that I could at last calm your anxieties, but now, to my sorrow, I see that I am about to increase them still further. But calm yourself: my nephew is not in danger; it cannot even be said that he is really ill. However, something extraordinary is surely taking place within him. I do not understand it, but I left his room with a feeling of sadness, perhaps even of alarm; I reproach myself for making you share it, yet I cannot help talking to you about it. Here is an account of what happened; you may be sure it is accurate, for if I live another eighty years I shall not forget the impression made on me by that sad scene.

When I went into his room this morning, I found him writing and surrounded by various piles of paper which seemed to be the object of his work. He was so absorbed in it that I was already in the middle of the room before he turned his head to see who had entered. As soon as he had seen me, I noticed as he stood up that he tried to compose his features, and it was perhaps that which made me pay closer attention to him. He was disheveled and unpowdered, it is true, but he still looked pale and wasted, and above all his face looked haggard. His eyes, which we have both seen so lively and gay, were sad and downcast. In short, be it said between you and me, I would not have wanted you to see him in that condition, for he looked very touching, and quite capable, I believe, of arousing that tender pity which is one of the most dangerous snares of love.

Although I was struck by my observations, I began the conversation as if I had noticed nothing. I first spoke to him of his health, and while he did not say it was good, neither did he say it was bad. I then complained of his retirement, which seemed a little like an eccentricity, and I tried to mingle some gaiety with my mild reprimand; but he answered earnestly, "It's another one of my wrongs, I admit it; but I shall make amends for it along with the others." His expression, even more than his words, dampened my cheerfulness a little, and I hastened to tell him that he was attaching too much importance to a friendly reproach.

We then began to talk quietly. A short time later he told me that a certain matter, "the most important one of his life," might soon recall him to Paris; but since I was afraid I might guess it, my dear beauty, and that this beginning might lead me to a confidence I did not wish to receive, I asked him no more questions and contented myself with replying that more distractions would be good for his health. I added that this time I would not insist, since I loved my friends for their own sake. At this simple remark he pressed my hands and said to me with a fervor I cannot convey to you, "Yes, aunt, love a nephew who respects and cherishes you; and, as you say, love him for his own sake. Do not be distressed over his happiness, and do not trouble by any regret the eternal tranquillity he hopes to enjoy soon. Tell me again that you love me, and that you forgive me. Yes, you will forgive me: I know your kindness; but how can I hope for the same indulgence from those I have offended so greatly?" Then he leaned over me, to hide, I think, the visible signs of a grief which he involuntarily revealed to me by the sound of his voice.

More deeply moved than I can tell you, I quickly stood up, and no doubt he noticed my alarm, for he immediately added, with more composure, "Forgive me, Madame; I have been carried away in spite of myself. Please forget my words and remember only my deep respect. I shall not fail to come and renew my expression of it before I go." It seemed to me that these last words required me to end my visit, and so I left.

But the more I think about it, the less I can guess what he meant. What is that matter, "the most important one of his life"? For what did he ask me to forgive him? What caused his involuntary emotion as he spoke to me? I have asked myself these questions a thousand times without being able to answer them. I see nothing in all this that has any relation to you; but since the eyes of love see more clearly than those of friendship, I wanted you to be fully informed of everything that took place between my nephew and me.

I have stopped and resumed writing this letter four times, and I would make it still longer if it were not for the fatigue I feel. Good-by, my dear beauty.

LETTER 123

~ *From Father Anselme to the Vicomte de Valmont*

Paris, October 25, 17—

I have received, Vicomte, the letter with which you have honored me, and yesterday, in accordance with your wishes, I went to the person in question. I informed her of the object and the motives of your request that I intercede with her for you. Although I found her firmly attached to her original wise decision, when I pointed out to her that by her refusal she might be placing an obstacle in the path of your happy return to virtue, and thus opposing, as it were, the merciful designs of Providence, she consented to receive your visit, on condition, however, that it be the last. She has asked me to tell you that she will be at home next Thursday, the twenty-eighth. If that day is not convenient for you, be so kind as to let her know, and choose another. Your letter will be received.

However, Vicomte, let me urge you not to delay without good reason, so that you can sooner and more wholeheartedly carry out the praiseworthy intentions you have announced to me. Remember that if we delay taking advantage of a moment of grace, we run the risk of its being withdrawn from us; that while divine goodness is infinite, its use is nevertheless regulated by justice; and that there may come a time when the God of mercy changes into a God of vengeance.

If you continue to honor me with your confidence, I beg you to believe that all my efforts will be yours to command whenever you so desire. No matter how great my occupations may be, my first concern will always be to fulfill the duties of the holy ministry to which I am particularly devoted, and the happiest moment of my life will come when I see my efforts crowned with success through the blessing of the Almighty. Weak sinners that we are, we can do nothing by ourselves! But the God who calls you back to Himself can do everything; and we shall both be indebted to His goodness: you for the constant desire to rejoin Him, I for the means of leading you to Him. It is with His aid that I hope soon to convince you that only our holy religion can give, even in this world, the solid and lasting happiness that is vainly sought in the blindness of human passions.

I have the honor of being, with respectful esteem, etc.

LETTER 124

~ *From Madame de Tourvel to Madame de Rosemonde*

Paris, October 25, 17—

In the midst of the astonishment into which I was thrown by the news I received yesterday, I have not forgotten the satisfaction it will surely give you, Madame, and I hasten to impart it to you. Monsieur de Valmont is no longer concerned with either me or his love, and his only desire is now to make amends, by a more edifying life, for the sins, or rather the errors, of his youth. I have been informed of this great change by Father Anselme, whom he has asked to direct him in the future, and also to procure him an interview with me, the principal object of which is apparently to give me back my letters, which he has so far kept in spite of my request to return them.

No doubt I can only applaud this happy change, and congratulate myself on it, if, as he says, I was responsible for it to some extent. But why did I have to be the instrument of it? Why did it have to cost me the tranquillity of my life? Could not Monsieur de Valmont's happiness have occurred without my misfortune? Oh, my indulgent friend, forgive me for this lament! I know that it is not for me to fathom God's decrees; but while I ask Him constantly and always vainly for the strength to overcome my unhappy love, He lavishes it upon a man who had not asked Him for it, and leaves me helpless and entirely abandoned to my weakness.

But I must stifle these sinful complaints. Do I not know that when the prodigal son returned he received greater favor from his father than the son who had never gone away? Can we demand a reckoning of Him who owes us nothing? And even if it were possible that we should have some rights with Him, what could mine be? Could I boast of a chastity which I now owe only to Valmont? He has saved me—shall I dare to complain of suffering for him? No, my sufferings will be dear to me if they bring about his happiness. No doubt he had to return some day to the universal Father. The God who created him must cherish His work. He did not create that charming man only to make him a reprobate. It is for me to bear the punishment of my audacious imprudence; should I not have realized that since it was forbidden for me to love him, I ought not to have allowed myself to see him?

My sin, or my misfortune, lies in having refused too long to accept that truth. You are my witness, my dear and worthy friend, that I submitted to that sacrifice as soon as I recognized its necessity; but what was lacking to make it complete was that Monsieur de Valmont should not share it. Shall I confess to you that this idea is now what torments me most? Oh, intolerable pride, which softens the pains we feel by those we inflict on others! But I shall overcome this rebellious heart, and accustom it to humiliations.

It was in order to achieve this that I finally consented to receive Monsieur de Valmont's painful visit next Thursday. I shall then hear him tell me himself that I no longer mean anything to him, that the faint and passing impression I had made on him has now been entirely effaced! I shall see his gaze rest on me without emotion, while the fear of revealing my own emotion will make me lower my eyes. I shall receive from his indifference those same letters which he refused so long to my repeated requests; he will return them to me as useless objects which no longer interest him, and when my shameful hands receive that shameful gift, they will feel that it is given to them by a calm, steady hand! Finally I shall see him go away . . . forever. . . . My eyes will follow him, and his will not turn back to me!

And I was destined to such humiliation! Ah, let me at least make it useful by employing it to fill myself with the sentiment of my weakness! . . . Yes, I shall treasure those letters he no longer cares to keep. I shall impose on myself the shame of rereading them every day, until my tears have washed away the last word; and I shall burn his letters as being infected with the dangerous poison that has corrupted my soul. Oh, what is love, if it makes us miss even the dangers to which it exposes us, if we can still be afraid of feeling it even when we have ceased to inspire it! Let us flee that baneful passion which leaves only a choice between shame and unhappiness, and often unites them both, and let us at least replace virtue with prudence!

How far away Thursday still is! If only I could consummate that painful sacrifice at this very moment, and forget both its cause and its object! That visit is a burden to me; I regret having promised to receive it. Why does he need to see me again? What are we to each other now? If he has offended me, I forgive him. I even congratulate him on his desire to make amends for his wrongs; I praise him for it. I shall do more: I shall imitate him; and, led astray by the same errors, I shall be saved by his example. But when his plan is to avoid me, why does he begin by seeking me out? Is it not true that the most urgent thing for each of us is to forget the other? Yes, and from now on it will be my sole concern.

With your permission, my gracious friend, I shall return to you to undertake that difficult labor. If I need help, perhaps even consolation, I want to receive it only from you. You alone can understand me and speak to my heart. Your precious friendship will fill my whole existence. Nothing will seem difficult to me if it is to second the efforts you are willing to make. I shall be indebted to you for my tranquillity, my happiness and my virtue; and the fruit of your kindness to me will be to have made me worthy of it at last.

I think I have allowed myself to be carried away in this letter; at least I presume so from the agitation I have felt during the whole time I have been writing it. If it contains sentiments for which I must blush, cover them with your indulgent friendship. I entrust myself to it entirely. I do not want to hide any of the emotions of my heart from you.

Good-by, my estimable friend. I hope to announce the date of my arrival within a few days.

❧ PART FOUR ❧

❧ *From the Vicomte de Valmont to the Marquise de Merteuil*

Paris, October 29, 17—

She is vanquished, that haughty woman who had dared to think she could resist me! Yes, my friend, she is mine, entirely mine; since yesterday she has had nothing more to grant me.

I am still too full of my happiness to be able to appreciate it, but I am amazed at the unknown charm I felt. Could it be true that virtue increases a woman's value even at the very time of her weakness? But let us relegate that puerile idea to the category of old wives' tales. Does one not nearly always encounter a more or less well-feigned resistance to the first triumph? And have I found nowhere else the charm of which I speak? Yet it was not the charm of love, for while it is true that occasionally, with that astonishing woman, I had moments of weakness which resembled that abject passion, I was always able to overcome them and return to my principles. Even if yesterday's scene carried me, as I think it did, a little further than I expected, and even if I shared for a moment the agitation and rapture I created, that passing illusion would have vanished by now, and yet the same charm remains. I confess, in fact, that yielding to it would give me rather sweet pleasure, if it did not cause me a certain anxiety. At my age, shall I be overwhelmed like a schoolboy by an involuntary and unknown feeling? No: before everything else, I must combat it and fathom it.

Perhaps I have already glimpsed its cause! At least this idea pleases me, and I would like it to be true.

Among the multitude of women with whom I have played the

part and fulfilled the functions of a lover, I had never before encountered a single one who was not at least as eager to yield to me as I was to make her do so; I had even become accustomed to giving the name of "prudes" to those who only met me halfway, as opposed to those many others whose provocative defense only imperfectly covers the advances they have made.

In this case, however, I found an initial unfavorable bias, later supported by the advice and reports of a venomous but clear-sighted woman; extreme natural timidity strengthened by enlightened modesty; an attachment to virtue that was directed by religion and could already count two years of triumph; and finally, resolute actions inspired by these various motives, and all with the object of eluding my pursuit.

And so this is not, as in my other adventures, simply a more or less advantageous surrender which is easier to profit by than to feel proud of; it is a complete victory, won at the cost of a laborious campaign and decided by skillful maneuvers. It is therefore not surprising that this success, which I owe to myself alone, should be more precious to me; and the additional pleasure which I felt during my triumph, and which I still feel, is only the sweet impression of the sentiment of glory. I cherish this viewpoint, for it spares me the humiliation of thinking that I might depend in some way on the slave I have subjugated, that I do not have the plenitude of my happiness in myself alone, and that the power of making me enjoy it in all its intensity resides in a single woman, to the exclusion of all others.

These sensible reflections will guide my conduct in this important situation, and you may be sure that I shall not allow myself to be so enchained that I cannot always break my new bonds at will and without effort. But I am already talking to you of breaking off with her, and you do not yet know how I have acquired the right to do so; read, then, and see what wisdom is exposed to when it tries to help folly. I gave such careful attention to my words and the replies I obtained that I hope to be able to report them both with an exactness that will satisfy you.

I am enclosing copies of two letters* which will show you the mediator I chose to bring me back to my fair lady, and the zeal with which the saintly personage strove to unite us. But I must also tell you something I had learned from a letter intercepted as usual: the fear and the little humiliation of being abandoned had shaken the austere prude's caution, and had filled her heart and

---

*Letters 120 and 123.

her head with feelings and ideas which, though lacking in common sense, were none the less significant. It was after these preliminaries, which it is necessary for you to know, that yesterday, Thursday the twenty-eighth, the day set in advance by my ingrate, I went to her as a timid and repentant slave, and left as a crowned conqueror.

It was six o'clock in the evening when I arrived at the house of my fair recluse (for since her return she had refused to see anyone). She tried to stand up when I was announced, but her trembling knees made it impossible and she immediately sat down again. The servant who had shown me in had some duty to perform in the room; she seemed to be impatient for him to leave. We filled in the interval with the customary exchange of courtesies. But in order not to waste a single moment of this precious time, I carefully examined the room, noting every detail of the scene of my victory. I might have chosen a more convenient one, for while there was a divan in the room, I noticed that opposite it there was a portrait of her husband, and I confess I was afraid that, with such a singular woman, one glance in that direction might destroy in a moment the result of all my painstaking efforts. At last we were left alone and I began my attack.

After telling her in a few words that Father Anselme must have informed her of the reasons for my visit, I complained of the harsh treatment she had given me, and I particularly stressed the "contempt" she had shown for me. She denied these charges, as I expected; and, as you would also have expected, I set out to prove them by citing the mistrust and fear I had aroused in her, the scandalous flight that had followed, her refusal not only to answer my letters, but even to receive them, etc., etc. When she began to justify herself, which would have been easy, I thought it best to interrupt her, and to make her forgive me for this brusqueness, I quickly covered it with flattery: "If all your charms," I said, "have made such a deep impression on my heart, your virtues have made an equally deep impression on my soul. Carried away, no doubt, by my desire to bring myself closer to them, I dared to think myself worthy of them. I do not reproach you for having judged otherwise; but I am being punished for my error." Since she maintained an embarrassed silence, I went on: "I wished, Madame, either to justify myself in your eyes or to obtain your forgiveness for the wrongs you ascribe to me, so that I might at least end with some tranquillity the days to which I no longer attach any value, since you have refused to embellish them."

At this point she tried to reply: "My duty did not permit me . . ." But the difficulty of completing the lie demanded by duty did not permit her to finish the sentence. I therefore continued in a tone of great tenderness: "Is it true, then, that you fled from me?"

"My departure was necessary."

"And that you refuse to see me any more?"

"I must."

"Forever?"

"I have no choice."

I do not need to tell you that during this short dialogue the tender prude's voice faltered and her eyes were not raised to mine.

I felt I ought to animate this languishing scene a little, so I stood up with a resentful expression and said, "Your firmness has given me back all my own. Yes, Madame, we shall be separated, separated, separated even more than you think, and you will congratulate yourself on your handiwork at leisure."

Somewhat taken aback by this reproachful tone, she tried to answer: "The resolution you have made . . ."

"Is only the result of my despair!" I retorted angrily. "You wanted me to be unhappy: I am going to prove to you that you have succeeded even beyond your wishes!"

"I desire your happiness," she said.

The sound of her voice was beginning to indicate rather strong emotion, so I threw myself at her feet and cried out in the dramatic tone with which you are familiar, "Ah, cruel woman, can there be any happiness for me which you do not share? Where could I find happiness away from you? No, never, never!" I confess that in this outburst I had counted heavily on the aid of tears, but whether because I was unfavorably disposed or merely because of the close attention I was constantly giving to everything, I was unable to weep.

Fortunately I recalled that all methods of subjugating a woman are equally good, and that the shock of any strong emotion is enough to make a deep and favorable impression on her. I therefore made up by terror for the sensibility I found lacking: remaining in the same position and changing only the inflection of my voice, I said, "Yes, I swear to you at your feet that I shall either possess you or die." As I spoke these last words, our eyes met. I do not know what the timid lady saw or thought she saw in mine, but she stood up with a look of alarm and freed herself from my arms, which I had placed around her. It is true that I did nothing to retain her, for I had noticed several times that when scenes of despair were carried out too energetically they became ridiculous as soon as they became long, or left only truly tragic resources which I was far from wishing to employ. However, as she was slipping away from me, I added in a low, sinister tone, but loudly enough for her to hear, "So be it, then: death!"

I then stood up, and after a moment of silence I cast wild glances at her which, however distraught they may have appeared to be, were none the less clear-sighted and observant. Her unsteady bearing, her heavy breathing, the contraction of all her muscles, her trembling, half-raised arms—everything about her proved to me that the effect was such as I had wanted to produce; but since in love nothing is completed except at very close quarters, and we were now rather far apart, the first thing that had to be done was to bring us closer together. For this purpose I passed as quickly as possible to an apparent tranquility, calculated to calm the effects of that violent state without weakening its impression.

My transition was: "I am very unfortunate. I wanted to live for your happiness, and I troubled it. I have devoted myself to your tranquillity, and again I have troubled it." Then, with more composure, but also some constraint: "Forgive me, Madame; since I am unaccustomed to the storms of the passions, it is difficult for me to hold them in check. If I was wrong to yield to them, remember at least that it will never happen again. Ah, please calm yourself, I beg you!" And during this long speech I had been gradually drawing nearer.

"If you want me to be calm," said the apprehensive beauty, "you must be calmer yourself."

"I shall, I promise you," I replied. I added in a weaker voice, "If the effort is great, at least it will not be long. But," I went on immediately, with a distraught expression, "I came to return your letters, did I not? Please deign to take them back. That painful sacrifice still remains for me to make; leave me nothing that can weaken my courage." I took the precious bundle from my pocket. "Here," I said, "is the collection of your deceitful assurances of friendship. It attached me to life; take it back. In so doing, you yourself will be giving the signal for my eternal separation from you."

Here she yielded entirely to her tender anxiety: "But Monsieur de Valmont, what is the matter? What do you mean? Is not the step you are now taking a voluntary one? Is it not the fruit of

your own reflections? And was it not those same reflections
which led you to approve of the necessary course I have followed from a sense of duty?''

"Your course has determined mine," I said.

"And what is it?"

"The only one which can both separate me from you and put
an end to my suffering.''

"But tell me, what is it?"

At this point I took her in my arms; she made no resistance
whatever. Judging from this forgetfulness of propriety how strong
and powerful her emotion was, I said to her, risking a show of
fervor, "Adorable woman, you have no idea of the love you
inspire! You will never know how much you were adored, and
how much dearer that sentiment was to me than life itself! May
all your days be fortunate and tranquil; may they be embellished
with all the happiness of which you have deprived me! At least
reward this sincere wish with a regret, with a tear; and believe
that the last of my sacrifices will not be the most painful to my
heart. Good-by.''

While I was speaking, I felt her heart palpitating violently; I
observed the discomposure of her face; I saw that tears were
choking her, yet flowing only seldom and with difficulty. It was
only then that I decided to pretend to go away. She held me by
force and said quickly, "No, listen to me!"

"Let me go," I replied.

"You will listen to me, I insist on it.''

"I must leave you, I must!''

"No!" she cried.

At this last word she threw herself, or rather fell, unconscious
into my arms. Since I still doubted such a stroke of good fortune,
I pretended to be greatly alarmed; but at the same time I led her,
or carried her, to the place I had previously chosen as the field of
my glory; and indeed she did not regain consciousness until she
had been entirely subjugated to the will of her happy conqueror.

So far, my fair friend, I believe you will find that I acted with
a purity of method which will please you, and you will see that I
in no way departed from the true principles of that kind of
warfare which we have often observed to be so similar to the
other kind. Judge me, then, as you would judge Turenne or
Frederick. I forced the enemy to fight when she wanted to avoid
action; by skillful maneuvers I gave myself the choice of terrain
and disposition; I inspired her with confidence, so that I could
overtake her more easily in her retreat; I made confidence give

way to terror before joining battle; I left nothing to chance, except from consideration of a great advantage in case of victory, and the certainty of resources in case of defeat; finally, I did not join battle until I had an assured retreat by which I could cover and hold everything I had previously conquered. I think that is all one can do. But now I am afraid I may have become softened like Hannibal in Capua. Here is what happened afterward.

I did not expect such a great event to take place without the customary tears and despair; at first I noticed a little more shame than usual, and a kind of inner meditation, but I attributed them both to her prudishness; so, without concerning myself with these slight differences, which I thought to be purely local, I simply followed the main road of consolation, convinced that, as usually happens, sensations would aid sentiment, and that one action would do more than endless words, although I did not neglect them either. But I found a resistance that was truly frightening, less because of its intensity than because of the form in which it was manifested.

Imagine a woman sitting stiff and motionless, with an unchanging face, apparently neither thinking, listening nor hearing, while tears flow almost continuously, but without effort, from her fixed eyes. Such was Madame de Tourvel while I spoke to her; but if I tried to recall her attention to me by a caress or even a completely innocent gesture, her apparent apathy immediately gave way to terror, suffocation, convulsions, sobs, and even a few cries at irregular intervals, but without a single word being spoken.

These crises returned several times, always with greater strength; the last one was so violent that I was utterly discouraged, and for a moment I was afraid I had won a useless victory. I fell back on the usual commonplaces, and among them was this: "Are you in despair because you have made me happy?" At this word, the adorable woman turned to me, and I saw that her face, though still a little distraught, had already regained its angelic expression. "Happy?" she said. You can guess my reply. "Are you really happy?" I redoubled my protestations. "And happy through me!" I added praise and tender words. While I spoke, all her limbs relaxed and she leaned limply against the back of her chair; then, abandoning to me the hand I had dared to take, she said, "That idea consoles and relieves me."

As you may well suppose, now that I had found the path again I did not leave it; it was really the right one, and perhaps the only one. When I began to attempt a second success, I encountered some resistance at first, and I was made cautious by what had happened before; but when I appealed to that same idea of my happiness, I soon experienced its favorable effects: "You are right," she said, "my life is now unbearable to me, except insofar as it serves your happiness. I devote myself to it entirely; from this moment I give myself to you, and you will meet with neither refusals nor regrets from me." With this naive or sublime candor, she yielded her person and her charms to me, and increased my happiness by sharing it. The ecstasy was complete and mutual; and, for the first time, my rapture outlasted my pleasure. I left her arms only to fall at her feet and swear eternal love to her; and I must admit that I meant it. Even after I had left her, the thought of her stayed with me, and I had to make an effort to distract myself from it.

Ah, why are you not here to balance the charm of my triumph by that of its reward? But I shall lose nothing by waiting, shall I? And I hope I can count on your consent to the happy arrangement I proposed to you in my last letter. You can see that I am carrying out my end of the bargain, and that, as I promised you, my affairs will have advanced far enough to enable me to give you part of my time. But hurry: dismiss your burdensome Belleroche, abandon the insipid Danceny and concern yourself with me alone. What can you be doing in the country that prevents you from even answering me? Do you know that I could easily scold you? But happiness inclines me to indulgence; and besides, I am not forgetting that in again placing myself among your suitors, I must again submit to your little whims. Remember, however, that the new lover does not wish to lose any of his old rights as a friend.

Good-by, as in the past. . . . Yes, "good-by, my angel, I send you all the kisses of love!"

P.S.—Do you know that Prévan has been forced to leave his corps after spending a month in prison? It is now the talk of Paris. He has truly been cruelly punished for a crime he did not commit, and your success is complete!

LETTER 126

~ *From Madame de Rosemonde to Madame de Tourvel*

Château de ———, October 30, 17—

I would have answered you sooner, my charming child, if the fatigue of my last letter had not brought back my pains, which deprived me of the use of my arm for several days. I was eager to thank you for the good news you have given me of my nephew, and I was equally eager to give you my sincere congratulations on your own account. We are forced to recognize in this a genuine act of Providence which, in touching one person, has also saved the other. Yes, my dear beauty, God wished only to try you, and He helped you just when your strength was exhausted; and despite your little complaint, I believe you have reason to thank Him. Not that I do not realize that it would have been more agreeable for you if that resolution had come to you first, and Valmont's had only been the result of it; it even seems, humanly speaking, that the rights of our sex would have been better preserved, and we do not want to lose any of them! But what are these slight considerations in comparison with the important ends that have been attained? Does a man who escapes from a shipwreck complain that he had no choice of means?

You will soon find, my dear daughter, that the suffering you dread will become lighter of itself; and even if it were to remain undiminished forever, you would still feel that it was easier to endure than the self-contempt and the remorse of crime. It would have been useless for me to speak to you with this apparent severity earlier: love is an independent sentiment which prudence can enable us to avoid, but cannot overcome, and which, once it has been born, lasts until it either dies a natural death or perishes from total lack of hope. The latter case applies to you, and that is what gives me the courage and the right to tell you my opinion freely. It is cruel to frighten a doomed invalid who responds only to consolations and palliatives; but it is wise to enlighten a convalescent on the dangers to which he has been exposed, in order to give him the prudence he needs, and make him submit to any advice that may still be necessary to him.

Since you have chosen me as your doctor, I shall speak to you as such and tell you that the slight discomforts which you now feel, and which may require some sort of remedy, are nothing compared to the frightful illness whose cure is now assured. Then, as your friend, as the friend of a sensible and virtuous woman, I shall tell you that the passion which had subjugated you, already so unfortunate in itself, was still more so because of its object. If I am to believe what I am told, my nephew, whom I admit that I may love with weakness, and who does indeed combine great charm with many praiseworthy qualities, is dangerous to women, has wronged many of them, and takes almost as much pleasure in ruining them as in seducing them. I believe you would have converted him; certainly no one was ever worthier of it. But there have been so many others who flattered themselves with being able to do so, and whose hopes were disappointed, that I am glad you were not reduced to that resource.

And now consider, my dear beauty, that instead of all the risks you would have had to run, you will gain not only peace and an undisturbed conscience, but also the satisfaction of having been the chief cause of Valmont's happy return to virtue. As for myself, I do not doubt that it was largely due to your courageous resistance, and that a moment of weakness on your part might have left him plunged into his errors forever. I like to think so, and I hope you will think the same: you will find your first consolations in it, and I shall find new reasons for loving you still more.

I am expecting you to arrive in a few days, my charming daughter, as you have told me you intend to do. Come and recover your calm and happiness in the same place where you lost them; above all, come and rejoice with your tender mother over having kept so well the promise you made to her: that you would never do anything unworthy of her and of you!

LETTER 127

～ *From the Marquise de Merteuil to the Vicomte de Valmont*

Château de ———, October 31, 17—

If I did not answer your letter of the nineteenth, Vicomte, it was not because I did not have time: it was merely because it annoyed me and struck me as being senseless. I therefore felt that the best thing I could do was to leave it in oblivion; but since you have returned to it and seem to insist on the ideas it contains, and since you mistake my silence for consent, I must clearly tell you my opinion.

I may occasionally have claimed to be able to replace a whole harem all by myself, but it has never suited me to be part of one. I thought you knew that. Now that I have told you so, at least, you will easily see how ridiculous your proposal seemed to me. Did you really expect me to sacrifice an inclination, and a new inclination at that, to concern myself with you? And how? By waiting my turn, like a submissive slave, for the sublime favors of Your Highness! When, for example, you wished to distract yourself for a moment from that "unknown charm" which only your "adorable" and "angelic" Madame de Tourvel has made you feel, or when you were afraid of damaging the superior idea which you are so glad to have your "delightful" Cécile retain of you, then you would descend to me; you would come to me for pleasures that would be less intense, to be sure, but would have the advantage of being without consequence; and your precious favors, though somewhat rare, would be more than sufficient for my happiness!

You are certainly rich in high regard for yourself, but apparently I am not rich in modesty, for no matter how closely I examine myself, I cannot feel that I have fallen as low as that. It may be one of my faults; but I warn you that I have many others.

Specifically, I have the fault of thinking that my "schoolboy," the "insipid" Danceny, concerned solely with me, sacrificing to me, without making a merit of it, a first passion even before it has been satisfied, and loving me as one loves at the age of twenty, could work more effectively than you, despite his youth, for my happiness and my pleasures. I shall even take the liberty of adding that if I should decide to give him an assistant, it would not be you, at least not for the moment.

You will no doubt ask me what my reasons are. First of all, there might be none at all, for the caprice that might make you preferred might just as well exclude you. Out of courtesy, however, I am willing to tell you the motive of my refusal. It seems to me that you would have too many sacrifices to make to me; and I, instead of having the gratitude for them that you would not fail to expect, would be capable of thinking that you owed me still more! You can see that we are so far apart in our way of thinking that we cannot come closer together in any way; and I am afraid it will take me a long time, a very long time, to change

my feelings. I promise to let you know when I have turned over
a new leaf. Until then, take my advice: make other arrangements
and keep your kisses; you have so many opportunities to make
better use of them! . . .

"Good-by, as in the past," you say? But it seems to me that
in the past you valued me more highly; you had not quite
relegated me to third roles; and above all you were willing to
wait until I had said yes before being sure of my consent. You
will therefore excuse me, if, instead of saying "Good-by, as in
the past," I say "Good-by, as of now."

Your humble servant, Vicomte.

LETTER 128

～   *From Madame de Tourvel to Madame de Rosemonde*

Paris, November 1, 17—

It was only yesterday, Madame, that I received your belated
reply. It would have killed me as soon as I read it if my
existence were still my own; but it belongs to another, and that
other is Monsieur de Valmont. You can see that I hide nothing
from you. Even if you should feel that I am no longer worthy of
your friendship, I am less afraid of losing it than of keeping it by
fraud. All I can tell you is that, having been placed by Monsieur
de Valmont between his death and his happiness, I have chosen
the latter. I neither boast of it nor condemn myself for it: I
simply state the fact.

After that, you will easily understand the effect produced on
me by your letter and the severe truths it contains. But do not
think that it aroused any regret in me, or that it can ever make
me change my feelings or my conduct. Not that I do not have
cruel moments; but when my heart is most torn, when I am
afraid I can no longer endure my torment, I say to myself,
"Valmont is happy," and everything vanishes before that idea,
or rather it changes everything into pleasure.

I have, then, devoted myself to your nephew; it is for him that
I have ruined myself. He has become the sole center of my
thoughts, feelings and actions. As long as my life is necessary to
his happiness, it will be precious to me, and I shall consider it a
fortunate one. If some day he decides otherwise . . . he will hear

no complaint or reproach from me. I have already dared to look upon that fateful moment, and my mind is made up.

You can now understand how little I am affected by the fear you seem to have that Monsieur de Valmont may some day ruin me, for before he wishes to do so, he will have ceased to love me, and what shall I then care about vain reproaches which I shall not hear? He alone will be my judge. Since I shall have lived only for him, my memory will rest in him; and if he is forced to recognize that I loved him, I shall be sufficiently justified.

You have now seen into my heart, Madame. I prefer the misfortune of losing your esteem by my frankness to that of making myself unworthy of it by the debasement of lying. I feel I owe this complete confidence to your former kindness to me. If I were to add another word, I might make you suspect that I have the arrogance to continue to count on it when, on the contrary, I do myself justice by abandoning all claim to it.

I am with respect, Madame, your most humble and most obedient servant.

LETTER 129

～ *From the Vicomte de Valmont to the Marquise de Merteuil*

Paris, November 3, 17—

Tell me, my fair friend, what can have caused that tone of rancor and sarcasm which reigns in your last letter? What is this crime I have committed, apparently without knowing it, which has put you in such a bad temper? You reproach me with seeming to count on your consent before having obtained it: but I thought that what might appear to be presumption to everyone else could never be taken as anything but confidence between you and me; and since when has that sentiment been harmful to either friendship or love? In combining hope with desire, I was only yielding to the natural impulse which always makes us place ourselves as close as possible to the happiness we seek; and you mistook an effect of my eagerness for one of arrogance. I know very well that respectful doubt is customary in such cases, but you know equally well that it is only a convention, a mere formality, and it seems to me that I had good reason to believe that those minute precautions were no longer necessary between us.

It even seems to me that this forthright and unrestrained manner of proceeding, when it is founded on a former intimacy, is incomparably preferable to the vapid flattery which so often makes love insipid. Or perhaps the value I find in this manner comes only from that which I attach to the happiness it reminds me of; but for that very reason it would be still more painful for me to have you think otherwise.

Yet, to my knowledge, that is the only wrong I have committed; for I do not imagine for a moment that you can have seriously thought that there was any woman in the world whom I might prefer to you, much less that I could have set such a small value on you as you pretend to believe. You have examined yourself, you tell me, and you do not feel that you have fallen as low as that. I believe you, and it merely proves that your mirror is accurate. But might you not have concluded more easily, and with more justice, that I certainly had not formed any such judgment of you?

I vainly seek a reason for that strange idea. I can only conclude that it must have something to do with the praises I have allowed myself to give to other women. At least that is what I infer from your affectation in quoting the epithets of "adorable," "angelic" and "delightful," which I used in speaking to you of Madame de Tourvel and Cécile Volanges. But do you not know that such words, usually taken at random rather than from reflection, express not so much one's opinion of the person as the situation in which one is speaking? And if, at the very time when I was so keenly affected by one or the other, I still desired you as much as ever; if I gave you a marked preference over both of them, since after all I could not renew our first intimacy except at the expense of the two others, I do not think I have given you any serious grounds for reproaching me.

Nor will it be difficult for me to justify myself with regard to the "unknown charm" which also seems to have offended you a little; for first of all, from the fact that it is unknown, it does not follow that it is stronger. Ah, what could surpass those delightful pleasures which you alone are able to make always new and always more intense? I merely meant to say that it was of a kind that I had never experienced before, but I had no intention of classifying it; and I added, as I now repeat, that no matter what it may be, I shall be able to combat it and overcome it. I shall do so with even more zeal if I can view that light labor as an homage I can offer you.

As for little Cécile, I think it is useless to speak to you of her. You have not forgotten that I took charge of that child at your request, and I await only your permission to get rid of her. I may have noticed her ingenuousness and freshness; I may even have considered her "delightful" for a moment, because one is always more or less pleased with one's own work; but there is certainly not enough to her in any way to hold my attention.

And now, my fair friend, I appeal to your sense of justice, to your first favors to me, to the long, perfect friendship and complete confidence which have tightened our bonds since then: have I done anything to deserve the harsh tone you have taken with me? But how easy it will be for you to compensate me for it whenever you choose! You have only to say a word and you will see whether there are any charms or attachments capable of keeping me here, not for a day, but even for a minute. I shall fly to your feet and into your arms, and I shall prove to you a thousand times and in a thousand ways that you are and always will be the true ruler of my heart.

Good-by, my fair friend; I await your reply with great eagerness.

LETTER 130

~· *From Madame de Rosemonde to Madame de Tourvel*

Château de ———, November 4, 17—

And why, my dear beauty, do you no longer wish to be my daughter? Why do you seem to be announcing to me that all communication between us is going to be broken off? Is it to punish me for not having guessed something that was contrary to all likelihood? Or do you suspect me of having hurt you voluntarily? No, I know your heart too well to think that you could have such an opinion of mine; so the pain your letter has caused me is related much more to you than to me!

Oh, my young friend! It hurts me to tell you this, but you are so worthy of being loved that love will never make you happy. What truly delicate and sensitive woman has not found misfortune in that same sentiment which promised her so much happiness! Do men know how to appreciate the women they possess?

Not that some of them are not honorable in their conduct and constant in their affection; but even among them, how few are able to put themselves in unison with our hearts! Do not believe, my dear child, that their love is like ours. They experience the same ecstasy, often with greater fury; but they know nothing of that anxious eagerness, that delicate solicitude, which in us produce those tender and continuous attentions whose sole object is always the man we love. A man enjoys the happiness he feels, a woman the happiness she gives. This difference, so essential and yet so seldom noticed, has a marked influence on the whole of their respective behavior. A man's pleasure is to satisfy desires, a woman's is chiefly to arouse them. To please is for him only a means of succeeding, whereas for her it is success itself. And coquettishness, for which women are so often reproached, is nothing but the excess of this way of feeling, and by that very fact proves its reality. Finally, that exclusive inclination which particularly characterizes love is, in a man, only a preference which serves at most to increase a pleasure that another object might weaken but would not destroy, whereas in a woman it is a profound sentiment which not only annihilates all alien desires but, being stronger than nature and beyond its control, lets her feel only repugnance and disgust where it would seem that sensual pleasure ought to be aroused.

And do not believe that the more or less numerous exceptions that can be cited are capable of successfully opposing these general truths! They are supported by public opinion, which, for men only, distinguishes between infidelity and inconstancy, a distinction of which they readily avail themselves when they ought to be humiliated by it, and which, for our sex, has never been adopted except by those depraved women who are its shame, and to whom any means seems good if they expect it to save them from the painful awareness of their baseness.

I thought, my dear beauty, that it might be useful for you to have these reflections to oppose to the illusory ideas of perfect happiness with which love never fails to deceive our imagination; we still cling to that deceitful hope even when we are forced to abandon it, and its loss intensifies and multiplies the sufferings, already too real, that are inseparable from any strong passion. This function of softening your sorrows, or diminishing their number, is the only one I am willing and able to fulfill at this time. In incurable illnesses, advice can only be directed to the regimen. All I ask of you is to remember that to pity an invalid is not to blame him. Ah, what are we, to blame one another? Let us leave the right of judgment to Him who reads in our hearts; and I even dare to believe that in His paternal eyes a multitude of virtues can redeem a single weakness.

But I beg you, my dear friend, to resist those violent resolutions which are less an indication of strength than of utter discouragement; do not forget that in allowing your existence to belong to another, to use your expression, you cannot deprive your friends of that part of it which already belonged to them, and to which they will never cease to lay claim.

Good-by, my dear daughter; think of your affectionate mother sometimes, and do not doubt that you will always be, above all else, the object of her dearest thoughts.

LETTER 131

~ *From the Marquise de Merteuil to the Vicomte de Valmont*

Château de ———, November 6, 17—

Well said, Vicomte, and this time I am more pleased with you than before; but now let us have a friendly discussion, and I hope to convince you that the arrangement you seem to desire would be a real folly for both of us.

Have you not yet noticed that, while pleasure is indeed the sole motive for the union of the two sexes, it is not sufficient to form a bond between them, and that if it is preceded by desire, which attracts, it is none the less followed by disgust, which repels? It is a law of nature that can be changed only by love, and can one have love at will? Yet it is always required, and this would be a serious problem if it had not been discovered that fortunately it is enough for love to exist on one side only. This reduces the difficulty by half, and without any great loss, for one enjoys the happiness of loving while the other enjoys that of pleasing; the latter is a little less intense, it is true, but to it is joined the pleasure of deceiving, which restores the balance, and thus all is well.

But tell me, Vicomte, which of us will undertake to deceive the other? You know the story of the two cheaters who recognized each other while gambling: "We can do nothing to each other," they said, "let us divide the stakes between us"; and they abandoned the game. Believe me, we must follow that prudent example, and not waste any time together that we can employ so well elsewhere.

To prove to you that my decision is based on your interest as much as on my own, and that I am not acting from spitefulness or caprice, I shall not refuse you the reward we have agreed upon. I know very well that for one evening we shall more than satisfy each other, and I have no doubt that we shall be able to embellish it so much that we shall see it end with regret. But let us not forget that this regret is necessary to happiness, and no matter how sweet our illusion may be, let us not believe that it could last.

You see that I, too, am carrying out my end of the bargain, and I am doing so even though you have not fulfilled all the conditions, for I was to have your first letter from your heavenly prude, and yet, whether because you still treasure it, or because you have forgotten the terms of the bargain, which may interest you less than you would like to make me believe, I have received nothing, absolutely nothing. And if I am not mistaken, she must write a great deal, for what else can she do when she is alone? She surely does not have the good sense to amuse herself. If I so desired, then, I could make a few little complaints to you, but I shall pass over them in silence to compensate for any ill-humor I may have shown in my last letter.

And now, Vicomte, I have only one request to make of you, and again it is as much for your sake as for mine: it is to postpone a moment which I desire perhaps as much as you do, but which I think should be delayed until my return to Paris. On the one hand, we would not have the necessary freedom here; and on the other, it would involve a certain risk for me, because it would take only a little jealousy to make my dismal Belleroche more firmly attached to me than ever, although he is now hanging only by a thread. He has already reached the point of having to make desperate efforts to love me, so that I now put as much malice as prudence into the caresses with which I overload him. But at the same time you can see that this would not be a sacrifice to make to you! A reciprocal infidelity will make the charm much more powerful.

Do you know that I sometimes regret that we are reduced to such resources? In the days when we loved each other—for I believe it was love—I was happy; and you, Vicomte? . . . But why think about a happiness that cannot return? No, whatever you may say, it is impossible. First of all, I would demand sacrifices which you surely could not or would not make to me, and which I may not deserve; and then, how could I hold you? Oh, no, no! I do not even want to consider that idea; and despite the pleasure I now feel in writing to you, I prefer to leave you abruptly. Good-by, Vicomte.

LETTER 132

~ *From Madame de Tourvel to Madame de Rosemonde*

Paris, November 7, 17—

I am deeply moved by your kindness, Madame, and I would abandon myself to it entirely if I were not restrained to some extent by the fear of profaning it by accepting it. When I find it so precious, why must I feel at the same time that I am no longer worthy of it? Ah, I shall at least dare to express my gratitude to you for it; I shall admire that indulgence of virtue which recognizes our weaknesses only to sympathize with them, and whose powerful charm holds such a sweet and strong dominion over our hearts, even beside the charm of love.

But can I still deserve a friendship which no longer suffices for my happiness? I say the same of your advice; I feel its value, yet I cannot follow it. And how could I not believe in perfect happiness when I am now experiencing it? Yes, if men are as you say, they must be avoided, they are hateful; but if so, how far Valmont is from resembling them! If he has that violence of passion which you call fury, how greatly it is surpassed in him by his extreme delicacy! Oh, my friend, you speak to me of sharing my sorrows; enjoy my happiness instead! I owe it to love, and the object of that love makes it still more precious to me. If only you knew him as I do! I love him to the point of idolatry, and even then it is less than he deserves. It is true that he has been led into certain errors, he himself admits it; but who has ever known real love as he does? What more can I tell you? He feels it as he inspires it.

You will think that this is one of those "illusory ideas with which love never fails to deceive our imagination"; but in that case, why would he have become more tender and ardent now that he no longer has anything left to obtain? I confess that I formerly saw in him an air of reflection and reserve which seldom left him and often brought me back, in spite of myself, to the false and cruel impressions I had been given of him. But now that he can abandon himself without constraint to the impulses of his heart, he seems to guess all the desires of mine. Who knows whether we were not born for each other, whether I was not destined to achieve my happiness in being necessary to his! Ah, if it is an illusion, may I die before it ends! But no, I want to live to cherish him, to adore him. Why should he stop loving me? What other woman could make him happier than I do? I myself feel that this happiness which one creates is the strongest of all bonds, the only one that really binds. Yes, it is that delightful sentiment which ennobles love, purifies it, as it were, and makes it truly worthy of a tender and generous soul, like Valmont's.

Good-by, my dear, my estimable, my indulgent friend. It would be useless for me to try to write any longer: it is now the time when he has promised to come, and every other thought has abandoned me. Forgive me, but you desire my happiness, and it is so great at this moment that I can scarcely contain it.

LETTER 133

~   *From the Vicomte de Valmont to the Marquise de Merteuil*

Paris, November 8, 17—

What are these sacrifices, my fair friend, which you think I would not make even though their reward would be to please you? You have only to let me know what they are, and if I so much as hesitate to offer them to you, I give you permission to refuse them. What opinion have you formed of me if, even in your indulgence, you doubt my feelings or my resoluteness? Sacrifices that I would not or could not make! So you consider me to be in love, and subjugated? And you suspect me of attaching to the person the value I originally set on the victory? I have not yet been reduced to that, thank heaven, and I offer to prove it to you. Yes, I shall prove it to you, even if it must be at the expense of Madame de Tourvel. After that, you will surely have no more doubts.

I have given some time, without compromising myself, I believe, to a woman who at least has the merit of belonging to a category one seldom encounters. Perhaps also the dead season in which this adventure occurred mad me throw myself into it more wholeheartedly, and even now, when the great current of society has scarcely begun to flow, it is not surprising that I should be almost entirely absorbed in it. But remember that I have only been enjoying for a week the fruit of three months of effort. I have so often lingered longer over women who were worth much less, and had not cost me so much! . . . And it never made you draw any adverse conclusions about me.

And then, would you like to know the real cause of my enthusiasm? Here it is. That woman is naturally timid; at first she constantly doubted her happiness, and that doubt was enough to trouble it, so I am only beginning to see how far my power can go in that direction. It is something I was curious to know, and it is more difficult to find the opportunity than is commonly believed.

First of all, for many women pleasure is always pleasure and nothing more; to them, no matter what the title with which they adorn us, we are never anything but laborers, mere agents whose sole merit is activity, and he who does most is always he who does best.

Another class of women, perhaps the most numerous today, are almost wholly concerned with their lover's celebrity, the pleasure of having taken him away from one rival, and the fear that he may be taken away by another. We have something to do, more or less, with the kind of happiness they enjoy, but it is related much more to the circumstances than to the person. It comes to them through us, not from us.

For my observations, then, I had to find a delicate and sensitive woman who would make love her sole concern, and who, in love itself, would see only her lover; a woman whose emotion, far from following the usual path, would always start from her heart to reach her senses; a woman who, for example, as I have actually seen (and I am not speaking of the first day), could emerge from pleasure in tears and then find sensuality a moment later in word that replied to her soul. Finally, she had to have a natural candor that had become insurmountable through the habit of yielding to it, and which would not permit her to dissimulate any of the sentiments of her heart. Now you will admit that such women are rare, and I can readily believe that I might never have known one if I had not met Madame de Tourvel.

It would therefore not be surprising if she should hold me longer than usual. And if the work I wish to do on her requires me to make her happy, perfectly happy, why should I refuse to do so, especially since it serves my purposes instead of thwarting them? But when the mind is occupied, does it follow that the heart is enslaved? Of course not. So the importance which I do not deny attaching to this adventure will not prevent me from pursuing others, or even sacrificing it to more agreeable ones.

I am so free that I have not even neglected little Cécile, for whom I care so little. Her mother is taking her back to Paris in three days, and yesterday I made sure of my communications in advance: the matter was arranged by a little money to the door-keeper and a few compliments to his wife. Can you understand why Danceny never discovered that simple means? And yet it is said that love makes one resourceful! On the contrary, it dulls the minds of those it dominates. And you think I cannot protect myself from it! Have no fear! . . . The impression I have received is perhaps too intense, but in a few days I shall weaken it by sharing it, and if sharing it with one is not enough, I shall share it with many.

I shall nevertheless be ready to hand over your pupil to her discreet Danceny whenever you see fit. It seems to me that you no longer have any reason to prevent it, and I am willing to render poor Danceny that outstanding service. It is the least I can do for him after all the services he has rendered me. He is now in a state of great anxiety to know whether he will be received in Madame de Volanges's house. I calm him as best I can by assuring him that, in one way or another, I shall make him happy the first day; and meanwhile I continue to take charge of the correspondence he wants to resume when "his Cécile" arrives. I already have six letters from him, and I shall have one or two more before the happy day. The boy must have a great deal of spare time!

But let us leave that childish couple and return to ourselves; let me dwell exclusively on the sweet hope your letter has given me. Yes, you will hold me, and I would not forgive you for doubting it. Have I ever ceased to be constant with you? Our ties were loosened, not broken; what we regarded as our parting was only an error of our imagination: our feelings and interests have remained united. Like a traveler who returns undeceived, I shall recognize that I had left happiness to pursue hope, and I shall say, like Harcourt, "The more foreigners I saw, the more I loved my country."*

Abandon your opposition to the idea, or rather the feeling that brings me back to you; and after having tried all pleasures in our

---

*Du Belloi. *Tragédie du Siège de Calais.*

different paths, let us enjoy the happiness of discovering that none of them can compare with the pleasure we felt in the past, which we shall find to be more delightful than ever!

Good-by, my charming friend. I consent to wait until your return, but hasten it, and do not forget how much I desire it.

LETTER 134

~ *From the Marquise de Merteuil to the Vicomte de Valmont*

Château de ———, November 11, 17—

Really, Vicomte, you are like children, before whom one must not say anything, and to whom one cannot show anything without their trying to snatch it away! A mere idea occurred to me and I warned you that I did not wish to pursue it; but, taking advantage of the fact that I mentioned it to you, you have brought my attention back to it, forced me to dwell on it when I want to be diverted from it, and made me share your foolish desires to some extent in spite of myself! Is it fair of you to leave me to bear the whole burden of prudence? I tell you again, and I repeat it to myself still more often: the arrangement you propose is really impossible. Even if you put into it all the generosity you are now showing, do you think that I do not have my delicacy also, and that I would accept sacrifices which would be harmful to your happiness?

Is it true, Vicomte, that you are still deluded about the sentiment which attaches you to Madame de Tourvel? It is love, or love never existed; you deny it in a hundred ways, but you prove it in a thousand. Consider, for example, the subterfuge you employ with yourself (for I believe you are sincere with me) when you attribute your wish to keep her, which you can neither hide nor overcome, to a desire for observation. As thought you had never made another woman happy, perfectly happy! Ah, if you doubt that, you have a very poor memory! But no, it is not that. It is simply that your heart deceives your mind and makes it accept false reasons; but I, who have a great interest in not being mistaken, am not so easily contented.

Thus, while I noticed your courtesy in carefully eliminating all the words you thought had displeased me, I saw that you had nevertheless retained the same ideas. She is no longer the adorable, the angelic Madame de Tourvel; but she is an "amazing woman," a "delicate and sensitive woman," and this to the exclusion of all others; and she is a "rare woman," so rare that one might never meet another like her. It is the same with that unknown charm which is "not the strongest." So be it; but since you had never found it before, we may assume that you will never find it again, and your loss of it would be irreparable. Either these are conclusive symptoms of love, Vicomte, or none will ever be found.

You may be sure that this time I am speaking to you without rancor. I have promised myself never to give in to it again; I have seen too clearly that it can be a dangerous snare. Believe me, it is better for us to remain friends and nothing more. But be grateful to me for my courage in restraining myself: yes, my courage, for it is sometimes needed to avoid doing something even when we know it would be a mistake.

It is therefore not in order to persuade you to accept my opinion that I am going to answer your questions about the sacrifices I would demand and you could not make. I deliberately use the word "demand" because I am sure that in a moment you will indeed think me too demanding; but so much the better! Far from being angered by your refusals, I shall thank you for them. I shall not dissimulate with you, although perhaps I need to.

I would demand—see how cruel I am!—that your rare, amazing Madame de Tourvel be no more to you than an ordinary woman, a woman such as she really is, for we must not be deceived: the charm we think we find in others exists in us, and it is love alone that embellishes its object so much. Although what I am asking is impossible, you would perhaps make the effort of promising, even swearing that you would do it; but I confess that I would not believe empty words. I could be convinced only by your whole conduct.

That is not all: I would be capricious. I would care nothing for the sacrifice of little Cécile which you so graciously offer me. I would ask you, on the contrary, to continue that laborious service until further orders from me, either because I would enjoy abusing my power in that way, or because, being more indulgent or more just, it would be enough for me to control your sentiments without thwarting your pleasures. In any case, I would insist on obedience, and my orders would be very harsh!

It is true that I would then feel obliged to thank you, and perhaps—who knows?—even to reward you. For example, I would certainly cut short an absence that would become unbearable to me. I would see you again, Vicomte, and I would see you . . . how? . . . But you have not forgotten that this is only a conversation, a mere account of an impossible plan, and I do not want to forget it alone. . . .

Do you know that I am a little worried about my lawsuit? I finally decided to find out exactly what I can count on; my lawyers quoted me a few laws and many "authorities," as they call them, but I do not see so much reason and justice in what they call them, but I do not see so much reason and justice in what they have told me. I have almost begun to regret having refused a compromise. However, I am reassured when I remind myself that the attorney is shrewd, the counselor eloquent, and the litigant pretty. If these three advantages were no longer decisive, the whole course of affairs would have to be changed, and what would become of respect for ancient customs?

This lawsuit is now the only thing that keeps me here. Belleroche's is now over: thrown out of court, both parties to share the costs. He has reached the point of regretting that he has missed this evening's ball—only an idle man could have such a regret! I shall give him his complete freedom when I return to Paris. I am going to make that painful sacrifice to him, and I am consoled for it by the generosity he sees in it.

Good-by, Vicomte; write to me often: the details of your pleasures will at least partially compensate me for the boredom I am now undergoing.

LETTER 135

〜 *From Madame de Tourvel to Madame de Rosemonde*

Paris, November 15, 17—

I shall try to write to you, but I do not yet know whether I shall be able to do so. Ah, dear God, when I think that in my last letter it was my extreme happiness that prevented me from continuing! It is now my extreme despair that overwhelms me; it leaves me only the strength to feel my pain, and deprives me of the strength to express it.

Valmont . . . Valmont no longer loves me, he never loved me. Love does not vanish in that way. He has deceived me, betrayed me, insulted me. I am enduring all the misfortunes and humiliations that can be gathered together, and they have come to me from him!

And do not think that this a mere suspicion: I was so far from having any! I am not fortunate enough to be able to doubt. I saw him: what could he say to justify himself? . . . But what does it matter to him! He will not even try. . . . Wretch that I am! What will he care about my tears and my reproaches? He is indifferent to me! . . .

It is true that he has sacrificed me, betrayed me. . . . And to whom? A vile creature. . . . But what am I saying? I have lost even the right to despise her! She has betrayed fewer duties, she is less guilty than I. Oh, how painful grief is when it is strengthened by remorse! I feel my torments redoubling. Good-by, my dear friend; however unworthy of your pity I may have made myself, you will have some of it left for me if you can form some idea of my suffering.

I have just reread my letter, and I see that it tells you nothing; I shall therefore try to have the courage to relate that cruel event to you. It was yesterday. For the first time since my return, I was to go out for supper. Valmont came to see me at five o'clock; never had he seemed more tender. He let me know that he was displeased by my intention of going out, and so, as you may well suppose, I soon decided to stay home. Two hours later, however, his expression and tone suddenly changed perceptibly. I do not know if something escaped from me which may have offended him, but in any case, a short time later he claimed to remember an engagement that obliged him to leave me, and he went away, though not without expressing keen regrets which seemed tender to me, and which I then thought to be sincere.

When I was left to myself, I thought it would be best to fulfill my original engagement, since I was now free to do so. I completed my toilet and got into my carriage. Unfortunately my coachman drove me past the opera, and we became entangled in the confusion of the exit. A short distance in front of me, in the line beside mine, I saw Valmont's carriage. My heart began to pound at once, but it was not from fear; my mind was occupied only by my desire for my carriage to go forward. Instead, his was forced to move back, and it stopped opposite mine. I leaned forward immediately: what was my surprise when I saw him sitting with a woman of ill repute, well known as such! I drew back, as you may well imagine; this alone was enough to pierce my heart, but what you will find difficult to believe is that the woman, apparently informed by an odious confidence, stayed at the carriage window and continued to look at me, laughing loudly.

Although I was in a state of prostration, I allowed my coachman to drive me to the house where I was to have supper; but it was impossible for me to stay there: I felt ready to faint at any moment, and I could not hold back my tears.

When I returned, I wrote a letter to Monsieur de Valmont and sent it to him immediately; he was not at home. Wishing, at any price, either to emerge from that state of death or confirm it forever, I sent my servant back with orders to wait, but he returned before midnight and told me that the coachman, who had come back, had said that his master would not be home until the following day. This morning I felt that I had no choice but to ask him to return my letters and never to come to my house again. I gave orders to that effect, but no doubt they were useless. It is now past noon: he has not come, and I have not received a word from him.

And now, my dear friend, I have nothing more to add; you are informed of everything, and you know my heart. My only hope is that I shall not have to distress your sensitive friendship much longer.

LETTER 136

~ *From Madame de Tourvel to the Vicomte de Valmont*

Paris, November 15, 17—

After what happened yesterday, Monsieur, you surely do not expect to be received in my house again, and you surely have little desire to be! The object of this note, then, is not so much to ask you not to come here again as to request the return of those letters which ought never to have existed, and which, although they may have interested you for a short time as proofs of the blindness you had created, can only be worthless to you now that it has been dispelled and they express nothing but a sentiment you have destroyed.

I recognize and admit that I was wrong to place in you a confidence which had made victims of so many other women before me; in this I blame only myself: but I thought I had at least deserved not to be exposed to contempt and insult by you. I thought that in sacrificing everything to you, and in losing for you alone my rights to the esteem of others and of myself, I could expect not to be judged more sternly by you than by the public, whose opinion still makes a sharp distinction between a weak woman and a depraved woman. These wrongs, which would apply to anyone, are the only ones of which I shall speak. I shall say nothing about those of love; your heart would not understand mine. Good-by, Monsieur.

LETTER 137

～   *From the Vicomte de Valmont to Madame de Tourvel*

Paris, November 15, 17—

Your letter has just been delivered to me, Madame; I shuddered as I read it, and it has left me scarcely enough strength to reply to it. What a horrible idea you have of me! Ah, certainly I have done wrong, so much so that I shall never forgive myself for it as long as I live, even if you should cover it with your indulgence! But how far from my soul the wrongs with which you reproach me have always been! What! Could I humiliate you, degrade you, when I respect you as much as I cherish you, when I have known pride only since you first judged me to be worthy of you? You have been misled by appearances, and I admit that they may have been against me: but did your heart lack what was needed to combat them? Did it not rebel against the mere idea that it might have reason to complain of mine? Yet you believed it was true! Not only did you judge me to be capable of that atrocious madness, but you even feared that you might have exposed yourself to it through your kindness to me. Ah, if you consider yourself so degraded by your love for me, I myself must be very vile in your eyes!

Oppressed by the painful feeling which this idea causes me, I waste in rejecting it the time I ought to employ in destroying it. I shall confess everything; but another consideration still restrains me. Must I recount facts which I would like to annihilate, and fix your attention and mine on a moment of error which I would like to redeem with the rest of my life, whose cause I still cannot understand, and whose memory will always bring me humiliation and despair? If, in accusing myself, I must arouse your anger, at least you will not have to seek far for your vengeance: it will be enough to leave me to my remorse.

And yet—who would believe it?—the first cause of that event was the all-powerful charm I feel in your presence. That was what made me forget too long an important matter which could not be postponed. I left you too late, and I did not find the person I had gone to meet. I hoped to find him at the opera, but my search there was unsuccessful. Emilie, whom I encountered there, and whom I had known at a time when I was far from knowing either you or love, did not have her carriage with her, and asked me to take her to her home a short distance away. Feeling that it was a matter of no consequence, I consented. But it was then that I met you, and I realized at once that you would be inclined to judge me guilty.

My fear of displeasing or distressing you is so powerful that it could not fail to be noticed. I admit that it made me try to restrain that woman from showing herself, but that precaution of my delicacy turned against my love. Accustomed, like all women of her condition, to never being certain of a power which is always usurped, except by the abuse she allows herself to make of it, Emilie had no intention of letting such an outstanding opportunity escape. The more she saw my embarrassment increase, the more conspicuously she showed herself; and her wild laughter, the memory of which makes me blush when I think that you believed yourself to be its object, was caused only by the cruel pain I felt, which was in turn caused by my respect and my love.

So far I am more unfortunate than guilty; and those wrongs, "which would apply to anyone," and are "the only ones of which you will speak," cannot be imputed to me, since they do not exist. But it is in vain that you say nothing about those of love; I shall not keep the same silence about them: too great an interest forces me to break it.

Not that, in my shame over that incomprehensible aberration, I can bring myself to recall it without extreme pain. Overwhelmed by my wrongs, I would consent to bear the punishment for them, or await forgiveness of them from time, from my eternal tenderness, and from my repentence. But how can I remain silent when what I have to say is important to your delicacy?

Do not think that I am seeking a roundabout way of excusing or palliating my offense: I admit my guilt. But I do not and never will admit that this humiliating error could be regarded as an offense against love. What can there be in common between a surprisal of the senses, a moment of self-forgetfulness soon followed by shame and regret, and a pure sentiment which can arise only in a delicate soul, can be sustained there only by esteem, and whose fruit is happiness! Ah, do not profane love thus! Above all, fear to profane yourself by bringing together, within the same point of view, things that can never be confused with one another. Let vile and degraded women dread a rivalry whose possibility they feel in spite of themselves, and let them endure the torments of a cruel and humiliating jealousy; but as for you, turn your eyes away from objects that would sully your gaze, and, pure as the Divinity, imitate it further in punishing the offense without resenting it.

But what punishment can you inflict on me which would be more painful than what I now feel, which could be compared to the regret of having displeased you, to the despair of having hurt you, or to the crushing idea of having made myself less worthy of you? You are thinking of punishment, and I ask you for consolation; not because I deserve it, but because it is necessary to me, and can come to me only from you.

If, suddenly forgetting my love and yours, and ceasing to place any value on my happiness, you should wish, on the contrary, to inflict eternal pain on me, you have the right to do so: strike. But if, more indulgent, or more sensitive, you still recall those tender sentiments which united our hearts; that exquisite pleasure of the soul, always reborn and always more keenly felt; those sweet, happy days which each of us owed to the other; and finally, all those treasures of love which it alone can bring, then, perhaps, you will prefer the power of recreating them to that of destroying them. What more can I say? I have lost everything, through my own fault; but I can regain everything through your benevolence. It is for you to decide now. I shall add nothing but this: only yesterday you swore to me that my happiness was certain as long as it depended on you! Ah, Madame, will you abandon me today to eternal despair?

LETTER 138

~ *From the Vicomte de Valmont to the Marquise de Merteuil*

Paris, November 15, 17—

I persist, my fair friend: no, I am not in love; and it is not my fault if circumstances force me to play the part. You have only to give your consent and come back: you will soon see for yourself how sincere I am. I gave proof of it yesterday, and it cannot be destroyed by what is happening today.

I went to see my tender prude, without any other engagement, because little Cécile, despite her condition, was to spend the whole night at Madame de V——'s early ball. At first, lack of anything better to do made me want to prolong the evening, and I even demanded a little sacrifice for that purpose; but scarcely had it been granted when the pleasure I was anticipating was disturbed by the thought of your stubborn belief that I am in love, or at least your stubborn persistence in accusing me of it, and from that moment my only desire was to assure myself and convince you that it was pure calumny on your part.

I therefore took decisive action: on a rather slight pretext, I suddenly abandoned my fair lady, leaving her in great surprise and no doubt still greater distress. I then calmly went off to meet Emilie at the opera; and she can tell you that no regrets troubled our pleasures from the time we met until we parted this morning.

Yet I would have had a rather good cause for anxiety if my perfect indifference had not saved me from it, for I was no more than four houses away from the opera, with Emilie in my carriage, when my pious beauty's carriage stopped exactly opposite mine, and a blockage kept us there beside each other for nearly ten minutes. We could see each other as plainly as at noon, and there was no way to escape.

But that is not all: I took it into my head to confide to Emilie that this was the woman of the letter (you may remember that prank, in which Emilie served as my desk*). She had not forgotten, and, being mirthful by nature, she insisted on having a good

*See Letters 47 and 48.

look at "that virtue personified," as she put it, with bursts of loud, offensive laughter.

And that is still not all: the jealous woman sent a messenger to my house that same evening. I was not there, but, in her obstinacy, she sent him back with orders to wait for me. As soon as I decided to stay with Emilie, I sent my carriage home with no orders to my coachman except to come for me at her house this morning; when he returned, he found the messenger of love, and thought it quite simple to tell him I was not coming home that night. You can imagine the effect of this news: when I returned, I found my dismissal expressed with all the dignity required by the circumstances.

And so you see that this adventure, which you consider endless, might have ended this morning; if I have not allowed it to do so, it is not, as you will believe, because I set any value on its continuation, but because I did not think it would be proper to let myself be abandoned, and also because I wanted to reserve the honor of that sacrifice for you.

I therefore replied to the stern note by a long letter full of sentiment; I gave lengthy reasons and relied on love to make them seem good. I have already succeeded. I have just received a second note: it is also severe and it confirms our eternal separation, as was to be expected, but its tone is not the same. She especially refuses to see me again: this resolution is announced four times in the most irrevocable manner. From this I concluded that I had no time to lose before paying her a visit. I have already sent my valet to deal with her doorkeeper, and in a moment I shall go myself to have my pardon signed, for in crimes of this kind there is only one form which gives a general acquittal, and it must be drawn up in person.

Good-by, my charming friend; I am off to attempt that great event.

LETTER 139

~ *From Madame de Tourvel to Madame de Rosemonde*

Paris, November 16, 17—, in the evening

How I reproach myself, my sensitive friend, for having spoken to you too much and too soon about my passing sorrows!

You are now grieved because of me; the distress that came to you from me still lasts, and I am happy. Yes, everything has been forgotten, forgiven; or, still better: everything has been restored. My pain and anguish have given way to calm and bliss. O joy of my heart, how shall I express you! Valmont is innocent; no one can be guilty with so much love. He did not commit those grave, offensive wrongs with which I reproached him so bitterly; and if I had to be indulgent on one point, did I not also have to atone for my own injustice?

I shall not tell you in detail the facts or reasons which justify him; perhaps the mind would not appreciate them: they can only be felt by the heart. If, however, you suspect me of weakness, I shall appeal to your own judgment in support of mine. You yourself have said that, for men, infidelity is not inconstancy.

I am well aware that although this distinction is authorized by public opinion, it is nevertheless offensive to delicacy; but of what could mine complain when Valmont's suffers even more? Do not think he has forgiven or consoled himself for the wrong I have forgotten; yet how fully he has made amends for that slight lapse by the abundance of his love and of his happiness!

I do not know whether my felicity is greater than before, or whether I have merely become more conscious of its value since I was afraid I had lost it; but I do know that if I felt that I had the strength to endure more torments as cruel as those I have just experienced, I would not consider it too high a price to pay for the wealth of happiness I now enjoy. O my tender mother, scold your thoughtless daughter for having grieved you by her hastiness; scold her for having rashly judged and slandered the man she should never have ceased to adore; but in recognizing that she is imprudent, see that she is happy, and increase her joy by sharing it.

LETTER 140

~ *From the Vicomte de Valmont to the Marquise de Merteuil*

Paris, November 21, 17—

Why is it, my fair friend, that I have had no answer from you? It seems to me that my last letter deserved one; I should have received it three days ago, yet I am still waiting! I am annoyed, to say the least, so I shall not speak to you at all about my great affairs.

That the reconciliation has had its full effect; that instead of reproaches and mistrust, it has produced only new tenderness; that it is now I who am receiving the apologies and reparations that are owed to me because suspicion was cast on my candor—I shall not say a word about any of these things, and if it were not for last night's unexpected event, I would not be writing to you at all. But since it concerns your pupil, and since she will probably not be able to tell you about it herself, at least not for some time, I shall do it for her.

For reasons which you may or may not guess, I had not been occupied with Madame de Tourvel for the past few days, and since those reasons could not exist with little Cécile, I had become more assiduous with her. Thanks to the obliging doorkeeper, I had no obstacles to overcome, and your pupil and I were leading a convenient and orderly life. But habit brings carelessness. During our first nights together, we could never take too many precautions for our safety; we trembled even behind bolted doors. Last night an incredible oversight caused the accident I am going to report to you; I escaped with nothing more than fright, but it cost her more dearly.

We were not asleep, but we were in the repose and abandon that follows pleasure, when we heard the door of the bedroom suddenly open. I immediately leapt for my sword, to defend her as well as myself. I went to the door and saw no one, but it was actually open. Since we had a light, I looked around and did not find a soul. Then I recalled that we had forgotten our usual precaution: the door, left unlocked, had no doubt opened of itself.

When I returned to calm my timid companion, I did not find her in the bed: she had fallen, or taken refuge, between it and the wall; in any case, she was lying on the floor unconscious, and without movement except for rather strong convulsions. Imagine my consternation! I succeeded in putting her back in bed, and even in bringing her back to consciousness, but she had been injured by her fall, and she soon felt the effects of it.

Violent pains in the back and stomach, along with other still more unmistakable symptoms, soon enlightened me about her condition; but in order to tell her about it, I first had to inform her of the condition in which she had been before, for she had not yet even suspected it. Never before, perhaps, had a girl ever kept so much innocence while doing everything necessary to get rid of it! Ah, there is one girl who wastes no time on reflection!

But she was now wasting a great deal of it on lamentations, and I knew that something had to be done. We agreed that I would go to the physician and the surgeon of the family, tell them that they would soon be sent for, and confide everything to them under the seal of secrecy; meanwhile she would ring for her maid and confide in her or not, as she chose, but in any case she would tell her to bring assistance and forbid her to awaken Madame de Volanges: a delicate and natural consideration on the part of a daughter who was afraid of upsetting her mother.

I ran my two errands and made my two confessions as quickly as I could, then I went home. I have not gone out since, but the surgeon, whom I already knew, came to me at noon to give me a report on the patient's condition. I was not mistaken; but he hopes that, if no accident happens, no one in the house will discover the truth. Her maid has been taken into the secret, the physician has given her illness a name, and this affair will be buried in silence like countless others, unless it should later suit our purposes to have it talked about.

But is there still any common interest between you and me? Your silence would make me doubt it, and I might even have ceased to believe it altogether, if my desire for it did not make me seek every means of retaining my hope of it.

Good-by, my fair friend; I kiss you, with rancor.

LETTER 141

~ *From the Marquise de Merteuil to the Vicomte de Valmont*

Château de ———, November 24, 17—

How you bother me with your obstinacy, Vicomte! What does my silence matter to you? Do you think I have been keeping it because I lack reasons with which to defend myself? God grant that it were so! But no, it is only because it is painful for me to tell them to you.

Tell me the truth: are you deluding yourself, or are you trying to deceive me? The difference between your words and your actions leaves me no choice except between those two explanations: which one is correct? What do you expect me to say to you, when I do not even know what to think?

You seem to make a great merit of your latest scene with

Madame de Tourvel, but what does it prove for your viewpoint, or against mine? I have certainly never told you that you loved her enough not to decieve her, not to seize any opportunity that might seem pleasant or easy to you; nor have I doubted that you would have almost no qualms about satisfying with another woman, the first woman who happened to be available, even those desires which she alone had aroused; and I am not surprised that, by a libertinism of the mind which it would be wrong to deny you, you have for once done be design what you have done countless other times from opportunity. Who does not know that it is simply the way of the world, and the usual practice of all men, from the wily scoundrel to the bungling fool? Anyone who abstains from it nowadays is regarded as romantic, and I do not think that is the fault with which I reproach you.

But what I said, and what I still believe, is that you are nevertheless in love with your Madame de Tourvel; not with a very pure or tender love, to be sure, but with the kind of love of which you are capable: the kind, for example, which makes you think a woman has the charms or qualities she lacks, which places her in a class apart and puts all other women in a second order, which keeps you attached to her even when you insult her; the kind of love, in short, that I imagine a sultan may feel for his favorite sultana, which does not prevent him from often preferring a lowly harem concubine to her. My comparison seems all the more accurate to me because, like the sultan, you are never a woman's lover or friend, but always her tyrant or slave. So I am quite sure that you humiliated and degraded yourself to return to your fair lady's good graces! And, overjoyed to have succeeded, as soon as you thought the time had come to obtain your forgiveness, you left me for "that great event."

If, in your last letter, you do not talk to me only about her, it is because you do not want to tell me anything about "your great affairs"; they seem so important to you that you feel you are punishing me by remaining silent about them. And it is after these many proofs of your preference for another woman that you calmly ask me if there is "still any common interest between you and me"! Be careful, Vicomte! Once I have given my answer, it will be irrevocable; and letting you know that I am afraid to give it now is perhaps already saying too much, so I absolutely refuse to discuss it any further.

All I can do is to tell you a story. Perhaps you will not have time to read it or give it enough attention to understand it properly; do as you please. At worse, it will only be a story wasted.

A man I know had become entangled, like you, with a woman who did him little honor. He occasionally had the good sense to realize that sooner or later this adventure would do him harm; but although he was ashamed of it, he did not have the courage to break it off. His embarrassment was all the greater because he had boasted to his friends that he was completely free, and because he was aware that one's ridiculousness increases in proportion as one denies it. Thus he spent all his time doing foolish things and invariably saying afterward, "It is not my fault." This man had a friend who was tempted for a moment to exhibit him to the public in this state of derangement, thus making his ridiculousness ineffaceable; but, more generous than malicious, or perhaps from some other motive, she decided to try one last means, so that in any event she could say, like him, "It is not my fault." She therefore sent him, without any explanation, the following letter, as a remedy whose application might be effective against his disease:

"One eventually becomes bored with everything, my angel; it is a law of nature, and it is not my fault.

"So if I am now bored with an adventure that has been my sole preoccupation for four deadly months, it is not my fault.

"If, for example, I had just as much love as you had virtue—and that is surely saying a great deal—it is not surprising that one should have ended at the same time as the other. It is not my fault.

"From it this follows that for some time I have been deceiving you; but I was more or less forced to do so by your implacable tenderness! It is not my fault.

"And now a woman with whom I am madly in love demands that I sacrifice you, It is not my fault.

"I realize that this gives you a fine opportunity to bewail my broken vows; but if nature has given men only persistence, while she has given women obstinacy, it is not my fault.

"Take my advice: choose another lover, as I have chosen another mistress. This is good advice, very good; if you consider it bad, it is not my fault.

"Good-by, my angel; I took you with pleasure, I am leaving you without regret, and perhaps I shall come back to you. So goes the world. It is not my fault."

*   *   *

This is not the time, Vicomte, to tell you the effect of this last attempt and what followed from it; but I promise to tell you in my next letter. You will also find it in my ultimatum on the renewal of the treaty you propose to me. Until then, good-by, without further qualification. . . .

By the way, I thank you for your details about little Cécile; it is an article which we must reserve for publication in the Gossip Gazette on the day after her wedding. In the meantime, let me offer you my condolences on the loss of your posterity. Good night, Vicomte.

LETTER 142

~ *From the Vicomte de Valmont to the Marquise de Merteuil*

Paris, November 27, 17—

Really, my fair friend, I do not know whether I misread or misunderstood your letter, the story you told me in it, and the model note that was included in it; but I do know that the latter struck me as original and likely to be effective, so I simply copied it and sent it to my heavenly prude. I did not waste a moment, for the tender missive was dispatched last evening. I preferred it thus, first of all because I had promised to write to her yesterday, and also because I felt she would need at least all night to collect her thoughts and meditate on "that great event" (I will use the expression even if you reproach me for it again).

I had hoped to be able to send you my beloved's reply this morning, but it is nearly noon and I have not yet received anything. I shall wait until three o'clock, and then, if I still have no news, I shall go to obtain some in person; for, especially in such matters, it is only the first step that is difficult.

And now, as you must realize, I am eager to learn the end of the story of that man you know who is so strongly suspected of being unable to sacrifice a woman when necessary. Has he not reformed? And has his generous friend not give him her pardon?

I am no less eager to receive your "ultimatum," as you so diplomatically express it! I am particularly curious to know whether you will still see love in this latest action of mine. Ah, there certainly is a great deal of love in it! But for whom?

However, I have no intention of making any claims; I look to your kindness for everything.

Good-by, my charming friend; I shall not close this letter until two o'clock, in the hope that I may be able to enclose the desired reply.

Two o'clock in the afternoon.

Still nothing, and time is pressing, so I can add no more; but this time will you continue to refuse the most tender kisses of love?

LETTER 143

~ *From Madame de Tourvel to Madame de Rosemonde*

Paris, November 27, 17—

The veil is torn, Madame: the veil on which the illusion of my happiness was painted. The sinister truth enlightens me, and shows me nothing but certain and imminent death, the path to which is laid out for me between shame and remorse. I shall follow it. . . . I shall cherish my torments if they shorten my existence. I am enclosing the letter I received yesterday; I shall add no reflections on it: it is self-explanatory. The time for complaining is past; I can now do nothing but suffer. It is not pity I need, but strength.

Receive, Madame, the only farewell I shall make, and grant my last request: it is to leave me to my fate, to forget me completely, and to consider me as no longer among the living. Unhappiness eventually reaches a point at which even friendship increases our suffering and cannot cure it. When wounds are mortal, all aid becomes cruel. Every feeling except despair is foreign to me. Nothing can befit me except the profound darkness in which I am going to bury my shame. There I shall weep for the wrong I have done—if I can still weep; for since yesterday I have not shed a tear. My withered heart can supply no more.

Good-by, Madame. Do not reply to me. I have sworn upon that cruel letter never to receive another.

LETTER 144

～   *From the Vicomte de Valmont to the Marquise de Merteuil*

Paris, November 28, 17—

Yesterday, my fair friend, at three o'clock in the afternoon, I finally lost patience at still having no news, so I went to the house of the forsaken beauty; I was told she had gone out. I saw this only as a refusal to receive me which neither angered nor surprised me; I left with the hope that my attempt would at least force such a polite woman to honor me with a word of reply. My desire to receive it made me stop by my house for that purpose at about nine o'clock, but I found nothing. Astonished by this unexpected silence, I told my valet to make inquiries and find out if the sensitive lady was dead or dying. When I returned later, he told me that Madame de Tourvel had left her house at eleven o'clock in the morning, that she had gone to the Convent of ———, and that at seven o'clock in the evening she had sent back her carriage and her servants, with instructions not to wait for her at home. She has certainly done the right thing: a convent is the proper refuge for a widow; and if she persists in her praiseworthy resolution, I shall have still another obligation to her: that of the fame which this adventure will have.

Some time ago I told you that, despite your worries, I would not make any reappearance on the stage of society until I was shining with a new luster. Let them show themselves, those stern critics who accused me of a romantic and unhappy love! Let them break off an affair more swiftly and brilliantly! But no, let them do better: let them present themselves as consolers, the path is already marked out for them. Let them merely set out on the course I have pursued to the end, and if one of them obtains the slightest success, I will yield first place to him. But they will find that when I make my best efforts, the impression I leave is indelible. This one will surely remain so; and I would count all my other triumphs as nothing if this woman should ever prefer a rival to me.

The course she has taken flatters my self-esteem, I admit it; but I regret that she found enough strength to cut herself off from me so sharply. What! Will there be obstacles between us other than those I have placed there myself? If I wished to return to her, could she no longer be willing? What am I saying? Could she no longer desire it, no longer make it her supreme happiness? Is that the way to love? And do you think, my fair friend, that I ought to allow it? Could I not, for example, and would it not be better, try to bring her back to the point of foreseeing the possibility of a reconciliation, which one always desires as long as one has hope? I could try it without attaching any importance to it, and therefore without offending you. On the contrary, it would simply be an attempt that we would make together; and even if I should succeed, it would only be a means of repeating, whenever you chose, a sacrifice that seems to have pleased you. And now, my fair friend, I have only to receive my reward for it, and all my wishes are for your return. Hurry back to your lover, your pleasures, your friends, and the current of adventures.

Little Cécile's adventure has turned out perfectly. Yesterday, when my anxiety did not allow me to stay in one place for long, in the course of my various activities I went to see Madame de Volanges. I found your pupil already in the drawing room, still dressed as an invalid, but in full convalescence, and looking all the fresher and more attractive. In a similar case, a woman would have spent a month on her chaise longue: long live young girls! This one really made me want to find out if her recovery was complete!

I must also tell you that her accident has almost driven your sentimental Danceny insane: first with grief, now with joy. "His Cécile" was ill! You can imagine how he lost his head in such a misfortune. He sent for news of her three times a day, and no day went by without his coming to the house in person; finally he sent an eloquent letter to Madame de Volanges asking permission to come and congratulate her on the convalescence of her dear daughter, and she consented. I therefore found the young man installed in her house as in the past, except for a certain familiarity which he did not yet dare to show.

It was from him that I learned these details, for I left at the same time he did, and I made him chatter to me. You have no idea of the effect that visit had on him. I could not describe his joy, his eager desires, his raptures. Since I like great emotions, I made him lose his head entirely by assuring him that within a few days I would make it possible for him to see his beloved at even closer range.

I have decided to hand her over to him as soon as I have made my experiment. I want to devote myself to you completely; and then, would it be worthwhile for your pupil to be mine also if she were to deceive only her husband? The master stroke is to deceive one's lover, especially one's first lover! For as to myself, I am not obliged to reproach myself with ever having said the word "love" to her.

Good-by, my fair friend; come back as soon as possible to enjoy your power over me, to receive the tribute of it, and to give me my reward.

LETTER 145

~   *From the Marquise de Merteuil to the Vicomte de Valmont*

Château de ———, November 29, 17—

Seriously, Vicomte, have you abandoned Madame de Tourvel? Have you sent her the letter I composed for her? Really, you are charming, and you have surpassed my expectations! I admit in good faith that this triumph flatters me more than any of the others I have obtained. You may think I am now valuing that woman very highly after previously thinking so little of her; not at all: I have not won a victory over her, but over you. That is the amusing part of this affair, and it is really delightful.

Yes, Vicomte, you were very much in love with Madame de Tourvel, and you still are; you are madly in love with her, but because I amused myself by making you ashamed of it, you bravely sacrificed her. You would have sacrificed a thousand women rather than endure one jest. See where vanity can lead us! The wise man is quite right when he says it is the enemy of happiness.

What would your situation be now if I had wanted to do more than play a trick on you? But I am incapable of deceit, as you well know; even if you should also reduce me to despair and drive me into a convent, I shall take that risk and yield to my conqueror.

Yet if I surrender, it is purely from weakness, for if I wanted to, how many points I could still quibble over! And perhaps you would deserve it. I am impressed, for example, by the adroitness, or the awkwardness, with which you cautiously suggest that I let you patch things up with Madame de Tourvel. It would suit you very well, would it not, to give yourself the merit of having broken off with her without losing the pleasures of possession? And then, when that apparent sacrifice would no longer be one at all, you offer to repeat it whenever I choose! By that arrangement, the heavenly prude would still think herself the sole choice of your heart, while I would pride myself on being the preferred rival; we would both be deceived, but you would be satisfied, and what does anything else matter?

It is a pity that, with so much talent for making plans, you have so little for carrying them out, and that by a single thoughtless act you yourself have placed an insurmountable obstacle between you and what you most desire.

What! You had the idea of winning her back after sending her the letter I composed? You must think that I, too, am very awkward! Believe me, Vicomte: when a woman strikes at another woman's heart, she seldom fails to find the sensitive spot, and the wound is incurable. As I was striking this one, or rather, as I was directing your blows, I did not forget that she was my rival, that for a time you had found her preferable to me; in short, that you had placed me beneath her. If I have made an error in my venegeance, I am willing to take the consequences of it, so I have no objection to your trying every possible means; I invite you to do so, in fact, and I promise not to be angered by your success, if you should have any. However, I am so confident in this matter that I do not wish to concern myself with it any more. Let us talk of other things.

Of little Cécile's health, for example. You will give me precise details of it when I return, will you not? I shall be glad to have them. After that, it will be for you to judge whether it will be better for you to give her back to Danceny, or to try to become a second time the founder of a new branch of the Valmonts, under the name of Gercourt. That idea seemed rather amusing to me, and although I am now leaving the choice to you, I ask you not to make any final decision before we have discussed it together. This will not involve a long delay, because I shall be back in Paris very soon. I cannot tell you exactly which day, but you may be sure that you will be the first to be informed of my arrival.

Good-by, Vicomte; despite my quarrels, my tricks and my reproaches, I still love you very much, and I am preparing to prove it to you. Until we meet again, my friend.

LETTER 146

~ *From the Marquise de Merteuil to the Chevalier Danceny*

Château de ———, November 29, 17—

At last I am leaving, my young friend, and tomorrow evening I shall be back in Paris. In the midst of all the confusion that a journey brings with it, I shall receive no one. However, if you have anything urgent to confide to me, I am willing to make you an exception to the general rule; but I shall except no one but you, so I ask you to keep my arrival a secret. Even Valmont will not be informed of it.

If anyone had told me only a short time ago that you would soon have my exclusive confidence, I would not have believed it. But yours has attracted mine. I might be tempted to think that you have employed adroitness, perhaps even seduction. That would be very wrong, to say the least! However, it would not be dangerous now: you have other things to do! When the heroine is on the stage, one forgets about the confidante.

And so you have not even had time to tell me about your new successes. When your Cécile was absent, the days were not long enough for all your tender complaints. You would have made them to the echoes if I had not been there to hear them. Later, when she was ill, you still honored me with an account of your anxieties; you needed someone to tell them to. But now that your beloved has returned to Paris and is in good health again, and especially now that you occasionally see her, she suffices for everything, and your friends no longer mean anything to you.

I do not blame you for this; it is the fault of your youth. Is it not well known that, from Alcibiades down to you, young people have never known friendship except in their sorrows? Happiness sometimes makes them indiscreet, but never confiding. I can truthfully say, like Socrates, "I like my friends to come to me when they are unhappy"*; but since he was a philosopher, he could do without them very well when they did not come. In that respect, I am not quite so wise as he, and I felt your silence with all a woman's weakness.

---

*Marmontel, *Conte Moral d'Alcibiade*.

But do not think I am demanding: I am far from it! The same sentiment which makes me notice these privations also makes me endure them with courage, when they are the proof or the cause of my friends' happiness. I therefore do not count on seeing you tomorrow evening unless love leaves you free and unoccupied; and I forbid you to make the slightest sacrifice for my sake.

Good-by, Chevalier; I am looking forward to seeing you again; will you come?

LETTER 147

~ *From Madame de Volanges to Madame de Rosemonde*

Paris, November 29, 17—

You will surely be as distressed as I am, my worthy friend, when you learn of Madame de Tourvel's condition. She has been ill since yesterday; her illness came upon her so suddenly, and with such grave symptoms, that I am truly alarmed.

A burning fever, a violent and almost constant delirium, an unquenchable thirst: that is all that can be observed. The doctors say they cannot yet make any prognosis, and the treatment will be all the more difficult because she stubbornly refuses every kind of remedy, so that she had to be held by force to be bled, and force has had to be used twice since then to put back her bandage, which, in her delirium, she always wants to tear off.

You who have seen her, as I have, so frail, so timid and so gentle, can you imagine that four people can scarcely restrain her, and that she flies into an indescribable fury whenever anyone tries to tell her anything? For my part, I am afraid it may be something more than delirium, that is may be a real mental derangement.

My fears on that subject are increased by what happened day before yesterday.

On that day she arrived at about eleven o'clock in the morning, with her maid, at the Convent of ———. Since she was brought up in that convent and has retained the habit of returning to it occasionally, she was received as usual, and she seemed calm and well to everyone. About two hours later she asked if the room she had occupied as a school girl was vacant, and when she was told that is was, she asked to see it again. The prioress and several other nuns accompanied her to it. She then told them that she had come back to live in that room, and that she should never have left it; she added that she would not leave it again "until death": that was her expression.

At first they did not know what to say, but when their first astonishment had passed, they pointed out to her that, as a married woman, she could not be allowed to stay there without special permission. This reason and countless others had no effect on her, and from then on she stubbornly refused to leave not only the convent, but even her room. Finally, at seven o'clock in the evening, they gave up and let her spend the night there. They sent back her carriage and her servants, and put off making any decision until the next day.

They say that during the whole evening there was nothing disorderly about her appearance or her behavior; on the contrary, both were composed and thoughtful. Four or five times, however, she sank into such a deep reverie that the nuns could not draw her out of it by speaking to her, and each time, before coming out of it, she raised both hands to her forehead, which she seemed to clasp tightly. When one of the nuns asked her if she had a headache, she looked at her for a long time before answering, then finally said, "The pain is not there!" A moment later, she asked to be left alone, and requested that no questions be asked of her in the future.

Everyone then withdrew, except for her maid, who fortunately had to sleep in the same room with her, since there were no other accommodations.

According to the maid's report, her mistress was fairly calm until eleven o'clock. She then said she wanted to go to bed, but before she was entirely undressed, she began pacing the floor with great animation and frequent gestures. Julie, who had witnessed what had happened during the day, was afraid to say anything, and waited in silence for nearly an hour. Finally Madame de Tourvel called her twice in rapid succession; she immediately ran over to her mistress, who fell into her arms and said, "I'm exhausted." She let Julie guide her to her bed, but would not take anything or allow her to go for help. She only had some water placed beside her, then she ordered Julie to go to bed.

Julie says she lay awake until two o'clock in the morning, and that during that time she heard neither movement nor complaints. But she says she was awakened at five o'clock by her mistress's speaking in a loud voice. She asked if she needed anything.

Having received no reply, she took a light and went over to her bed. Madame de Tourvel did not recognize her, but she broke off the incoherent words she was saying and cried out, "Leave me alone, leave me in darkness! It is darkness that befits me!" I myself noticed yesterday that she often repeats this.

Julie took advantage of this order to go out and bring help; but Madame de Tourvel refused everything with the fury and delirium which have returned to her so often since.

The difficulty in which this had placed the whole convent made the prioress decide to send for me at seven o'clock in the morning. . . . It was not yet daylight. I hurried to the convent immediately. When I was announced to Madame de Tourvel, she seemed to recover her senses and replied, "Ah, yes, let her come in." But when I was beside her bed she stared at me, clutched my hand and said to me in a strong but somber voice, "I am dying because I did not believe you." Immediately afterward, she hid her eyes and returned to her most frequent words: "Leave me alone," etc. Then she lost all consciousness.

This remark which she made to me, and a few others which have escaped from her in her delirium, make me fear that her cruel illness has a still more cruel cause. But let us respect our friend's secrets and content ourselves with pitying her misfortune.

The whole of yesterday was equally stormy, and was divided between terrifying fits of delirium and moments of lethargic prostration, the only moments when she takes or gives any rest. I did not leave her bedside until nine o'clock in the evening, and I shall go back this morning to spend the day there. Certainly I shall not abandon my unfortunate friend; but what is disheartening is her stubborn refusal of all care and assistance.

I shall enclose last night's report on her, which I have just received, and which, as you will see, is anything but comforting. I shall take care to send all the reports to you.

Good-by, my worthy friend; I am going back to the invalid. My daughter, who is fortunately nearly well now, sends you her respects.

LETTER 148

~~   *From the Chevalier Danceny to the Marquise de Merteuil*

Paris, December 1, 17—

O you whom I love! O you whom I adore! O you who began
my happiness! O you who have completed it so abundantly!
Sensitive friend, tender lover, why does the memory of your
sorrow come to trouble the charm I feel? Ah, Madame, calm
yourself, it is friendship that asks it of you. O my beloved, be
happy: that is the prayer of love.

With what can you reproach yourself? Believe me, your delicacy deceives you. The regrets it causes you and the wrongs of
which it accuses you are equally illusory; and I feel in my heart
that there has been no other seducer between us than love. Fear
no longer to abandon yourself to the feelings you inspire, to let
yourself be imbued with all the ardor you arouse. What! Can our
hearts be less pure because they were enlightened later? Certainly not. On the contrary, it is seduction which, never acting
except by design, can co-ordinate its advances and its means,
and foresee events from afar. But true love does not allow us to
meditate and reflect thus: it diverts us from our thoughts by our
feelings; its power is never greater than when it is unrecognized,
and it is in darkness and silence that it binds us with the ties that
are as impossible to perceive as they are to break.

Thus, only yesterday, despite the keen emotion aroused in me
by the idea of your return, and despite the extreme pleasure I felt
in seeing you again, I still thought I was called and guided only
by friendship; or rather, I was so absorbed in the sweet feelings
of my heart that I gave very little attention to distinguishing their
origin or cause. Like me, my tender friend, you felt, without
recognizing it, that imperious charm which delivered our souls to
the sweet impressions of tenderness, and we both recognized
love only when we emerged from the ecstasy into which that god
had plunged us.

But that in itself justifies us instead of condemning us. No,
you have not betrayed friendship, not have I abused your confidence. We were both unaware of our sentiments, it is true; but
we felt that illusion without seeking to create it. Ah, far from

complaining of it, let us think only of the happiness it has brought us! And, without troubling that happiness by unjust reproaches, let us concern ourselves with increasing it still more by the charm of trust and confidence. O my beloved, how dear that hope is to my heart! Yes, henceforth freed from all fear, and entirely absorbed in love, you will share my desires, my transports, the ecstasy of my senses, the rapture of my soul; and each moment of our happy days will be marked by a new pleasure.

Farewell, you whom I adore! I shall see you this evening, but shall I find you alone? I dare not hope it. Ah, you do not desire it as much as I!

LETTER 149

~ *From Madame de Volanges to Madame de Rosemonde*

Paris, December 2, 17—

I hoped almost all day yesterday, my worthy friend, that by this morning I could give you more favorable news of our dear invalid's health; but that hope was destroyed last evening, and I have nothing left but the regret of having lost it. An event, quite unimportant in appearance, but very cruel in its consequences, has made her condition at least as bad as before, if not worse.

This sudden change would have been incomprehensible to me if our unhappy friend had not fully confided in me yesterday. Since she told me that you are also aware of all her misfortunes, I shall speak to you without reserve about her sad situation.

When I arrived at the convent yesterday morning, I was told that she had been asleep for more than three hours, and her sleep was so deep and tranquil that for a moment I was afraid she might be in a coma. Some time later, she awoke and drew back the bed curtains herself. She looked at all of us with an air of surprise, and as I was standing up to go over to her, she recognized me, called me by name and asked me to come to her. Without giving me time to question her, she asked me where she was, what we were doing there, whether she was ill, and why she was not at home. At first I thought she was having a new, though calmer, attack of delirium, but then I saw that she understood my answers quite well. She had recovered her reason, but not her memory.

She questioned me in great detail about everything that had
happened to her since she had been in the convent, to which she
did not remember coming. I answered her truthfully, omitting
only what might have alarmed her too much; and when I asked
her how she felt, she replied that she was not suffering at that
moment, but that she had been tormented in her sleep and felt
tired. I urged her to be calm and speak little, then I partially
closed the curtains and sat down beside her bed. At the same
time she was offered some broth; she accepted it and ate it with
relish.

She remained thus for about half an hour, speaking only to
thank me, with her usual charm and graciousness, for the care I
had given her. Then she maintained an absolute silence for some
time, breaking it only to say, "Ah, yes, I remember coming
here"; and a moment later she cried out sorrowfully, "My
friend, my friend, pity me! All my grief has returned!" When I
moved closer to her, she seized my hand, pressed her head
against it and said, "Dear God, why can I not die?" Her
expression, even more than her words, moved me to tears; she
noticed this from my voice and said, "You pity me! Ah, if you
only knew . . ." She interrupted herself: "Ask them to leave us
alone together, and I shall tell you everything."

As I think I have indicated to you, I already had some
suspicion as to what she might confide to me; I was therefore
afraid that this conversation, which I expected to be long and
sad, might be harmful to her condition, so I refused at first,
saying that she needed rest. But she insisted, and I yielded to her
entreaties. As soon as we were alone, she told me everything;
you have already learned it from her, so I shall not repeat it to you.

Finally, in speaking of the cruel way in which she had been
sacrificed, she said to me, "I thought I was quite certain to die
of it, and I had the courage to do so; but it will be impossible for
me to survive my misery and shame." I tried to combat her
discouragement, or rather her despair, with the weapons of
religion, hitherto so powerful over her; but I soon felt that I did
not have the strength for those august functions, and I limited
myself to proposing that Father Anselme be sent for, since I
knew he had her entire confidence. She consented, and even
seemed to desire it greatly. He was sent for, and he came
immediately. He stayed with her for a long time, and when he
came out he said that if the doctors were of the same opinion, he
thought the ceremony of the sacraments could be postponed, and
that he would return the next day.

It was then about three o'clock in the afternoon, and until five o'clock our friend was fairly tranquil, so that we all regained hope. Unfortunately a letter was then brought to her. At first she refused to take it, saying that she would not receive any letters, and no one insisted. But from that moment she seemed more agitated. Soon afterward, she asked where the letter had come from. It was not postmarked. Who had brought it? No one knew. On whose behalf had it been delivered? The doorkeeper had not been told. She remained silent for a time, then began to speak again; but her incoherent words told us only that her delirium had returned.

However, there was another interval of calm which lasted until she asked to be given the letter that had been brought for her. As soon as she saw it she cried out, "From him! Oh, dear God!" And then, in a strong but oppressed voice: "Take it back. Take it back." She immediately had her bed curtains closed and forbade anyone to approach her, but a few moments later we were forced to return to her. Her delirium had set in again with greater violence than ever, and this time it was accompanied by truly frightful convulsions. These symptoms continued all evening, and this morning's report informs me that the night was no less stormy. Her condition is such that I am surprised that she has not succumbed to it, and I shall not conceal from you that I have very little hope.

I suppose that unfortunate letter is from Monsieur de Valmont, but what can he still dare to say to her? Forgive me, my dear friend; I shall refrain from making any comments, but it is extremely painful to see a woman perish so wretchedly when she enjoyed such great happiness before, and was so worthy of it.

LETTER 150

From the Chevalier Danceny to the Marquise de Merteuil

Paris, December 3, 17—

While awaiting the happiness of seeing you again, my tender friend, I shall indulge in the pleasure of writing to you; it is by thinking of you that I charm away the regret of being separated from you. It delights my heart to recall your feelings and remind you of mine, and in doing so I give countless treasures to my love even during the time of my deprivation. Yet, if I am to believe you, I shall obtain no reply from you: this letter, in fact, will be the last, and we shall deprive ourselves of a correspondence which, according to you, is dangerous, and which "we do not need." I shall certainly believe you if you persist, for you can wish nothing that I shall not wish for that very reason. But before you come to a final decision, will you not allow me to discuss it with you?

As for the danger involved, you alone must judge it; I can make no calculations, and I limit myself to begging you to take care of your safety, for I cannot be calm if you are worried. In this respect, it is not we two who are one, it is you who are both of us.

It is not the same with the "need." Here we can have only a single thought, and if we differ in opinion, it can only be from lack of having explained ourselves or of having understood each other. Here, then, is my point of view.

No doubt a letter seems unecessary when we can see each other freely. What could it say which a word, a look, or even a silence could not express a hundred times better? This seems to me so true that when you spoke to me of no longer writing to each other, the idea slipped easily over my soul; it may have annoyed it slightly, but it had no further effect. It was almost the same as when I wish to place a kiss over your heart and encounter a ribbon or a thin veil: I merely push it aside without feeling that it is an obstacle.

But since then we have parted, and as soon as you were no longer with me, the idea of letters returned to torment me. "Why that additional privation?" I asked myself. What! Have we nothing more to say to each other, simply because we are apart? Let us suppose that favorable circumstances allow us to spend a whole day together: should we spend in conversation some of the time we could devote to pleasure? Yes, pleasure, my tender friend, for with you even moments of rest bring delightful pleasures. In any case, no matter how long we are together, eventually we must part, and then I am so lonely! It is then that a letter is precious! If one does not read it, at least one looks at it. . . . Yes, one can look at a letter without reading it, just as it seems to me that in the dark it would still give me some pleasure to touch your portrait. . . .

Your portrait, did I say? But a letter is a portrait of the soul. It does not have, like a cold image, that stagnation which is so far removed from love; it lends itself to all our emotions; it alternately becomes animated, enjoys pleasure, rests. . . . Your feelings are so precious to me! Will you deprive me of a means of gathering them?

Are you sure you will never be tormented by the need to write to me? If in solitude your heart swells or is oppressed, if a surge of joy reaches your soul, if an involuntary sadness should trouble it for a moment, will you not pour out your happiness or your sorrow to your friend? Will you have a feeling which he does not share? Will you leave him to wander, lonely and pensive, far from you? My friend . . . my tender friend! But it is for you to decide. I only wanted to discuss the matter, not to exert influence on you. I have only given you reasons; I dare to think that entreaties would have been more effective. I shall therefore try not to be afflicted if you persist; I shall try to say to myself what you would have written to me. But no: you will say it better than I could, and it will give me greater pleasure to hear it from you.

Good-by, my charming friend; the hour is at last approaching when I can see you: I shall leave you quickly, so that I can come to you all the sooner.

LETTER 151

～ *From the Vicomte de Valmont to the Marquise de Merteuil*

Paris, December 3, 17—, in the evening

Surely, Marquise, you do not consider me so inexperienced as to think that I could have been deceived about the private conversation in which I found you this evening, and about the "amazing chance" which had brought Danceny to your house! It is true that your practiced features were able to take on a perfect expression of calm and serenity, and that you did not betray yourself by any of the remarks which sometimes escape from embarrassment or regret. I also admit that your docile eyes served you perfectly, and that if they had been able to make themselves believed as well as they made themselves understood, I would not have had or retained the slightest suspicion, and I would not have doubted for a moment that you were greatly annoyed by the presence of that unwelcome intruder. But in order not to display such great talents in vain, in order to obtain the success you expected and produce the illusion you were trying to create, you should have trained your novice lover more carefully beforehand.

Since you have become an educator, teach your pupils not to blush and become disconcerted at the slightest jest, and not to deny so vehemently about one woman the same things they deny so feebly about all others. Teach them also to be able to hear praise of their mistress without feeling obliged to accept it as an honor to themselves; and if you allow them to look at you in company, at least make sure that they know how to disguise that look of possession which is so easy to recognize, and which they so awkwardly confuse with a look of love. Then you can let them share your public appearances without their conduct harming their modest teacher; and I myself, only too glad to contribute to your fame, promise to draw up and publish the program of this new school.

But I confess that I am surprised that it should be I whom you have undertaken to treat like a schoolboy. Oh, how quickly I would have taken vengeance if it had been any other woman but you! What pleasure it would have given me, and how far it would have surpassed the pleasure she thought she was making me lose! Yes, it is with you alone that I can prefer reparation to vengeance; and do not think I am restrained by the slightest doubt or uncertainty: I know everything.

You came back to Paris four days ago; you have seen Danceny every day since then, and you have seen no one but him. Even today your door was still closed to visitors, and your doorkeeper would have prevented me from reaching you if his self-assurance had been as great as yours. But in your letter you assured me that I would be the first to be informed of your arrival—of that arrival whose date you could not tell me while you were writing to me on the eve of your departure. Will you deny these facts, or try to excuse yourself? Both are impossible; and yet I still restrain myself! You may recognize your power in that, but take my advice: be content with having tested it, and do not abuse it any longer. We know each other, Marquise; that piece of advice ought to be enough for you.

You have told me that you will be out all day tomorrow. Well and good, if it is true; and you may be sure that I shall know. But you will return in the evening; and for our difficult reconciliation, we shall not have too much time between then and the following morning. Let me know whether we are to make our numerous reciprocal expiations in your town house or in the other one. Above all, no more Danceny. Your perverse head had become filled with the idea of him, and it is possible for me not to be jealous of that delirium of your imagination; but remember that what was only a whim before would, from now on, be a marked preference. I do not think I am made for that humiliation, and I do not expect it from you.

I even hope that this sacrifice will not appear to be one to you. But even if it should cost you something, I think I have given you a good enough example! I believe that a beautiful, sensitive woman who lived only for me, and who may be dying of love and regret at this very moment, is worth at least as much as a schoolboy who, I grant, is by no means ugly or stupid, but lacks experience and resolution.

Good-by, Marquise; I shall say nothing about my feelings for you: all I can do at this moment is not to scrutinize my heart. I await your reply. When you make it, bear this clearly in mind: it will be easy for you to make me forget the offense you have given me, but a refusal on your part, or merely a delay, would indelibly engrave it in my heart.

LETTER 152

～ *From the Marquise de Merteuil to the Vicomte de Valmont*

Paris, December 4, 17—

Please be careful, Vicomte, and treat my extreme timidity with more consideration! How do you expect me to endure the overwhelming idea of incurring your indignation, or not to succumb entirely to the fear of your vengeance? Especially since, as you know, if you were to do anything unkind to me, it would be impossible for me to retaliate. No matter how much I talked, your life would be as glorious and peaceful as ever. After all, what would you have to fear? Being forced to leave the country, if you were given time to do so. But does one not live abroad the same as one lives here? On the whole, provided the Court of France left you in peace at the foreign court where you had taken up refuge, you would only have changed the scene of your triumphs. Now that I have tried to restore your cool-headedness by these moral considerations, I shall return to our affairs.

Do you know, Vicomte, why I have never remarried? It is certainly not because I could not have found advantageous matches; it is solely because I do not want to give anyone the right to criticize my actions. I am not even afraid that I might not be able to do as I pleased if I were married, for I would always succeed in doing so sooner or later, but it would annoy me if someone even had a right to complain of it; and then, I want to deceive only for my pleasure, not from necessity. And now you have written me the most marital letter imaginable! You speak of nothing but wrongs on my side and forgiveness on yours! But I cannot understand how it is possible to fail in one's duties toward someone to whom one owes nothing!

Come now, what is the great problem? You found Danceny in my house, and that displeased you? So be it; but what could you conclude? Either that he was there as the result of chance, as I told you, or that he was there at my invitation, as I did not tell you. In the first case, your letter is unjust; in the second, it is ridiculous—so in either case it was not worth writing! But you are jealous, and jealousy does not reason. Well, I shall reason for you.

Either you have a rival or you have not. If you have one, you must please me in order to be preferred to him; if not, you must please me to avoid having one. Your conduct should be the same in either case, so why torment yourself? And especially, why torment me? And you are not able to be the more charming of the two? Are you no longer sure of your successes? Come, Vicomte, do yourself justice. But no, it is not that: it is that you do not consider me to be worth all that trouble. You want my favors less than you want to abuse your power over me. You are an ingrate! Is that your idea of sentiment? If I were to continue along that line, this letter might become very tender; but you do not deserve it.

Neither do you deserve any effort on my part to justify myself. To punish you for your suspicions, I shall let you keep them; and so I shall tell you nothing about the date of my return, or about Danceny's visits. You went to a great deal of trouble to gather information about them, did you not? Well, are you any better off for it? I hope it gave you great pleasure; it did not damage mine.

All I can say in reply to your threatening letter is that it has failed either to please me or to intimidate me, and that for the moment I could not be less inclined to grant your requests.

If I were to accept you as you have now shown yourself to me, I would be truly unfaithful to you. I would not be returning to my former lover: I would be taking a new one who is worth far less than the other. I have not forgotten the first one enough to make such a mistake. The Valmont I loved was charming; I shall even go so far as to say that I have never met a more charming man in my life. If you find him again, Vicomte, please bring him to me: he will always be well received.

But tell him that under no circumstances will it be today or tomorrow. His double has harmed him to some extent; if I hurried too much, I would be afraid of having accepted the wrong man. Or perhaps I have promised to spend those two days with Danceny, and your letter has shown me that you take it quite seriously when someone breaks a promise, so you can see that you must wait.

But what does it matter to you? You can always avenge yourself on your rival. He will do nothing worse to your mistress than you would do to his, and after all, is not one woman as good as another? Such are your principles. Even a "tender and sensitive woman who lived only for you and would finally die of love and regret" would be sacrificed to your first whim, or to the fear of being laughed at for a moment. And yet you expect me to make sacrifices for you! Ah, that is unfair!

Good-by, Vicomte; make yourself pleasant again. I ask nothing better than to find you charming, and I promise to prove it to you as soon as I am sure of it. Really, I am too kind.

LETTER 153

〜 *From the Vicomte de Valmont to the Marquise de Merteuil*

Paris, December 4, 17—

I am answering your letter immediately, and I shall try to be clear, which is not easy with you once you have made up your mind not to understand.

It was not necessary to make long speeches to establish the fact that since each of us has all that is needed to ruin the other, we both have an equal interest in treating each other with consideration; so that is not the question. But between the violent course of ruining each other, and the assuredly better course of remaining united as before and becoming still more so by resuming our former intimacy, there are countless others that might be adopted. It was therefore not ridiculous to tell you, and it is not ridiculous to repeat, that from this day on I shall be either your lover or your enemy.

I am well aware that this choice will annoy you, that it would suit you better to temporize, and that you have never liked to be placed between yes and no; but you must realize that I cannot let you out of this narrow circle without running the risk of being duped, and you must have foreseen that I would not tolerate that. It is now for you to decide; I can leave you the choice, but I cannot remain in uncertainty.

I warn you, however, that you will not delude me by your arguments, whether they are good or bad, that you will not beguile me by any flattery with which you may try to sweeten your refusals, and that the time for frankness has come. I ask nothing better than to set the example for you, and I tell you with pleasure that I prefer peace and union; but if both must be broken, I think I have the right and the means to do it.

I therefore add that if you raise the slightest obstacle I shall take it as an open declaration of war. You can see that the answer I am asking of you does not require long or flowery speeches. One word will suffice.

> *Reply from the Marquise de Merteuil, written at the bottom of the above letter:*

Very well, then: war.

LETTER 154

~ *From Madame de Volanges to Madame de Rosemonde*

Paris, December 5, 17—

The reports have been informing you better than I could do, my dear friend, of our invalid's sad condition. Entirely occupied by the care I am giving her, I take time to write to you only when there are events other than those of her illness. Here is one which I certainly did not expect. I have received a letter from Monsieur de Valmont. He has seen fit to choose me as his confidante, and even as his mediator between him and Madame de Tourvel. He enclosed a letter for her; I returned it to him when I replied to the letter he wrote to me, which I am sending to you. I think you will agree with me that I had to refuse to do what he asked. Even if I had been willing, our unfortunate friend would have been in no condition to understand me. Her delirium is continuous. But what do you think of this despair of Monsieur de Valmont's? Should we believe in it, or does he only want to deceive everyone until the end?* If he is sincere this time, he may well tell himself that he has caused his own unhappiness. I do not think my answer will please him; but I confess that the more I learn about this appalling situation, the more indignant I am with the man who created it.

Good-by, my dear friend; I shall now return to my sad efforts, which are made still sadder by the weakness of my hope of seeing them succeed. You know my feelings for you.

LETTER 155

~ *From the Vicomte de Valmont to the Chevalier Danceny*

Paris, December 5, 17—

I have been to your house twice, my dear Chevalier, but since you have abandoned the role of a tender suitor for that of a Don Juan, it has naturally become impossible to find you. Your valet assured me that you would come home this evening and that he had orders to wait for you, but I know your plans, so I realized that you would come home only for a moment, to put on the proper costume, then immediately set off again on your victorious course. Well and good: I can only applaud you for it; but perhaps this evening you will be tempted to change its direction. You still know only half of your affairs; you must learn about the other half, then make up your mind. Take time to read this letter. It will not distract you from your pleasures: on the contrary, its sole object is to give you a choice in them.

If I had had your complete confidence, if you had told me about that part of your secret which you have left me to guess, I would have been informed in time, and my zeal, being less clumsy, would not impede your progress today. But let us start

---

*Since the rest of this correspondence contains nothing capable of resolving this doubt, Monsieur de Valmont's letter has been omitted.

from where we are now. Whatever you may decide, anyone else would be made happy by even your worst choice.

You have a rendezvous for tonight, have you not? With a charming woman whom you adore? For at your age, what woman does one not adore, at least for the first week! The setting of the scene will add still more to your pleasures. A delightful private house, which has been "taken especially for you," will embellish sensuality with the charms of freedom and mystery. Everything has been agreed upon; you are expected, and you are eager to go! That is what we both know, although you have told me nothing about it. And now, here is what you do not know, and what I must tell you.

Since my return to Paris I have been trying to find a way of bringing you and Mademoiselle de Volanges together. I promised you to do so, and the last time I spoke to you about it I had reason to think, from your replies, I might almost say from your raptures, that I was working toward your happiness. I could not succeed unaided in that rather difficult enterprise; after I had prepared the means, I left the rest to your zeal. In her love she has found resources that my experience lacked, and, to your misfortune, she has succeeded. She told me this evening that all the obstacles had been overcome for the past two days, and your happiness now depends only on you.

Also, for the past two days she has been expecting to tell you this news herself, and despite her mother's absence, you would have been received; but you have not even come to call! And, to tell you everything, whether from caprice or reason, she seemed a little annoyed by this lack of eagerness on your part. In any case, she also succeeded in finding a way for me to approach her, and she made me promise to deliver the enclosed letter to you as soon as possible. From her own eagerness, I am willing to bet that her letter deals with a rendezvous for this evening. Be that as it may, I promised on my honor and friendship that you would have the tender missive today, and I cannot and will not break my word.

And now, young man, what are you going to do? Having been placed between coquetry and love, between pleasure and happiness, which will you choose? If I were speaking to the Danceny of three months ago, or even a week ago, I would be sure of his heart and therefore of his actions; but the Danceny of today is sought after by women, he is engrossed in intrigues, and, as is customary, he has become something of a scoundrel: will he prefer a timid young girl, who has nothing in her favor except her beauty, her innocence and her love, to the charms of a perfectly experienced woman?

For my part, my dear friend, it seems to me that even with your new principles, which I confess are also mine to some extent, circumstances would make me choose the young girl. First of all, she will be one more conquest; and then there is novelty to consider, as well as the fear of losing the fruit of your efforts by neglecting to pluck it: for you would be truly missing your opportunity, and it does not always return, especially when it is a question of a first weakness. In such cases it takes only a moment of annoyance, a jealous suspicion, or even less, to cut short the finest triumph. Drowning virtue sometimes clutches a branch, and once it has escaped, it is on its guard and is not easily taken by surprise.

On the other side, however, what will you risk? Not even a separation; at most a quarrel, after which a few attentions will be rewarded by the pleasure of a reconciliation. Once a woman has already yielded, what choice except indulgence is open to her? What would she gain by severity? The loss of her pleasures, without benefit to her reputation.

If, as I suppose, you adopt the course of love, which also seems to me that of reason, I think it would be prudent not to send any excuse for missing your rendezvous; simply let her wait for you: if you risk giving a reason, she may be tempted to investigate it. Women are curious and stubborn; everything might be discovered: as you know, I myself have just been an example of this. But if you leave her with hope, which will be supported by vanity, she will not lose it until long after the time for inquiries has passed, and tomorrow you can choose the insurmountable obstacle that prevented you from coming: you will have been ill, or dead if necessary, or anything else; but whatever it may be, you will be heartbroken over it, and your reconciliation will be assured.

But no matter what your decision, please tell me about it; since my own interest is not involved, I shall approve of anything you do. Good-by, my dear friend.

I must add that I miss Madame de Tourvel; I am in despair at being separated from her, and I would give half my life for the happiness of devoting the other half to her, Ah, believe me, we are happy only through love!

LETTER 156

~ *From Cécile Volanges to the Chevalier Danceny*
(Enclosed with the preceding letter)

Paris, December 4, 17—, in the evening

Why is it, my dearest, that I have ceased to see you when I have not ceased to desire it? Do you no longer want to see me as much as I want to see you? I am so sad now, sadder than when we were separated completely! My grief was caused by others then, but now it comes to me from you, and that makes it much worse.

For several days now, my mother has been away from home nearly all the time, as you well know. I hoped you would take advantage of this time of freedom, but you do not even think of me! I am very unhappy! You have told me so often that I loved you less than you loved me! I knew it was not true, and now you have proved it. If you had come to see me, you would actually have seen me, for I am not like you: I think only of what can unite us. If I treated you as you deserve, I would tell you nothing about all the difficult efforts I have made to bring us together; but I love you too much, and I want to see you so much that I cannot help telling you. And then, I shall see afterward if you really love me!

As the result of my efforts, the doorkeeper is now on our side, and he has promised me that whenever you come, he will let you enter as though he did not see you. We can trust him, because he is a very honorable man. The only other problem is to make sure that you are not seen in my house, and that will be easy if you come only in the evening, when there will be nothing at all to fear. For example, since my mother has been going out every day, she has been going to bed at eleven o'clock every evening, so we shall have plenty of time.

The doorkeeper says that when you want to come like that, instead of knocking on the door you must tap on his window, and he will let you in immediately. You will easily find the little staircase, and since you cannot carry a candle with you, I shall leave my bedroom door ajar, which will give you a little light. Be careful not to make any noise, especially when you are passing my mother's door. As for my maid's door, it makes no difference, because she has promised not to wake up: she is a very good girl! It will be the same when you leave. And now we shall see whether you come.

Oh, why does my heart beat so fast when I write to you! Is it because something terrible is going to happen to me? Or is it the hope of seeing you again that agitates me like this? All I know is that I have never loved you so much before, and that I have never wanted so much to tell you so. Come to me, my dearest; let me tell you a hundred times that I love you, that I adore you, and that I shall never love anyone but you.

I have found a way to let Monsieur de Valmont know I have something to tell him, and since he is a very good friend, he will surely come tomorrow, and I shall ask him to give you this letter immediately. So I shall expect you tomorrow evening, and you will come without fail if you do not want your Cécile to be very unhappy.

Good-by, my dearest; I kiss you with all my heart.

LETTER 157

～ *From the Chevalier Danceny to the Vicomte de Valmont*

Paris, December 5, 17—

Do not doubt either my heart or my actions, my dear Vicomte: how could I resist a desire on the part of my Cécile? Ah, it is she and she alone whom I love, whom I shall always love! Her ingenuousness and tenderness have a charm for me from which I may have been weak enough to allow myself to be distracted, but which nothing will ever efface. Although I have become involved in another adventure without realizing it, so to speak, the memory of Cécile has often come to trouble me even amid the sweetest pleasures, and perhaps my heart has never paid her truer homage than at the very moment when I was unfaithful to her. But let us spare her delicacy, my friend, and hide my wrongs from her, not to abuse her good faith, but to avoid grieving her. Her happiness is my most ardent desire; I would never forgive myself if I had done something which cost her a single tear.

I know I deserve your jest about what you call my new

principles, but you can believe me when I tell you that I am not acting in accordance with them now, and I am determined to prove it tomorrow. I shall confess my error to the woman who caused and shared it; I shall say to her, "Read in my heart: it has the most tender friendship for you; and friendship combined with desire resembles love so strongly! . . . We have both been mistaken; but although I am liable to error, I am incapable of bad faith." I know my friend: she is as honorable as she is indulgent. She will do more than forgive me: she will commend me. She has often reproached herself with having betrayed friendship, and her delicacy has often frightened her love; wiser than I, she will strengthen in my soul those useful fears which I rashly tried to smother in hers. I shall be indebted to her for making me better, just as I shall be indebted to you for making me happier. Oh, my friend, share my gratitude! The thought of owing my happiness to you makes it more precious to me.

Good-by, my dear Vicomte. My extreme joy does not prevent me from thinking of your sorrows and sympathizing with them. If only I could help you! Is Madame de Tourvel still inexorable? She is said to be seriously ill. How I pity you! May she recover both her health and her indulgence, and make you happy forever. These are the wishes of friendship; I dare to hope that they will be granted by love.

I would like to talk with you longer, but time is pressing and perhaps Cécile is waiting for me already.

LETTER 158

~ *From the Vicomte de Valmont to the Marquise de Merteuil*

Paris, December 6, 17—, in the morning

Well, Marquise, how are you after last night's pleasures? Are you not a little tired? You must admit that Danceny is charming! The young man performs wonders! You did not expect it of him, did you? Yes, I am forced to admit that such a rival deserves to be given preference over me. Seriously, he is full of good qualities, but he is particularly admirable for his love, his constancy, his delicacy! Ah, if he should ever love you as much as he loves his Cécile, you would have no rivals to fear: he proved hat to you last night! By persistent coquetry, another woman might succeed in taking him away from you for a moment, since young man is seldom able to reject provocative advances, but ne word from the woman he loves is enough to dispel that llusion, as you have seen; so you have only to become the woman he loves in order to be perfectly happy.

You will certainly not be misled in this matter; you are too perceptive for that. But the friendship that unites us, as sincere on my part as it is well rewarded on yours, made me desire last night's test for your sake. It was the work of my zeal and it succeeded, but please do not thank me: I do not deserve it, because nothing could have been easier.

After all, what did it cost me? A slight sacrifice and a little adroitness. I consented to share the favors of the young man's mistress with him; but then he has as much right to them as I, and I cared so little about them! I dictated the letter she sent to him, but it was only to gain time, because we had better ways of spending it. As for the letter I sent with it—oh, it was nothing, almost nothing: only a few friendly reflections to guide the new lover's choice. But really they were useless; I must tell the truth: he did not hesitate for a moment.

And then, in his candor, he will come to you today to tell you everything, and that will surely give you great pleasure! He will say, "Read in my heart," he has already told me so himself; and you can see that that will set everything right. When you read in his heart whatever he wants you to see there, I hope you will also read that such young lovers have their dangers, and that it is better to have me as a friend than as an enemy.

Good-by, Marquise, until the next occasion.

LETTER 159

~ *From the Marquise de Merteuil to the Vicomte de Valmont (A note)*

Paris, December 6, 17—

I do not like bad jokes added to spiteful actions; that is neither in my style nor to my taste. When I have reason to complain of someone, I do not mock him; I do something better: I take vengeance. However pleased with yourself you may be now,

remember that this would not be the first time you had ever
congratulated yourself in advance, and all alone, in the expectation of a triumph which escaped you just as you were gloating
over it. Good-by.

LETTER 160

~ *From Madame de Volanges to Madame de Rosemonde*

Paris, December 6, 17—

I am writing to you from the bedroom of our unfortunate
friend, whose condition is still almost the same. This afternoon
there is to be a consultation of four doctors. Unfortunately, as
you know, this is more often a proof of danger than a means of
aid.

It seems, however, that she briefly recovered her reason last
night. Her maid told me this morning that her mistress had called
her at about midnight, said she wanted to be alone with her, and
dictated a rather long letter to her. Julie added that while she was
making the envelope, Madame de Tourvel's delirium returned,
and so the girl did not learn to whom the letter was to be
addressed. I expressed surprise that the letter itself had not
sufficed to tell her this; when she replied that she was afraid she
might be mistaken, and that her mistress had ordered her to send
it at once, I took it upon myself to open the envelope.

I found the enclosed letter, which is addressed to no one, yet
is addressed to too many people. I think, however, that it was to
Monsieur de Valmont that our unfortunate friend wished to write
at first, but that she yielded, without realizing it, to the disorder
of her ideas. In any case, I decided that the letter should not be
delivered to anyone. I am sending it to you because it will show
you, better than I could tell you, the thoughts that are occupying
our invalid's mind. As long as she remains so violently affected,
I shall have scarcely any hope. It is difficult for the body to
recover when the mind is so agitated.

Good-by, my dear and worthy friend. I am glad for your sake
that you are removed from the sad spectacle I constantly have
before my eyes.

LETTER 161

~   *From Madame de Tourvel to ———*
    (Dictated by her and written by her maid)

Paris, December 5, 17—

Cruel and malevolent being, will you never tire of persecuting me? Is it not enough for you to have tormented me, degraded me, debased me? Do you want to rob me even of the peace of the grave? What! In this abode of darkness in which ignominy has forced me to bury myself, is pain without respite, is hope unknown? I do not implore a mercy I do not deserve; I shall suffer without complaint if only my suffering does not exceed my strength. But do not make my torments unbearable. In leaving me my grief, take away the cruel memory of the treasures I have lost. You have already robbed me of them; do not hold their heartbreaking image before my eyes. I was innocent and unperturbed: it was from having seen you that I lost my peace of mind; it was from having listened to you that I became criminal. You are the author of my sins: what right have you to punish them?

Where are the friends who cherished me, where are they? My misfortune terrifies them. None of them dares to approach me. I am crushed, and they leave me without aid. I am dying, and no one weeps for me. All consolation is refused to me. Pity stops on the brink of the abyss into which the criminal plunges. He is torn by remorse, and his cries are not heard!

And you whom I have outraged, you whose esteem intensifies my ordeal, you who alone have the right to avenge yourself, why are you so far from me? Come and punish your faithless wife. Let me suffer deserved torments at last. I would already have submitted to your vengeance if I had not lacked the courage to tell you of the dishonor I have brought upon you. It was not dissimulation, it was consideration. May this letter at least tell you of my repentance. Heaven has taken up your cause and avenged you for a wrong of which you are ignorant. It was Heaven which bound my tongue and restrained my words, fearing that you might forgive a sin it wished to punish. It has removed me from your indulgence, which would have offended its justice.

Merciless in its vengeance, it has given me over to the very man who ruined me. It is for him and through him that I suffer. I vainly try to flee from him; he follows me, he is there, he constantly obsesses me. But how different he is from himself! His eyes now express only hatred and contempt. His lips utter only insults and reproaches. His arms embrace me only to rend me. Who will save me from his savage fury?

But what! It is he . . . I am not mistaken: it is he whom I see again. Oh, my dearest! Take me in your arms, hide me in your bosom: yes, it is you, it is really you! What sinister illusion made me fail to recognize you? How I have suffered in your absence! Let us never part again! Let me breathe. Feel how my heart is palpitating. Ah, it is no longer from fear, but from the sweet emotion of love. Why do you refuse my tender caresses? Turn your gentle gaze to me! What are those bonds which you seek to break? For whom are you preparing that garb of death? Why are your features so contorted? What are you doing? Leave me: I shudder! Dear God, it is the monster again!

My friends, do no abandon me. You who urged me to flee from him, help me to combat him! And you who, more indulgent, promised to lessen my pain, come to me! Where are you both? If I am not permitted to see you again, at least answer this letter, let me know that you still love me.

Leave me, cruel one! What new fury animates you? Are you afraid that a sweet feeling may penetrate to my soul? You redouble my torments, you force me to hate you. Oh, how painful hatred is! How it corrodes the heart that distills it! Why do you persecute me? What can you still have to say to me? Have you not made it impossible for me to listen to you or answer you? Expect nothing more of me. Good-by, Monsieur.

LETTER 162

～ *From the Chevalier Danceny to the Vicomte de Valmont*

Paris, December 6, 17—, in the evening

I am informed, Monsieur, of your conduct toward me. I also know that, not content with having basely duped me, you have

ared to boast of it, to congratulate yourself on it. I have seen
roof of your betrayal written by your own hand. I admit that it
ut me to the heart, and that I felt some shame at the thought that
 myself had aided you so much in your odious abuse of my
lind confidence. Yet I do not envy you that shameful advan-
ige; I am only curious to know if you will keep all advantages
ver me. I shall learn this if, as I hope, you will meet me at the
ate of the Bois de Vincennes, Village of Saint-Mandé, between
ight and nine o'clock tomorrow morning. I shall see to it that
verything necessary for settling our differences will be available
ere.

The Chevalier Danceny

LETTER 163

From Monsieur Bertrand to Madame de Rosemonde

Paris, December 7, 17—

ladame,

It is with great regret that I perform the sad duty of announc-
ng to you an event which will cause you such cruel grief. Allow
ie first to exhort you to that pious resignation which everyone
as so often admired in you, and which alone can enable us to
ndure the ills with which our wretched life is strewn.

Your nephew . . . Dear God, must I inflict such pain on such
n estimable lady! Your nephew has had the misfortune to perish
a a duel which he fought this morning with the Chevalier
)anceny. I do not know the cause of their quarrel, but from the
ote which I found in the Vicomte's pocket, and which I have
ie honor of sending to you, it appears that he was not the
ggressor. And it had to be he whom Heaven permitted to
erish!

I was waiting for him in his house at the very time when he
*as brought home. Imagine my alarm when I saw him being
arried by two of his servants, covered with his own blood! He
ad two sword wounds in his body, and was already very weak.
Ionsieur Danceny was also there, and was even weeping. Ah,
o doubt he must weep, but it is too late for tears when one has
aused an irreparable misfortune!

As for me, I could not contain myself, and despite my humble

condition I told him exactly what I thought of him. But it wa
then that the Vicomte showed himself to be truly great. H
ordered me to be silent; he took the hand of his murderer, calle
him his friend, embraced him in front of all of us and said to us
"I order you to treat this gentleman with all the respect that i
owed to a brave and gallant man." He then ordered that Mor
sieur Danceny be given, in my presence, a voluminous pile c
papers with which I was not acquainted, but to which I know h
attached great importance. After that, he asked to be left alon
with Monsieur Danceny for a moment. Meanwhile I had sent fc
aid, both spiritual and temporal, but alas, the ill was irremedia
ble. Less than half an hour later, he lost consciousness. He wa
able only to receive extreme unction, and scarcely was th
ceremony over when he breathed his last.

Dear God, when I received into my arms at his birth tha
precious scion of such an illustrious family, could I have see
that he would die in my arms, and that I would have to weep fc
his death? A death so untimely and so unfortunate! My tear
flow in spite of myself. Please forgive me, Madame, for darin
thus to mingle my grief with yours; but no matter what his ran
may be, a man has a heart and sensibility, and I would be ver
ungrateful if I did not weep all my life for a noble lord who wa
so kind to me, and who honored me with so much confidence.

Tomorrow, after the body is taken away, I shall have seal
placed on everything, and you can rely completely on my services
You are aware, Madame, that this unfortunate event puts an en
to the entail and leaves you free to dispose of your property a
will. If I can be of any assistance to you, I beg you to be so kin
as to send me your orders: I shall devote all my zeal to executin
them punctually.

I am, with the deepest respect, Madame, your most humble, etc

                                                      Bertrand

LETTER 164

~ *From Madame de Rosemonde to Monsieur Bertrand*

                        Château de ———, December 8, 17—
I have just received your letter, my dear Bertrand, and learne
from it the terrible event of which my nephew has been th

unfortunate victim. Yes, I shall certainly have orders to give you, and it is only because of them that I can turn my attention to something other than my mortal grief.

The note from Monsieur Danceny which you sent me is a convincing proof that it was he who provoked the duel, and it is my will that you shall immediately lodge a complaint against him in my name. In forgiving his enemy, his murderer, my nephew acted in accordance with his natural magnanimity; but I must avenge his death, humanity, and religion. The severity of the law cannot be too strongly urged against this remnant of barbarism which still infects our customs; and I do not think that this is a case in which forgiveness of wrongs is enjoined upon us. I therefore expect you to pursue this matter with all the zeal and vigor of which I know you to be capable, and which you owe to the memory of my nephew.

Before all else, you will see Monsieur de ———, the magistrate, on my behalf, and confer with him. I am not writing to him, for I am in haste to give myself up entirely to my grief. You will give him my apologies and show him this letter.

Good-by, my dear Bertrand; I praise and thank you for your good sentiments, and I am devoted to you for life.

LETTER 165

~ *From Madame de Volanges to Madame de Rosemonde*

Paris, December 9, 17—

I know that you have already been informed, my dear and worthy friend, of the loss you have just suffered; I knew your affection for Monsieur de Valmont, and I sincerely share the grief you must be feeling. I am truly grieved to be obliged to add new sorrows to those you have already, but alas, there is now nothing left but tears for you to give our unfortunate friend. We lost her last night at eleven o'clock. By a turn of fate which seemed to mock all human prudence, the short time she survived Monsieur de Valmont was long enough for her to learn of his death, and for her not to succumb to the weight of her misfortunes, as she herself said, until their measure had been filled to overflowing.

You already know that she had been completely unconscious

for over two days; and yesterday morning, when her doctor arrived and we both went to her bedside, she recognized neither of us and we were unable to obtain a word or the slightest sign from her. But when we had gone over to the fireplace and the doctor had begun to give me the sad news of Monsieur de Valmont's death, she fully regained consciousness, whether because nature alone produced the change, or because the repetition of the words "Monsieur de Valmont" and "death" may have recalled to her the only ideas that had occupied her mind for so long.

In any case, she suddenly opened her bed curtains and cried out, "What! What are you saying? Monsieur de Valmont is dead!" Hoping to make her think she was mistaken, I assured her at first that she had not heard correctly; but, far from allowing herself to be persuaded of this, she demanded that the doctor begin the cruel narrative again, and when I made another attempt to dissuade her, she called me to her and said in a low voice, "Why try to deceive me? Was he not already dead for me!" I had to yield.

At first our unfortunate friend listened rather calmly, but soon she interrupted: "Enough! I know enough." She immediately asked that her bed curtains be closed; and when the doctor tried to give her his professional services again, she would not let him come near her.

As soon as he was gone, she also sent away her nurse and her maid. When we were alone together, she asked me to help her kneel on her bed, and then to support her. She remained thus for some time in silence, and with no other expression than that of her abundant tears. Finally, clasping her hands and raising them toward Heaven, she said in a weak but fervent voice, "Almighty God, I submit to thy justice; but forgive Valmont. Let him not be blamed for my misfortunes, which I recognize as having been deserved, and I shall bless thy mercy!" I have allowed myself, my dear and worthy friend, to enter into these details of a subject which I know must renew and augment your sorrow, because I feel certain that Madame de Tourvel's prayer will also bring great consolation to your soul.

After our friend had spoken these few words, she fell back into my arms; and scarcely was she in her bed again when she sank into another swoon which, though long, eventually yielded to the usual remedies. As soon as she regained consciousness, she asked me to send for Father Anselme, and she added, "He is now the only doctor I need; I feel that my ills will soon be ended.'' She complained of great difficulty in breathing, and was scarcely able to speak.

A short time later she had her maid give me a small chest, which I am sending to you. She told me it contained some of her papers, and that I was to send it to you immediately after her death.* Then she spoke to me of you and your friendship for her, as much as her condition would allow, and with great feeling.

Father Anselme arrived at about four o'clock and stayed nearly an hour with her. When we went back into her room, her face was calm and serene; but it was easy to see that Father Anselme had wept a great deal. He remained to be present during the last ceremonies of the Church. This spectacle, always so imposing and painful, was made still more so by the contrast between her tranquil resignation and the profound grief of her venerable confessor, who burst into tears beside her. The emotion became general; and the woman for whom we all wept was the only one who did not weep.

The rest of the day was spent in the customary prayers, interrupted only by the invalid's frequent swoons. Finally, toward eleven o'clock at night, her breathing became more difficult and she seemed to be in greater pain. I reached out for her arm; she still had strength enough to take my hand and place it over her heart. I could not feel it beating; our unfortunate friend had expired at that very moment.

Do you remember, my dear friend, that during your last stay here, less than a year ago, we were talking of several people whose happiness seemed to be more or less assured, and we dwelt with satisfaction on the fate of the same woman whose misfortunes and death we are now mourning? So many virtues, praiseworthy qualities and charms; such a gentle and easy character; a husband whom she loved, and who adored her; a circle of friends whose company pleased her, and who were delighted by hers; beauty, youth, wealth—all those combined advantages were lost through a single imprudence! O Providence, doubtless we must worship thy decrees, but how incomprehensible they are! But I must stop, lest I increase your sadness by yielding to my own.

I shall now leave you and go to my daughter, who is somewhat indisposed. When I informed her this morning of the sudden death of two people with whom she was acquainted, she felt faint, and I sent her to bed, I hope, however, that this slight

---

*This chest contained all the letters relating to her affair with Monsieur de Valmont.

indisposition will have no serious results. At her age, one is not yet accustomed to grief, so its effect is sharper and stronger. That active sensibility is no doubt a praiseworthy quality; but how much we are taught to fear it by everything we see each day! Good-by, my dear and worthy friend.

LETTER 166

～   *From Monsieur Bertrand to Madame de Rosemonde*

Paris, December 10, 17—

Madame,

In obedience to the orders you have done me the honor of sending to me, I have had that of seeing Monsieur de ————, and I have shown him your letter, informing him that, in accordance with your wishes, I would do nothing without his advice. That respectable magistrate has asked me to point out to you that the complaint you intend to lodge against the Chevalier Danceny would compromise the memory of your nephew, and that his honor would necessarily be stained by the judgment handed down by the court, which would undoubtedly be a great misfortune. It is therefore his opinion that no steps ought to be taken, and that if any were taken, their goal should be, on the contrary, to prevent the Public Prosecutor from taking notice of this unfortunate matter, which has already become too widely known.

These observations seemed so wise to me that I have decided to await further orders from you.

Allow me to beg you, Madame, when you send them to me, to be so kind as to add a few words about the state of your health, for I am extremely apprehensive of the effect which so many sorrows may have upon it. I hope you will forgive me this liberty in view of my attachment and my zeal.

I am, with respect, Madame, your, etc.

LETTER 167

~ *Anonymous, to the Chevalier Danceny*

Paris, December 10, 17—

Monsieur,

I have the honor of informing you that this morning, at the Office of the Public Prosecutor, the King's legal advisors discussed your encounter with the Vicomte de Valmont a few days ago, and that there is reason to fear that the Public Prosecutor may take action. I thought this warning might be useful to you in enabling you to urge your protectors to stop those regrettable proceedings, or, if that should be impossible, to take measures for your personal safety.

If you will allow me to give you some advice, I think you would do well, for a time, to show yourself less than you have been doing for the past two days. One should always pay this respect to the law, even though the kind of affair in question is usually treated with indulgence.

This precaution is particularly necessary in your case, for I have heard that a Madame de Rosemonde, who is said to be Monsieur de Valmont's aunt, intends to lodge a complaint against you, and that if she does so, the Public Prosecutor cannot refuse her demand. It might be advisable for you to have someone speak to her.

Private reasons prevent me from signing this letter. But I hope that, although you do not know from whom it has come, you will nevertheless render justice to the sentiment which has dictated it.

I have the honor of being, etc.

LETTER 168

~ *From Madame de Volanges to Madame de Rosemonde*

Paris, December 11, 17—

Extremely surprising and disturbing rumors, my dear and worthy friend, are being spread here about Madame de Merteuil.

I am certainly far from believing them, and I would wager that they are nothing but vicious slander, but I know so well how even the most implausible gossip can easily gain credence, and how difficult it is to efface the impression it leaves, that I am alarmed by these stories, however easily I think they may be disproved. I wish they could be stopped early, before they have gained wider circulation. But it was only late yesterday that I learned of these horrors, which are only beginning to be repeated; and when I sent a servant to Madame de Merteuil's house this morning, she had just left for the country, where she is to spend two days. No one could tell me to whose estate she had gone. Her second maid, whom I asked to come and speak to me, told me that her mistress had merely given orders to expect her next Thursday, and none of the servants she has left here know more than that. I myself cannot imagine where she might be; I cannot think of anyone she knows who remains in the country this late in the year.

Be that as it may, I hope that you will be able, by the time she returns, to obtain some information which may be useful to her, for these odious stories are based on certain circumstances of Monsieur de Valmont's death; if these circumstances are true, you have probably already been informed of them, or at least it will be easy for you to find out about them, which I beg you to do. Here are the rumors; they are still only a murmur, but it will surely not be long before they are circulated more openly.

It is said that the quarrel between Monsieur de Valmont and the Chevalier Danceny was the work of Madame de Merteuil, who was deceiving them both; that, as nearly always happens, the two rivals began by fighting and did not discuss their differences until afterward; that this discussion produced a sincere reconciliation; and that, to complete the Chevalier Danceny's knowledge of Madame de Merteuil, and also to justify himself entirely, Monsieur de Valmont added to his words a large number of letters, forming a regular correspondence that he had maintained with her, in which she relates extremely scandalous anecdotes about herself in the most immodest style.

It is also said that Danceny, in his first indignation, showed these letters to anyone who wished to see them, and that they are now passing from hand to hand all over Paris. Two of them* are mentioned in particular: one in which she tells the whole story of her life and her principles, and which is said to be utterly

---

*Letters 81 and 85 in this collection.

abominable; the other entirely justifies Monsieur de Prévan, whose story you will remember, by giving proof that he merely yielded to the most active advances on her part, and that she had agreed to the rendezvous.

Fortunately there is strong evidence for assuming that these charges are as false as they are odious. First of all, we both know that Monsieur de Valmont was certainly not involved with Madame de Merteuil, and I have every reason to believe that Danceny was not involved with her either, so it seems obvious to me that she could have been neither the subject nor the instigator of the quarrel. Nor do I understand how it could have been to the interest of Madame de Merteuil, who is supposed to have been in agreement with Monsieur de Prévan, to make a scene which could not fail to be unpleasant for her because of the attention it would attract, and which might have been very dangerous to her, since she would thereby have made an irreconcilable enemy of a man who knew part of her secret, and who had many supporters at the time. Yet it should be noted that since that adventure not one voice has been raised in favor of Prévan, and that he himself has made no protest.

These reflections incline me to suspect him as the author of the rumors that are now circulating, and to regard those slanderous accusations as the work of the hatred and vengeance of a man who, seeing himself ruined, hopes in this way at least to spread doubts, and perhaps to cause a useful diversion. But no matter where those spiteful stories may have originated, the most urgent thing is to destroy them. They will collapse of themselves if it is learned that, as is likely, Monsieur de Valmont and Monsieur Danceny did not speak to each other after their unfortunate duel, and that no papers were given to Monsieur Danceny.

In my impatience to verify these facts, I sent my footman to Monsieur Danceny's house this morning, but he, too, has left Paris. His servants told my footman that he left last night, in accordance with a communication he had received yesterday, and that the place where he is staying is a secret. Apparently he is afraid of the consequences of his duel. It is therefore only through you, my dear and worthy friend, that I can obtain the information which interests me, and which may become so necessary to Madame de Merteuil. I again ask you to let me have it as soon as possible.

P.S.—My daughter's indisposition had no serious results; she sends you her respects.

LETTER 169

~ *From the Chevalier Danceny to Madame de Rosemonde*

Paris, December 12, 17—

Madame,

You will perhaps feel that the action I am now taking is very strange, but I beg you to listen to me before judging me, and not to see impudence and temerity where there is only respect and confidence. I do not conceal from myself the wrong I have done you, and I would never forgive myself for it if I could think for a moment that it would have been possible for me to avoid it. But you may be sure, Madame, that while I consider myself free from blame, I am not free from regrets, and I can even add with sincerity that the regrets I have caused you have contributed greatly to those I feel. To believe in the sentiments of which I dare to assure you, it will be enough for you to do justice to yourself, and to be aware that although I do not have the honor of being known by you, I have that of knowing you.

And yet, while I am lamenting the fatality which has caused your grief and my misfortune, there are those who would have me fear that, obsessed by a desire for vengeance, you are seeking means of satisfying it even through the severity of the law.

Allow me first to point out to you that you are misled by your grief, since my interest in this respect is essentially bound up with that of Monsieur de Valmont, who would also be involved in any condemnation you might arouse against me. It would therefore seem to me, Madame, that I could expect aid from you, rather than opposition, in the steps I may be obliged to take in order to make sure that this unfortunate event will remain buried in silence.

But this resource of complicity, which suits the guilty and the innocent alike, cannot suffice for my delicacy; while I wish to avoid having you as my opponent, I claim you as my judge. The esteem of those we respect is too precious for me to allow yours to be taken away from me without defending it, and I think I have the means of doing so.

If you agree that vengeance is permissible, or is even a duty, when one's love, friendship and confidence have been betrayed, my wrongs will vanish in your eyes. Do not rely on my words, but read, if you have the courage, the correspondence I am placing in your hands.* The number of original letters it contains seems to authenticate those which exist only in the form of copies. Moreover, I received these letters, just as I have the honor of sending them to you, from Monsieur de Valmont himself. I have added nothing to them, and I have removed only two of them which I have taken the liberty of making public.

One of them was necessary to the common vengeance of Monsieur de Valmont and myself, to which we both had a right, and which he expressly asked me to carry out. I felt, furthermore, that I was rendering a service to society in unmasking a woman so truly dangerous as Madame de Merteuil, for she alone, as you will see, is the true cause of what took place between Monsieur de Valmont and myself.

A sense of justice also led me to reveal the second letter, for the justificiation of Monsieur de Prévan, whom I scarcely know, but who by no means deserved the severe punishment he received, or the still more severe judgment of the public from which he has suffered since that time, without having anything with which to defend himself.

You will therefore find only copies of those two letters, whose originals it is my duty to keep. As for the remainder, I do not think I could place in safer hands a collection which it is important for me not to have destroyed, but which I would be ashamed to misuse. In confiding it to you, Madame, I believe I am serving the people concerned as well as if I gave it to them; and I am saving them from the embarrassment of receiving it from me, and knowing that I am informed of certain matters which they no doubt wish to remain unknown to everyone.

I think I ought to tell you that the enclosed correspondence is only a part of a much more voluminous collection from which Monsieur de Valmont took it in my presence; when the seals are broken, you will find this collection under the title, which I saw, of: "Account opened between the Marquise de Merteuil and the Vicomte de Valmont." You will deal with it in whatever way your prudence suggests.

---

*It was from this correspondence, as well as from the letters sent to Madame de Rosemonde after Madame de Tourvel's death, and those confided to her by Madame de Volanges, that this collection was formed. The originals are in the possession of Madame de Rosemonde's heirs.

I am with respect, Madame, etc.

P.S.—Certain warnings I have received, and the advice of my friends, have made me decide to leave Paris for some time, but the place of my retirement, kept secret from everyone else, will not be a secret for you. If you honor me with a reply, send it by P—— to the Commandery of ————, in care of Commander ————. It is from his house that I have the honor of writing to you.

LETTER 170

~ *From Madame de Volanges to Madame de Rosemonde*

Paris, December 13, 17—

I go from surprise to surprise, my dear friend, and from sorrow to sorrow. Only a mother can have any idea of what I suffered all morning yesterday; and although my most painful anxieties have since been calmed, I retain a keen affliction whose end I cannot foresee.

Yesterday morning at about ten o'clock, surprised at not yet having seen my daughter, I sent my maid to learn the reason for her lateness. She came back a few moments later in great alarm, and alarmed me still more by telling me that my daughter was not in her room, and that her maid had not seen her there all morning. Imagine my state on hearing this! I called together all my servants, particularly my doorkeeper: they all swore that they knew nothing and could tell me nothing about my daughter's absence. I immediately went to her room. The disorder that reigned in it showed me that she had apparently left only that morning, but I found nothing that could give me any other information. I examined her wardrobes and her writing desk; I found everything in place, and all her clothes except the dress she had been wearing when she left. She had not even taken the small amount of money she had in her room.

Since it was only the day before that she had heard all that is being said about Madame de Merteuil, to whom she is strongly attached, so much so that she wept all evening, and since I remembered that she did not know Madame de Merteuil was in the country, my first idea was that she had wanted to see her friend, and that she had been foolish enough to go to her house

lone. But the time that went by without her returning brought
back all my anxieties. Each moment increased my pain, and
although I was dying to know where she was, I did not dare to
make any inquiries, for fear of attracting attention to an event
which I might later want to hide from everyone. No, I have
never suffered so much in my life!

It was not until after two o'clock that I received a letter from
my daughter and also one from the Mother Superior of the
Convent of ———. My daughter's letter said only that she had
been afraid I might oppose the vocation she felt to be a nun, and
that she had not dared to speak to me about it; the rest was only
apologies for having taken that step without my permission. She
added that I would surely not disapprove of her decision if I
knew her reasons for it, although she begged me not to ask her
what they were.

The Mother Superior informed me that, seeing a young lady
arrive alone, she had at first refused to receive her, but that when
she had questioned her and learned who she was, she had felt
that she would be rendering me a service by giving shelter to my
daughter in order to spare her other journeys, which she seemed
determined to make. While she naturally offered to return my
daughter to me if I asked her to, she urged me, in accordance
with her condition, not to oppose a vocation which she called
'so decided''; she also told me that she had not been able to
inform me of this occurrence sooner because she had had great
difficulty in persuading my daughter to write to me, her plan
having been that no one should know where she had gone. The
unreasonableness of children is a cruel thing!

I went to the convent immediately, and after seeing the Mother
Superior I asked to see my daughter; at first she did not want to
come, and she was trembling when she finally arrived. I spoke to
her in front of the nuns, and then alone; all I was able to draw
from her, amid many tears, was that she could be happy only in
a convent. I decided to let her stay there, but without yet being a
postulant, as she had requested. However much I respect a
religious vocation, I could not see my daughter become a nun
without sorrow, and even fear. It seems to me that we already
have enough duties without creating new ones, and furthermore
that at her age we hardly know what is best for us.

What redoubles my perplexity is that Monsieur de Gercourt
will soon return. Should I break off such an advantageous marriage? How can we make our children happy if it is not enough
to desire their happiness and devote all our efforts to it? You

would greatly oblige me if you would tell me what you would do
if you were in my place. I cannot come to any decision: I find
nothing so frightening as to have to decide the fate of others,
and in this situation I am equally afraid of showing the severity
of a judge or the weakness of a mother.

I constantly reproach myself for increasing your sorrows by
speaking to you of mine; but I know your heart: the consolation
you can give to others is for you the greatest you can receive.

Good-by, my dear and worthy friend; I await your two replies
with great impatience.

LETTER 171

~   *From Madame de Rosemonde to the Chevalier Danceny*

Château de ———, December 15, 17—

After what you have made known to me, Monsieur, there is
nothing left but to weep and be silent. I regret still being alive
when I have learned such horrors; I am ashamed of being a
woman when I have seen one capable of such enormities.

I gladly agree, Monsieur, insofar as I am concerned, to leave
in silence and forgetfulness anything that may be related to those
sad events, and anything that might cause them to have further
consequences. I even hope that they will never cause you any
sorrows other than those which are inseparable from the disastrous victory you won over my nephew. Despite his faults,
which I am forced to recognize, I feel that I shall never be
consoled for his loss; but my eternal affliction will be the only
vengeance I shall allow myself to take on you: it is for your heart
to be aware of its magnitude.

If you will allow me, at my age, to make an observation
which one almost never makes at yours, I shall say that if one
had clear knowledge of one's true happiness, one would never
seek it outside of the limits laid down by the law and religion.

You may be sure that I shall faithfully and gladly keep the
letters you have confided to me, but I ask you to authorize me
not to give them to anyone, not even to you, Monsieur, unless
they should become necessary for your justification. I dare to
believe that you will not refuse this request, and that you no

nger feel that one often suffers from having yielded to even the
ost just vengeance.

I shall not stop in my requests, for I am now convinced of
our generosity and your delicacy; it would be worthy of both if
ou would also give me Mademoiselle de Volanges's letters,
/hich you have apparently kept, and which are undoubtedly of
o further interest to you. I know that she has wronged you
reatly, but I do not believe you intend to punish her for it; if
nly from self-respect, you will not debase the girl you once
oved so much. I therefore have no need to add that the consider-
tion which she does not deserve should at least be shown for her
nother, that respectable woman to whom you have many amends
o make; for, after all, however one may try to delude oneself with
so-called delicacy of sentiment, the man who first tries to lead
stray a heart that is still virtuous and simple makes himself, by
hat very attempt, the first instigator of its corruption, and must be
orever held accountable for any excesses and failings that follow.

Do not be surprised, Monsieur, by this severity on my part; it
s the greatest proof I can give you of my perfect esteem. You
vill acquire new rights to that esteem if you will consent, as I
lesire, to the preservation of a secret which would harm you if it
vere known, and would bring death into a mother's heart that
ou have already wounded. I wish to render my friend that service, Monsieur, and if I were afraid you might refuse me that
consolation, I would ask you first to consider that it is the only
ne you have left me.

I have the honor of being, etc.

LETTER 172

~ *From Madame de Rosemonde to Madame de Volanges*

Château de ———, December 15, 17—

If I had been obliged, my dear friend, to send to Paris and
wait for the information you request concerning Madame de
Merteuil, it would not yet be possible for me to give it to you,
and it would no doubt have been only vague and uncertain; but
nformation has come to me which I did not expect, which I had
o reason to expect, and it is all too certain. Oh, my friend, how
hat woman has deceived you!

It is repugnant to me to enter into any of the details of that mass of horrors, but no matter what is being said about her, you may be sure that the truth is still worse. I hope, my dear friend, that you know me well enough to take my word for this, and that you will not demand that I give you any proof. Let it suffice you to know that there is abundant proof, and that I now have it in my possession.

It is not without extreme pain that I also request you not to force me to give you my reasons for the advice you ask me concerning Mademoiselle de Volanges. I urge you not to oppose the vocation she shows. Surely there can be no justification for forcing a girl to become a nun when she has no vocation for it, but sometimes it is very fortunate that she should have one; and your daughter herself has told you that you would not disapprove of her decision if you knew her reasons for it. He who inspires our sentiments knows better than our vain wisdom what is best for each of us, and often what appears to be an act of His severity is, on the contrary, an act of His clemency.

My advice, which I know will grieve you, and which for that very reason you must believe is not given to you without great reflection, is that you should leave Mademoiselle de Volanges in the convent, since that is her choice; that you should encourage rather than oppose the plan she seems to have formed; and that, in the expectation of its execution, you should not hesitate to break off the marriage you have arranged for her.

Having fulfilled these painful duties of friendship, and being powerless to add any consolation, I have only one favor to ask of you, my dear friend, and that is not to question me about anything relating these sad events: let us leave them in the forgetfulness that befits them; and, without seeking useless and distressing explanations, let us submit to the decrees of Providence and believe in the wisdom of its designs, even when it does not permit us to understand them. Good-by, my dear friend.

LETTER 173

~ *From Madame de Volanges to Madame de Rosemonde*

Paris, December 18, 17—

Oh, my friend, what a frightening veil you cast over my daughter's fate! And you seem to fear that I may try to raise it! What does it hide that could pain a mother's heart more than the terrible suspicions to which you abandon me? The more I recall your friendship and indulgence, the more my torments increase. Since yesterday I have decided a dozen times to do away with these cruel uncertainties and ask you to tell me the truth bluntly and frankly; but each time I shuddered with fear, remembering your request that I refrain from questioning you. I have finally decided on a course which leaves me some hope, and I count on your friendship to make you grant my request: I ask you to answer me if I have more or less understood what you may have to tell me, and not to be afraid to tell me anything to which maternal indulgence can apply, and which is not irreparable. If my misfortunes exceed that measure, I consent to let you explain yourself only by your silence. Here, then, is what I have learned already, and how far my fears extend.

My daughter showed some inclination for the Chevalier Danceny, and I have been informed that she went so far as to receive letters from him, and even to answer him, but I thought I had made sure that this childish error would have no dangerous consequences. Today, when I fear everything, I recognize the possibility that my vigilance may have been evaded, and I am afraid that my daughter may have been led so far astray as to carrying her failings to the uttermost limit.

I recall several circumstances which strengthen this fear. I have told you that my daughter felt faint when she heard the news of Monsieur de Valmont's misfortune; perhaps the only object of her sensibility was the thought of the danger to which Monsieur Danceny had been exposed in the duel. When she later wept so much on learning everything that was being said about Madame de Merteuil, perhaps what I thought was the grief of friendship was only the effect of jealousy or regret at having found her lover to be unfaithful. Her latest step, it seems to me, may also be explained in the same way. We often feel that we are called to God merely because we feel revulsion against men. Finally, supposing that these facts are true and that you were aware of them, no doubt you would have thought them sufficient to warrant the severe advice you have given me.

However, if this is so, while I blame my daughter, I think I still owe it to her to try every means of saving her from the torments of an illusory and temporary vocation. If Monsieur Danceny has not lost all sense of decency, he will not refuse to right a wrong of which he is the sole author, and I venture to believe that his marriage to my daughter would be so advantageous that he as well as his family could be flattered by it.

That, my dear and worthy friend, is my one remaining hope; hasten to confirm it, if it is possible for you to do so. You can understand how much I want you to reply, and what a terrible blow your silence would be to me.*

I was about to close this letter when a man of my acquaintance came to see me and told me about the cruel scene Madame de Merteuil underwent day before yesterday. Since I have seen no one for the past few days, I had heard nothing of the incident. Here is an account of it, as it was told to me by an eyewitness.

On returning from the country day before yesterday, Thursday, Madame de Merteuil went to the Comédie Italienne, where she had a box. She was alone and, as must have seemed extraordinary to her, no man came to her box during the entire performance. When it was over, she went, as usual, to the little drawing room, which was already filled with people. A murmur arose at once, but she apparently did not think she was the cause of it. She saw an empty place on one of the benches and went to sit down in it; but immediately all the women who were there already rose in unison and left her entirely alone. This marked display of general indignation was applauded by all the men and increased the murmurs, which, it is said, became outright denunciation.

Then, to make her humiliation complete, her misfortune willed that Monsieur de Prévan, who had not shown himself anywhere since his adventure, should enter the little drawing room at the same moment. As soon as he was seen, everyone, men and women alike, gathered around him and applauded him; and he was carried, as it were, in front of Madame de Merteuil by the people surrounding them. I was told that she seemed not to see

---

*This letter remained unanswered.

r hear anything, and that her expression did not change at all!
ut I think that must be an exaggeration. In any case, this
tuation, truly ignominious for her, lasted until her carriage was
nnounced; and as she was leaving, the vehement denunciations
:doubled. It is terrible to be a relative of that woman. That
ame evening, Monsieur de Prévan was given a warm welcome
y all the officers of his corps who were there, and no one doubts
aat he will soon be restored to his former post and rank.

The same man who gave me these details also told me that
Madame de Merteuil was seized with a violent fever that night.
At first it was thought to be a result of the trying situation in
vhich she had been placed, but yesterday evening it became
pparent that she was afflicted with confluent smallpox of a very
erious kind. I really believe it would be fortunate for her if she
ied of it. It is said that this incident may do her great harm in
er lawsuit, which will soon come up for judgment, and in
vhich she is said to need a great deal of favor.

Good-by, my dear and worthy friend. I see in all this that the
vicked are punished, but I find no consolation in it for their
unfortunate victims.

LETTER 174

~ *From the Chevalier Danceny to Madame de Rosemonde*

Paris, December 26, 17—

You are right, Madame, and I shall certainly not refuse you
anything which depends on me and to which you seem to attach
any value. The packet I have the honor of sending to you
ontains all of Mademoiselle de Volanges's letters. If you read
hem, I think you will be surprised to see that so much ingenuousness can be combined with so much perfidy. At least that is
what struck me most during the last reading I have just given
hem.

But above all, can one resist feeling the keenest indignation
against Madame de Merteuil when one recalls the horrible pleasure she took in her efforts to abuse so much innocence and
candor?

No, I am no longer in love. I retain nothing of a sentiment that
was so infamously betrayed, and it is not love that makes me

seek to justify Mademoiselle de Volanges. And yet, would no
that simple heart, that gentle, pliable character, have been in
clined more easily toward good than they were led into evil
Would any other young girl have resisted such criminal guile an
better when she had just come from a convent, without experi
ence and almost without ideas, bringing with her into society, a
almost always happens, only an equal ignorance of good an
evil? Ah, in order to be indulgent it is enough to reflect on the
circumstances, independent of us, which affect the frightening
alternative of the delicacy or depravity of our sentiments! You
did me justice, Madame, in thinking that although I have keenly
felt the wrongs done by Mademoiselle de Volanges, they inspire
me with no idea of vengeance. It is enough to be forced to give
up loving her; it would cost me too much to hate her.

It required no reflection on my part to desire that everything
that concerns her and might harm her should remain forever
unknown to everyone. If I have seemed to delay for some time in
complying with your wishes in this matter, I think I need no
conceal my motive from you: I first wanted to be sure I was no
going to be prosecuted for the consequences of my unfortunate
duel. At a time when I was asking for your indulgence, when I
even dared to think I had some right to it, I was afraid of
seeming to be trying to buy it, so to speak, by granting your
request; and, being sure of the purity of my motives, I was proud
enough, I confess, to want you to be unable to doubt it. I hope
you will forgive this delicacy, which was perhaps too sensitive,
in view of the veneration I have for you, and the value I place on
your esteem.

The same sentiment makes me ask you, as a last favor, to be
so kind as to tell me whether you feel that I have fulfilled all the
duties imposed on me by the unfortunate circumstances in which
I have been placed. Once I am satisfied on that point, my course
is clear: I shall go to Malta, where I shall gladly make and
religiously keep the vows that will separate me from a world of
which, though still young, I already have so much reason to
complain; I shall go there and try to forget, beneath a foreign
sky, the idea of so many horrors whose memory could only
sadden and wither my soul.

I am, with respect, Madame, your most humble, etc.

LETTER 175

~ *From Madame de Volanges to Madame de Rosemonde*

Paris, January 14, 17—

Madame de Merteuil's destiny seems to have been fulfilled at last, my dear and worthy friend, and it is such that her worst enemies are divided between the indignation she deserves and the pity she inspires. I was right to say that it would be fortunate for her if she died of her smallpox. She has survived, it is true, but she is horribly disfigured and has lost one eye. I have not seen her again, as you may well suppose, but she is said to be truly hideous.

The Marquis de ———, who never misses a chance to make a spiteful remark, said yesterday, in speaking of her, that her illness had turned her inside out, and that her soul was now on her face. Unfortunately everyone felt that it was an apt expression.

Another event has just added to her disgrace and her wrongs. Her lawsuit came up for judgment day before yesterday, and she lost it by a unanimous vote. Costs, damages, restitution of profits—everything was awarded to the minors, so that the small portion of her fortune that was not involved in the lawsuit was more than absorbed by its expenses.

As soon as she heard this news, even though she had not yet fully recovered from her illness, she made her arrangements and left, alone and at night, by stagecoach. Her servants now say that not one of them was willing to go with her. She is thought to be on her way to Holland.

Her departure has aroused even more indignation than all the rest, for she took with her the valuable diamonds that were to have reverted to her husband's estate, her silverware, her jewels: in short, everything she could; and she has left debts amounting to nearly fifty thousand francs. It is a real bankruptcy.

The family is to gather tomorrow to discuss making arrangements with the creditors. Although I am a very distant relative, I have offered to participate; but I shall not attend the meeting, for I must be present at a still sadder ceremony. Tomorrow my daughter will become a postulant at the convent. I hope you will not forget, my dear friend, that the silence you have kept toward me is my only reason for thinking myself obliged to make this great sacrifice.

Monsieur Danceny left Paris nearly two weeks ago. It is said that he is going to Malta and intends to remain there. Perhaps there would still be time to detain him. . . . My friend! . . . Is it true, then, that my daughter is very guilty? . . . You will surely forgive a mother for yielding only with difficulty to that terrible certainty.

What is the fatality that has been spreading around me for some time, and has struck me through what I hold most dear? My daughter and my friend!

Who could fail to shudder in thinking of the misfortunes that can be caused by a single dangerous association! And what sorrows we could avoid if we reflected on this more often! What woman would not flee at a seducer's first words? What mother would not tremble to see anyone but herself talking to her daughter? But these belated reflections never come until after the event, and one of the most important and perhaps most generally recognized truths remains stifled and neglected in the whirl of our irresponsible morals.

Good-by, my dear and worthy friend; I am now keenly aware that our reason, so incapable of warding off our misfortunes, is still less capable of consoling us for them.*

---

*Private reasons, and certain considerations which we shall always regard it as our duty to respect, force us to stop here.

At this time we can neither give the reader the sequel to Mademoiselle de Volanges's adventures nor inform him of the sinister events which climaxed the misfortunes, or completed the punishment, of Madame de Merteuil.

Perhaps some day we shall be permitted to complete this work, but we can give no assurances on the matter; even if we could, we would still feel obliged first to consult the taste of the public, whose reasons for being interested in reading about these events are not the same as ours.

(Publisher's note)